A Practical Approach to Motor Vehicle Engineering

A Practical Approach to Motor Vehicle Engineering

Derek Newbold
Formerly of Hinckley College

Allan Bonnick *Formerly of Eastbourne College*

A member of the Hodder Headline Group
LONDON

First published in Great Britain in 2000 by
Arnold, a member of the Hodder Headline Group,
338 Euston Road, London NW1 3BH

http://www.arnoldpublishers.com

© 2000 Derek Newbold and Allan Bonnick

Whilst the advice and information in this book are believed to be true and
accurate at the date of going to press, neither the author[s] nor the publisher
can accept any legal responsiblity or liability for any errors or omissions
that may be made.

British Library Cataloguing in Publication Data
A catalogue record for this book is available from the British Library

ISBN 0 340 69231 6

1 2 3 4 5 6 7 8 9 10

Commissioning Editor: Siân Jones
Production Editor: Wendy Rooke
Production Controller: Sarah Kett
Cover design: Stefan Brazzo

Typeset by J&L Composition Ltd, Filey, North Yorkshire
Printed and bound in Great Britain by The Bath Press, Bath

What do you think about this book? Or any other Arnold title?
Please send your comments to feedback.arnold@hodder.co.uk

Contents

Foreword

Although this book has been written mainly for those who wish to gain an NVQ in motor vehicle work, it is equally suitable for a wide variety of people who are undertaking the City & Guilds, BTEC as well those who just want to know about cars to enable them to undertake their own servicing with a greater degree of confidence. It can be used in schools, colleges and garage workshops as each task is being undertaken.

It covers the fundamental principles for each system found in the motor vehicle. It is by no means exhaustive, but it does allow the student to take simple steps in understanding how each system works.

The NVQ qualification is not as daunting as many people think. The main problem seems to be in the gaining of evidence and the assembling of a portfolio, so, with this in mind, there are a number of exercises at the end of each section for the student to complete. The evidence required by the NVQ assessor from the student will be gained gradually and built into a student portfolio. Each completed job sheet (suitably signed after the job has been checked) should show evidence of what you have done, how you did it and that it was completed to a satisfactory standard. When the student feels confident enough to complete the task alone then he or she may request an assessment. Examples of assessments are given in the book to show what might be required by the assessor.

The text has a number of words and sentences that are highlighted when they first appear in the text. These are mostly key words that will help the student to remember what is essential from the text. No matter how much the student 'waffles' when answering questions, unless he or she understands the subject and uses the key words, it will be very difficult for the assessor to give marks. Remember the key words and you will be half-way there. Some of the words used are specific to the motor vehicle and to the NVQ. We have tried to explain those relating to the motor vehicle in the text and those relating to the NVQ in a glossary at the end of the book.

There are a number of practical assignments and learning tasks in each chapter. If these are undertaken in a realistic way, they will enable the student to complete the task repeatedly, up to an acceptable standard, without supervision, which is the requirement of the NVQ.

The workshop job sheet should contain all the elements of the performance criteria as requested in the NVQ. They should be signed by both the person undertaking the task (you) and the assessor/supervisor to say the task has been completed satisfactorily.

The illustrations have been selected to give the maximum amount of support when learning about new topics. We advise students to attempt the learning tasks when they have completed the related section of their training and education.

This book is based on many years of teaching and helping students and apprentices who have gone on to become successful and valued mechanics. Some of them have become owners of their own motor vehicle workshops, each in turn has appreciated the training that was given to them in their early years. Our hope is that this book will enable a wider variety of people to achieve their hopes and ambitions.

Derek Newbold
Allan Bonnick

Acknowledgements

Thanks are due to the following companies who supplied information and in many cases permission to reproduce photographs and diagrams:

- Audi UK Ltd
- Champion Spark Plugs Ltd
- Crypton Technology Group
- Cummins Engine Company Inc.
- Delmar Publishers Inc.
- Dunlop Holdings Ltd
- Ford Motor Company UK Ltd
- Haynes Publications
- Honda UK Ltd
- Lucas Automotive Ltd
- Rover Group
- Vauxhall Motors Ltd
- Volvo Group (UK)
- Toyota GB Ltd
- Zahnradfabrik Friedrichshafen AG

Special thanks are due to the following for supplying much useful information, and with permission to reproduce pictures and diagrams from:

The Automotive Chassis: Engineering principles 2nd edition, J Reimpell & H Stoll (Vogel-Buchverlag, Würzburg, 1995)

If we have used information or mentioned a company name in the text, not listed here, our apologies and acknowledgements

Introduction

Interacting with customers and colleagues

Selling vehicles to the public and then providing the support services that maintain and repair those vehicles is a major industry in industrialized countries such as the United Kingdom. Motor trade businesses exist in many forms, from very large companies with many branches, to small businesses operated by the owner. The structure of a multiple branch company is likely to be far more complicated than that of a small company (firm) employing two or three people. However, because these firms are all engaged in very similar work, there are certain features that are common to them all. It is these common features that are covered here.

This book is mainly about the engineering aspects of the vehicle trade and, as such, it is aimed primarily at those who are working to become qualified vehicle service technicians. However, this does not mean that we can disregard the business side, because all organizations need to be efficient, to work within their budget and, if appropriate, to make a satisfactory profit. In order to achieve these ends, it is necessary for a firm to be organized so that each member knows what their position is and what they have to do to make their expected contribution to the satisfactory operation of the business.

Organization of the firm

A company, or firm as it is often called, will often display its structure in the form of an organization chart. For any group of people who are engaged in some joint activity it is necessary to have someone in charge and for all members of the 'team' to know what their role is and which person they should speak to when they need advice. Just as a football team is organized and each person is given a position on the field so a business is organized so that people can work as a team.

The 'line chart' (Fig. A.1) shows how the work is divided up into manageable units, or areas of work, and how the personnel in those areas relate to each other. In this example the managing director is the 'boss'. Under the managing director come the accountant, the service manager, the parts department manager and the sales manager; these are known as 'line' managers. Below these line managers, in the hierarchical structure that is used in many businesses,

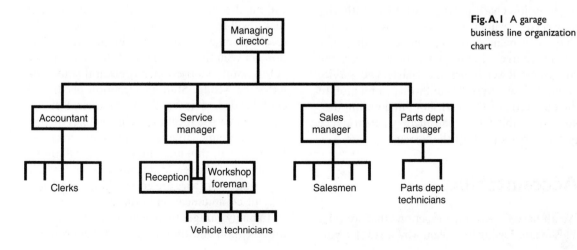

Fig. A.1 A garage business line organization chart

are supervisors (foremen/women) and then come the technicians, clerks, etc.

Policy

A policy is a set of rules and guidelines that should be written down so that everyone in an organization knows what they are trying to achieve. Policy is decided by the people at the top of an organization, in consultation with whoever else they see fit. It is important for each employee to know how policy affects them and it should be suitably covered in a contract of employment. For example, every firm must have a 'safety policy'. It is the duty of every employee to know about safety and firms are subject to inspection to ensure that they are complying with the laws that relate to health and safety at work, and similar legislation.

Discipline

Standards of workmanship, hours of work, relations with other employees, relations with customers and many other factors need to be overseen by members of the firm who have some authority because, from time to time, it may be necessary to take steps to change some aspect. For example, it may be the case that a particular technician is starting to arrive late for work; it will be necessary for someone to deal with this situation before it gets out of hand and this is where the question of 'authority' arises.

Authority

Authority is power deriving from position. The organization chart illustrates who has authority (power) over whom. The vertical position on the chart of a member of staff indicates that they are in charge of, and have power over, the employees lower down the chart. The service manager in a garage has authority in relation to the operation of the workshop; in addition they are responsible for the satisfactory performance of the workshop side of the business.

Accountability

We all have to account for actions that we take. This means having to explain why we took a par-

ticular line of action. We are all responsible for the actions that we take. This means that we did certain things that led to some outcome. By having to explain why something 'went wrong', i.e. by having to account for our behaviour, we are made to examine our responsibility. We are 'responsible' for seeing that we get to work on time, for making sure that we do a job properly and safely, and for helping to promote good working relationships.

Delegating

It is often said that you can delegate (pass down) authority but not responsibility. So, if you are a skilled technician who has a trainee working with you and you have been given a major service to do, it will be your responsibility to ensure that the job is done properly. You will have had some authority given to you to instruct the trainee, but the responsibility for the quality of the work remains with you.

Having introduced some ideas about business organization and the working relationships that are necessary to ensure success, we can turn our attention to the business activities that are the immediate concern of the service technician. In order to place some structure on this section it is probably a good idea to start with 'reception'.

Reception

Reception in a garage is the main point of contact between customers and the services that the workshop provides. It is vitally important that the communication between the customers and reception and between reception and the workshop is good. It is at reception that the customer will hand over the vehicle and it is at reception that it will be handed back to the customer. The reception engineer is a vital link in the transaction between the customer and the firm and it is at this point that friction may occur if something has gone wrong. Staff in reception need to be cool headed, able to think on their feet and equipped with a vocabulary that enables them to cope with any situation that may 'crop up'. From time to time they may need to call on the assistance of the service manager and it is vitally important that there are good relations and clear lines of communication in this area.

In many garages there will be an area set aside for reception and the staff placed there will have set duties to perform. In the case of small garages employing, perhaps, one or two people reception may take place in the general office and the person who is free at the time may perform the function. In either case, certain principles apply and it is these that are now addressed.

Customer categories

Because a good deal of skill and tact is required when dealing with customers it is useful to categorize them as follows:

- informed
- non-informed
- new
- regular

Informed customers

Informed customers are those who are knowledgeable about their vehicle and who probably know the whole procedure that the vehicle will follow before it is returned to them. This means that the transaction that takes place between them and the receptionist will largely consist of taking down details of the customer's requirements and agreeing a time for the completion of the work and the collection of the vehicle. Depending on the status of the customer, i.e. new or regular, it will be necessary to make arrangements for payment. It may also be necessary to agree details for contacting the customer should some unforeseen problem arise while work on the vehicle is in progress, so that details can be discussed and additional work and a new completion time agreed.

Non-informed customers

The non-informed customer probably does not know much about cars or the working procedures of garages. This type of customer will need to be treated in quite a different way. The non-informed customer will – depending on the nature of the work they require for their vehicle – need to have more time spent on them. A proportion of this extra time will be devoted to explaining what the garage is going to do with their vehicle and also what the customer has to do while the vehicle is in the care of the garage. The latter part will largely consist of making arrangements for getting the customer to some chosen destination and for collecting the vehicle

when the work is completed. On handing the car back to the 'non-informed' customer it will probably be necessary to describe, in a non-patronizing and not too technical way, the work that has been done and what it is that they are being asked to pay for.

New customers

A 'new' customer may be informed or non-informed and this is information that should be 'teased' out during the initial discussions with them. Courtesy and tact are key words in dealing with customers and they are factors that should be uppermost in one's mind at the new-customer-introduction stage. The extent of the introductory interview with the new customer will depend on what it is that they want done and the amount of time that they and the firm have to give to the exercise. If it is a garage with several departments it may be advisable to introduce the new customer to relevant personnel in the departments that are most likely to be concerned with them. Customers may wish to know that their vehicle will be handled by qualified staff and it is common practice for firms to display samples of staff qualification certificates in the reception area. At some stage it will be necessary to broach the subject of payment for services and this may be aided by the firm having a clearly stated policy. Again, it is not uncommon for a notice to be displayed which states the 'terms of business'; drawing a client's attention to this is relatively easy.

Regular customers

Regular customers are valuable to a business and they should always be treated with respect. It hardly needs saying that many of the steps that are needed for the new customer introduction will not be needed when dealing with a regular customer. However, customers will only remain loyal (regular) if they are properly looked after. It is vitally important to listen carefully to their requests and to ensure that the work is done properly, and on time and that the vehicle is returned to them in a clean condition.

Workshop activities

Reception will have recorded the details of the work that is to be done on the vehicle, and they will have agreed details of completion time, etc.

with the workshop. At some point in the process a 'job card' will have been generated. The instructions about the work to be done must be clear and unambiguous. In some cases this may be quite brief, e.g. 10 000 mile service. The details of the work to be performed will be contained in the service manual for the particular vehicle model. In other cases it may be rather general, e.g. 'Attend to noisy wheel bearing. Near side front.' Describing exactly what work is required may entail further investigation by the technician. It may be that the noise is caused by the final drive. The whole thing thus becomes much more complicated and it may be necessary to conduct a preliminary examination and test of the vehicle before the final arrangements are made for carrying out the work.

Once the vehicle has been handed over to the workshop with a clear set of instructions about the work to be done, it becomes the responsibility of the technician entrusted with the job and their colleagues to get the work done efficiently and safely and to make sure that the vehicle is not damaged. This means that the workshop must have all necessary interior and exterior protection for the vehicle such as wing and seat covers, etc. Figure A.2 shows a suggested layout for a service bay.

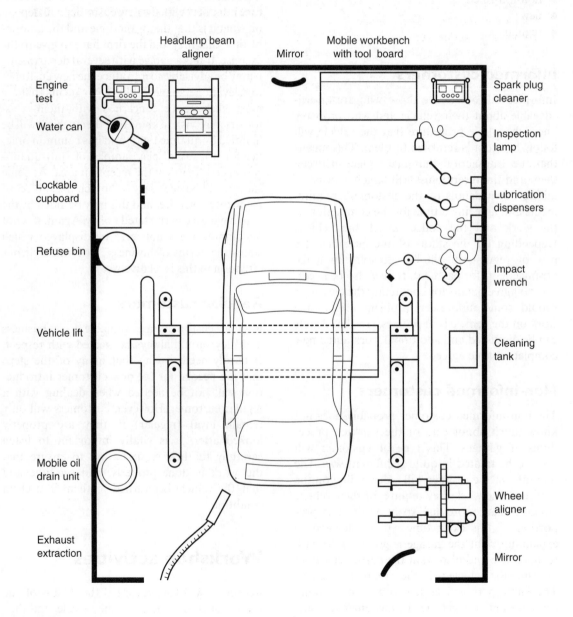

Fig. A.2 A service bay

Records

As the work proceeds a record must be made of materials used and time spent because this will be needed when making out the invoice. In large organizations the workshop records will be linked to stock control in the parts department and to other departments, such as accounts, through the company's information system which will probably be computer based.

Quality control

Vehicle technicians are expected to produce work of high quality and various systems of checking work are deployed. One aspect of checking quality that usually excites attention is the 'road test'. It is evident that this can only be performed by licensed drivers and it is usually restricted to experienced technicians. A road test is an important part of many jobs because it is probably the only way to ensure that the vehicle is functioning correctly. It is vitally important that it is conducted in a responsible way. Figure A.3 illustrates the point that there must be a good clear road in front of and behind the vehicle.

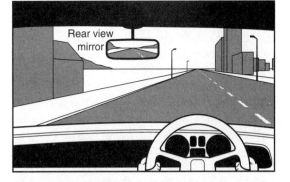

Fig.A.3 The front and rear view of the road when road testing

Returning the vehicle to the customer

On satisfactory completion of the work, the vehicle will be taken to the customer's collection point; the covers and finger marks and other small blemishes should be removed. In the meantime the accounts department will, if it is a cash customer, have prepared the account so that everything is ready for completion of the transaction when the customer collects the vehicle.

Section One

I
Engines and lubrication

1.1 Light vehicles

Vehicles classified in this category have a laden mass of less than three tonnes. A wide range of different body shapes and sizes are used in this category from simple two-seater cars to mini-buses and small trucks.

1.2 Layout of components

The power units used in the light vehicle can be fitted in a number of different places (Fig. 1.1). The source of power is provided by an **internal combustion engine**. The petrol or spark ignition (SI) engine is the most common, although the diesel or compression ignition (CI) engine is becoming more widely used. These are of the conventional design, where the pistons move up and down in the cylinders. Several other designs have been used; for example the Wankel engine used by Mazda in the RX7 and by Norton in their motor cycle. Another method of propulsion is

electricity; the electric vehicle is gaining popularity as there is very little pollution of the atmosphere and it can therefore meet the more stringent regulations coming into force each year.

The layout of the main components may conform to one of the following:

- **front engine front wheel drive** (FWD)
- **front engine rear wheel drive** (RWD)
- **mid-engine rear wheel drive**
- **rear engine rear wheel drive** (Fig. 1.2)
- one of the above but **four wheel drive** (4WD)

1.3 Location of major components

> *Learning task*
>
> Make a simple sketch in plan view of a front engine FWD vehicle. Label the main components: engine, clutch, gearbox, drive shafts, driving wheels, radiator, fuel tank.

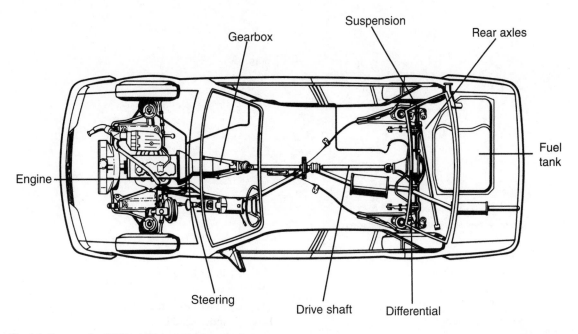

Fig. 1.1 Front engine RWD with integral body mountings

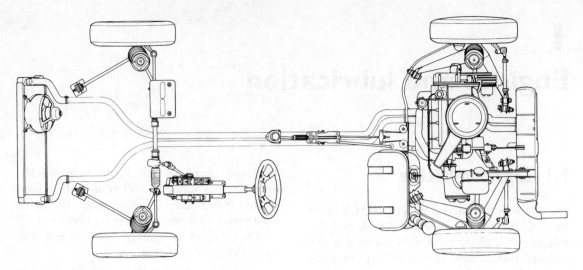

Fig. 1.2 Rear engine RWD ideal layout for a two seater coupe

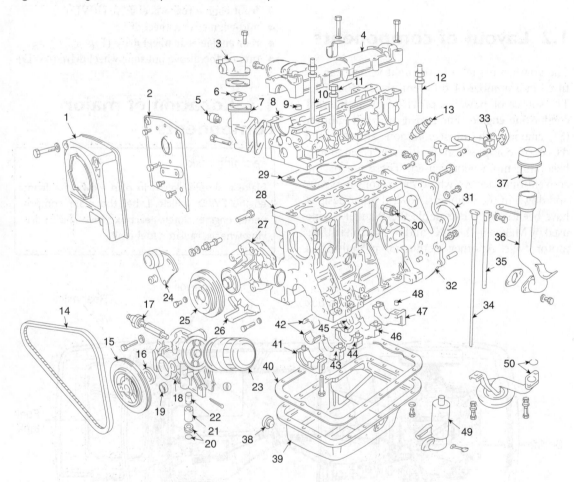

Fig. 1.3 Exploded view of engine block components

1 –	Timing belt cover	7 –	Thermostat housing
2 –	Timing belt cover back plate	8 –	Cylinder head
3 –	Thermostat outlet	9 –	Dowel
4 –	Camshaft cover	10 –	Cylinder head stud – long
5 –	Coolant thermistor	11 –	Cylinder head bolt
6 –	Thermostat	12 –	Cylinder head stud – short

13 – Spark plug
14 – Alternator/water pump belt
15 – Crankshaft pulley
16 – Oil seal
17 – Oil pressure switch
18 – Oil pump
19 – Oil pump plug
20 – Plug and 'O' ring
21 – Oil pressure relief valve spring
22 – Oil pressure relief valve plunger
23 – Oil filter cartridge
24 – Timing belt tensioner
25 – Water pump pulley
26 – Deflector
27 – Water pump
28 – Cylinder block
29 – Cylinder head gasket
30 – Knock sensor
31 – Crankshaft rear oil seal
32 – Gearbox adapter plate
33 – Crankshaft sensor
34 – Dipstick
35 – Dipstick tube

36 – Oil filler tube
37 – Oil filler cap
38 – Sump plug
39 – Oil sump
40 – Oil sump gasket
41 – Front main bearing cap
42 – Main bearing shells
43 – Intermediate main bearing cap
44 – Centre main bearing cap
45 – Thrust washers
46 – Intermediate main bearing cap
47 – Rear main bearing cap
48 – Dowel
49 – Oil separator
50 – Oil strainer and 'O' ring

Learning task

By using the information shown on Fig. 1.3 identify from Fig. 1.4 the following numbered components: 4, 5, 15, 27, 28, 29, 31, 32, 39, 41.

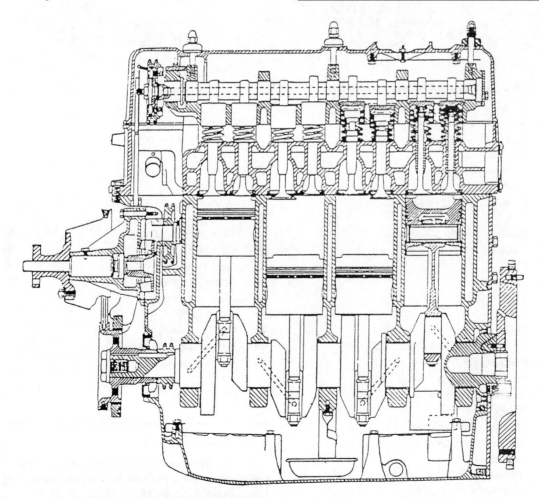

Fig. 1.4 Four cylinder in-line engine cross-section view

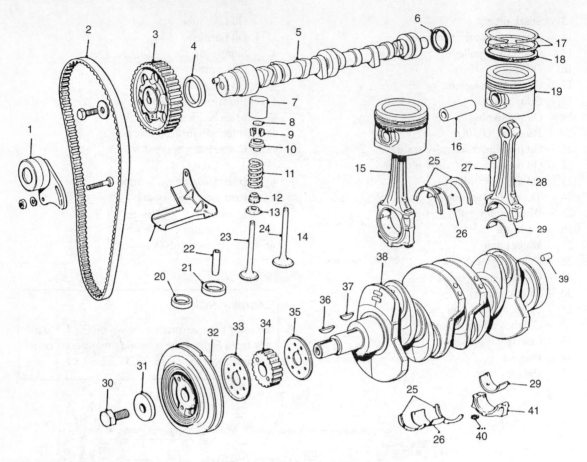

Fig. 1.5 Exploded view of internal engine components

1 – Timing belt tensioner
2 – Timing belt
3 – Camshaft gear
4 – Camshaft front oil seal
5 – Camshaft
6 – Camshaft rear oil seal
7 – Tappet
8 – Shim
9 – Cotters
10 – Cup
11 – Spring
12 – Valve stem seal
13 – Seat
14 – Deflector
15 – Connecting rod and piston – LH
16 – Gudgeon pin
17 – Compression rings
18 – Oil control ring
19 – Piston
20 – Exhaust valve seat insert
21 – Inlet valve seat insert
22 – Valve guide
23 – Exhaust valve
24 – Inlet valve
25 – Crankshaft washers

26 – Main bearing shell
27 – Connecting rod bolt
28 – Connecting rod – RH
29 – Big-end bearing shell
30 – Pulley bolt
31 – Washer
32 – Crankshaft pulley
33 – Gear flange
34 – Crankshaft gear
35 – Gear flange
36 – Pulley and gear key
37 – Oil pump key
38 – Crankshaft
39 – Flywheel dowel
40 – Connecting rod nut
41 – Connecting rod cap

Learning task

By using the information shown on Fig. 1.5 identify from Fig. 1.6 the following numbered components: 5, 7, 11, 15, 16, 19, 23, 32, 38, 39.

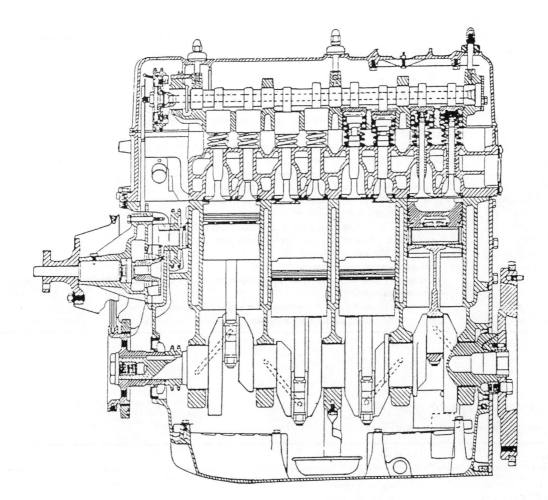

Fig. 1.6 Cross-sectioned view

1.4 Functional requirements of engine components

These are shown in Table 1.1.

1.5 Definition of terms used in motor vehicle engines

These are given in Table 1.2.

1.6 Cycles of operation

The basic function of an engine is to convert chemical energy (the fuel) into mechanical energy and to produce usable power and torque (this is the ability to turn the driving wheels and move the vehicle). The spark ignition (SI) engine operates on the principle of the Otto four-stroke cycle or the Clerk two-stroke cycle of operations.

Table 1.1 Functional requirements of engine components

Component	Function or purpose
Camshaft cover	Encloses the camshaft and valve mechanism
Camshaft carrier	Locates the camshaft and provides upper bearing locations
Camshaft	Operates the valves and provides a means of driving the auxiliaries
Cylinder head	Provides for (in some cases) the combustion space, inlet and exhaust gas ports, supports the valve gear and part of the cooling system passages
Cam followers	Provide a bearing surface between the rotating camshaft and valve stem
Collets	Lock the valve spring to the valve
Valve spring	Keeps the valves closed, but allows them to be opened when required
Valve	Controls the flow of mixture into and out of the cylinder
Camshaft gear	Provides the drive to the camshaft at half crankshaft speed
Tensioner	Ensures the drive belt is maintained at a constant tension
Timing belt	Transmits the drive from the crankshaft to the camshaft without slipping
Pistons	Transmit the pressure of combustion down to the con-rod
Piston rings	These form a gas- and oil-tight seal
Gudgeon pin	Connects the piston to the con-rod
Connecting rod	Connects the piston to the crankshaft and converts the straight line motion of the piston to the rotary motion of the crankshaft
Crankshaft	Transmits the power from all the cylinders to the flywheel and transmission
Shell bearings	These form the bearing surface for the crankshaft journals

Table 1.2 Definitions of motor vehicle engine terms

Term	Definition
OHV	Over head valve
OHC	Over head camshaft
TDC	Top dead centre
BTDC	Before top dead centre
ATDC	After top dead centre
BDC	Bottom dead centre
BBDC	Before bottom dead centre
ABDC	After bottom dead centre
Bore	Diameter of the cylinder
Stroke	Distance moved by piston from TDC to BDC
Cylinder capacity	Stroke of the piston multiplied by the cross-sectional area of the bore
Swept volume (SV)	Volume created by the area of the bore times the stroke
Clearance volume (CV)	Volume left by piston when at TDC
Compression ratio (CR)	Ratio of swept volume (SV) and clearance volume (CV) against clearance volume (CV). This is expressed as $\dfrac{(SV + CV)}{CV}$
Engine capacity	Capacity of all the cylinders
IVO	Inlet valve opens
IVC	Inlet valve closes
EVO	Exhaust valve opens
EVC	Exhaust valve closes
Valve lead	The amount in crankshaft degrees the valves open before TDC or BDC
Valve lag	The amount in crankshaft degrees the valves close after TDC or BDC
Valve overlap	The amount in degrees the valves are open together measured at TDC
Valve timing	The point at which the valves should open in relation to piston/crankshaft movement
Valve clearance	The distance between the camshaft and valve stem, allows the valve to close
Ignition timing	The time at which the distributor opens the points in relation to the pistons
Combustion	This is the burning of the petrol and air mixture in the cylinder
Energy	Capacity for doing work
Power	Rate of doing work

Four-stroke cycle of operations

To complete the cycle of operations, four strokes of the piston are used. This involves two complete revolutions of the crankshaft, the inlet and exhaust valves being mechanically opened and closed at the correct times. Starting with the piston at TDC and the crankshaft rotating clockwise (looking from the front of the engine), the strokes operate as follows.

First stroke

With the inlet valve open and the exhaust valve closed the piston moves in a downwards direction drawing in a mixture of petrol vapour and air. This is called the **induction** stroke.

Second stroke

The piston moves up with both valves closed, thus compressing the mixture into the combustion chamber at the top of the cylinder. This is the **compression** stroke.

Third stroke

At the end of the compression stroke a spark occurs at the sparking plug. This ignites the mixture which burns very rapidly heating the gas to a very high temperature which also raises its pressure. This forces the piston down the cylinder and is called the **power** stroke.

Fourth stroke

As the piston begins to rise the exhaust valve opens and the spent gases are forced out of the cylinder. This is called the **exhaust** stroke. At the end of this stroke the exhaust valve closes and the inlet valve opens.

This cycle of induction, compression, power and exhaust operates on a continuous basis all the time the engine is running. As can be seen the complete cycle of operations of a four-stroke engine occupies two complete revolutions of the crankshaft. The SI engine draws into the cylinder a mixture of petrol and air which is compressed and burnt. The CI engine draws air only into the cylinder which is compressed to a very high pressure. This also raises its temperature and when fuel is sprayed into the combustion chamber it self-ignites. The four-stroke cycle is illustrated in Fig.1.7.

Learning task

Read about the diesel four-stroke engine and describe in your own words the cycle of operations.

Two-stroke cycle of operations

By using both sides of the piston the four phases (induction, compression, power, and exhaust) are completed in two strokes of the piston and one revolution of the crankshaft. No valves are used as ports in the cylinder are covered and uncovered by the piston as it moves up and down the cylinder. When describing how this type of engine works it is best to look at what is happening above the piston and then below the piston.

First stroke (piston moving down the cylinder)

Events above the piston

The expanding gases which have been ignited by the spark plug force the piston down the cylinder. About two-thirds of the way down the **exhaust port** is uncovered and the burning gases leave the cylinder. As the piston continues to move downwards, the **transfer port** is uncovered; this allows a fresh mixture into the cylinder.

Events below the piston

The decending piston covers the **inlet port**. The air and fuel trapped in the crankcase is compressed.

Second stroke (piston moving up the cylinder)

Events above the piston

The transfer port is closed first, quickly followed by the closing of the exhaust port. Further movement of the piston compresses the mixture now trapped in the upper part of the cylinder.

Events below the piston

As the piston moves upwards, the depression created in the crankcase draws a fresh mixture in through the inlet port as it is uncovered by the piston.

The two-stroke cycle is shown in Fig. 1.8.

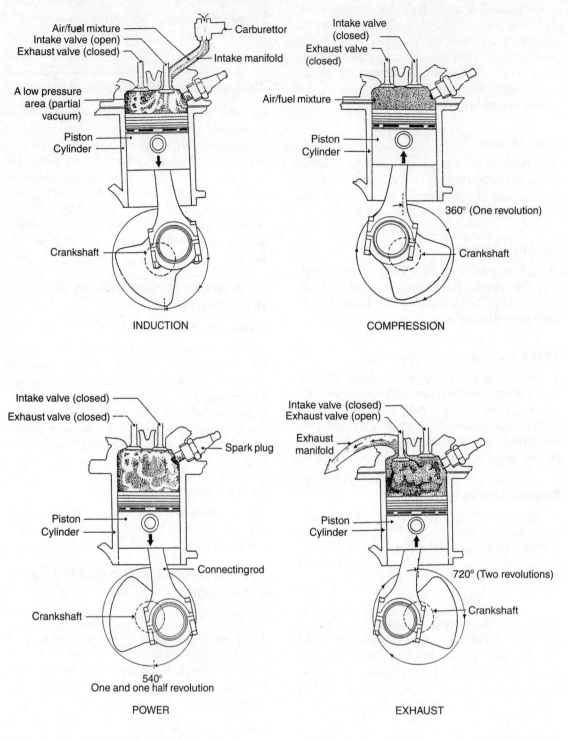

Fig. 1.7 The four-stroke cycle of operations

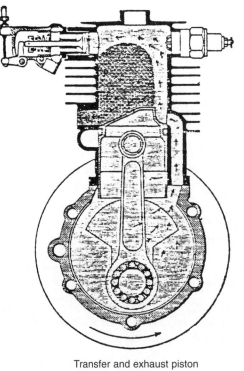

Transfer and exhaust piston
at BDC

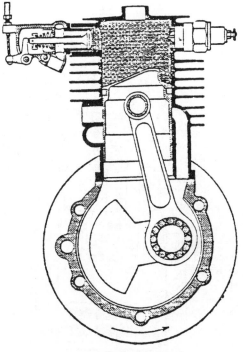

Both ports closed
piston rising on compression

Fig. 1.8 The two-stroke cycle of operations

Two-stroke compression ignition engine

First stroke (piston moving upwards)

The cylinder is filled with air under pressure from the pressure charger. The piston rises covering the inlet ports; the **exhaust valves** are also closed. The air is compressed and fuel is sprayed into the cylinder. It mixes rapidly with the air until self-ignition occurs near TDC.

Second stroke (piston moving downwards)

The rapidly expanding gases force the piston downwards. The exhaust valves are arranged to open just before the piston uncovers the inlet ports. A new charge of air is forced into the cylinder through the open inlet ports forcing the spent gases out of the open exhaust valves and filling the cylinder with a fresh charge of air.

With the diesel two-stroke it is necessary to pressure charge the engine as there is no actual induction stroke. With the short port-opening period it is essential to fill the cylinder with a large mass of air to create the compression pressure and temperature rise to self-ignite the fuel when it is injected. This gives the following advantages:

- high power-to-weight ratio
- higher engine speeds
- simpler in construction
- good scavenging of exhaust gases

Its main disadvantages are:

- higher fuel consumption
- lower **volumetric efficiency**
- less complete combustion
- good **scavenging** of exhaust gases

Figure 1.9 shows the two-stroke CI engine.

Learning tasks

1. Take a look at the main components of a diesel engine and a petrol engine and list the major differences.
2. Make a simple list of the differences between a petrol SI engine and a diesel CI engine. To help you with this, one main difference is that the CI engine does not have a carburettor, it has an injection pump and a set of injectors, one for each cylinder.
3. With the aid of service manuals, list the differences in service intervals, components that require servicing and life expectancy before major overhaul is required.

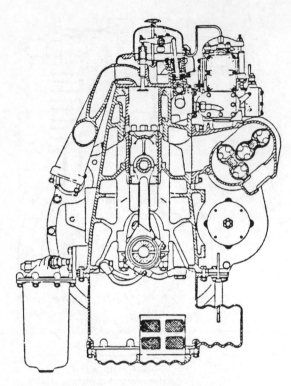

Fig. 1.9 Cross-section of a two-stroke diesel engine

1.7 The process of combustion

The process of combustion in a diesel engine differs from that in a petrol engine and therefore the two must be considered separately.

Combustion of the petrol/air mixture

Air and fuel are drawn into the cylinder and compressed into the combustion chamber by the rising piston. Just before TDC a spark at the spark plug ignites the mixture which burns rapidly across the combustion chamber in a controlled manner.

Combustion of the diesel/air mixture

Air only is drawn into the cylinder and compressed by the rising piston. The compression pressure, and therefore the temperature of the air, is very much higher in the CI engine than in the SI engine. Fuel in the form of very fine droplets is injected into the cylinder; towards the end of the compression stroke this fuel heats up and self-ignites. This causes a very rapid temper-

ature and pressure rise forcing the piston down on its power stroke. The amount of fuel injected will determine the power developed by the engine.

Figure 1.10 shows the layout of a single-cylinder engine. The **reciprocating** motion of the piston is converted to **rotary** motion of the crankshaft by the connecting rod.

As the piston moves downwards the connecting rod is forced to move the crankshaft in a clockwise direction. In this way the linear (straight line) motion of the piston is converted into rotary motion of the crankshaft.

Capacity, swept volume, compression ratio

The following questions show how engine **capacities** are worked out mathematically.

1. The swept volume of a cylinder in a four-cylinder engine is 298 cm^3. Calculate the total volume of the engine.

   Total volume = volume of 1 cylinder × 4
   = 298 × 4
   = 1192 cm^3

2. The swept volume of a cylinder in a six-cylinder engine is 330 cm^3. Calculate the total volume of the engine.

   Total volume = volume of 1 cylinder × 6
   = 330 × 6
   = 1980 cm^3

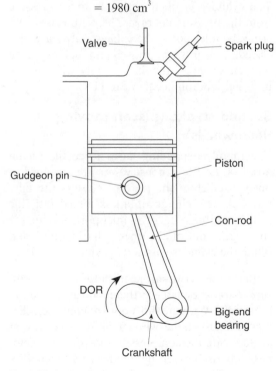

Fig. 1.10 Single-cylinder engine

3. The total volume of a four-cylinder engine is 1498 cm³. Calculate the swept volume of one cylinder.

$$\text{Volume of 1 cylinder} = \frac{\text{total volume}}{4}$$
$$= \frac{1498}{4}$$
$$= 374.5 \text{ cm}^3$$

4. The cross-sectional area (CSA) of the piston crown is 48.5 cm² and the stroke is 12 cm. Calculate the swept volume of the cylinder and the capacity of the engine if it has six cylinders.

$$
\begin{aligned}
\text{Swept volume} \quad &= \text{CSA} \times \text{length of stroke} \\
&= 48.5 \times 12 \\
&= 582 \text{ cm}^3 \\
\text{Capacity} \quad &= \text{SV} \times \text{no of cylinders} \\
&= 582 \times 6 \\
&= 3492 \text{ cm}^3
\end{aligned}
$$

Learning tasks

1. Calculate the SV of an engine in the workshop by removing a cylinder head and measuring the bore diameter and stroke. Check your results by looking in the manufacturer's manual.
2. What advantages are there to having an over-size cylinder (the diameter of the cylinder larger than the stroke)?
3. What are the constructional differences between the combustion chamber of an SI engine and a direct injection CI engine?
4. What safety aspects should be observed when working with petrol or diesel?

1.8 Cylinder arrangements and firing orders

There are three arrangements which may be used for an engine.

- **In-line engine** The cylinders are arranged in a single row, one behind the other. They may be vertical, as in most modern light vehicles, horizontal as used in coaches where the engine is positioned under the floor, or inclined at an angle to allow for a lower bonnet line, as shown in Fig. 1.4.
- **Vee engine** The cylinders are arranged in two rows at an angle to one another. The angle for two-, four- and eight-cylinder engines is usually 90°. For six- and twelve-cylinder engines

the angle is usually 60°. This is illustrated in Fig. 1.11.
- **Opposed piston or cylinder engine** This is where the cylinders are at an angle of 180° apart and usually positioned horizontally (see Fig. 1.12.)

Learning task

Take a look at each type of engine and draw up a simple list of the main advantages and disadvantages, e.g. is it easier to work on for the mechanic? Does it allow for a lower bonnet line? Is the exhaust system easier to arrange? If so, what advantage/disadvantage is there in this?

Firing orders

When considering multi-cylinder engines and firing orders, the power strokes should be spaced at equal intervals to give the smoothest possible

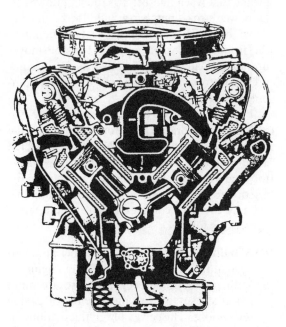

Fig. 1.11 A high-performance V eight-cylinder engine

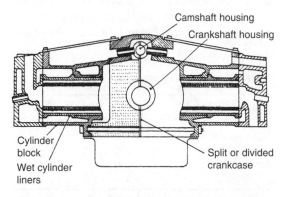

Fig. 1.12 Horizontally opposed cylinders with divided crankcase

running of the engine. Each interval is equal to the number of degrees per cycle of operation. This will be 720° for a four-stroke engine. This is then divided by the number of cylinders, e.g. 720/4 = 180°. Therefore the **firing interval** for a four-cylinder in-line engine will be **180°** and that for a six-cylinder in-line engine will be 720/6 = **120°**. The firing order is determined by two things.

- The position of the cylinders and the cranks on the crankshaft (this determines the *possible* firing orders).
- The arrangement of the cams on the camshaft (this must be in accordance with *one* of the possible firing orders).

The arrangements on the crankshaft are such that the **pistons** on a four-cylinder in-line engine are moved in pairs, e.g. numbers 1 and 4 form one pair and 2 and 3 form the other pair. This means that when number 1 is moving down, on its power stroke, number 4 will also be moving down, but on its induction stroke. Depending on the firing order, when number 2 piston moves upwards it will either be on its exhaust or compression stroke, number 3 will be on its compression or exhaust stroke.

From this then we can see that there are two possible firing orders for a four-cylinder in-line engine. These are 1342 or 1243, both of which are in common use today. Table 1.3 below shows the events in each of the cylinders for the two firing orders. The reasons for using more than one cylinder are very complex but in simple terms they are as follows.

- A multi-cylinder engine has a higher power-to-weight ratio than a single-cylinder engine.
- With multi-cylinder engines there are more power strokes for the same number of engine revolutions. This gives fewer fluctuations in torque and a smoother power output.
- A better acceleration is achieved due to smaller moving parts and more firing impulses.
- The crankshaft is balanced better; the crank-

shaft of a single-cylinder engine cannot be perfectly balanced. Very good balance is obtained with six or more cylinders.

- The piston crown cannot be adequately cooled on large single-cylinder engines; as the piston gets larger the centre of the crown becomes more difficult to keep cool.

Figure 1.13 shows firing orders for a range of different engines.

Speed relationship between crankshaft and camshaft

The movement ratio between the crankshaft and the camshaft is *always* 2:1 on all four-stroke engines. This can be simply determined either by counting the number of teeth on each gear or by measuring the diameter of the gears and dividing the driven gear by the driving gear. From this it will be seen that the camshaft gear is *always* twice as large as the crankshaft gear.

Learning task

Describe two methods you could use to determine the TDC position of number 1 cylinder on its firing stroke.

Cylinder arrangements

In-line cylinders

The four-cylinder in-line is the most popular design in Europe. It has the advantages of having easy access for its size and providing enough power for most applications. The larger six-cylinder engines provide for better acceleration and give better engine balance, and smoother running.

Horizontally opposed cylinders

In this layout the engine has little secondary imbalance giving very smooth running and long

---

Table 1.3 Firing orders: 1342 and 1243

Cylinder number	1		2		3		4	
1st Stroke	I	I	C	E	E	C	P	P
2nd Stroke	C	C	P	I	I	P	E	E
3rd Stroke	P	P	E	C	C	E	I	I
4th Stroke	E	E	I	P	P	I	C	C

P – Power; I – Induction; E – Exhaust; C – Compression

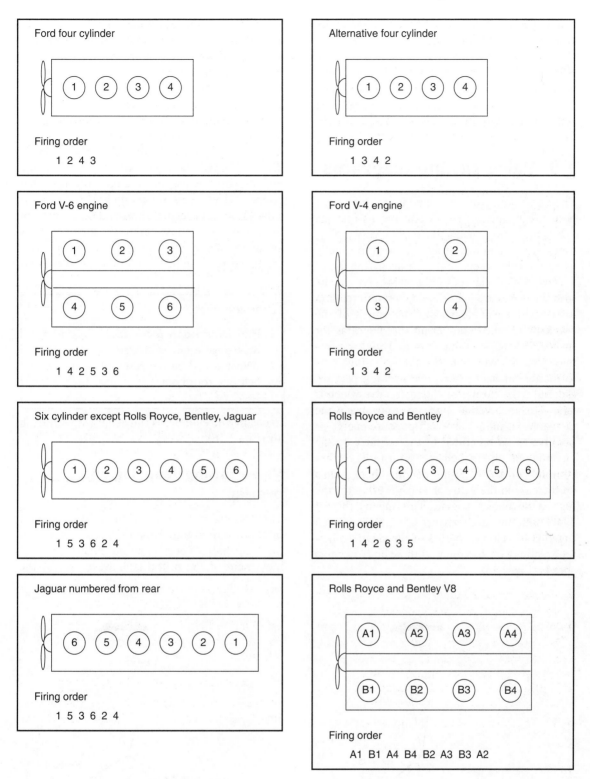

Fig. 1.13 Firing order diagrams for different engines

engine life. It also has a lower centre of gravity allowing for a lower bonnet line.

Vee cylinder arrangements

With this layout the engine is more compact than an in-line engine of the same number of cylinders and the vee 6, 8 and 12 are well balanced.

1.9 Valve-timing diagrams

The valve timing of an engine is set to give the best possible performance. This means that the valves must be opened and closed at very precise times. The traditional way of showing exactly when the valve opens and closes is by the use of a valve-timing diagram (Fig. 1.14). As can be seen the valves are opened and closed in relation to the number of degrees of movement of the crankshaft. When comparing the diagrams for the petrol engine of medium and high performance cars, it will be noticed that the high performance car has larger valve opening periods, especially the closing of the inlet valve which is later. This is so that at high operating speeds the increased lag allows as much pressure energy as possible to be generated in the cylinder by the incoming air and fuel charge, prior to its further compression by the rising piston. There is also an increase in the value of valve overlap for the high performance engine. This means that at TDC both inlet and exhaust valves will be open together for a longer period of time giving a better breathing of the engine at these higher engine speeds (Fig. 1.15).

In the two-stroke petrol engine port timing is the equivalent to valve timing. It must take into account the time lapse before the ports are either fully opened or fully closed, and also the inertia effect of the incoming and outgoing flows of the crankcase and cylinder gases.

In the two-stroke diesel engine the main point to be noticed in comparison with that for a two-stroke petrol engine is that the exhaust event need no longer be symmetrical. This is made possible by the use of mechanically operated poppet valves. An early opening of the exhaust valves initiates (begins) thorough scavenging of the exhaust gases just before the air inlet ports are uncovered by the piston. The exhaust valves are timed to close just before the air inlet ports

---

Learning task

1. Find information for a sports engine and draw a valve-timing diagram.
2. What would be the result of fitting a cam belt one tooth out?

---

to ensure the cylinder is fully charged with fresh air (Fig. 1.16).

Valve timing: lead, lag and overlap

The opening and closing of the valves is pre-set by the position and shape of the cam lobes on the camshaft. Their position relative to the movement of the piston is, however, set by the

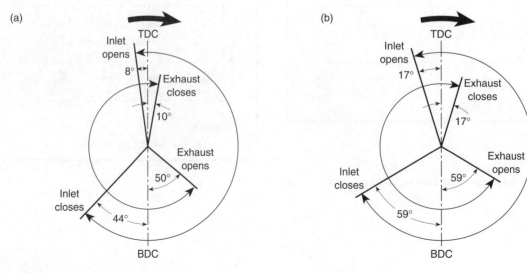

Fig. 1.14 Valve-timing diagrams (a) medium-performance engine, (b) high-performance engine

(a)

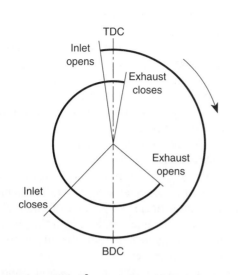

(b)

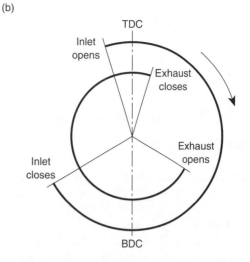

Swept volume 848 cm³
Compression ratio 8.3:1
Max. torque – 62 Nm at 2900 rev/min
Max. power – 31.3 kW at 4500 rev/min

Swept volume 1955 cm³
Compression ratio 9.2:1
Max. torque – 151 Nm at 3500 rev/min
Max. power – 72 kW at 5200 rev/min

Fig. 1.15 Valve-timing diagrams (a) four-cylinder OHV engine, (b) four-cylinder OHC engine

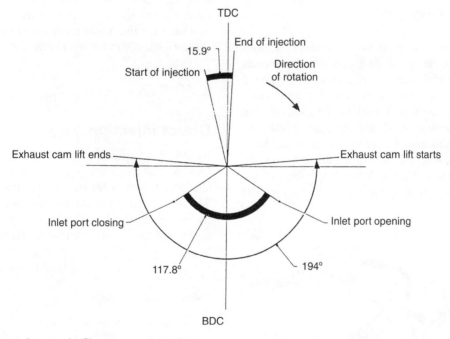

Fig. 1.16 A typical two-stroke CI engine port-timing diagram

correct positioning of the chain or belt connecting the camshaft to the crankshaft.

The effects on the engine if the valves were set to open **too early** would be loss of power and 'popping back' in the inlet manifold. If the valves were set to open **too late** the effects would be loss of power, overheating, poor starting and exhaust backfiring.

In both cases it could be possible for a valve

to hit the piston as it passes TDC on the end of the exhaust stroke and start of the inlet stroke. This is known as valve overlap when shown on the valve-timing diagram.

Ignition timing

Correct setting of the ignition timing is vitally important, and, as described earlier, ignition takes place as the piston nears TDC towards the end of the compression stroke. Accuracy is necessary to gain the best power output and economy from an engine. Ignition is described in detail in Chapter 10.

1.10 Combustion in a petrol engine

As the piston reaches TDC the fuel is ignited by the spark at the spark plug and the burning process of the mixture begins. As the gases rapidly expand the piston is forced down the cylinder on the power stroke. The speed of the flame front must not exceed the speed of the power stoke. Figure 1.17 shows the combustion process occurring in a wedge-shaped combustion chamber of a petrol engine.

1.11 Combustion in a diesel engine

Combustion in a petrol engine originates (begins) at the spark plug and then progresses across the combustion chamber in a controlled manner. In the case of the diesel engine, combustion of the fuel is initiated (started) by the heat of the air in the chamber. As the droplets of fuel pass through the air they absorb the heat, and, if the temperature is high enough, the fuel will **vaporize** and **ignite**. Wide distribution of the fuel during the heating phase means that the burning process (combustion) starts at many different points in the chamber.

In direct injection systems, once ignition has started, most of the burning will tend to concentrate in zones fairly close to the injector. These zones must be fed with air in order to sweep away the burnt gases and supply the oxygen necessary for complete combustion. Any lack of oxygen in the combustion region will lead to black smoke in the exhaust.

A common and essential objective of all CI or diesel engine combustion systems is to achieve the maximum degree of mixing of the fuel, in the form of very fine droplets, with the air. This happens during injection of the fuel into the combustion chamber.

Injection will occur in the period approximately 15° BTDC on the compression stroke to approximately 10° ATDC. Mixing can be achieved by giving the air movement, either by shaping the inlet port, or by masking the inlet valve to give rotary movement to the incoming air charge about the axis of the cylinder. This movement of the air is called **swirl**.

There are two main methods of introducing fuel into the combustion chamber:

- direct, and
- indirect.

Direct injection

In the 'direct injection' system (Fig. 1.18) the fuel is injected directly into the combustion chamber which is formed in the piston crown. The air is made to rotate in this cavity at 90° to the incoming swirl by the squeezing out of the air from between the cylinder head face and the

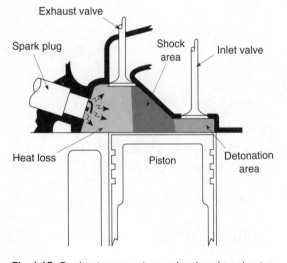

Fig. 1.17 Combustion zones in a wedge-shaped combustion chamber

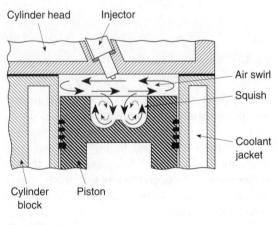

Fig. 1.18 Direct injection

piston crown as the piston approaches the end of its compression stroke. This rapid movement of the air is called **turbulence**.

Maximum cylinder pressures are high, causing diesel knock, rough running and higher exhaust smoke. However, easier starting, no starting aids, high thermal efficiency and fairly constant torque output are the main advantages. Also, because of the low surface area/volume ratio giving low heat losses, a characteristic of the system is a considerable saving in fuel giving good fuel consumption results. A disadvantage is a reduction in volumetric efficiency, due to the necessity of giving the incoming air the swirling movement as it passes into the cylinder. This effect can be largely overcome by the use of the 'indirect injection' system.

Indirect injection

In this arrangement the required movement of the air is made by transferring it, towards the end of the compression stroke, from the cylinder space into a small chamber (usually located in the cylinder head) via a restricting throat, arranged so as to give rapid rotation of the air in the chamber. The fuel is injected into the chamber at a point where the passage of air past the tip of the injector will give the maximum degree of mixing. This is shown in Fig. 1.19.

1.12 Phases of combustion

There are three distinct periods or phases.

First phase – ignition delay period

This is the time taken between the start of the injection of the fuel to the commencement of combustion. During this important period, the injected fuel particles are being heated by the hot air to the temperature required by the fuel to self-ignite.

Second phase – pressure rise or flame spread

The flame spread causes a sharp pressure rise due to the sudden combustion of the fuel that was injected during the first phase. The rate of pressure rise governs the extent of the combustion knock (diesel knock).

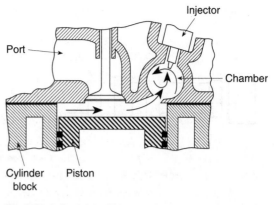

Fig. 1.19 Indirect injection

Third phase – direct or controlled burning

Direct burning of the fuel as it enters the chamber gives a more gradual pressure rise. The rate of combustion during this phase is directly controlled by the quantity of fuel injected into the cylinder. Combustion and expansion of the gases takes place as the piston descends on its power stroke producing a sustained torque on the crankshaft during the time the gases are burning.

Learning tasks

1. From what you have learned so far describe in your own words the main differences between combustion in a petrol engine and combustion in a diesel engine.
2. Examine the combustion chamber of a direct injection engine and make a sketch of the main components, e.g. piston positioned in the cylinder at TDC, the inlet and exhaust valves positioned in the cylinder head.

1.13 The main components used in the construction of the engine

Camshafts

As we have seen, the function of the camshaft is to open the valves at the correct time in the cycle of operations of the engine. It is also used as a drive for various auxiliary units such as the distributor, fuel pump and oil pump.

The position of the camshaft can be in the

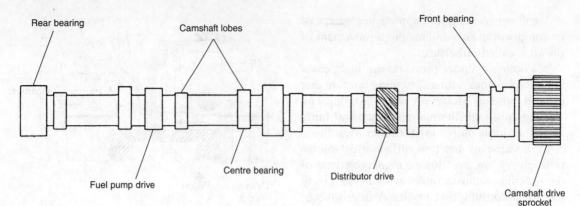

Fig. 1.20 The camshaft. The shape of a camshaft lobe is designed to give required performance with least strain on valve gear

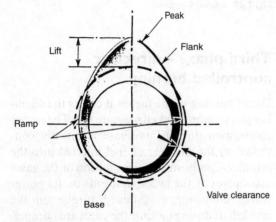

cylinder block (often termed as side-mounted). The main advantage of this arrangement is that the timing is not disturbed when the cylinder head is removed. An alternative position is on the top of the cylinder head (termed the over head cam or OHC). This has the advantage of there being a considerable reduction in components that are required to transmit the movement of the camshaft to open the valves.

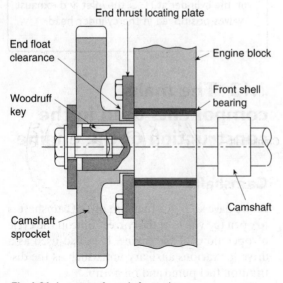

Fig. 1.21 Location of camshaft sprocket

Figure 1.20 shows a typical camshaft for a four-cylinder engine. The camshaft driving gear or sprocket is located on the shaft by means of a woodruff key or dowel peg to ensure correct fitting, and therefore correct timing, and to give a positive location of the driving gear (see Fig. 1.21).

Camshaft drives

Several methods are employed to transmit the drive from the crankshaft to the camshaft, these are chain, gear and toothed belt (Fig. 1.22). The most common one in use on modern OHC engines is the toothed belt drive. This has the advantages of being silent in operation, requiring no lubrication and being fairly easy to remove and replace.

> *Learning tasks*
>
> 1. From the manuals of over head camshaft engines, make a simple sketch of how the camshaft and crankshaft timing marks should be lined up.
> 2. When next in the workshop remove the timing belt from an engine. Rotate the crank shaft and re-align the timing marks, replace the belt and apply the correct tension.

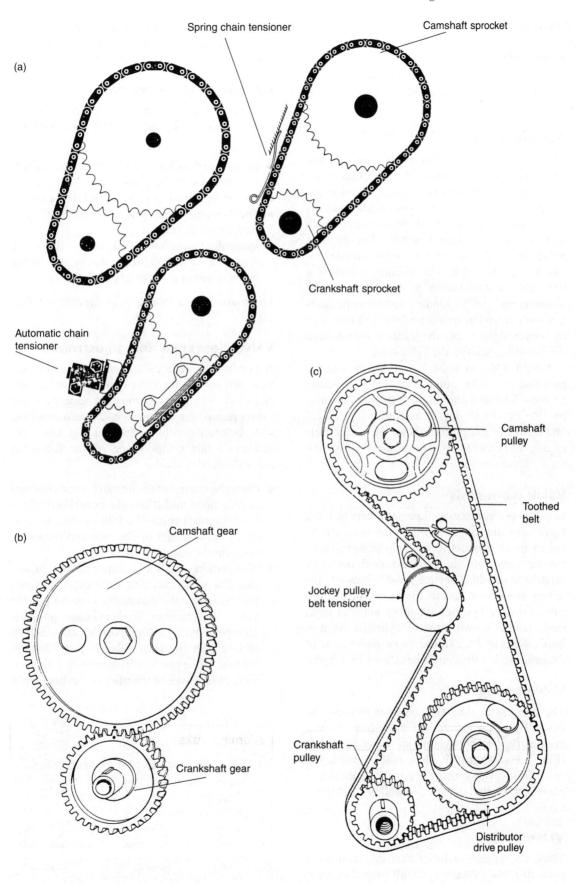

Fig. 1.22 Camshaft drives (a) chain driven, (b) gear driven, (c) toothed belt

Valves

Inlet valve

This is made from high tensile alloy steels, e.g. those containing nickel, chromium and molybdenum.

Exhaust valve

This is also made from high tensile alloy steels, e.g. those containing alloys of cobalt chromium and silicon chromium, silicon chromium austenitic steel, all of which resist oxidation, corrosion and wear. Under full power it can reach temperatures of around 650 °C. For extreme operating conditions the valve stem is made hollow and partly filled with sodium, which is a very soft metal having a melting point of approximately 98 °C. Under running conditions it is molten, and in splashing from end to end of the valve stem it assists the transfer of heat from the hot valve head to the valve stem.

Several types of valve have been used in the past and are to be found in current production engines. The most common are the poppet valve on the four-stroke engine as shown in Fig. 1.5 and the reed valve on the two-stroke motor cycle engine. The other types to have been tried are the rotary valve and the sleeve valve.

Valve stem seals

Because a clearance is necessary between the valve stem and the guide, valve stem seals are fitted to prevent excessive oil from passing down the stem and into the combustion chamber or exhaust manifold. They are most commonly fitted on the inlet valves as this is on the suction side of the combustion chamber and the oil is more readily drawn into the cylinder. As it is burnt it causes blue smoke to be passed out of the exhaust into the atmosphere. See Fig. 1.24(a).

Valve springs

The purpose of the valve spring is to close the valve. They also prevent the valve from bouncing open at the wrong time in the engine cycle (Fig. 1.23). Always fit close coils towards the valve head. The springs are made from either plain high-carbon steel or a low alloy chromium-vanadium steel.

Valve guides

These are usually made of cast iron and are a press fit in the cylinder head, although bronze is sometimes used, particularly for exhaust valves,

because of its better heat conducting properties. If the cylinder head is made of cast iron then the guide will be part of the same casting.

Operation of the valves

A number of different methods are used to open and close the valves, the most common methods are:

- **pushrod and rocker**   used where the camshaft is positioned in the cylinder block;
- **rocker, lever or finger**   used on OHC engines;
- **direct acting**   used where the camshaft acts directly on the tappet;
- **hydraulic operation**   used where the valve clearance is automatically taken up during normal running of the engine.

These are shown in Fig. 1.24 (a)–(c) and Fig. 1.25.

Valve clearance and adjustment

A number of methods are used to position the camshaft so that the valve clearance can be correctly set. The follower must be resting on the lowest part of the cam profile, i.e. the base of the cam, before any adjustment can take place. To determine this position one of the following methods may be used.

- Turn the engine until the valve to be adjusted is fully open and rotate the crankshaft a further complete turn. The follower will now be on the lowest part of the cam and the clearance can be correctly set.
- The 'rocking method' is a quicker way of setting the valve clearances although it is not quite so accurate. Rotate the engine until the valves on number four cylinder are just changing over, i.e. the exhaust valve is just closing and the inlet valve is just opening. Numbers one and four pistons will now be at TDC, the valves on number one cylinder will

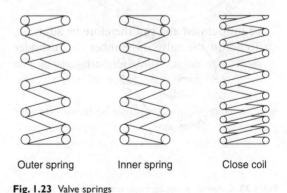

| Outer spring | Inner spring | Close coil |

Fig. 1.23 Valve springs

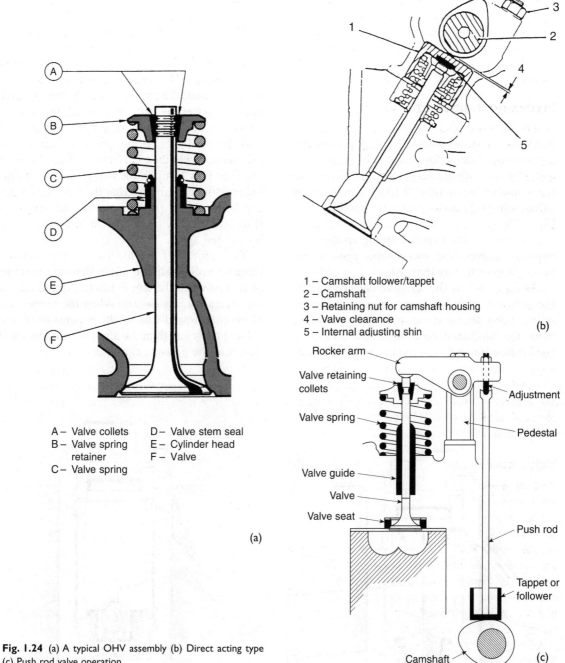

A – Valve collets
B – Valve spring
    retainer
C – Valve spring
D – Valve stem seal
E – Cylinder head
F – Valve

(a)

1 – Camshaft follower/tappet
2 – Camshaft
3 – Retaining nut for camshaft housing
4 – Valve clearance
5 – Internal adjusting shin

(b)

Fig. 1.24 (a) A typical OHV assembly (b) Direct acting type (c) Push rod valve operation

be fully closed and can therefore be adjusted. To adjust the valve on number four cylinder rotate the engine one full turn (360°). The same method can be used to set numbers two and three cylinders.

● The 'rule of nine' can also be used. Number the valves from the front of the engine one to eight. Rotate the crankshaft until number one valve is fully open; number eight valve will be fully closed and can therefore be adjusted, $1 + 8 = 9$. In this way if the numbers are

made to add up to nine the valves can be accurately set using the following method:

number 1 valve fully open, set number 8	$1 + 8 = 9$
number 2 valve fully open, set number 7	$2 + 7 = 9$
number 3 valve fully open, set number 6	$3 + 6 = 9$
number 4 valve fully open, set number 5	$4 + 5 = 9$
number 5 valve fully open, set number 4	$5 + 4 = 9$
number 6 valve fully open, set number 3	$6 + 3 = 9$
number 7 valve fully open, set number 2	$7 + 2 = 9$
number 8 valve fully open, set number 1	$8 + 1 = 9$

The above three methods can only be used on four-cylinder, four-stroke, in-line engines. For other layouts and cylinder arrangements, reference will need to be made to the manufacturer's manual to give the correct procedure to follow.

Hydraulic tappet operation

When the valve is closed, oil from the engine lubrication system passes through a port in the tappet body, through four grooves in the plunger and into the cylinder feed chamber. From the feed chamber the oil flows through a non-return valve (ball type) into the pressure chamber (A in Fig. 1.25).

The load of the cylinder spring enables the plunger to press the rocker arm against the valve, eliminating any free play.

As the cam lifts the follower the pressure in the pressure chamber rises, causing the non-return valve to close the port feed chamber. Since the oil cannot be compressed it forms a rigid connection between the tappet body, cylinder and plunger so that these parts rise together to open the valve.

The clearance between the tappet body and the cylinder is accurately controlled to allow a specific amount of oil to escape from the pressure chamber. Oil will only pass along the cylinder bore when the pressure is high during valve opening. After the valve has closed, this loss of oil will produce a small amount of free play; and also there will not be any pressure available in the pressure chamber. Oil from the feed chamber can then flow through the non-return valve into the pressure chamber so that the tappet cylinder can be raised by the pressure of the spring to eliminate the play in the system before the valve is operated again.

The amount of oil flowing into the pressure chamber will be slightly more than the amount of oil lost when the tappet has to expand due to the increased play (wear). When the tappet has to be compressed due to the expansion of the valve slightly less than the amount of oil lost will flow into the pressure chamber.

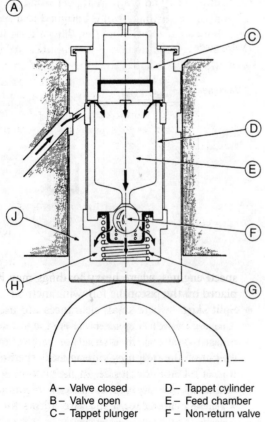
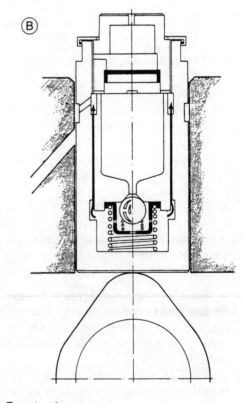

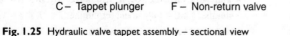

A – Valve closed	D – Tappet cylinder	G – Tappet spring
B – Valve open	E – Feed chamber	H – Pressure chamber
C – Tappet plunger	F – Non-return valve	J – Tappet body

Fig. 1.25 Hydraulic valve tappet assembly – sectional view

Note: If the engine is started up after standing unused for a lengthy period of time a chattering noise may be heard from the valve operating system. This is normal and will disappear after a few seconds when the tappets are pressurized with oil.

Cylinder head

Function

This forms the cover that is fitted on the top of the cylinder block. It may contain the combustion chamber which is formed in the space remaining when the piston reaches the top of its stroke. On some designs this space is formed in the top of the piston and the cylinder head is flat. The head will also contain the spark plugs, inlet and exhaust valves together with their operating mechanism, a number of ports which allow gases into and out of the cylinders, bolt holes to enable components to be bolted to the head and the head to be attached to the cylinder block. It may also contain part of a water jacket which forms part of the cooling system. The materials from which the cylinder head is made are often the same as the cylinder block, e.g. cast iron or aluminium. The cylinder head is illustrated in Fig. 1.26.

Cylinder head tightening sequence

To avoid distorting either the cylinder head or the head gasket the **tightening sequence** (order) must be followed. The torque settings must also be correct to prevent over-stretching of the bolts and studs or stripping of the threads. The manufacture's manual must always be referred to and the procedure followed; this will ensure that the above problems are not encountered when reassembling the cylinder head to the engine. In some cases it may be necessary to fit new bolts or nuts as these become stretched and cannot be used a second time. Figure 1.27 shows a typical tightening sequence.

Learning tasks

1. Why is the inlet valve larger in diameter than the exhaust valve?
2. What are the reasons for using hydraulic tappets?
3. Under what circumstances would it be necessary to **decoke** a cylinder head? Name any special tools or equipment that you would use.
4. Give the correct procedure for checking and adjusting the valve clearances for an OHC engine.
5. How would you check the serviceability of the valves and their seats?
6. When refitting the cylinder head, why is it necessary to tighten the bolts/nuts in the correct sequence? What would happen if this sequence was not followed?
7. Why is it necessary to have a gap between the valve stem and operating mechanism? What would happen if the engine was operated with no valve clearance?
8. Remove and refit a cylinder head from an engine, make out a job sheet and record any special tools used, faults found and safety procedures that were followed. Draw up an operations schedule for the task.

Piston

The main function of the piston is to provide the movable end of the cylinder, so as to convert the expansion of the burning gases on the power stroke into mechanical movement of the piston, connecting rod and crankshaft. On some types of engines the piston crown is designed to a specific shape instead of being flat. This allows for the shape of the combustion chamber to be included in the piston crown instead of in the cylinder head, and may also have an effect on the flow of gases into and out of the cylinder. Figure 1.28 shows an example of the shape of the combustion chamber being included in the piston crown.

Piston skirt

Several shapes are used in the manufacture of the lower part of the piston, called the piston skirt, e.g.

● **Solid skirt** used in both CI and SI high speed engines, where heavy loadings may be placed on the piston;
● **Split skirt** where small clearances are used to reduce piston slap when the engine is cold;
● **Slipper type** which is used to reduce the weight of the piston by cutting away the bottom of the non-thrust sides of the piston skirt; at the same time it reduces the area in contact with the cylinder wall, and also allows for a reduction in the overall height of the engine as BDC is now closer to the crankshaft.

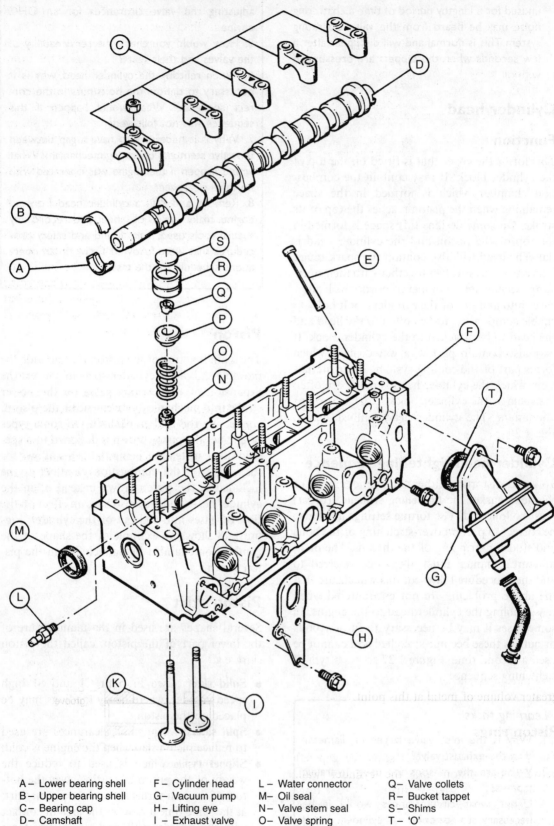

A – Lower bearing shell
B – Upper bearing shell
C – Bearing cap
D – Camshaft
E – Vacuum pump plunger

F – Cylinder head
G – Vacuum pump
H – Lifting eye
I – Exhaust valve
K – Inlet valve

L – Water connector
M – Oil seal
N – Valve stem seal
O – Valve spring
P – Valve spring retainer

Q – Valve collets
R – Bucket tappet
S – Shims
T – 'O'

Fig. 1.26 Cylinder head – exploded view

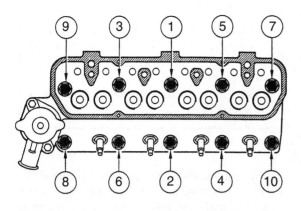

Fig. 1.27 Cylinder head bolt tightening sequence

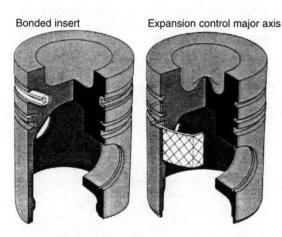

Bonded insert   Expansion control major axis

Fig. 1.28 Combustion chambers

A piston skirt is illustrated in Fig. 1.29. When cold, the piston head is smaller in diameter than the skirt. When the engine is operating at its normal temperature the piston head expands more than the skirt due to its being closer to the very hot gases and also the fact that there is a greater volume of metal at this point.

Piston rings

The piston ring (Fig. 1.30) seals the gap left between the piston and the cylinder wall. Made from high-grade centrifugally cast iron, it is split to enable the ring to be assembled onto the piston. Some rings may be coated on their outer edge with chromium to give better wear characteristics and longer life. Normally

three rings are fitted. The **top compression ring** takes most of the compression pressure and forms the first defence against the heat and escaping gases. It may be stepped so that it misses the ridge that tends to form in the cylinder bore at TDC. The second is also a compression ring that completes the sealing against compression loss. The third ring is the **oil control ring**. It is this ring that removes the excess oil from the cylinder wall, passing it back to the sump through holes drilled in the oil control ring groove of the piston. This ring may be made up from a number of steel rails that have radiused chromium plated edges. A crimped spring fitted in the ring groove next to the piston expands the rails against the cylinder wall. This type are commonly fitted where the piston comes very close to the oil in the sump, i.e. short stroke engines, or where some wear has taken place in the cylinder bore but not enough to warrant reboring the engine and fitting new pistons and rings.

Connecting rod

The con-rod connects the piston to the crankshaft. Its action converts the linear (straight line) movement of the piston into the rotary movement of the crankshaft. It is attached to the piston by the gudgeon pin via the **little-end** and to the crankshaft journal by the **big-end**. They are manufactured in the shape of an 'H' as this gives the greatest resistance to the stresses under which it operates whilst at the same time being as light as possible.

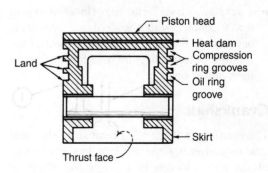

Piston head
Heat dam
Compression ring grooves
Oil ring groove
Land
Skirt
Thrust face

Fig. 1.29 Piston skirt

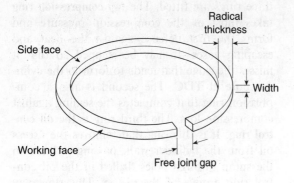

Fig. 1.30 Piston ring

Cylinder block

The cylinder block (Fig. 1.31) contains the pistons, liners, crankshaft together with its bearings and sometimes the camshaft. It may also contain the oil pump and galleries to direct the oil to the bearings and the water jacket for the cooling system. It is normally cast in a mould using **cast iron** or **aluminium** and machined to fine tolerances.

Cylinder liners

Cylinder liners are used to allow the engine block to be manufactured from a different kind of material, e.g. an aluminium block and cast iron liners. The liners, being made of cast iron, have a much better wear resistance than many other materials. The block can be made from a lighter material than cast iron therefore saving weight. Two of the most common types of liners used are:

- a dry-type liner which forms a lining in the cylinder and is a press fit in the block;
- a wet liner, which forms the cylinder and is in direct contact with the coolant; with seals between the liner and the cylinder block at the top and bottom they are held in position by the cylinder head.

Crankshaft

The crankshaft (Fig. 1.32) represents the final link in converting the straight line movement of the piston to one of rotating movement at the flywheel. In the case of a multi-cylinder engine, the crankshaft also controls the relative movement of the pistons from TDC to BDC whilst at the same time receiving their power impulses.

Learning tasks

1. Take a look at an engine with cylinder liners and make a simple sketch to show how they are kept in place. Show one other way of doing this.
2. Give three reasons for fitting liners in a cylinder block.

The crankshaft rotates in plain bearing shells in the crankcase, held in position by bearing caps. Oil under pressure from the oil pump is forced into the bearings to lubricate the moving surfaces.

A one piece construction is most commonly used for the motor vehicle crankshaft. It extends the whole length of the engine and must therefore be fairly rigid. The drive for the camshaft is normally taken from the front end of the crankshaft, as is the pulley and belt drive for the engine auxiliaries such as the water pump and alternator.

The flywheel is fitted to the other end of the crankshaft as shown in Fig. 1.33. Its purpose is to store the energy given to it on the power

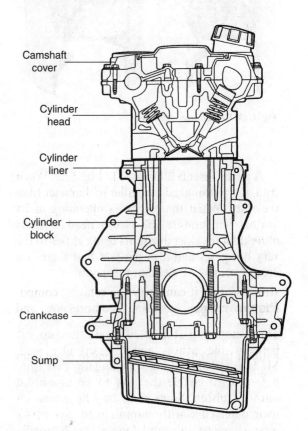

Fig. 1.31 Cylinder block and crankcase assembly

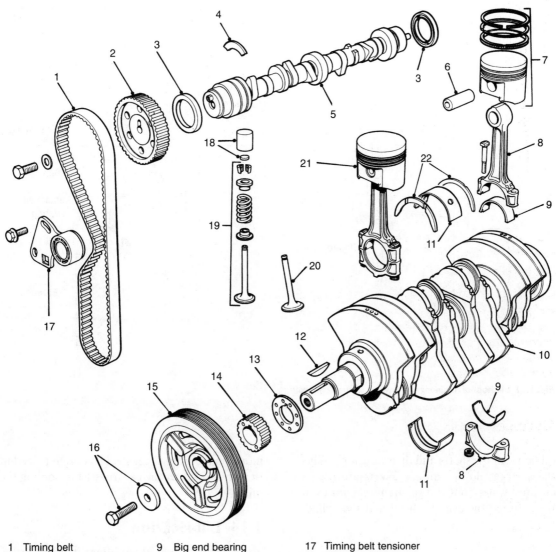

1	Timing belt	9	Big end bearing	17	Timing belt tensioner	
2	Camshaft gear	10	Crankshaft	18	Tappet and shim	
3	Camshaft oil seal	11	Main bearing	19	Inlet valve, oil seal, spring, cap and cotters	
4	Camshaft locating plate	12	Key – pulley and gear	20	Exhaust valve	
5	Camshaft	13	Guide plate	21	Piston and connecting rod assembly	
6	Gudgeon pin	14	Crankshaft gear	22	Crankshaft thrust and washers	
7	Piston rings and piston	15	Crankshaft pulley			
8	Connecting rod and cap	16	Pulley bolt and special washer			

Fig. 1.32 A four-cylinder, five main bearing crankshaft

stroke so that it can carry the rotating components over the induction, compression and exhaust strokes (these strokes do not produce any useable power but the engine cannot operate without them). It is also a convenient point from which to pass the drive to the clutch. The starter ring gear is commonly fitted to the outer circumference to enable the engine to be rotated during starting. Several methods of locating the flywheel to the crankshaft are used, such as dowel, key, flange and taper with slotted washer. The attachment must be positive and secure, and preferably in one position only. This provides for balance of both crankshaft and flywheel together.

Seals

Oil seals (Fig. 1.34) are placed at each end of the crankshaft and camshaft to prevent the loss of

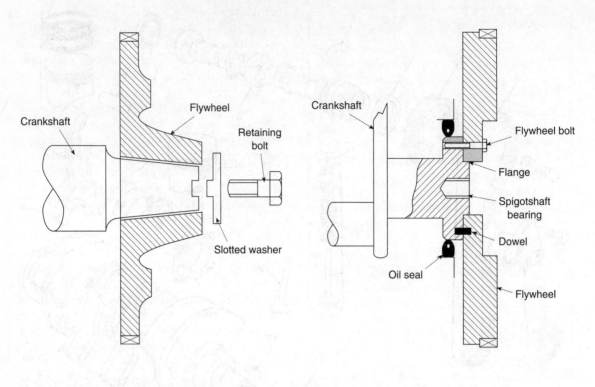

Fig. 1.33 Methods of mounting the flywheel to the crankshaft

oil between the shafts and their housings. Where the surfaces do not move, gaskets are used to ensure a water-, oil- and gas-tight seal, for example between the cylinder head and the cylinder block.

Sump

The bottom of the engine is enclosed by a sump which normally contains the engine oil. Com-

monly made from sheet steel it is often placed in the air flow under the car to assist in cooling the oil.

1.14 Lubrication

To understand how the oil does its work in the operation of the engine and other parts of the motor vehicle, we first need to understand what is meant by **friction**. The term friction is defined

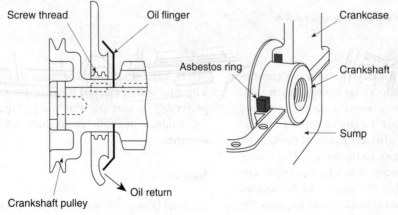

Fig. 1.34 Crankshaft oil seals

as a resistance to movement between any two surfaces in contact with each other.

In some cases friction on a vehicle is useful (Fig. 1.35). The type of friction which keeps our feet from slipping when we are walking also provides the frictional grip that is required between the tyres and the surface of the road, the brake pads and the brake disc, the drive belt and the pulleys of the fan and crankshaft.

If friction occurs in the engine it can cause serious problems as it destroys the effectiveness of the engine components due to the heat generated. This in turn causes wear and early failure of components such as bearings and their journals. It follows then that this type of friction must be reduced to a minimum to allow the engine to operate satisfactorily.

Many years ago it was found that considerable effort was required to drag or push a heavy stone along the ground. It was found to be much easier to roll the stone (Fig. 1.36). It was later discovered that when the stone was put onto a raft and floated on water it was easier still to transport the same stone (Fig. 1.37).

It was almost impossible to move the stone by sliding it along the ground because **dry sliding** friction creates a lot of resistance. This type of friction is used in the brakes and so is useful (Fig. 1.38). When the stone was rolled it was found to be easier to move. **Rolling** friction creates a lot less resistance and therefore far less heat. This type of friction exists in the ball-and-roller-type wheel bearing (Fig. 1.36).

When the stone was placed on a raft and floated on the water it made the work lighter still. This is called **fluid** friction and exists in the sliding bearings under certain conditions as it does in the crankshaft bearings.

Note: The fact that the raft floats on the water is not the most important factor. When the water comes between the raft and the bed of the river the only force resisting the movement of the raft carrying the stone is the resistance caused by one particle of water sliding over another. This resistance is a lot less than the resistance of dry friction when an object is in direct contact with the solid ground (Fig 1.38).

(a)　　　　　　　　　　　　(b)

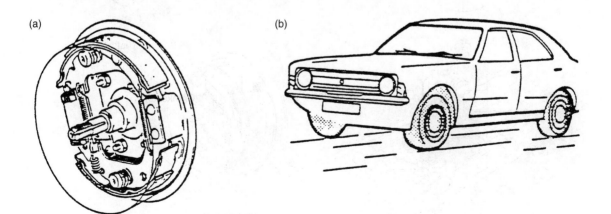

Fig. 1.35 Useful friction in the motor vehicle. (a) Friction between brake linings and brake drum. (b) Friction between tyres and road surface.

Ball/roller bearing

Fig. 1.36 Examples of rolling friction

To summarize, less force is required to overcome rolling friction than sliding friction. However, when no lubricant is present, the same **wear**, **heat** or eventual **seizure** of the surfaces in contact will occur, but to a lesser degree in the case of rolling friction. From this we can see that friction can be classified into four basic types.

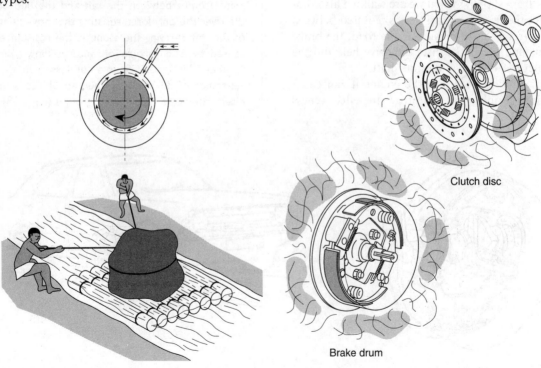

Fig. 1.37 Examples of fluid friction

Clutch plate   Disc brake

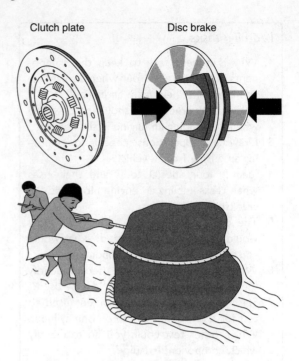

Fig. 1.38 Examples of dry sliding friction

● **Dry friction** This is friction between two materials without any type of lubrication. It can generate a large amount of heat (Fig. 1.39).

Clutch disc

Brake drum

Fig. 1.39 Heat is generated by dry friction

- **Boundary friction** This is friction between two materials where very little lubrication is present (Fig. 1.40).
- **Fluid friction** (hydrodynamic friction) A film of fluid prevents contact between two materials, for example between the rotating crankshaft journal and the bearing. A film of oil under pressure ensures that the two metal surfaces slide over one another. The only friction that occurs is between the oil particles themselves. These have less resistance to sliding over one another than solid surfaces have. This reduces friction to a minimum resulting in minimum heat and therefore minimum wear (Fig. 1.41).
- **Mixed friction** This is friction between two materials with a good oil film which is not quite thick enough to prevent contact occurring between the metal surfaces. Here the metal itself can touch the surface of the sec-

ond metal for a short time but this is not long enough to produce much heat; therefore wear is limited. This type of friction takes place in ball and roller bearings (Fig. 1.42). The more mixed friction moves towards boundary friction the more heat is produced, this causes more wear and eventually complete seizure.

Learning tasks

1. Name three areas on the motor vehicle where you will find the following types of friction:
   (a) dry friction
   (b) boundary friction
   (c) mixed friction
2. What can change fluid friction to mixed friction and mixed friction to boundary friction?

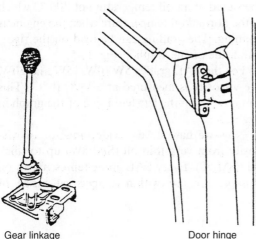

Gear linkage   Door hinge

Fig. 1.40 Areas of boundary friction

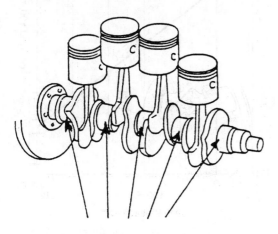

Fig. 1.41 Points of fluid friction

Engine oil – SAE viscosity classification

When selecting oil for an engine it is important that the one chosen is suitable for the engine itself and the conditions under which it will be used. Two important factors determining the choice of oil are:

- that the oil meets the quality requirements;
- that the oil has the right 'thickness' or **viscosity**.

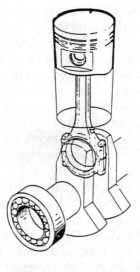

Fig. 1.42 Mixed friction occurs in this ball and roller bearing

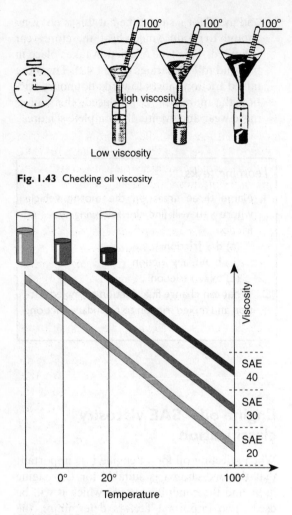

Fig. 1.43 Checking oil viscosity

Fig. 1.44 SAE grading of engine oil

nents. This would cause the oil film, which must be present to keep the components apart, to break down.

The most significant characteristic of lubricating oil is its viscosity. This can be measured in different ways. One way, shown in Fig. 1.43, is to check the quantity of oil which passes through a hole in a tube of standard size during a certain length of time at a given temperature.

A widely used system of grading oil, based upon viscosity, has been worked out by the American Authorities for Standardization (SAE – Society of Automotive Engineers). Various oils are grouped into viscosity grades marked with SAE numbers. These indicate the **viscosity index** of the oil (see Fig. 1.44).

For engine oils the **SAE grades** are numbered: 5W, 10W, 15W, 20W, 30, 40, 50. The lower numbers indicate thin oils and the higher numbers indicate thicker, or higher-viscosity, oils. For the SAE grades 20, 30, 40 and 50, the viscosity is measured at an oil temperature of 100°C which is the normal oil temperature when the engine is running. The grading can be read on the right-hand side of the graph in Fig. 1.45.

For the SAE grades 5W, 10W, 15W and 20W, the viscosity is measured at −18°C (0°F). This can be seen on the left-hand side of the graph in Fig. 1.46.

Now we have a very wide range of oil viscosity from very thin oil (SAE5W) up to thick oil (SAE50). Every SAE grade represents an oil suitable for use within a specified range of

The term viscosity refers to the relative thickness of a liquid. A thin free-flowing liquid has a low viscosity, and a thick, slow-flowing liquid has a high viscosity. It will be seen that the viscosity of a liquid like oil changes as the temperature changes. At high temperatures the oil becomes thinner (giving a low viscosity) and at low temperatures the oil becomes thicker (giving a high viscosity). The correct oil viscosity is essential for the efficient operation of the engine because when the oil is too thick (high viscosity) it causes resistance and too much power is needed to turn the engine, making it difficult to start when cold.

Thick oil does not circulate freely enough during the starting period, causing insufficient lubrication of the bearings and thus increasing wear. Oil which is too thin (low viscosity) combined with a high temperature and a heavy load has the risk of oil being pressed out from between the bearings or other engine compo-

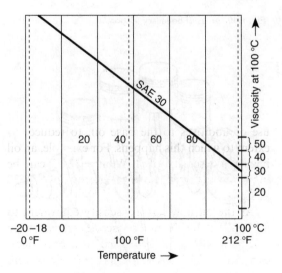

Fig. 1.45 SAE 30 single grade oil

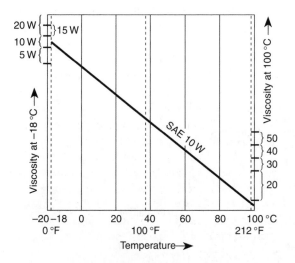

Fig. 1.46 SAE 10W single grade oil

temperatures and for a certain type of engine, e.g. oils within the viscosity range SAE 5W, 10W and 20W are suitable for use in climates with temperatures ranging from very low to moderate. SAE 20 and 30 are suitable for use in moderate to hot climates. SAE 40 and 50 oils are mostly used in old engines designed for rather thick oil or in badly worn engines with high oil consumption.

However, many engines operate in climates where the temperature varies considerably from season to season. In addition it is always preferable for any engine to run on low-viscosity oil during the starting period when the engine is cold, and on high-viscosity oil when the engine is hot and fully loaded. For practical reasons it is not possible to use a low-viscosity oil for starting and then change to a high-viscosity oil when the engine is hot. Therefore, we need an oil which is thin enough at low temperatures, but will also have a sufficiently high viscosity at high temperatures – that is a **multi-viscosity** or **multi-grade** oil.

We cannot change the fact that oil becomes thinner as it is heated, but it is possible, by the use of additives to the base oil, to reduce the extent to which this happens. For example, an oil having a viscosity of 10W at −18 °C can be improved so that it also has a viscosity of SAE30 at 100 °C.

As the oil now has a viscosity equivalent to SAE10W at −18 °C and a viscosity equivalent to SAE30 at 100 °C, it is marked with both numbers, that is SAE 10W/30. Oils are available with a very wide viscosity range, e.g. 10W/50 which may be used in any climate enables the cold

engine to start on a thin oil (SAE10W) and, when hot, to run on a sufficiently thick oil (SAE50).

Oils that meet the specification for more than one SAE grade are often referred to as multi-viscosity, **all season** or multi-grade oils. Remember that the SAE grades only tell you the viscosity of the oil and not the quality. The correct method for selecting the oil with the right SAE number corresponding to the temperature and running conditions would be to check in the specifications for the engine. Oil producers have worked out, together with the engine manufacturers, recommendations for the oil viscosity most suitable for given conditions.

It is important that only the correct grade of oil is used in a given vehicle and the information about that is given in the driver's handbook or the workshop manual. In most modern engines multi-grade oils are recommended regardless of temperature. An SAE10W/40 oil, for instance, can be used in most climates thus simplifying the selection of oil. It is important to know that the SAE grades only give information on the viscosity of the oil and not the quality. This can be found by making reference to the API (American Petroleum Institute) classification.

Lubrication system

There are three main types of lubrication systems in common use on internal combustion engines. These are:

- **wet sump**
- **dry sump**
- **total loss**

The object of the lubrication system is to feed oil to all the moving parts of the engine to reduce friction and wear and to dissipate heat. Modern oils also clean the engine by keeping the products of combustion, dirt, etc. in suspension. This makes it essential that oil and filters are changed in accordance with the manufacturers' instructions. It can be seen from this that the oil performs four important functions.

- It keeps friction and wear on the moving parts to a minimum.
- It acts as a coolant and transfers the heat from the moving parts.
- It keeps the moving parts clean and carries the impurities to the oil filter.
- It reduces corrosion and noise in the engine. It also acts as a sealant around the piston and rings.

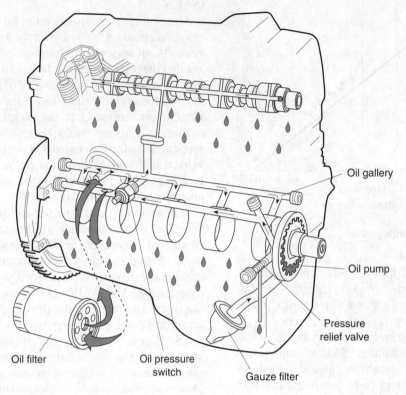

Oil gallery

Oil pump

Pressure
relief valve

Oil filter

Oil pressure
switch

Gauze filter

Fig. I.47 Lubrication circuit for an
OHC engine

Main components in the lubrication system

The lubrication system is mostly pressurized and consists of the following main components.

- **Oil pump** draws the oil from the sump and delivers it under pressure to the engine lubrication system.
- **Relief valve** limits the maximum pressure of the oil supplied by the pump to the system.
- **Sump** serves as a reservoir for the oil.
- **Oil galleries** are channels or drillings through which the oil passes to the different lubrication points in the engine.
- **Oil pressure indicator** shows whether the oil pressure is being kept within the manufacturers' limits.
- **Oil filter** filters the oil removing impurities to keep it clean.

A typical lubrication system works in the following way.

1. Oil is drawn from the sump by the oil pump.

2. The pump pressurizes the oil and passes it through the oil filter into the oil galleries and passages which lead to the crankshaft and camshaft bearings and, in some engines, the rocker shaft and rocker arms.
3. The oil splashed from the crankshaft lubricates the pistons and other internal parts of the engine.
4. After lubricating the moving components the oil drips back down into the sump. Figure 1.47 shows the oil flow in an engine lubrication system.

Function of the oil

When looking at the working surfaces of, say, the crankshaft (A in Fig. 1.48) and the main bearings in which it runs (B) they appear to be blank and smooth. But when observed under a

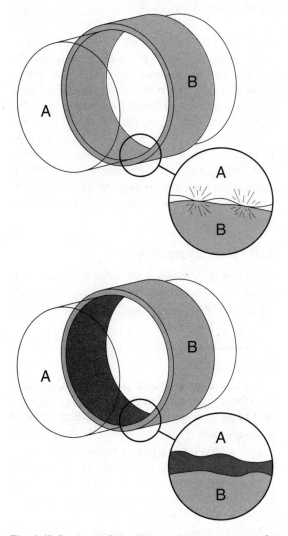

Fig. 1.48 Bearing surface shown under a microscope. Oil under pressure keeps the surfaces apart

powerful microscope they will be seen to be uneven and rough. When oil is introduced between these surfaces, it fills up the slight irregularities and forms a thin layer, called an oil film. It is this oil film that separates the surfaces and, when the components are rotating, prevents metal-to-metal contact. When the engine is operating the oil must be strong enough to withstand the heavy loads imposed on all the moving parts. The oil is therefore delivered under pressure to the bearings and, to enable it to enter, a very small clearance between the shaft and bearing is necessary.

The clearance must be sufficient for the oil to enter, but small enough to resist the heavy loadings to which the bearings are subjected. This clearance is approximately 0.05 mm for a shaft of 60–70 mm diameter. When the shaft is not rotating but is resting on the bearings only a very thin film of residual oil separates the surfaces. As the engine starts the only lubrication for the first revolution is provided by this thin film of oil; as the revolutions increase, the oil pump starts to deliver the oil under pressure to the bearings. The oil is drawn round by the rotating shaft which, together with the pressure, forms an oil wedge which lifts the shaft up from the bearing. The shaft then rotates freely, separated from the bearings by this thin film of oil. A correct bearing clearance is shown in Fig. 1.49.

It is important that the bearings have the correct clearance. Too much will cause the oil to escape from the bearing without being able to create the required **oil wedge**; too little will restrict the oil from entering the bearing, causing metal-to-metal contact. In both cases wear will increase.

The oil which is pressed out from the bearings is splashed around and forms an oil mist which lubricates the cylinder and piston (Fig. 1.50). In some cases a hole is drilled from the side of the connecting rod into the bearing shell to spray oil onto the thrust side of the cylinder wall.

Function of the sump

When the engine is filled with oil, it flows down through the engine into a container called the sump. This is attached to the bottom of the engine block with a series of small bolts, usually with a gasket between the block and the sump. It is commonly formed from sheet steel pressed to a shape that has one end slightly lower to form the oil reservoir. In the bottom of the sump is the drain plug. **Baffle plates** are fitted to

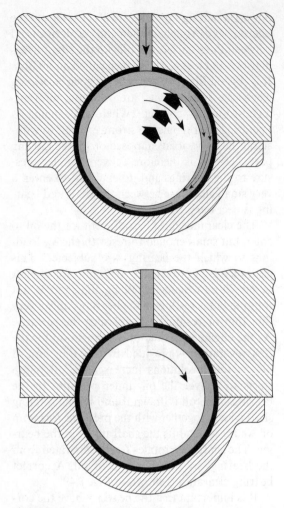

Fig. 1.49 Bearing clearance correct

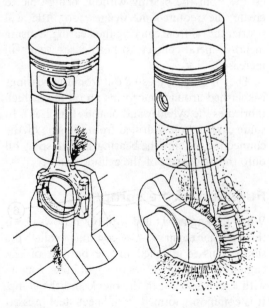

Fig. 1.50 Splash lubrication from the big-end bearing

prevent the oil from splashing around or surging when the vehicle is accelerating and braking or

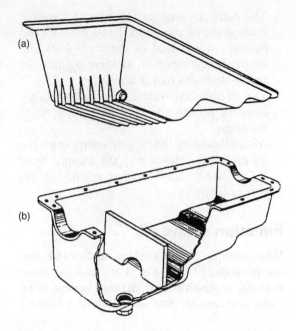

Fig. 1.51 Types of sump (a) aluminium cast, (b) pressed steel

going round corners. If all the oil is allowed to move to the rear or to the side of the sump, the oil pick-up may become exposed causing air to be drawn into the lubrication. The sump also acts as an oil cooler because it extends into the air stream under the vehicle. To assist with the cooling process there may also be small fins formed on the outside to increase its surface area. Aluminium is sometimes used to give a more rigid structure to support the crankshaft and crankcase of the engine. Two types of sump are shown in Fig. 1.51.

Oil level indicators

The level in the sump is checked by means of a dipstick on which the maximum and minimum oil levels are indicated. A number of vehicles fit

---

Learning tasks

1. What would be the effects of running an engine with the oil level (a) above the maximum, and (b) below the minimum on the dipstick?
2. A vehicle is brought into the workshop with a suspected oil leak from the sump. Suggest one method of checking exactly where the leak is coming from and describe the procedure for correcting the fault.
3. How should a resistance-type oil level indicator be checked for correct operation?

indicators to show the driver the level of oil in the engine without having to lift the bonnet and remove the dipstick manually. One of the popular types used is the 'hot wire' dipstick where a resistance wire is fitted inside the hollow stick between the oil level marks. The current is only supplied to the wire for about 1.5 seconds at the instant the ignition is switched on. If the wire is not in the oil it overheats and an extra electrical resistance is created which signals the ECU (electronic control unit) to operate the driver's warning light. This is illustrated in Fig. 1.52.

Oil pump

The oil enters the pump via a pipe with a strainer on the end which is immersed in the oil reservoir in the sump. This strainer prevents larger particles from being sucked into the lubrication system. The oil pump creates the required pressure that forces the oil to the various lubrication points. The quantity of oil delivered by the pump varies greatly from vehicle to vehicle and also depends

on engine speed but will be approximately 120 litres when the speed of the vehicle is 100 km/h.

The most common types of pumps used in the motor vehicle engines are the **gear**, **rotary** or **vane**.

Gear pump

Shown in Fig. 1.53, this consists of two gears in a compact housing with an inlet and outlet. The gears can be either **spur** or **helical** in shape (the

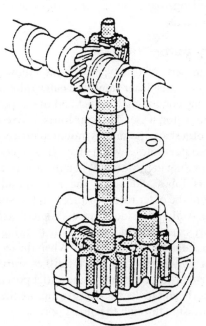

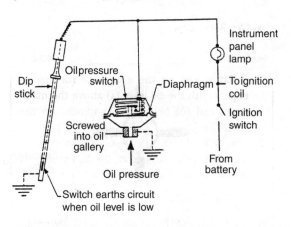

Fig. 1.52 Combined oil pressure and low oil level warning circuit

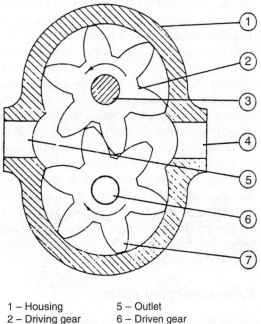

1 – Housing	5 – Outlet
2 – Driving gear	6 – Driven gear
3 – Driving shaft	7 – Gear lobe
4 – Inlet	

Fig. 1.53 Gear-type pump

helical being quieter in operation). The pump drive shaft is mounted in the housing and fixed to this is the driving gear. Oil is drawn via the inlet into the pump. It passes through the pump in the spaces between the gear teeth and pump casing and out through the outlet at a faster rate than is used by the system. In this way pressure is created in the system until the maximum pressure is reached at which time the pressure-relief valve will open and release the excess pressure into the sump.

Rotary pump

The main parts of this type of pump (shown in Fig. 1.54) are the **inner rotor**, the **outer rotor** and the **housing** containing the inlet and outlet ports. The inner rotor, which has four lobes, is fixed to the end of a shaft; the shaft is mounted off-centre in the outer rotor which has five recesses corresponding to the lobes. When the inner rotor turns, its lobes slide over the corresponding recesses in the outer rotor turning it in the pump housing. At the inlet side the recess is small; as the rotor turns the recess increases in size drawing oil up from the sump into the pump. When the recess is at its largest the inlet port finishes, further movement of the rotor reveals the outlet port and the recess begins to decrease in size forcing the oil under pressure through the outlet port.

Vane-type pump

This pump, shown in Fig. 1.55, takes the form of a driven rotor that is eccentrically mounted (mounted offset) inside a circular housing. The rotor is slotted and the **eccentric vanes** are free to slide within the slots, a pair of thrust rings ensuring that the vanes maintain a close clearance with the housing. When in operation the vanes are pressurized outwards by the centrifugal action of the rotor rotating at high speed. As the pump rotates the volume between the vanes at the inlet increases, thus drawing oil from the sump into the pump; this volume decreases as the oil reaches the outlet, pressurizing the oil and delivering it to the oil gallery. This type has the advantage of giving a continuous oil flow rather than the pulsating flow that is rather characteristic of the gear-type pump.

Pressure-relief valve

As engine speed increases the oil pump produces a higher pressure than is required by the engine lubrication system. A **pressure-relief valve** (see Fig. 1.56) is therefore fitted in the system to take

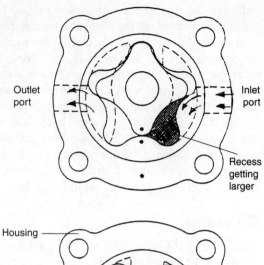

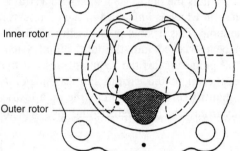

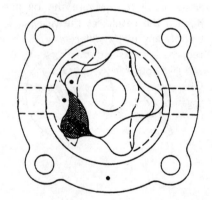

Fig. 1.54 Rotary pump

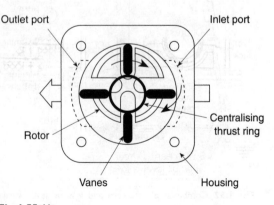

Fig. 1.55 Vane pump

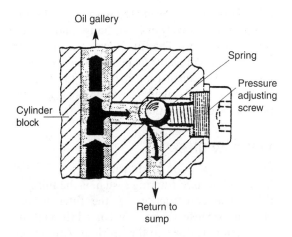

Fig. 1.56 Oil pressure-relief valve

away the excess pressure and maintain it at a level appropriate for the bearings and seals used. It will be seen then that the relief valve performs two important functions: first, it acts as a pressure regulator; and second, it acts as a safety device in the lubrication system. The main types in use are the ball valve, the plate and the plunger or poppet valve. Each is held in the closed position by a spring. As the oil pressure in the oil gallery rises above the setting for the relief valve, the valve opens against spring pressure allowing the oil to bypass the system and return back to the sump via the return outlet. The force on the spring determines the oil pressure in the lubrication system.

Oil filter

When the oil passes through the engine it becomes contaminated with carbon (the by-product of the combustion process), dust (drawn in from the atmosphere), small metal particles (from components rubbing together), water and sludge (a combination of all these impurities mixed together). All these will cause engine wear if they remain in the oil, so the engine must be equipped with a filtering system that will remove them and keep the oil as clean as possible. Most modern engines are equipped with a filtering system where all the oil is filtered before it reaches the bearings. This arrangement is called the **full-flow** system. There is another system also in use where only a portion of the oil passes through the filter, called the **bypass** filter system. The two systems are shown in Fig. 1.57.

The importance of filtering the oil is shown by the results of an investigation into the wear

---

Learning tasks

1. When next in the workshop, dismantle a vane-, rotor- and gear-type oil pump. Using the manufacturers' data measure and record the tolerances for each type and give your recommendations on serviceability.

2. Remove the oil pressure switch from the oil gallery of an engine and attach the appropriate adapter to measure the oil pressure. Record the results at the relevant speeds. Identify any major differences between the recorded results and the manufacturer's data and give your recommendations.

3. Give two reasons for low oil pressure together with recommedations for correcting the fault.

(a)

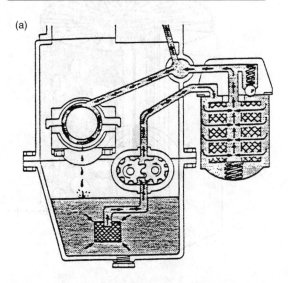

(b)

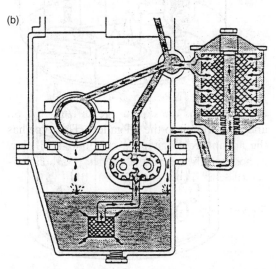

Fig. 1.57 Lubrication systems (a) full flow system, (b) by-pass system

on the cylinder and piston, using the two filtering systems. It was found that maximum wear (100%) occurs in engines working without an oil filter. When a bypass filter is used, wear is reduced to about 43% on the cylinder and 73% on the piston, which means that the life of the piston and cylinder are almost doubled. Minimum wear occurs when a full-flow filter is used, wear is again reduced by a further 15% on the cylinder and 22% on the piston. This means that the life of the piston and cylinder is four to five times longer than in an engine working without a filter. A good oil filter must be capable of stopping the flow of very small particles without restricting the flow of oil through the filter. To meet this requirement different materials are used as the filtering medium. Resin-impregnated paper is widely used, the paper being folded in order to make a large surface area available for the oil to flow through; particles are left on the paper and clean oil is passed to the lubrication system. In this way when the filter is changed the impurities are removed at the same time. In other types of oil filters different kinds of fibrous materials are used. The filtering material is enclosed in perforated cylinders, one outer and one inner to form a filter element (Fig. 1.58).

The oil enters through the perforations in the cylinder, passes through the filtering element and leaves through the central tube outlet. Many modern filters are now the cartridge-type which is removed complete. The advantages of this disposable type are that it cleans the oil very efficiently, it is relatively easy to change and it is less messy to remove. The filter element can also be located in a removable metal container. With the replaceable-element-type it is only the element itself that is changed, the container is thoroughly cleaned and the 'O' ring replaced.

Full-flow filter

Oil filter operation is shown in Fig. 1.59. The most widely used filtering system is the full-flow filter. The construction of the filter is very efficient because all the oil is passed through the filter before it flows to the bearings. After a certain length of time the element becomes dirty and less efficient and must therefore be changed. If the element is not changed regularly the impurities will accumulate and the element will become clogged, restricting or preventing the oil from passing through the filter. For this reason a relief valve is fitted into the filter which opens and allows the oil to bypass the clogged filter element and flow directly to the bearings unrestricted. If the condition is allowed to continue, unfiltered oil will carry abrasive particles to the bearings causing rapid wear.

Cartridge filter

In the cartridge filter the relief valve is in the filter (shown in the open position in Fig. 1.60). Many of the filters now contain a valve under-

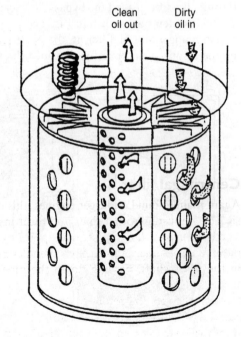

Clean oil out   Dirty oil in

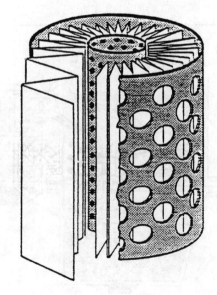

Fig. 1.58 The oil filter and pleated element

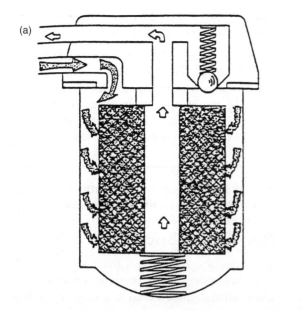
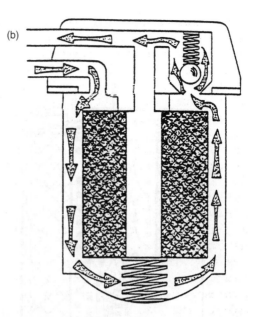

Fig. 1.59 Oil filter operation (a) oil being filtered, (b) oil filter blocked

neath the inlet hole which opens when oil pressure forces oil into the filter. When the engine stops and the oil flow ceases, the valve closes and the oil is kept within the filter. This prevents it

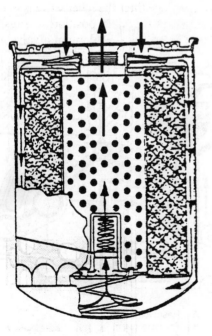

Fig. 1.60 Cartridge oil filter with oil relief valve open

from draining back into the sump. It also has the advantage of enabling the engine to develop the oil pressure more quickly when starting from cold. Correct operation is shown in Fig. 1.61.

Disc filter

This type of full-flow filter (shown in Fig. 1.62) is used in large diesel engines. The oil is filtered by being forced through very narrow gaps (0.05 mm) between thin steel discs which form an assembly which can be rotated. The narrow gap between the discs prevents impurities in the oil from passing through. The deposits accumulate on the outside of the discs, which are kept clean by scrapers which scrape off the deposits as the disc assembly rotates. In most cases the assembly is connected to the clutch pedal; each time the pedal is operated the disc assembly is rotated a small amount. The filter must be drained as per manufacturers' recommendations, this being done by removing the drain plug allowing dirt and some oil to be flushed out.

Centrifugal filter

Again mainly found on larger engines, this consists of a housing with a shaft and rotor inside. The oil is forced through the inlet ports by the pump and fills the rotor through the inlet holes in the rotor shaft, passing down the pipes to the jets. Due to the force of the oil passing through the jets the rotor rotates at very high speed. Owing to the centrifugal force, the impurities (which are heavier than the oil) accumulate on the walls of the rotor. The filter must be

Fig. 1.61 Cartridge oil filter operating correctly

> *Learning tasks*
>
> 1. Draw up a lubrication service schedule for a 12 000 mile major service.
> 2. Complete a lubrication service on a vehicle using the above service schedule. Identify any faults found, such as oil leaks, and complete the report on the workshop job card.

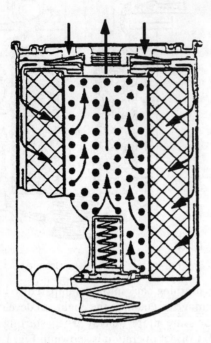

periodically cleaned by dismantling the filter and washing with a suitable cleaning fluid.

Dry-sump lubrication

This type of system (Fig. 1.63) is fitted to vehicles where the engine is mounted on its side, or where greater ground clearance is required. It is also used for motor cycle engines, cross-country vehicles and racing engines where under certain conditions the pick-up pipe could be exposed for a period of time and therefore the oil supply to the engine lubrication system could be interrupted. To overcome this problem a dry sump system is often fitted.

The oil is stored in a separate oil tank instead

Scrapers
Steel discs
Drain plug

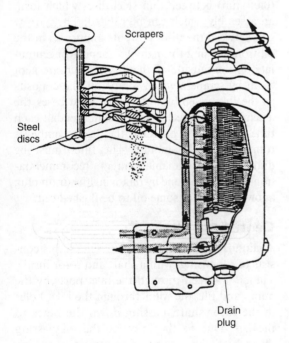

Fig. 1.62 Disc-type oil filter

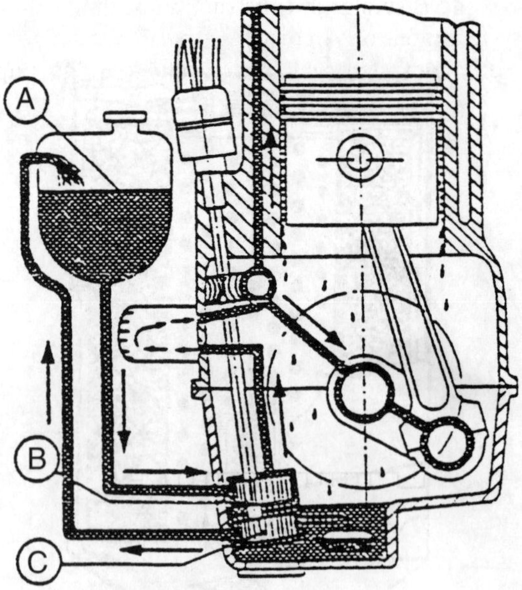

A
B
C
A – Reservoir
B – Pressure pump
C – Scavenge pump

Fig. 1.63 Operation of dry-sump lubrication system

of in the sump. The oil pump takes the oil from the tank and passes it to the lubrication system. The oil then drops down to the crankcase where a separate scavenge oil pump often running at a higher speed than the pressure pump returns it back to the oil tank. This means that the sump remains almost dry. The faster speed of the scavenge pump is due to the fact that it must be capable of pumping a mixture of air and oil (which has a larger volume than just oil) back to the tank.

Oil coolers (sometimes called heat exchangers)

Two types of oil coolers are fitted where the heat is removed from the oil: one is the oil-to-air where the heat is passed directly to the air; the other is the oil-to-water where the heat from the oil is passed to the water cooling system. Both types are shown in Fig. 1.64. On the water-cooled engines the oil cooler is normally located in front of, and sometimes combined with, the radiator. The advantage of the water-type heat exchanger is that the oil and water are operating at roughly the same temperature and each is maintained at its most efficient working temperature under most operating conditions. On air-cooled heat exchanger engines the cooler is usually located in the air stream of the cooling fan and is similar in construction to the cooling system radiator. An oil cooler bypass valve is fitted in the system which allows the oil to heat up more rapidly from cold by initially restricting its circulation to the engine only.

Total loss lubrication

There is one system commonly used that has so far not been mentioned; that is the total loss system. This is where the oil used to lubricate the piston, main and big-end bearings, is burnt during the combustion stroke and therefore lost through the exhaust system to the atmosphere. One example of this is the two-stroke petrol engine used in the motor cycle.

Learning tasks

1. Remove the pump from a motor cycle engine and identify the type of pump fitted and method of operation. After reassembling immerse the pump in clean engine oil and test the pumping side for pressure and the scavenge side for suction. Record the results.
2. Give two methods used in the total loss lubrication system of introducing oil into the engine.
3. How should engine oil be removed from the workshop floor?
4. List the main safety precautions that should be observed when working on the lubrication system.

(a)
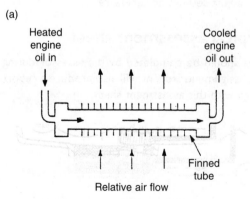

(b)
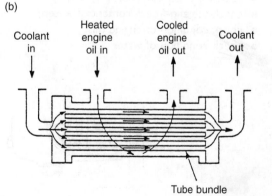

Fig. 1.64 Basic principles of oil coolers (a) oil-to-air, (b) oil-to-water

Practical assignment – removing and refitting the cylinder heads

Objective

To visually check the condition of:

- the valves and valve seats
- the cylinder head for cracks and distortion
- the piston crowns for build-up of carbon
- the cylinder bores for scoring and excessive wear

Vehicle/engines used

This exercise should be carried out on both OHC and push-rod operated engines.

Equipment required

- Specialist test equipment
- Small hand tools, e.g. spanners, sockets, etc.
- Valve spring compressors
- Torque spanner
- Relevant repair manual
- Drain trays

Task

Before removing the cylinder head the following checks/tests should be carried out:

- compression test
- cylinder leakage test
- cylinder balance test
- pressure check the cooling system
- check the anti-freeze content of water
- check condition of engine oil
- check condition of water

Activity

1. Drain both engine oil and water.
2. Remove ancillary components, e.g.
   (a) all electrical connections
   (b) accelerator and choke cables
   (c) water and air intake hoses/connections
   (d) cam belt OHC (having set camshaft timing) inlet and exhaust manifolds
3. Remove camshaft (OHC) or rocker shaft and push rods.
4. Remove cylinder head (ensure bolts/nuts are released in the correct order).
5. Remove all the inlet and exhaust valves (ensure these are kept in the correct order).
6. Thoroughly clean all the componets.
7. Visually inspect valve seats for pitting on seats and measure for wear on stems.
8. Visually check cylinder head for cracks and distortion.
9. Visually check valve seats in cylinder head for pitting and burning.
10. Reface valves and seats or replace as necessary.
11. Regrind valves into cylinder head.
12. Reassemble valves into cylinder head using new valve stem seals. Adjust clearances as necessary OHC.
13. Refit cylinder head to engine using new gaskets and bolts where required.
14. Tighten cylinder head bolts to the correct torque using recommended procedure.
15. Replace all ancillary equipment/components.
16. Fill with fresh oil and where appropriate water/anti-freeze.
17. Check operation by starting and running engine.
18. Check for water and oil leaks, check levels and adjust settings as necessary.

Typical assessment sheet

This should be completed by the assessor during the assignment. Student will also produce a report to go with this assessment sheet.

Name								Date	from to

Practical assignment

Tutor/assessor

General comments

Tasks	Chooses correct tools and operates equipment properly	General cleanliness of work/task	Uses safe working practices	Identifies components correctly	Locates and uses technical information	Completes task successfully	Identifies any problems	Compiles report on completed task	
Test equipment									Comments on specific tasks
Removing ancillaries									
Removing/ refitting valves									
Refitting cylinder head									
Checking and running engine									

2
Cooling systems

During combustion, when the engine is operating at full throttle, the maximum temperature reached by the burning gases may be as high as 1500–2000 °C. The expansion of the gases during the power stroke lowers their temperature considerably, but during the exhaust stroke the gas temperature may still be approximately 800 °C. All the engine components with which these hot gases come into contact will absorb heat from them in proportion to:

● the gas temperature
● the area of surface exposed to the gas
● the duration of the exposure

Engine operating temperatures are shown in Fig. 2.1.

2.1 Over-heating

For all these reasons the heat will raise the temperature of the engine components. If the temperature even of the exhaust gas is above red heat it will be above the melting point of metals such as aluminium from which the pistons are made. Unless steps are taken to reduce these temperatures a number of serious problems could arise.

● The combustion chamber walls, piston crown, the upper end of the cylinder and the region of the exhaust port are exposed to the hottest gases and will therefore reach the highest temperatures. This will create distortion causing a leakage of gas, water or oil. It may even cause the valve to burn or the cylinder head to crack and as a consequence there will be a loss of power output.
● The oil film will be burnt causing excessive carbon to form. The loss of lubrication of the piston and rings will cause excessive wear or the piston to seize in the cylinder.
● Power output will be reduced because the incoming mixture will become heated so reducing its density. It may also cause **detonation** (this is an uncontrolled explosion in the cylinder) making it necessary to reduce the compression ratio.
● Some part of the surface of the combustion chamber could become hot enough to ignite the incoming charge before the spark occurs (called **pre-ignition**) which could cause serious damage to the engine if allowed to continue.

For these reasons the engine must be provided with a system of cooling, so that it can be maintained at its most efficient practicable operating temperature. This means that the average temperature of the cylinder walls should not exceed

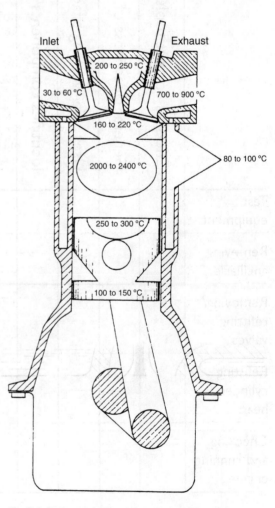

Fig. 2.1 Engine operating temperature ranges

about 250 °C, whereas the actual temperature of the gases in the cylinder during combustion may reach ten times this figure. One of the other things to remember is that the engine should not be run too cool as this would reduce **thermal efficiency** (this is how good the engine is at producing heat), increase fuel consumption and oil dilution and cause wear and corrosion of the engine.

2.2 Heat transfer

The cooling system works on the principles of **heat transfer**. Heat will always travel from hot to cold (e.g. from a hot object to a cold object, this would be by conduction). This transfer occurs in three different ways:

- conduction
- convection
- radiation

Conduction is defined as the transfer of heat between two solid objects, e.g. valve stem to valve guide as shown in Fig. 2.2. Since both objects are solid, heat is transferred from the hot valve stem to the cool valve guide by conduction and also from the guide to the cylinder head.

Convection is the transfer of heat by the circulation of heated parts of a liquid or gas. When the hot cylinder block transfers heat to the coolant it produces a change in its density and causes the warmer less dense water to rise, thus setting up convection currents in the cooling system.

Radiation is defined as the transfer of heat by converting it to radiant energy. Radiant heat is emitted by all substances and may be reflected or absorbed by others. This ability will depend upon the colour and nature of the surface of the objects, e.g. black rough ones are best for absorption of heat and light polished ones best for reflection of heat.

The cooling system relies on all three of these principles to remove excess heat from the engine.

Learning tasks

1. Take a look at three different types of radiators and check the colour and texture of the surface finish. Why are they finished like this?
2. How is the heat taken away from the top of the piston and spark plug? Which of the three methods named above are used?

2.3 Over-cooling

As we have seen, various problems can occur if the engine temperature gets too high but if the temperature becomes too low then another set of problems can occur.

- Fewer miles per gallon as the combustion process will be less efficient.
- There will be an increase in the build-up of carbon (as the fuel enters the cylinder it will condense and cause excessive build-up of carbon on the inlet valves).
- There will be an increase in the varnish and sludges formed within the lubrication system. Cooler engines make it easier for these to form.
- A loss of power, because if the combustion process is less efficient the power output will be reduced.
- The fuel not being burned completely which will cause fuel to dilute the oil and cause excessive engine wear.

The purposes of the cooling system can be summarized as follows:

- to maintain the highest and most efficient operating temperature within the engine;
- to remove excess heat from the engine;

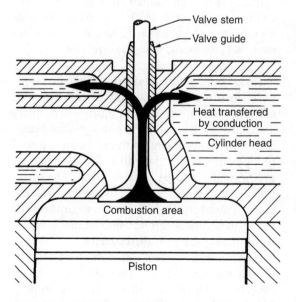

Fig. 2.2 Heat is transferred by conduction from the valve stem to the valve guide. Both objects are solid

● to bring the engine up to operating temperature as quickly as possible – in heavy duty driving, an engine could theoretically produce enough heat to melt an average 100 kg engine block in 20 minutes.

2.4 Types of cooling systems

There are two main types of cooling systems in common use, air and water. Both dissipate (radiate) heat removed from the cylinder into the surrounding air. Air cooling is described below and water cooling in Section 2.6.

Air cooling

In this system heat is radiated from the cylinder and head directly into the surrounding air. The rate at which heat is radiated from an object is dependent on:

1. the difference in temperature between the object and the surrounding air;
2. the surface area from which the heat is radiated, (since (1) must be limited, the surface area of the cylinder and head exposed to the air must be increased, by forming fins on their external surfaces) (Fig. 2.3);
3. the nature of the surface.

It is also necessary to remove the heated air from around the cylinder and deliver a constant supply of cool air around and between the fins. This means that the cylinders must be sufficiently widely spaced to permit a suitable depth

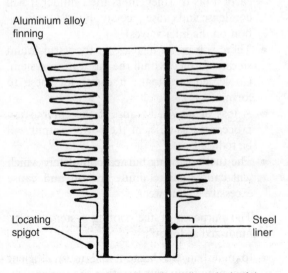

Fig. 2.3 Air-cooled finned cylinder wall method of heat transfer

of finning all around them, and the engine must be placed where the movement of the vehicle can provide the necessary supply of cool air. A large **fan** is often used and the engine is surrounded by large **cowls** to direct air to where it is required, e.g. around the cylinder head and valve area.

The choice of air or liquid cooling has always been controversial. Air is cheaper, lighter and more readily obtainable than water – though to remove a given quantity of heat demands four times the weight and 4000 times the volume of air than it does water. It also gives less control of the engine temperature and air-cooled engines tend to be noisier. But air can be collected and rejected, whereas water must be carried on the car and the jacketing, hoses, pump and radiator of a water-cooled engine will probably weigh more than the substantial fins of an air-cooled engine.

However, the fins force the cylinders of an air-cooled engine to be more widely separated than those of a water-cooled engine, so the crankshaft and crankcase must be longer and therefore heavier. For an engine of many cylinders, this is one of the greatest objections to air cooling.

2.5 Engine air-cooling system

Circulation of cooling air

With air cooling the engine structure is directly cooled by forcing air over its high-temperature surfaces. These are finned to present a greater cooling surface area to the air, which in non-motor-cycle applications is forced to circulate over them by means of a powerful fan.

The engine structure is almost entirely enclosed by sheet metal ducting (called a cowl), which incorporates a system of partitions (called **baffles**); these ensure that the air flow is properly directed over the cylinders and cylinder heads. To obtain uniform temperatures the air is forced to circulate around the entire circumference of each cylinder and its cylinder head. The direction of air flow will be along the cooling fins, the greatest number of which are found towards the top of the cylinder (around the exhaust valve) as this is the hottest part of the engine.

The complete system forms what is known as the **plenum chamber** in which the internal air pressure is higher than that of the atmosphere. The heated air is discharged from the plenum chamber to the atmosphere, or redirected to heat the car interior. Figure 2.4 shows a modern, air-cooled diesel engine. In order to provide the necessary air flow around the cylinders of an enclosed engine, a powerful fan is essential.

Types of air-cooling fans

Axial flow

This is a simple curved blade type in which the direction of air flow is parallel to the axis of the fan spindle (Fig. 2.5).

Radial flow

Often called a **centrifugal** this type (Fig 2.6) is more commonly used because it is more effective and a fan of smaller diameter can be used for a given air flow. This type of fan has a number of curved radial vanes mounted between two discs, one or both having a large central hole. When

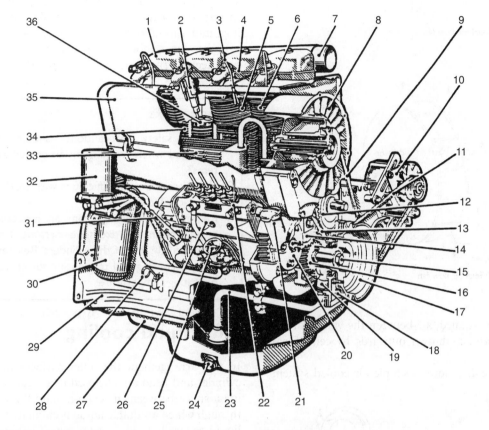

1 – Rocker chamber cover
2 – Injector
3 – Injection line to no.3 cylinder
4 – Back-leakage line
5 – Cylinder head anti-fatigue bolt (four bolts securing each cylinder head with cylinder to crankcase)
6 – Cylinder head (light alloy)
7 – Air intake manifold
8 – Cooling blower (V-belt driven)
9 – Cooling blower V-belt
10 – Generator (dynamo or alternator)
11 – Generator V-belt
12 – Camshaft gear
13 – Oil gallery
14 – Idler gear (driving injection pump and camshaft)
15 – Anti-fatigue bolt (securing V-belt pulley to crankshaft)
16 – Crankshaft gear
17 – V-belt pulley
18 – Vibration damper
19 – Oil pump
20 – Injection pump drive gear with advance/retard unit
21 – Oil filler neck
22 – Overflow line
23 – Oil suction pipe
24 – Oil drain plug
25 – Fuel feed pump
26 – Bosch in-line injection pump with mechanical centrifugal governor
27 – Oil sump (sheet metal or cast iron)
28 – Oil dipstick
29 – Crankcase (cast iron)
30 – Oil filter
31 – Speed control lever
32 – Fuel filter
33 – Integral oil cooler
34 – Finned cylinder (grey cast iron), separately removable
35 – Removable air cowling
36 – Piston

Fig. 2.4 Cut-away view of modern air-cooled diesel engine

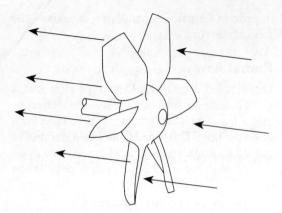

Fig. 2.5 Axial air flow fan

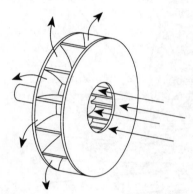

Fig. 2.6 Radial air flow fan

the fan is rotated, air between the vanes rotates with it and is thrown outwards by centrifugal force.

Figure 2.7 shows a simple air cooled system

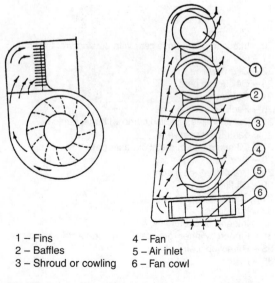

1 – Fins   4 – Fan
2 – Baffles   5 – Air inlet
3 – Shroud or cowling   6 – Fan cowl

Fig. 2.7 Simple in-line air cooled engine using a radial type fan

for a four-cylinder in-line engine. A centrifugal fan, driven at approximately twice crankshaft speed, is mounted at the front of the engine and takes in air through a central opening (5) in the fan casing. This air is delivered into the cowl (3) where it is directed over the fins of the cylinders (1). Baffles (2) ensure that the air passes between the fins where it picks up heat, thus cooling the cylinders.

The in-line engine is the most difficult to cool by air. Vee-type or horizontally opposed engines are easier to cool as the cylinders are spaced further apart to leave room for the crankshaft bearings and this allows more room between the cylinders for a good air flow whilst at the same time keeping the total engine length fairly short.

Learning tasks

1. What safety precautions should be observed when working on air-cooled systems?
2. What are the main difficulties with working on air-cooled engines?
3. Remove the cowling from an air-cooled engine, clean any excessive dirt, etc. from between the fins of the cylinders. Reassemble the cowling and test engine for correct operating temperature.

2.6 Liquid cooling

In this arrangement the outer surfaces of the cylinder and head are enclosed in a jacket, leaving a space between the cylinder and the jacket through which a suitable liquid is circulated. The liquid generally used is water, which is in many ways the most suitable for this purpose, even though it has a number of drawbacks. Whilst passing through the jacket the water absorbs heat from the cylinder and head, and it is cooled by being passed through a radiator before being returned to the jacket.

Thermo-syphon system

When heated, the water becomes less dense and therefore lighter than cold water. Thermo-syphon is the action of the water being heated, rising and setting up convection currents in the water. The thermo-syphon system is no longer used in the modern motor vehicle as it has a number of disadvantages.

- To ensure sufficient circulation the radiator must be arranged higher than the engine to ensure that the heated coolant will rise into the top of the radiator header tank and the cooled water in the radiator will flow into the bottom of the engine.
- Water circulation will be slow, so a relatively large amount of water must be carried.
- Large water passages must be used to allow an unrestricted flow of water around the system.

This system is usually now confined to small stationary engines such as those used to power narrow boats, small generators, water pumps etc.

Pump-assisted circulation

Most modern engines use a pump to provide a positive circulation of the coolant. This is shown in Fig. 2.8 and gives the following advantages:

1. a smaller radiator can be used than in the thermo-syphon system;
2. less coolant is carried as the water is circulated faster and therefore the heat is removed more quickly;
3. smaller passages and hoses are used because of (2) above;
4. the radiator does not need to be above the level of the engine, giving a lower bonnet line;

this also has the advantage of less wind resistance giving a better fuel consumption;
5. because the water flow is given positive direction the engine will operate at a more even temperature.

2.7 Comparison of air - and water-cooled systems

Advantages of air cooling

- An air-cooled engine is generally lighter than an equivalent water-cooled engine.
- It warms up to its normal running temperature very quickly.
- The engine can operate at a higher temperature than a water-cooled engine.
- The system is free from coolant leakage problems and requires no maintenance.
- There is no risk of damage due to freezing of the coolant in cold weather.

Disadvantages of air cooling

- A fan and suitable cowls are necessary to provide and direct the air flow. The fan can be noisy and absorbs a large amount of engine

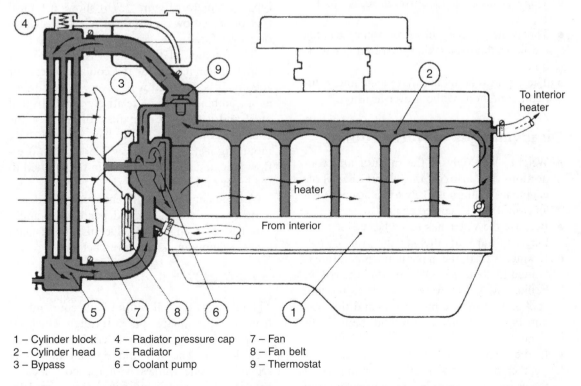

1 – Cylinder block	4 – Radiator pressure cap	7 – Fan
2 – Cylinder head	5 – Radiator	8 – Fan belt
3 – Bypass	6 – Coolant pump	9 – Thermostat

Fig. 2.8 Coolant is pumped from the water pump, through the cylinder block and heads, through the thermostat into the radiator, and back to the water pump

power. The cowl makes it difficult to get at various parts of the engine when servicing is required.

- The engine is more liable to over-heating under difficult conditions than a water-cooled engine.
- Mechanical engine noises tend to be amplified by the fins.
- The cylinders usually have to be made separately to ensure proper formation of the fins. This makes the engine more costly to manufacture.
- Cylinders must be spaced well apart to allow sufficient depth of fins.
- It is more difficult to arrange a satisfactory car-heating system.

Advantages of water cooling

- The temperatures throughout the engine are more uniform, thus keeping distortion to a minimum.
- Cylinders can be placed closer together making the engine more compact.
- Although a fan is usually fitted to force air through the radiator, it is much smaller than the type required for an air-cooled engine. It therefore absorbs less power and is quieter in operation.
- There is no cowl to obstruct access to the engine.
- The water jacket absorbs some of the mechanical noise making the running engine quieter.
- The engine is better able to operate under difficult conditions without over-heating.

Disadvantages of water cooling

- Weight – not only of the radiator and connections but also of the water; the whole engine installation is likely to be heavier than an equivalent air-cooled engine.
- Because the water has to be heated, it takes longer to warm up after starting from cold.
- If water is used, the maximum temperature is limited to about 85–90 °C to avoid the risk of boiling away the water. However, modern cooling systems are pressurized and this permits higher temperatures and better efficiency.
- If the engine is left standing in very cold weather, precautions must be taken to prevent the water freezing in the cylinder jackets and cracking them.

- There is a constant risk of a coolant leakage developing.
- A certain amount of maintenance is necessary, e.g. checking water level, anti-frost precautions, cleaning out deposits, etc.

Learning task

Using the above information write a short paragraph to explain the main components and their purpose in the water cooling system.

2.8 Radiator and heater matrix

The purpose of the radiator is to provide a cooling area for the water and to expose it to the air stream. A reservoir for the water is included in the construction of the radiator. This is known as the header tank and is made of thin steel or brass sheet and is connected to the bottom tank by brass or copper tubes; these are surrounded by 'fins'. This assembly is known as the **matrix**, **core**, **block** or **stack**. The more modern radiator uses plastic for the tanks and aluminium for the matrix. Shown in Fig. 2.9(a) is a conventional type of radiator. Figure 2.9(b) shows a typical type of cross-flow radiator which has an integral oil cooler fitted.

The function of the radiator as we have said is to transfer heat from the coolant to the air stream. It is designed with a very large surface area combined with a relatively small frontal area, and it forms a container for some of the coolant in the system. The radiators usually have mounting feet or brackets, a filler cap, an overflow pipe and sometimes a drain tap is fitted to the lower tank.

A large number of different types of radiator matrix are in common use depending on application size of engine, etc. Details of the main types in common use are given below.

Film core

The tubes are the full width of the core and are bent to form square spaces through which air can pass. They are sometimes crinkled to extend their length. The top and bottom tanks are secured to side frames with the core located between them and a fan cowl often completes the unit.

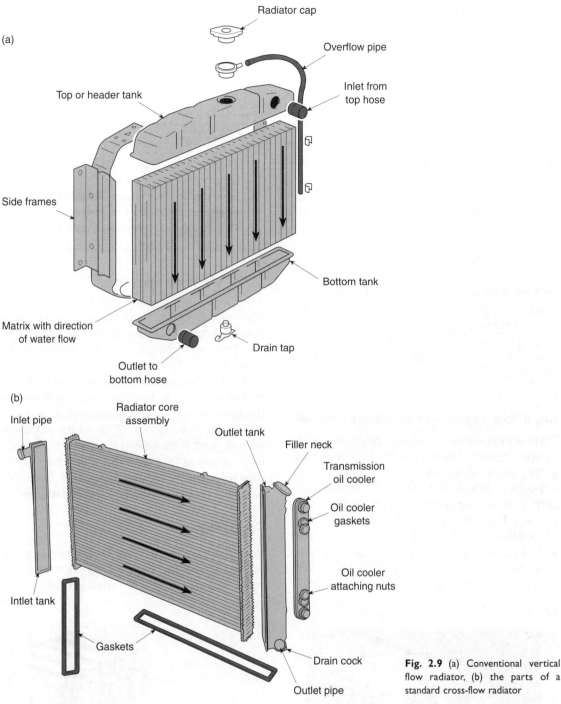

(a)

Radiator cap

Overflow pipe

Inlet from
top hose

Top or header tank

Side frames

Bottom tank

Matrix with direction
of water flow

Drain tap

Outlet to
bottom hose

(b)

Radiator core
assembly

Inlet pipe

Outlet tank

Filler neck

Transmission
oil cooler

Oil cooler
gaskets

Oil cooler
attaching nuts

Intlet tank

Gaskets

Drain cock

Outlet pipe

Fig. 2.9 (a) Conventional vertical flow radiator, (b) the parts of a standard cross-flow radiator

Tube and fin

This consists of copper or brass tubes of round, oval or rectangular cross-section. The tubes pass through a series of thin copper fins with the top and bottom tanks attached to the upper and lower fins, respectively. The fins secure the tubes and increase the surface area from which the heat can be dissipated. The tubes are placed edge on to the air flow for minimum air resistance and they are now produced from strip lock-seaming.

Tube and corrugated film

Sometimes used as an alternative to the tube and fin, the corrugated separator filming is made from copper and laid between the tubes to provide an airway. Each face of the filming is louvred to increase air turbulence as the air passes through. This improves the cooling efficiency of this design. A commonly used form of radiator matrix (core) construction is shown in Fig. 2.10.

Separate tubes

Radiators with separate coolant tubes are occasionally used. They provide a stronger core than the other types but they are more costly to build, heavy, time-consuming to repair and because of this are mainly confined to commercial vehicle applications. The tanks and side frames are usually bolted together and locate the thick walled tubes of rectangular or circular cross-section. The tubes are made watertight in the upper and lower tanks with rubber and metal seals, and they have bonded copper fins or a spiral copper wire wound over their complete length to increase their ability to dissipate the heat. Tube removal and refitting may be done by two methods depending on their construction. One is to remove top and bottom tanks from their side frames, the other is to spring the tubes in and out, which is only possible because of their flexibility.

Separate expansion or header tanks

Separate expansion or header tanks are now commonly used. These allow the radiator to be fitted lower than the engine and, on a commercial vehicle, to be fitted in a more accessible position for checking and refilling the coolant. The tank is also used to reduce the risk of **aeration** (this is air bubbles forming in the water) of the coolant when the engine is running. The early types of radiators were all of the conventional type, e.g. the coolant flows from

the top of the radiator to the bottom (vertically). Many vehicles now use a cross-flow type in which the coolant flows horizontally through the core from the top of one side tank across to the bottom of the other side tank as shown in Fig. 2.11.

Learning tasks

1. What are the advantages of a cross-flow radiator?
2. How should the radiator be tested for leaks when removed from the vehicle?
3. Why is the radiator painted matt black?

2.9 Water pump

The purpose of the water pump is to provide a positive means of circulating the water (it gives a direction to its flow, it does not pressurize the system).

The body of the pump is usually made of cast iron or aluminium. In most cases it is bolted to the front of the engine block and draws cool water from the bottom of the radiator via the bottom hose. This cooler water is directed into the water jacket and over the hottest part of the engine such as the exhaust valve seats. Two types of pump are used, **axial flow** and **radial flow**.

Axial flow

With the axial flow, when the pump is full of water, the rotating impeller carries with it the water contained in the spaces between the

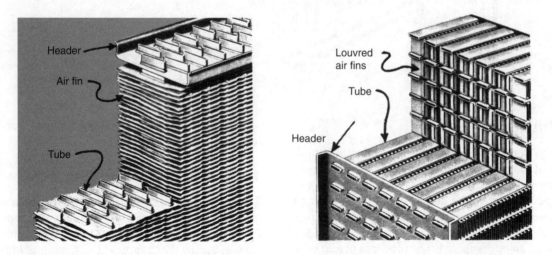

Fig. 2.10 Inside the radiator there are small tubes through which the coolant flows, helping to remove the heat into the air

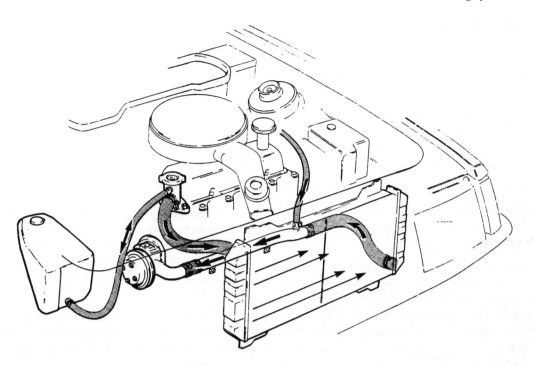

Fig. 2.11 Cooling system water flow

impeller blades and the casing. This water is subjected to centrifugal force which causes it to flow outwards from inlet to outlet. A carbon ring bonded to a rubber sleeve is fitted into the housing and pressed into light contact with a machined face on the impeller by a light spring.

This provides a water-tight seal along the shaft. The pump is driven by a belt from the crankshaft via a pulley which is a press fit on the end of the pump spindle. The fan is then bolted to the pulley which draws air through the radiator.

Radial flow

The radial flow centrifugal pump operates with a slightly higher flow and therefore the circulation is slightly faster. This type is fitted to commercial vehicles. The construction of such a water pump is shown in Fig. 2.12.

Learning tasks

1. What are the symptoms of the water pump not working? What could be the cause of this fault and how should it be repaired?
2. How should the drive belt to the pump be checked? Remove the belt, check for signs of wear or cracking. Replace and correctly tension the belt.

---

3. Remove one type of water pump from an engine, check for premature bearing failure, signs of water leaks and general serviceability. Replace the pump, refill with coolant and pressure test the system.

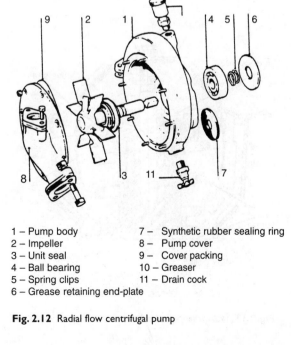

1 – Pump body	7 – Synthetic rubber sealing ring
2 – Impeller	8 – Pump cover
3 – Unit seal	9 – Cover packing
4 – Ball bearing	10 – Greaser
5 – Spring clips	11 – Drain cock
6 – Grease retaining end-plate	

Fig. 2.12 Radial flow centrifugal pump

2.10 Thermostat

This is a temperature sensitive valve that controls the water flow to the radiator. There are two main reasons for its use:

- to enable the engine to warm up quickly from cold;
- to control the rate of flow and so maintain a constant temperature in the engine.

Two types are in common use, the **bellows** type and the **wax** type.

Wax type

This is used in the pressurized system as it is not sensitive to pressure like the bellows type. A special wax is used, contained in a strong steel cylinder. The reaction pin is surrounded by a rubber sleeve and is positioned inside the cylinder.

As the temperature increases the wax begins to melt, changing from a solid to a liquid, and at the same time it expands. This forces the rubber against the fixed reaction pin, opening the valve against spring pressure thus allowing the water to circulate through the radiator. There is a small hole in the valve disc to assist in bleeding the system as filling takes place. The 'jiggle pin' closes the hole during engine warm-up. This thermostat is shown in Fig. 2.13.

Bellows type

Shown in Fig. 2.14. This consists of a flexible metal bellows which is partly filled with a liquid which has a boiling point that is lower than that of water (e.g. alcohol, ether or acetone). Air is removed from the bellows, leaving only the liquid and its vapour. The pressure in the bellows is then only due to the vapour pressure of the liquid. This varies with temperature, and is equal to atmospheric pressure at the boiling temperature of the liquid, less at lower temperatures and more at higher temperatures. As the temperature of the water increases, the liquid in the bellows begins to turn to a vapour and increase in pressure; this expands the bellows and opens the valve allowing water to pass to the radiator.

> *Note:* This type is not suitable for pressurized systems as the valves are pressure-sensitive. The wax element type does not have this disadvantage.

Testing thermostats

The thermostat cannot be repaired and so must be replaced if found to be faulty. It can be tested by placing the thermostat in a beaker of water and gradually heating it. A thermometer is used to check the temperature of the water (Fig. 2.15). The thermostat should begin to open

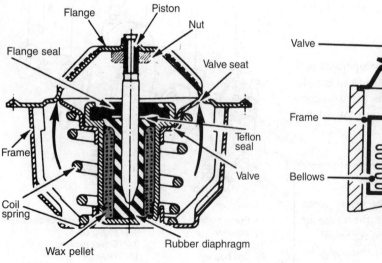

Fig. 2.13 Wax pellet-type thermostat

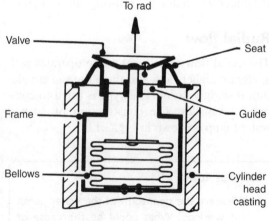

Fig. 2.14 Bellows-type thermostat

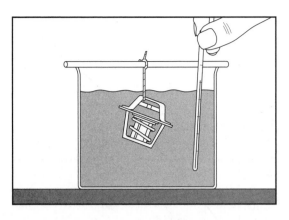

Fig. 2.15 Thermostat suspended in water container

Learning tasks

1. Write a schedule for removing, testing and replacing a thermostat that is suspected of being faulty.
2. What is the symptom, fault, cause and remedial action that should be taken when the driver complains of the heater blowing hot and cold?
3. Remove, test and replace a thermostat according to your work schedule drawn up at (1) above. State the type of unit fitted, the temperature at which it opened/closed and check with the manufacturer's data.

---

when the temperature marked on the valve is reached. An increase of approximately 10–20 °C will elapse before the valve is fully open.

2.11 Pressurized cooling systems

Pressurised cooling systems are used because they allow the engine to operate at a higher temperature. Figure 2.16 shows the layout and main components of a modern pressurized system.

Pressure cap

The cap contains two valves; one is the **pressure valve** the other is the **vacuum valve**. As the temperature of the water increases it expands and in a sealed system this expansion increases the pressure until it reaches the relief pressure of the cap. As the system cools down it contracts and opens the vacuum valve drawing in air. If no vacuum valve was fitted the depression in the system, caused by the contracting effect of the water as it cools, could cause the rubber hoses in the system to collapse. Most pressure caps operate at 28–100 kN/m. The pressure is usually stamped on the cap indicating the maximum relief pressure for the system to which it is fitted. Figure 2.17(c) shows a pressure cap in the open position.

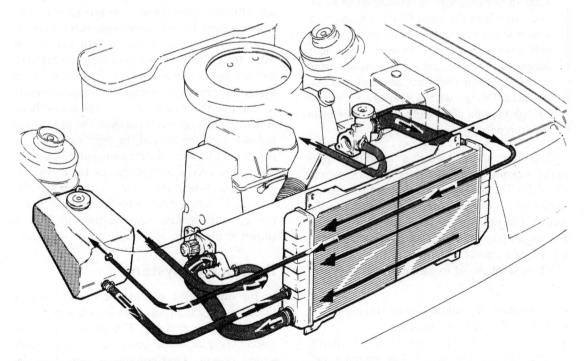

Fig. 2.16 'Degas' system with coolant at normal operating pressure and temperature

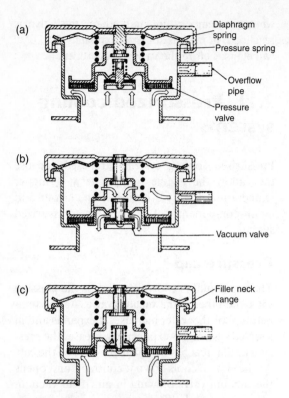

Fig. 2.17 Open-type pressure cap used in the semi-sealed system. (a) Pressure-relief valve open, (b) vacuum-relief valve open and (c) cap-removal precaution action

Safety note

Never remove the cap when the coolant temperature is above 100 °C as this will allow the water to boil violently: the resulting jet of steam and water from the open filler can cause very serious scalds. The system should be allowed to cool down and the cap removed slowly. It is designed so that the spring disc remains seated on the top of the filler neck until after the seal has lifted. This allows the pressure to escape through the vent pipe before it can escape from the main opening.

The temperature at which a liquid boils rises as the pressure acting on it rises. This is shown in Fig. 2.18. The cooling system's pressure is maintained by the use of a pressure cap fitted to the top of the radiator or expansion bottle. This closes the system off from the atmosphere creating a sealed system.

The advantages of using a pressurized system are:

- elimination of coolant loss by surging of the coolant during heavy braking;
- prevention of boiling during long hill climbs, particularly in regions much above sea level;

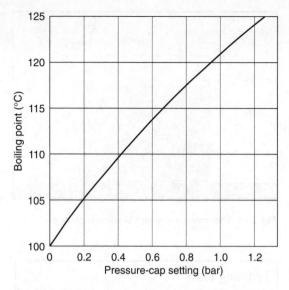

Fig. 2.18 Variation of boiling point of water with pressure

- raising of the working temperature improving engine efficiency;
- allowing the use of a smaller radiator to dissipate the same amount of heat as a larger one operating at a lower temperature.

Semi-sealed system

The advantage of the modern sealed cooling system is that it reduces the need for frequent inspection of the coolant level and the risk of weakening the anti-freeze solution by topping up. Although the pressure cap provided a semi-sealed system the fully sealed system has in effect a means of recovering the coolant that is lost when the engine is at its operating temperature and the pressure cap is lifted. It consists of an **expansion tank** that is mounted independently from the radiator and vented to the atmosphere. A flexible hose connects the overflow pipe of the radiator to a dip tube in the overflow tank. As the coolant heats up the pressure valve in the cap opens and excess coolant passes to the expansion tank. When the system cools down the coolant is drawn back into the radiator again through the vacuum valve in the cap. This is shown in Fig. 2.19.

Fully sealed system

In the fully sealed system, the pressure cap is fitted to the expansion tank and a simple cap is used on the radiator. The operation of the system is much the same as in the semi-sealed system. The reservoir is vented to the

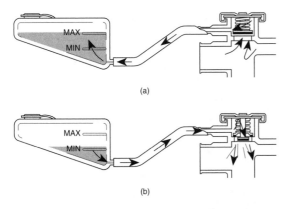

(a)

(b)

Fig. 2.19 Operating function of the overflow bottle. (a) Water heating up, (b) water coolong down.

atmosphere and should be approximately two-thirds full. If the coolant falls below the minimum level indicated on the tank air may be drawn into the radiator.

Learning tasks

1. What is the correct method for testing the pressure and vacuum valves in the cap? What would be the effect of fitting a cap with: (a) a stronger spring? (b) a weaker spring?

2. How would you test for water/oil contamination and which component would you suspect to be faulty?

2.12 Fans and their operation

Fans and temperature control

An important aspect of the cooling capabilities of the radiator is the volume of air, in unit time, which can be caused to flow through the matrix. Hence, the purpose of the cooling fan is to maintain adequate air flow through the matrix, at low and engine idling speeds. The speed of the fan ranges from slightly less to rather more than that of the engine. Excessive fan speeds are avoided because of noise and the power required to drive it.

Electrically driven fans

With this type of fan arrangement an electric motor is used together with a fan and a temperature-sensitive control unit. The advantages of this arrangement are:

- the fan only operates when the engine reaches its predetermined temperature;
- the engine will be more efficient as the fan is not being driven all the time;
- the radiator and fan can now be fitted in any convenient position, ideal for transversely mounted engines;
- the fan assembly can be mounted in front of or behind the radiator;
- engine temperature is more closely controlled as the temperature sensor will automatically switch the fan on and off within very close limits as required.

A typical layout is shown in Fig.2.20.

To improve the efficiency of the fan a cowl is often fitted. Its function is to prevent heated air from reversing its flow past the fan and recirculating through the matrix which could lead to engine overheating. The fan can be formed from some of the following materials:

- one piece steel pressing
- aluminium casting
- plastic moulding with a metal insert

An uneven number of irregularly spaced blades (Fig.2.21) are often employed to minimize fan noise. In all applications the fan assembly must be accurately balanced and the blades correctly aligned to avoid vibration.

Flexible fan blades

Used to reduce frictional power loss from the fan, these are made from fibreglass, metal and moulded plastic such as polypropylene. The plastic fans are lighter, easier to balance, look better, are more efficient aerodynamically, have a reduced noise level, a reduction in vibration and offer less risk of serious injury. They are also cheaper to manufacture. For these reasons the plastic fan is the most common of this type fitted to light vehicles.

A number of vehicles have a cover surrounding the fan (called a **shroud**) fitted to make sure the fan pulls air through the *entire* radiator. Figures 2.20 and 2.22 show arrangements commonly used. When no shroud is used the fan will only pull air through the radiator directly in front of the blades. There is very little air moving through the corners of the matrix.

With flexible fan blades, as the speed of the engine increases the blades flatten and therefore move less air, this give a reduction in the power lost to friction. An example of a flexible fan with a shroud is that used in the Mini; the air is forced

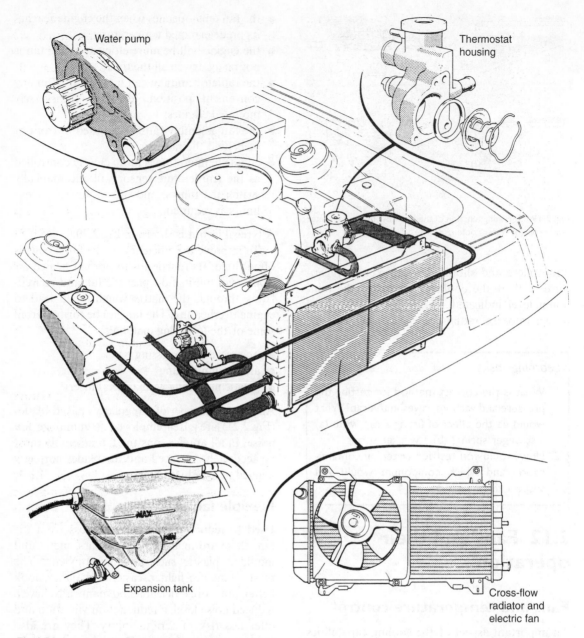

Water pump

Thermostat housing

Expansion tank

Cross-flow radiator and electric fan

Fig. 2.20 Layout for the Ford transverse engine

through the radiator, not drawn through as in most vehicles.

Cooling fan with swept tips

The flexible tips of the fan tend to straighten out as speed increases and this has the effect of reducing the amount of air drawn through the fan.

Cooling fan surrounded by cowl or shroud attached to the radiator

The shroud is a close fit around the radiator and fan to prevent the air from just circulating around the fan and not passing through the radiator matrix and cooling the water.

Directly driven fans

Directly driven fans are not normally used in light vehicles because they have the following disadvantages:

● rising noise level
● increase in power used
● tendency to over-cooling at higher speeds

Some engine manufacturers still use directly driven fans mainly because of the type of engine

Fig. 2.21 Unevenly spaced fan blades

fitted or because space is limited. The opposed piston engine often has the fan blades bolted directly on the end of the crankshaft, usually with some means of limiting the maximum speed of the fan. LGVs may also use the same method of driving the fan.

Fan drives

The drive for the fan is normally located on the water pump shaft. Its purpose is to draw sufficient air through the matrix for cooling purposes in heavy traffic on a hot day and to ensure adequate cooling at engine idling speeds.

At moderate speeds, say, driving down the motorway, the engine does not require the same amount of assistance from the fan, as the natural flow of air passing through the radiator will often be sufficient to cool the water. Power would be lost unnecessarily to the fan under

these conditions. A number of different methods of controlling fan operation and speed are becoming more popular.

Automatically-controlled fans are generally classified into four types:

- **free-wheeling**
- **variable-speed**
- **torque-limiting**
- **variable-pitch**

Free-wheeling

The free-wheeling-type is mounted on the coolant pump shaft and may form part of an **electromagnetic clutch** with the drive pulley. Connected into the electrical supply circuit to the clutch assembly is a thermostatically controlled switch. When the fan is no longer required, the supply to the electromagnet is interrupted, so that it disengages and allows the fan to free-wheel on the pump shaft.

Variable-speed

The variable-speed-type generally has a **viscous coupling**, which permits motion or **slip** to occur between the driving and the driven members. The driving member consists of a disc mounted on the pump shaft. Attached to the fan is a sealed cylindrical casing or chamber, freely mounted on the pump shaft. The driving disc revolves within the coupling chamber, which is partially filled with a highly stable **silicone fluid** (this means it retains a nearly constant viscosity with varying operating temperatures). The disc initially revolves in the stationary mass of fluid and sets up a **drag**, so that the fluid begins to circulate in the chamber. As a result of centrifugal force it moves outwards to fill the gaps between the drive faces of the coupling members. Since

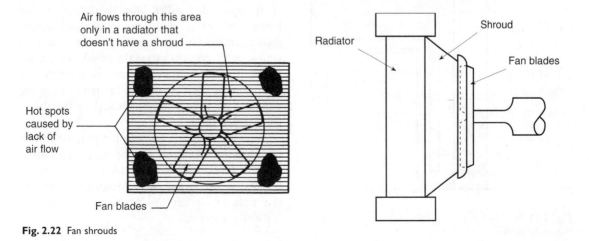

Fig. 2.22 Fan shrouds

these faces are very close to one another, drive is transmitted between them by the viscous drag of the silicone fluid. This drag is maintained with increasing fan speed, until the resisting torque imposed upon the fan by the air flow rises to an extent that causes shear breakdown of the fluid film, and the coupling slips. Fan speed is thus controlled by the slipping action of the coupling, which is predetermined by the viscosity of the fluid and the degree to which the coupling is filled. Where no provision is made for the quantity of oil, the coupling is termed a torque-limiting type. The layout of a viscous fan drive is shown in Fig. 2.23.

Torque-limiting

The torque-limiting-type has the disadvantage of operating within a fixed speed range, regardless of cooling system demands. Thus air circulation may be inadequate when car speed is low and engine speed is high. To overcome these difficulties, a temperature sensitive fan control is used in some installations.

Variable-pitch

In the variable-pitch fan the volume of air displaced is controlled by twisting its blades. The term pitch is considered as the distance the blade can twist, if it were turning one revolution in a solid substance (that is with no slip taking place). When the least amount of cooling is required, the blades are automatically adjusted to a low pitch, thereby reducing airflow to a minimum. The variable-pitch fan may be actuated by one of the following methods:

- centrifugal
- torque-limiting
- thermostatic means

An alternative to the engine driven fan is a separate electrically driven fan, which can be controlled automatically by the thermostat that responds to changes in engine coolant temperature. Although fan installations of this type absorb no engine power, they do impose an electrical load upon the car battery. It has a fixed higher operating speed and it may be noisier than a conventional driven fan, but it has the advantages of greater convenience of mounting position.

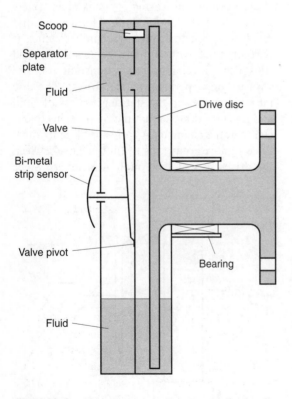

Fig. 2.23 Simplified diagram showing internal details of a viscous fan drive

Scoop

Separator plate

Fluid

Valve

Bi-metal strip sensor

Valve pivot

Fluid

Drive disc

Bearing

Learning tasks

1. Give reasons for the use of an electrically driven fan over other methods of operation.
2. Draw up in logical sequence the way an electric fan should be tested, apart from running the engine up to its normal operating temperature.
3. How should a viscous coupling be tested/repaired?

Radiator blinds and shutters

A very simple arrangement of controlling the air flow through the radiator is shown in Fig. 2.24. A spring-loaded **roller blind** is carried at the lower end of a rectangular channel-section frame attached to the front of the radiator. A simple cable control raises the blind to close off as much of the radiator as may be necessary to maintain the correct running temperature of the engine. This is normally operated by the driver from inside the cab.

Another method of controlling the air flow is by the use of a **shutter**. This operates in a similar way to a venetian window blind, each shutter rotates on a separate shaft. Mounted in front of the radiator it can be manually or thermostatically operated.

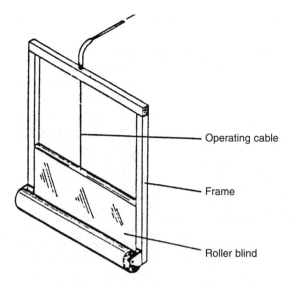

Fig. 2.24 A simple radiator blind

Fan belts

Most fan belts are of the V-type in construction and use the friction produced between the sides of the belt and pulley to provide the drive. The **vee** belt has a larger area of contact and therefore provides a more positive drive between the belt and the pulley. Another popular type is the flat **serpentine** belt; about 35 mm wide it has several grooves on one side. A larger area is provided by the grooves to give a more positive grip. This type is also used to transmit a drive around a smaller pulley than a conventional vee belt.

2.13 Corrosion in the cooling system

This can be very damaging to the engine. It can be caused in several different ways.

Direct attack

This means the water in the coolant is mixed with oxygen from the air. This process produces rust particles which can damage water pump seals and cause increased leakage.

Electromechanical attack

This is a result of using different metals in the construction of the engine. In the presence of the coolant, different metals may set up an electrical current in the coolant. If this occurs, one metal may deteriorate and deposit itself on the other metal. For example, a core plug may deteriorate to the point of causing a leak.

Cavitation

Cavitation is defined as high shock pressure developed by collapsing vapour bubbles in the coolant. These bubbles are produced by the rapid spinning of the water pump impeller. The shock waves cause small pin holes to form in nearby metal surfaces such as the pump impeller or the walls of the wet-type cylinder liner which could reach all the way through into the cylinder.

Mineral deposits

Calcium and silicate deposits are produced when a hard water is used in the cooling system. Both deposits restrict the conduction of heat out of the cooling system. As can be seen from Fig. 2.25 the deposits cover the internal passages causing uneven heat transfer.

2.14 Anti-freeze

Function

When an **ethylene-glycol** anti-freeze solution is added to the coolant many corrosion problems are overcome. Chemicals are added to the anti-freeze to reduce corrosion. It is not therefore necessary to add a corrosion inhibitor to the coolant when using an anti-freeze solution. In some cases, mixing different corrosion inhibitors or anti-freezes produces unwanted sludges within the cooling system.

Fortunately the freezing point of water can be lowered quite considerably by the simple addition of certain liquids such as ethylene-glycol. The recommended mixture varies with each manufacturer but is usually 33–50% of anti-freeze in the cooling water.

Checking the level

The proportion of ethylene-glycol-based anti-freeze present in a cooling system can be determined by checking the **specific gravity** of the coolant and by reference to its temperature. The percentage of anti-freeze is measured by the use of a hydrometer and a thermometer.

The graph in Fig. 2.26 shows what happens to

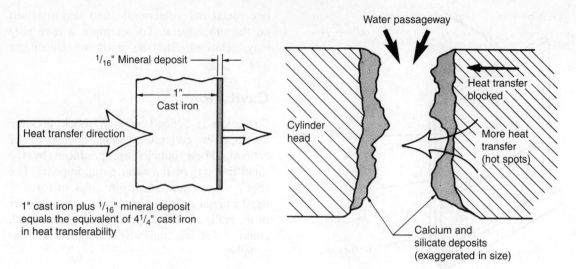

Fig. 2.25 Build-up of deposits in the cooling system

water when an anti-freeze solution is added. The water changes from a liquid to a mush before becoming solid ice. This ability to form mush before becoming ice gives some warning of freezing and consequently of the danger of damage to the engine.

Methanol-based anti-freeze is also used but has the disadvantage of losing its anti-freeze effect due to evaporation. It is also inflammable. Both types are toxic, and if spilt on the paint work of the vehicle would damage it.

Figure 2.27 shows how to check the anti-freeze content using the 'Bluecol' hydrometer. The coolant is drawn into the hydrometer to a level between the two lines. Note the letter on the float at the water line and the temperature of the

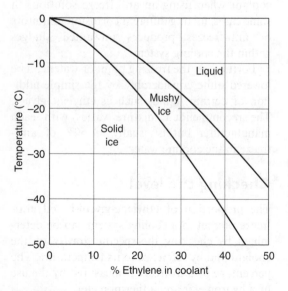

Fig. 2.26 Variation of freezing range with different strengths of anti-freeze

coolant on the thermometer. Using the slide rule, line up the two readings of temperature and letter. The true percentage content of anti-freeze can be identified at the 'read off' point.

Faults and their possible courses are shown in Table 2.1

2.15 Temperature indicators

Several types are used the most simple of which is a sensor which is placed in the coolant. As the temperature rises the heat causes an electrical circuit to close inside the sensor. This earths the system causing the lamp to light.

Thermal temperature units

These use **bi-metal elements** at both the temperature measuring end and in the indicator. The transmitter is in the form of a voltage stabilizer in which the contacts open and close at a rate which depends upon temperature. This causes a large or small amount of current to flow deflecting the needle a large or small amount on the indicator as shown in Fig. 2.28.

Thermistor units

Thermistor units are **semi-conductors**. As the temperature increases the resistance is reduced allowing more current to pass to the indicator. Semi-conductors are covered in more detail in Chapter 9.

Table 2.1 Liquid cooling systems fault chart

Fault	Possible cause
External leakage	1. Loose hose clips or split rubber hose
	2. Damaged radiator (cracked joints or corroded core)
	3. Water pump leaking (bearing worn)
	4. Corroded core plugs
	5. Damaged gaskets
	6. Interior heater, hoses, valves
	7. Temperature sensor connection leaking
Internal leakage	1. Defective cylinder head gasket
	2. Cylinder head not correctly tightened
	3. Cracked water jacket internal wall
	4. Defective cylinder liner seals
Water loss	1. Boiling
	2. Leaks – internal and external
	3. Restriction in radiator
	4. Airways in radiator matrix blocked
Dirty coolant (corrosion)	1. Excessive impurity in coolant water
	2. Infrequent draining and flushing of system (where required)
	3. Incorrect anti-freeze mixtures
	4. Lack of inhibitor
Over-heating	1. Loose, broken, worn or incorrect fan belt tension
	2. Defective thermostat
	3. Water pump impeller loose on shaft
	4. Restricted circulation – through radiator, hoses, etc.
	5. Radiator airways choked
	6. Incorrect ignition timing
	7. Incorrect valve timing
	8. Tight engine
	9. Low oil level
	10. Insufficient coolant in system
Over-cooling	1. Defective thermostat
	2. Temperature gauge incorrect
	3. Electric fan operating continuously

Bourdon tube gauge

This uses an electrical sensor in the coolant. As the temperature rises, a liquid inside the sensor vaporizes, producing a pressure rise that is transmitted to the Bourdon tube through a connecting pipe. The tube tends to straighten out and in doing so, via a toothed quadrant, moves a needle across a scale shown on the gauge. These are now rather old fashioned and so are no longer used.

Learning tasks

1. Explain in your own words what is meant by semi-conductor.
2. How should the temperature sensor/transmitter be checked for correct operation?

(a)

Fig. 2.27 (a) 'Bluecol' hydrometer, (b) slide rule for use with it

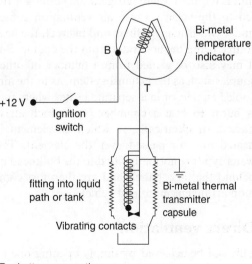

B – battery connection
T – transmitter connection

Fig. 2.28 Thermal temperature sensing device

Name any special equipment that might be required.

3. Remove a temperature sensor and test for electrical resistance, both when cold and when hot, note the readings and check your results with the manufacturer's data. Make recommendations on serviceability.

4. Where in the cooling system would a temperature sensor be located? Why would it be fitted in this position?

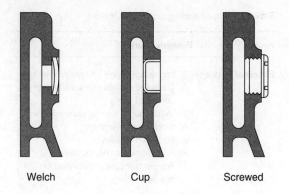

Welch   Cup   Screwed

Fig. 2.29 Types of core plugs fitted to the engine block

2.16 Engine core plugs

These are fitted for the following reasons:

● they may blank off the holes left by the jacket cores during casting or machining;
● they may be removed for cleaning out corrosive deposits from the jacket.

The plugs may be of the **welsh plug**, drawn **steel cup** or, less commonly, the **screwed plug** type. The first two are expanded and pressed into core holes that have been machined to size. All three are shown in Fig. 2.29.

2.17 Heating and ventilation

The most common method of providing a comfortable atmosphere in the car is through the heating and ventilation system. In some countries it could mean that a full air-conditioning unit is required where refrigeration cooling is fitted to the vehicle. Fresh air ventilation comes under two headings, **direct** and **indirect,** the heat source being the hot water from the engine. But it may also be gained from a number of other sources such as the exhaust system, as in the air-cooled engine, or in a separate heater where fuel is burnt to heat a chamber over which air is passed, or electrically, in which an element is heated and air passed over the element. The water type are normally fitted to the bulkhead or behind the facia panels and are the most common arrangement in light vehicles.

Direct ventilation

This can be achieved by simply opening one or more of the windows, but this could cause draughts, noise and difficulties in sealing against rain when closed. A number of different methods have been tried to overcome these problems, such as the swivelling quarter light window, but this created problems with water leaking in when the window was shut.

Indirect ventilation

This is routed through a **plenum chamber** located at the base of the windscreen. The internal pressure in the chamber is higher than that of the surrounding atmosphere. It is important therefore that the position of the plenum chamber and its entrance is chosen to coincide with a high-pressure zone of air flow over the car body, and also where it is free from engine fumes. A heating and ventilation system is shown in Fig. 2.30.

The air flow through the interior of the car can be derived simply from the ram effect of air passing over the car and spilling into the plenum chamber or, at low speeds, it may be boosted by the use of an electrically driven fan connected into the intake of the plenum chamber. Directional control for the air flow is adjustable by deflectors fitted to the outlets on the facia.

Provision for the extraction of the stale air is provided for in grills incorporated in the rear quarter panels of the body, their siting coinciding with **neutral pressure zones** in the air flow over the car.

Learning tasks

1. The volume of air delivered by the interior heater is controlled by the speed of the fan. Identify two methods that are used to control the temperature of the air delivered by the heater.

2. How would you check for the correct operation of the three-speed switch which operated the fan at only two speeds?
3. What symptoms would indicate that the cooling system needs bleeding?
4. How would you identify a suspected problem with a noisy heater fan? Suggest methods you would use to rectify the fault?

2.18 Routine maintenance

The reasons for carrying out routine maintenance are:

- to maintain engine efficiency
- to extend the life of the engine
- to reduce the risk of failure in the cooling system
- to reduce the time the vehicle is off the road when a failure does occur

There are a number of simple checks that should be made when a routine service is carried out on the cooling system. Check the water level, the condition of hoses and clips and the heater/radiator matrix for blockages. Drain and flush the system and refill with fresh anti-freeze mixture. Check the anti-freeze content, adjust the belt tension, pressure-test the system, test the thermostat and flow-test the radiator. Bleed the heater system and adjust the control, check the fan cowling and thermostatically controlled components for correct operation.

2.19 Heat Losses

These occur when heat transfers from a hot body to a cold body. This process of transfer continues until all the parts are at the same temperature. Heat is measured in **joules** and can be directly converted or expressed as mechanical energy, e.g.

1 newton metre (N m) = 1 joule (J)

When a mass of 1 kg is used as a standard the heating value is called the **specific heat capacity** (SHC). This is the amount of heat required to raise the temperature of a substance through 1 °C.

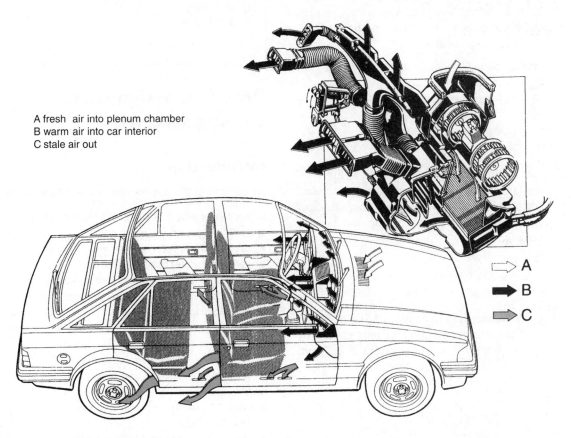

A fresh air into plenum chamber
B warm air into car interior
C stale air out

⟹ A
➡ B
⟹ C

Fig. 2.30 Heating and ventilation system

The SI unit of heat capacity is the **joule per degree C**. As an example the heat required to raise 1 kg of water through 1 °C is 4.18 kJ. Therefore the SHC of water is 4.18 kJ/kg°C.

Different materials accept or lose heat at different rates. Therefore for a similar mass they will increase or decrease their temperature at different rates.

Table 2.2 shows the SHC of various substances.

The quantity of heat transferred from one substance to another can be calculated from mass, SHC and temperature change.

Calculations

One litre of water has a mass of 1 kg. The formula used in calculating the heat lost or gained by a substance is:

$$Q = m \times c \times t$$

where: Q = heat loss
m = mass
c = SHC
t = temperature change

1. A pump circulates 150 litres of water through a cooling system in two minutes. The temperature at the top of the radiator is 90 °C, and at the bottom 70 °C. Calculate the heat energy radiated per second.

$$Q = \frac{m \times c \times t}{\text{time}}$$
$$= \frac{150 \times 4.18 \times (90 - 70)}{60 \times 2}$$
$$= 1.25 \times 4.18 \times 20$$
$$= 104.5 \text{ kJ/sec}$$

2. An impeller unit circulates two litres of coolant to the radiator per second. Calculate the heat lost to air per second, when the temperature difference between top and bottom tank is 25 °C

$$Q = m \times c \times t$$
$$= 2 \times 4.18 \times 25$$
$$= 209 \text{ kJ/sec}$$

3. a) A cooling system contains 15 kg of water. Calculate the quantity of heat gained by the water if its temperature rises from 12 °C to 88 °C on starting.

$$Q = m \times c \times t$$
$$= 15 \times 4.18 \times (88 - 12)$$
$$= 15 \times 4.18 \times 76$$
$$= 4765.2 \text{ kJ}$$

Table 2.2 The specific heat capacity of substances used in motor vehicles

Substance	SHC kJ/kg°C	Substance	SHC kJ/kg°C
Water	4.18	Steel	0.48
Lub. Oil	1.70	Brass	0.40
Aluminium	0.88	Lead	0.13

b) What heat is lost during cooling if the flow rate is two litres per second and the temperature at the bottom of the radiator is 53 °C?

$$t = 88 - 53 = 35°C$$
$$Q = m \times c \times t$$
$$= 2 \times 4.18 \times 35$$
$$= 292.6 \text{ kJ/sec}$$

Learning task

State the meaning of the following terms:

(a) heat transfer
(b) conduction
(c) convection
(d) radiation
(e) air-cooled
(f) liquid-cooled
(g) corrosive
(h) anti-freeze
(i) centrifugal pump
(j) heat exchanger
(k) core plug
(l) pressure
(m) vacuum
(n) shroud
(o) matrix

Practical assignment – cooling systems

Introduction

At the end of this assignment you will be able to:

- recognize water cooling and heater systems
- test the system for leaks
- test the system for anti-freeze content
- remove and test the thermostat
- test the pressure and vacuum valves
- check the operation of the temperature sensor and electric fan
- remove and check the drive belts for serviceability
- refit and set drive belt tension
- remove the radiator and test the flow rate
- bleed the cooling and heater system
- remove the water pump and state the type of impeller fitted
- flush the cooling and heater system

Tools and equipment

- A water-cooled engine
- Suitable drain trays
- Selection of tools and spanners
- Cooling system pressure tester
- Equipment for testing thermostat
- Hydrometer for testing anti-freeze content
- Relevant workshop manual or data book

Objective

- To check the correct operation of each of the components in the cooling system
- To prevent loss of water and over-heating which could cause damage to the engine
- To prevent freezing of the water during very cold weather

Activity

1. Before starting the engine, remove the radiator pressure cap and pressure test the cooling system.
2. Test the pressure and vacuum valves that are situated in the cap. Note any leaks which occur in tests 1 and 2 on the report sheet.
3. Remove the thermostat and check for correct operation using the equipment provided.
4. Remove the drive belts and check for cracks, splits, wear and general serviceability.
5. Remove the radiator, reverse flush it and where necessary complete a flow test. Remove any dirt, leaves, etc. from between fins of the matrix.
6. Remove the water pump, check the bearings for play and the seal for signs of leakage.
7. Refit the thermostat, water pump (using new gaskets), radiator and drive belts, setting the correct torque on the bolts and drive belt tension.
8. Flush the heater system, refit all the hoses and refill with water/anti-freeze mixture, bleeding the system as necessary.
9. Check the operation of the temperature sensor by running the engine up to its normal operating temperature.
10. Remove the fan. If it is an electric fan check for any play or tightness in the bearings, undue noise or loose mountings. Check for damage to the fan blades. Where necessary lubricate the bearings and refit the fan.
11. Complete the report sheet on the cooling system, identify any faults and report on serviceability.
12. Answer the following questions:

    (a) State the types of cooling systems used on motor vehicles and give two advantages for each.

    (b) State the purpose of:
    - (i) the pressure valve
    - (ii) the vacuum valve
    - (iii) the thermostat
    - (iv) the temperature sensor
    - (v) the water pump

    (c) What is the purpose of pressurizing the cooling system?

    (d) Give two advantages of fitting an electric fan compared with belt driven fans.

    (e) Describe a possible cause and the corrective action to be taken for the following faults:
    - (i) Squealing noise from the front of the engine.
    - (ii) External leak from the bottom of the radiator.
    - (iii) Internal leak in the engine.
    - (iv) Over-heating with no loss of water.
    - (v) Heater does not get warm enough.
    - (vi) Coolant is very dirty.

Checklist

Vehicle

Visual checks on:
Type of radiator fitted
Type of fan fitted
Type of cooling system

Practical tests on the cooling system
Anti-freeze content
Pressure test of cap
Pressure test of system
Fan belt tension and condition
Operation of heater
Operation of fan
Operation of thermostat
Radiator flow test
Manufacturer's technical data

Comments on serviceability

Student's signature

Supervisor's signature

Practical assignment – liquid cooling systems

Objective

To carry out a number of tests on the cooling system to ascertain its serviceability.

- Thermostat setting.
- System pressure testing.
- Radiator flow test.

Tools and equipment

- Running engine/vehicle
- Assorted hand tools
- Thermostat testing equipment
- Pressure tester
- Header tank, drain tank and fittings
- Stopwatch.

Safety aspects

- Cables, hands, hair and loose clothing must be kept clear of fans and other rotating parts. Stationary engines require guards to be fitted to the fan drive.
- Keep hands clear of hot parts of the engine.
- If a vehicle is used, the gear lever must be in the neutral position, the hand brake applied and the wheels chocked before operating the starter motor.
- Arrangements must be made for the exhaust gases to pass directly out of any enclosed space.
- Remove radiator cap *slowly* and cover with a cloth if the engine is hot.

Safety questions

1. Why must the exhaust gases not be discharged into the garage?
2. What are the dangers from unguarded fan blades and fan belts?
3. What is likely to happen if the radiator cap is removed quickly when the engine is hot?

Activity

1. (a) Disconnect hoses and housing and remove the thermostat from the engine.
   (b) Place the thermostat in the tester and heat the water to the opening temperature of the thermostat, watch for commencement of opening and fully open point, note the temperatures and record the results.

Note: it may be necessary to first subject the thermostat to boiling water so that the fully open position can be assessed.)

   (c) The recommended opening temperatures should be obtained from the data book.
   (d) Replace the thermostat in the correct position, refit the housing using a new gasket as required, fit hoses and tighten hose clips, run engine and check for water leaks.
2. (a) Remove radiator cap. (Observe safety instructions.)
   (b) Fit pressure testing equipment in place of the radiator cap, operate pump to pressurize system to recommended pressure.
   (c) Carry out visual inspection of components in the cooling system and joints for coolant leakage.

Note: look for a steady reading of the pressure tester gauge; if the pressure falls steadily and there is no coolant leakage then an internal leakage of the coolant can be suspected. (Check that the tester unit is fully sealed on the radiator neck.)

   (d) To identify internal leakage there are products on the market which can be mixed with the coolant, the system is closed and the engine is run until it reaches its normal operating temperature. After the system cools the radiator cap is removed and the colour of the coolant is inspected. The chemical changes colour when it comes into contact with oxygen. Therefore if the colour of the coolant changes it can be assumed that air is entering the system, most probably through the cylinder head gasket.
   (e) The radiator cap can be checked for correct operation by fitting the correct adaptor to the pump and fitting the cap in place on the tester. The pressure is then raised by operating the pump and recorded when the stage is reached for the seal and the spring in the cap to lift and so relieve the pressure.
3. To flow test the radiator.
   (a) Remove the radiator and fit it to the test rig.
   (b) Fill the header tank of the rig with a known quantity of water.
   (c) Open the tap to discharge the water through the radiator and measure the draining time with a stop watch. Compare this with the manufacturing data (20 litres

takes approximately 20 seconds for a car radiator with a water head of 0.7 metres).

(d) The mineral deposits in the coolant tend to block the water ways, so an approximation of the flow rate can be ascertained by comparing the mass of the radiator under test with the mass of a new radiator of the same type. The deposits are heavy so a 25% increase in weight will give an indication of several mineral deposits.

Questions

1. What are the effects of pressurizing the cooling system?
2. Explain the function of the two valves in the pressure cap.
3. List five reasons for an engine becoming overheated.

3
Fuel systems

3.1 Petrol fuel

Petrol is a colourless liquid and is one of the fuels most commonly used in the motor vehicle engine. This is because it is a clean liquid, is easily stored and flows freely. It gives off an inflammable vapour even at very low temperatures and when burnt gives off a large amount of heat.

Before petrol can be burnt it must be **atomized** (that is it has to be broken down into very small droplets like a mist) so that it can be mixed with a suitable quantity of air. This is usually done by the carburettor. The **combustion** process (the burning of the air/fuel mixture) involves the chemical combination of a fuel with oxyge; during this process heat is given off. This heat given off by the complete combustion of a unit mass of a fuel is called the **calorific value** of a fuel, e.g. an average sample of petrol has a calorific value of 44 MJ/kg. Crude petroleum, from which petrol is refined, is a mixture of various compounds of hydrogen and carbon (called **hydrocarbons**).

The mass of air per kilogram of fuel in a mixture of air and fuel gives the air/fuel ratio. For complete combustion the chemically correct mixture is approximately 14.7 parts of air to 1 part of fuel (**14.7:1**). Ratios of less than about 8:1 (rich) or more than 22:1 (weak) cannot normally be ignited in petrol engine cylinders. The air/fuel ratio has a considerable effect on the engine's performance and power output. The chemically correct ratio does not always give the best results: for instance, under cold starting conditions, an air/fuel ratio as low as 2:1 may be required; for acceleration a ratio of say 12:1; and for the most economical running 17 or 18:1 may be required.

Any change in the air/fuel ratio also changes the composition of the exhaust gases. Under normal operating conditions a ratio of approximately 14.7:1 will give the least toxic exhaust gas. With a richer mixture the exhaust gas will contain more **carbon monoxide**, with a weaker mixture **oxides of nitrogen** will be present. Both these gases are harmful to the human body, especially in confined spaces.

Learning tasks

1. What are the main dangers associated with petrol? What safety regulations must be observed in the workshop when working on the fuel system?
2. How may fuel be used or stored in the garage environment?
3. List the dangers of running a petrol engine in the workshop and any safety precautions that should be taken.
4. Complete a survey of the local service stations and garages in your area. Identify the types of fuel and services offered, stating price and grade of fuel, e.g. diesel, petrol, leaded, unleaded, super, etc. From your survey draw up a graph to show price and variety of services offered.
5. Identify the main differences between leaded and unleaded fuels, and give the advantages of each. What effect (if any) does each have on the running of the vehicle, e.g. power output, MPG, service intervals, engine wear, etc?

3.2 Layout of the petrol fuel system

A complete fuel system consists of the following components.

- **Fuel tank** in which to store the fuel. This also contains a **sensor unit** to indicate to the driver how much fuel the tank contains.
- **Pipelines** that connect the tank to the lift pump and carburettor and return excess fuel back to the tank. This helps to reduce the formation of vapour locks in the system, which in warm weather may stop the engine from running.
- **Fuel filter** to remove unwanted sediment (particles of dirt and water) from the fuel before it reaches the carburettor.

- **Fuel lift pump** to transfer the fuel from the tank to the carburettor or fuel injection unit.
- **Carburettor or fuel injection unit** which meters the fuel and mixes it with the air in the correct proportions to suit the engine needs.
- **Inlet manifold** which directs the mixture to the inlet ports in the cylinder head.
- **Air filter** to remove small particles from the air as it is drawn into the inlet manifold via the carburettor.

A typical carburettor-type fuel system is shown in Fig. 3.1.

Learning task

1. Take a look at one of the vehicles in the workshop and identify the main units. Draw and label a simple block diagram to show the layout of the system and how the points are connected together. Show on the diagram the direction of the fuel flow.
2. What personal safety precautions should the mechanic take when working on the fuel system?

3.3 The fuel tank

Several types of materials are commonly used in the manufacture of the fuel tank. One type is the pressed steel, often coated on the inside with lead/tin to prevent corrosion. They normally have either welded joints and seams or soldered joints (where the tin is cut and bent to shape and the seams are rolled before being soldered). Another type uses expanded synthetic rubber or flame-resistant plastic, moulded to the required shape. This gives a high resistance to damage as it

will bend or distort fairly easily. It is also lighter than those made from steel and is rust proof.

The tank is usually fitted with **baffles** (these are partitions inside the tank) to prevent the fuel surging from side to side, especially when the tank is not full. Holes are positioned in the side or top of the tank to allow for the location of the fuel-gauge sensor unit, the supply and return pipes and the filler pipe. A coarse gauze filter is positioned over the fuel feed pipe to prevent large particles of dirt from blocking the pipe. A **vent pipe** is also fitted to relieve the vapour pressure and allow air to enter as fuel is drawn from the tank. The filler tube usually contains the vent pipe and the overflow pipe near to the filler cap end. No petrol vapour is allowed to pass into the atmosphere, so a non-venting filler cap is fitted; it contains a one-way valve allowing air into the tank and preventing the fuel and its vapour from escaping.

Safety note

If fuel tank repairs are necessary it is recommended that these are only undertaken by the specialist. Any heat could ignite the fuel vapour and cause a serious explosion and possible personal injury or fire, even if the tank has been empty for some months.

Learning task

1. Draw up an operations schedule for removing a fuel tank from a vehicle. Include any safety recommendations.
2. What would be the symptoms of a blocked valve in the filler cap?
3. Remove and refit a fuel tank using the operations schedule you have drawn up, taking special note of any safety precautions that must be observed.

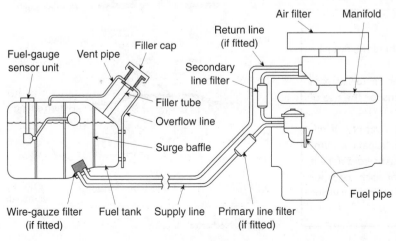

Fig. 3.1 Carburettor-type fuel system

3.4 Fuel pipe lines

Both supply and return lines may be made from plastic or steel piping which is clipped to the body between the tank and the engine. Flexible hoses are used to connect the rigid pipe to the engine, this allows for the movement of the engine on its mountings. Plastic pipes must be protected from heat or there could be a serious risk of fire, especially if welding is to be carried out on the bodywork close to any part of the fuel system.

When the **needle valve** in the carburettor float chamber closes, the fuel passes via the return line back to the tank. A **restrictor** is fitted in the return to prevent too much fuel bypassing the float chamber. In this way a continuous flow of fuel through the system is maintained which reduces the possibility of a **vapour lock** occurring and keeps the fuel at a fairly constant temperature.

3.5 Fuel filters

The idea of fitting a fuel filter is to prevent particles of dirt, water, etc. from entering the main components and creating a blockage, causing excessive wear or premature failure to occur. Although the fuel produced by the petrol companies is clean, it is possible for particles of dust or dirt to enter the tank when filling, and for moisture-laden air to condense into water droplets inside the tank and be drawn into the fuel system. A combination of coarse filters on the inlet and fine filters on the outlet sides of the pump is used, as shown in Fig. 3.1.

Learning tasks

1. At what service intervals should the filter be checked, cleaned or replaced?
2. Inspect a filter and state the material from which it is made. Give reasons for the use of these materials.
3. Fuel filters may be fitted in a variety of different places in the system. Inspect a number of vehicles and list at least two different places giving an advantage for each together with any changes in their servicing requirements.

3.6 Fuel lift pumps

The two main types of fuel lift pumps in common use are:

- The **mechanical** lift pump – fitted to and operated by the engine.
- The **electrical** lift pump – fitted in any convenient position on the vehicle and operated electrically.

Mechanical lift pump

Figure 3.2 shows a **diaphragm-type lever-operated** petrol pump, which draws fuel from the tank and lifts it under pressure to the carburettor float chamber. It is bolted to the engine so that the lever arm rests on an **eccentric** on the **camshaft**. As the lever arm is lifted a diaphragm is operated inside a sealed chamber. This upper chamber contains **inlet** and **outlet valves**. The fuel is drawn from the tank through the inlet valve as the diaphragm is pulled down. On releasing the lever the inlet valve closes and the diaphragm forces the fuel through the outlet valve under pressure from the return spring to the carburettor; as the lever is lifted again the outlet valve closes preventing fuel from passing back into the pump. This sequence is repeated each time the lever is operated until the float chamber is full.

Electrical fuel pump

As with the mechanical fuel pump the electrical pump is of the **positive-displacement** type. This means it displaces a definite volume of fuel with

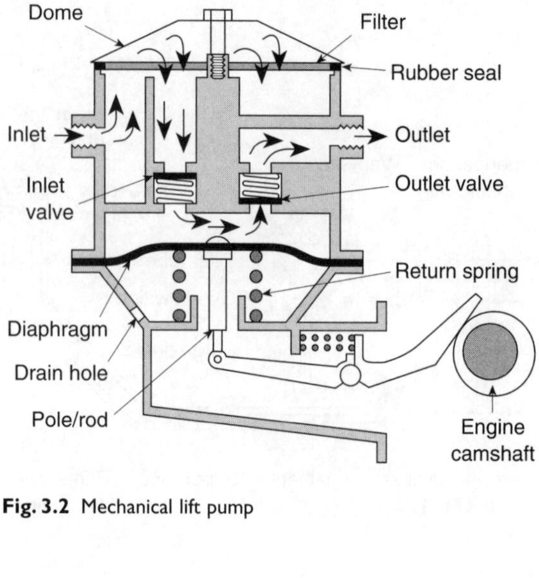

Fig. 3.2 Mechanical lift pump

each movement of the diaphragm. The main advantages of the electrical pump are that it can **prime** the system (that is pump fuel into the system) from the moment the ignition is switched on, ensuring that there is fuel in the carburettor before the engine is turned over, and it can be fitted anywhere on the vehicle between the fuel tank and the carburettor. The main disadvantages of the electrical fuel pump are:

- it is more expensive to manufacture and service;
- it is more complicated;
- it has a greater risk of fire in the event of an accident – many vehicles using this pump now incorporate a fuel cut-off switch which cuts off the electrical feed to the pump in the event of an accident.

Fig. 3.3 shows the SU (Skinners Union type of electrical fuel pump which consists of two parts, the pumping chamber (which is very similar to the mechanical pump) and the electrical unit. The diaphragm is attached to the **armature** which operates as an **electromagnet**. When **energized** it moves inside the coil towards the points/**toggle switch** and fuel is drawn into the pump through the inlet valve. At the end of its stroke the toggle spring assembly clicks open the points cutting off the electrical supply to the coil. The return spring forces the fuel through the outlet valve to the carburettor. As the armature reaches the end of its return stroke the toggle spring assembly clicks the points closed and the coil becomes energized, once again overcoming the return spring pressure and the cycle is repeated.

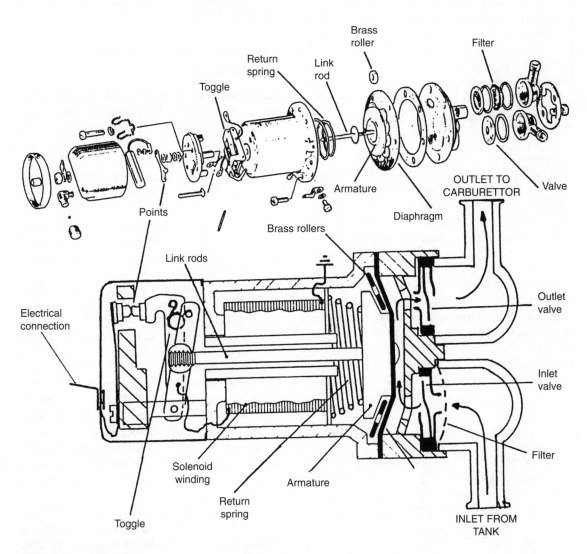

Fig. 3.3 SU electrical fuel pump

3.7 Carburation

Carburation is one of the two methods most commonly used to introduce the fuel into the air that is drawn into the cylinder. The other is fuel injection (see Section 3.9). Before considering any system some explanation of the term carburation, which is the mixing and delivery of, in this case, petrol and air into the cylinders, is necessary.

The mixing of the fuel with the air is done by the carburettor in the **venturi** or **choke tube** (Fig. 3.4). The venturi has a lower pressure at the narrowest section which will draw fuel into the air stream if the outlet from the float chamber is positioned at this point. This drop in pressure is caused by the molecules of air which flow faster

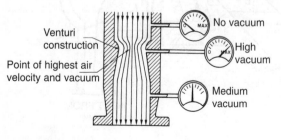

Fig. 3.4 Venturi pipe

Venturi construction

Point of highest air velocity and vacuum

No vacuum

High vacuum

Medium vacuum

at the narrowest section and, at the same time, move further apart thus lowering the pressure. The fuel in the float chamber has atmospheric pressure acting on its surface and so fuel is forced through the outlet into the air stream in the form of very fine droplets. This mixes with the air. The resulting mixture is drawn into the cylinders through the inlet manifold.

3.8 The carburettor

The function of the carburettor is to control the quantity of fuel and air mixture entering the cylinders, to atomize the fuel into very fine droplets, mix it with the incoming air and vaporize this fine spray into a combustible mixture. The chemically correct ratio of air to fuel is approximately 14:1 by weight, that is 14 parts of air to one part of fuel (this is called the **stoichiometric air-fuel ratio**).

Variable or fixed choke carburettor

Sometimes referred to as **variable vacuum** carburettors, these have a **fixed diameter venturi** and contain jets which enable the engine to operate over a wide range of both engine speeds and loads.

The simple fixed choke carburettor has a float chamber that provides a constant level of fuel, just below the outlet from the jet. This level is maintained by means of the float and needle. The float chamber has a small hole in the top to allow atmospheric pressure to act on the top of the fuel. A choke tube or venturi is fitted in the mixing chamber around the jet outlet to increase the speed of the air at this point and create a depression. This causes the atmospheric pressure acting on the fuel in the float chamber to force fuel via the outlet into the fast moving air stream. The **throttle butterfly valve** regulates the quantity of mixture passing to the cylinders and is operated by the driver pressing the accelerator pedal. However, in some cases it can be operated by hand, as on motor cycles or where a constant engine speed is required, as on some types of heavy vehicles that have a hydraulic pump fitted to operate a crane.

The **simple** carburettor will provide the correct mixture for one engine speed/load only, at higher engine speeds the mixture will progressively become too rich (too much fuel mixed with the air) and at lower engine speeds the mixture becomes too weak (that is not enough fuel is mixed with the air). When starting from cold a smaller proportion of fuel is evaporated and some may condense onto the cold surfaces of the inlet manifold before reaching the combustion chamber. Because of this a mixture richer than the chemically correct ratio is required. As the engine revs are increased the flow rate of the air does not match that of the fuel and consequently the air/fuel mixture becomes progressively too rich. Because of these problems the simple carburettor is not suitable for the modern motor car, although the basic principles of operation still apply. This type of carburettor is shown in Fig. 3.5.

Learning tasks

1. On which types of engines would the simple carburettor be used? Give reasons for your answer.
2. Give two reasons why a simple carburettor is unsuitable for the modern motor vehicle.
3. Dismantle a simple carburettor. State how many jets are fitted and what they are called. Clean and reassemble the carburettor, adjust the slow running jet and maximum and minimum revs to suit the engine.

Mixture correction

The simple carburettor attempts to meter both the fuel and the air. Air, which is a gas, flows very easily; petrol is a liquid which has particles that try to stick together and to the surface of the passages through which it must flow. If a suitable size jet is used for a fixed engine speed/load then if the speed is increased the larger depression would cause more fuel to flow creating a rich mixture.

To overcome the problem of the mixture getting richer as the engine speed increases an air bleed is fitted in the system. Methods of mixture correction all use the same basic principle, i.e. as the engine speed increases air is introduced into the fuel system to gradually weaken the mixture by reducing the amount of fuel entering the venturi. This gives a fairly constant mixture strength over a wider range of engine speeds and is shown in Fig. 3.6(a).

Air bleed compensation

With this arrangement a well of petrol, fed from the main jet, is subject to the depression in the venturi. As the fuel level is lowered **air bleed holes** are progressively uncovered, thereby admitting more air which reduces the depression acting on the jet which prevents enrichment of the mixture as the depression in the venturi increases. The tube, which contains a number of holes drilled down its length, is sometimes called the **emulsion** or **diffuser tube** as it tends to premix the fuel and air. The level in the well is at the same level as the float chamber when the engine is not running. Some systems have an **air bleed jet** (sometimes called an **air correction jet**) to enable the size of the jet to be altered. This is for tuning purposes and under normal circumstances would not be removed except for cleaning.

Slow-running (idling) systems

When the engine is running slowly, say at tickover, the depression in the venturi is not high

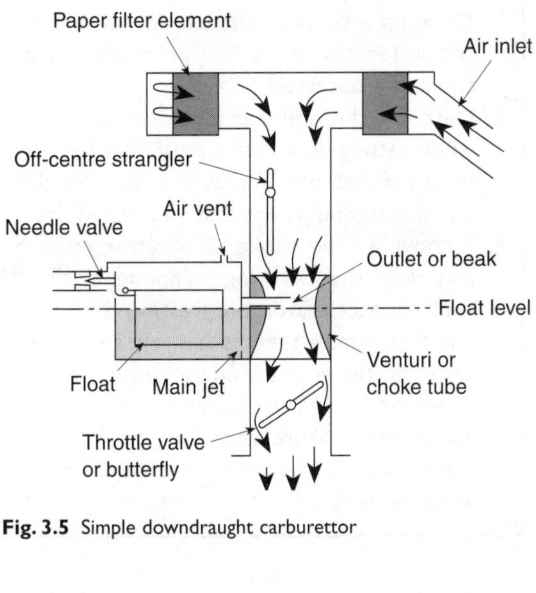

Fig. 3.5 Simple downdraught carburettor

Paper filter element
Air inlet
Off-centre strangler
Air vent
Needle valve
Outlet or beak
Float level
Float   Main jet
Venturi or choke tube
Throttle valve or butterfly

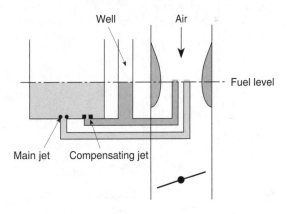

Fig. 3.6(a) Compensating jet action

Well   Air
Fuel level
Main jet   Compensating jet

enough to draw fuel out of the main jet and atomize it into very fine droplets. The speed of the air will also be too slow to keep the fuel in suspension in the air stream (it will tend to fall out of suspension onto the inlet manifold). Because of this the engine will have difficulty in idling and some means of keeping it operating is required. This is the purpose of the slow-running system.

As can be seen from Fig. 3.6(b) the circuit has a jet with a suitable size hole in it and a means of adjusting the volume of air/fuel mixture; and the outlet is positioned on the engine side of the throttle butterfly, where the inlet depression is at its highest. Here it mixes with the air stream as it passes between the throttle butterfly and the wall of the carburettor; in this way the venturi and main jet are bypassed and the engine is fed through the slow-running system to maintain a fairly constant tick-over.

Air bleed and idling mixture arrangements

When the two systems are incorporated into one carburettor then the system permits the mixture to be controlled over a wide range of engine speeds and loads to give the best possible fuel consumption and the least harmful exhaust gases.

Progression jets and acceleration devices

When the throttle butterfly is opened the depression at the slow running outlet is reduced while at the same time a larger volume of air is passed into the inlet manifold. The depression at the main jet outlet is not enough to draw fuel into the air stream. The result of this is a sudden weakening of the mixture strength, causing the engine revs to drop even further before they begin to pick up again.

To overcome this problem a series of holes (usually two or three) are drilled up the side of the body of the carburettor above the throttle butterfly. As the throttle opens it causes the depression to pass over the progression outlets, bypassing the **volume control screw** and drawing the emulsified fuel directly into the air stream. This enriches the mixture, increasing the engine revs until a point is reached where the depression is sufficient to operate the main jet in the mixing chamber (the venturi). This is shown in Fig. 3.7(a).

If the throttle is opened suddenly to full throttle neither the slow-running, progression jets or the main jet will operate. This is because there is no depression at the slow-running or progression jets as the throttle is fully open and the depression is not enough to operate the main jet. This causes what is known as a **flat spot** (this is where the driver is thrust forwards and then backwards as the engine almost stalls before the vehicle takes off). To overcome this problem an enrichment device or **acceleration pump** is fitted, linked to the throttle linkage. As the throttle is operated quickly the pump delivers neat fuel directly into the venturi, just at the time when the depression is insufficient to draw fuel from the other systems. If the throttle is opened slowly the accelerator pump will not operate. This is shown in Fig. 3.7(b).

Learning tasks

1. How would the driver notice if there was a hole in item 35 of the Weber carburettor shown in Figure 3.8
2. Draw up a service schedule for the carburettor. Identify any safety precautions that should be observed.
3. Describe the steps that should be taken when setting up a carburettor that has just been refitted after major overhaul. Itemize any special equipment that you would use.
4. Remove a fixed choke carburettor, remove and clean the following components: slow-running, accelerator, progression and main jets. Reassemble the jets and refit the carburettor to the engine. Run the engine and set tick-over, manual/automatic choke and adjust the mixture according to manufacturer's data. Complete a job card to record all work done.

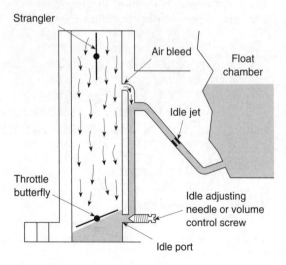

Strangler

Air bleed

Float chamber

Idle jet

Throttle butterfly

Idle adjusting needle or volume control screw

Idle port

Fig. 3.6(b) Simple idling circuit

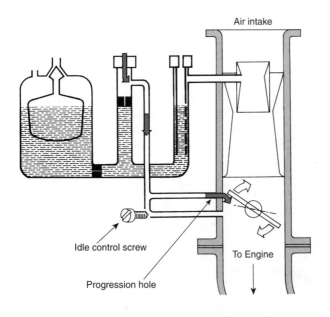

Air intake

Idle control screw

Progression hole

To Engine

Fig. 3.7(a) The principle of the progression hole

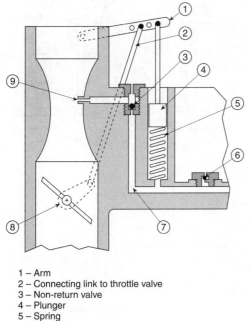

1 – Arm
2 – Connecting link to throttle valve
3 – Non-return valve
4 – Plunger
5 – Spring
6 – Non-return valve
7 – Drilling
8 – Throttle valve lever
9 – Outlet into venturi

Fig. 3.7(b) Mechanically operated acceleration pump

Cold starting devices

There are two main problems to overcome when starting from cold to ensure the engine will start. First, the speed at which the starter will turn the engine will not be fast enough to create sufficient depression in the venturi to ensure that fuel is drawn from the fuel jet. In cold weather the problem is made worse by the drag of the oil in the bearings and sump, oil being at its thickest when the weather is cold.

Second, there is no heat to assist in vaporizing the fuel which is delivered to the cylinders. The effective mixture of fuel vapour and air will be far too weak to be readily ignited by the spark at the sparking plug.

The simplest way of overcoming these two problems is to temporarily supply an excess of fuel to ensure that a proportion of fuel which will vaporize at this cold temperature will also form an ignitable mixture with the incoming air. To keep the engine running, some excess of fuel will still be required until the engine warms up, and a greater quantity of mixture will be required to off-set the increase in oil drag until the oil warms up. The excess fuel that does not evaporate will be deposited on the cylinder walls. Whilst a small amount of this may be helpful by thinning the oil down, too much will wash the oil film off altogether causing metal-to-metal contact and severe wear to occur. Thus any excess fuel must be no more than is absolutely necessary and must be discontinued as soon as possible.

Cold starting devices may be **automatic** or **manually operated**. The simplest is the manual strangler (Fig. 3.9(a)) where the driver pulls out the choke which is flexibly connected to the

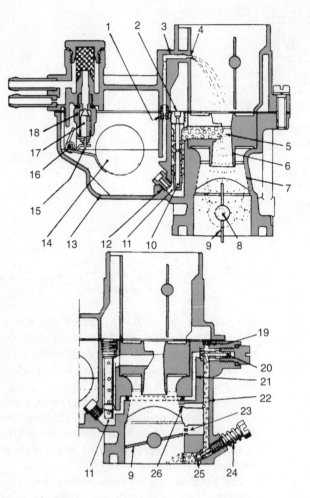

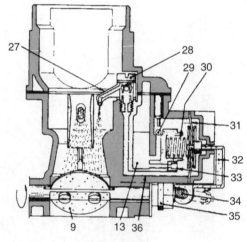

1 – Calibrated bushing	19 – Idle air metering bushing
2 – Air bleed jet	20 – Idle jet
3 – High speed orifice passage	21 – Fuel passage
4 – High speed orifice	22 – Idle passage
5 – Spray nozzle	23 – Transfer orifices
6 – Auxiliary venturi	24 – Idle adjusting screw
7 – Venturi	25 – Idle feed bushing
8 – Throttle shaft	26 – Idle air calibrated orifice
9 – Throttle valve	27 – Pump jet nozzle
10 – Emulsion tube	28 – Delivery valve
11 – Emulsion tube well	29 – Ball valve
12 – Main jet	30 – Intake control spring
13 – Fuel bowl	31 – Diaphragm
14 – Float	32 – Accelerating pump control lever
15 – Hook, needle return to float tang	33 – Calibrated bushing, excess fuel discharge
16 – Float hinge pin	34 – Throttle return spring
17 – Valve needle	35 – Throttle control lever
18 – Needle valve	36 – Fuel delivery passage

Fig. 3.8 Weber 32IBA unit

carburettor choke control. This has the effect of reducing the air supply and enriching the mixture drawn into the engine cylinders.

A simple automatic cold start control (Fig. 3.9(b)) has a **bi-metal spring** wound round the strangler (butterfly) spindle. One end of the spring is attached to the spindle; the other end is attached to the carburettor body in such a way that the butterfly is held in the closed position when the engine is cold. As the engine warms up the spring gradually unwinds and releases the strangler to the normal run position. The fast idle cam increases the engine speed to enable it to run when the strangler is in operation.

A number of other types of automatic cold start are used by manufacturers. The most common is the **water heated** type where the bi-metal strip is surrounded by a water jacket. As the engine cooling system heats up the heat is transferred to the bi-metal strip. Other methods use **exhaust gas** or **heated air** for this purpose

Variable-choke carburettor

This is sometimes called the constant-vacuum or constant-depression carburettor. The principle of the variable-choke carburettor is to employ a means whereby the effective choke area moves according to the engine speed as required. This will have the effect of having a constant air velocity (air speed) and therefore a constant depression over the jet. One of the most common carburettors of this type is called the SU carburettor, (S.U. stands for Skinners Union as in the original carburettor instead of the dashpot a diaphragm made from cow hide (leather to you and me) was used).

SU carburettor

This is a **side draught** type and has a tapered needle which is attached to the underside of the piston which moves vertically in a dashpot. The lower part of the piston rests on a flat portion of the venturi (sometimes called the bridge) and forms the moveable part of the variable choke area. The jet is also mounted in the bridge and the tapered needle passes through the middle of the jet. As the engine starts the depression in the inlet manifold is felt above the piston in the suction chamber, through the holes drilled on the engine side of the lower part of the piston. This causes the piston and needle to rise lifting the piston. The resulting air flow over the bridge draws fuel from the jet and mixes it with the incoming air in the correct air/fuel ratio. When the throttle is opened and engine revs increase, the piston lifts higher giving a greater choke area together with a larger jet area. With careful calibration of jet with tapered needle size this type of carburettor can be used on a wide range of engines. It is shown in Fig. 3.10.

Acceleration and mixture enrichment

When the throttle is opened quickly the piston will also rise quickly causing a 'flat spot' to occur just when you wanted the engine to accelerate. To overcome this problem the piston has a **damper** fitted in the central spindle which guides its vertical movement. This is filled with oil. This means that when the throttle is opened quickly the rate at which the piston rises is slowed because the oil has to be displaced through the

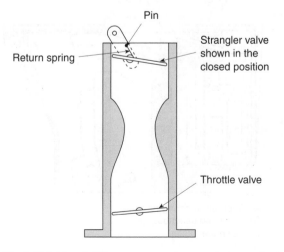

Fig. 3.9(a) Manual choke

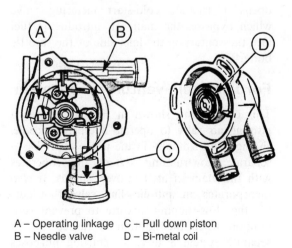

A – Operating linkage C – Pull down piston
B – Needle valve D – Bi-metal coil

Fig. 3.9(b) Automatic choke and bi-metal housing assemblies

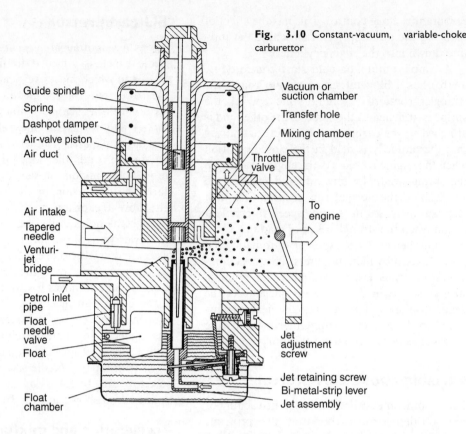

Fig. 3.10 Constant-vacuum, variable-choke carburettor

Labels on figure: Guide spindle, Spring, Dashpot damper, Air-valve piston, Air duct, Air intake, Tapered needle, Venturi-jet bridge, Petrol inlet pipe, Float needle valve, Float, Float chamber, Vacuum or suction chamber, Transfer hole, Mixing chamber, Throttle valve, To engine, Jet adjustment screw, Jet retaining screw, Bi-metal-strip lever, Jet assembly

valve. This will have the effect of increasing the depression over the jet, drawing more fuel for the same amount of air and giving a richer mixture for acceleration purposes.

Cold starting

In cold conditions the driver pulls the choke lever out to operate the cold start. The lever is connected via a flexible cable to a linkage which either lowers the jet in the body to increase the jet area and therefore the amount of fuel, or opens a separate cold-start metering valve which bypasses the main jet, introducing fuel into the venturi on the inlet side of the throttle butterfly.

Ford variable-venturi carburettor

This carburettor, shown in Fig. 3.11, uses a **pivoting air valve** to operate a tapered needle, sliding it horizontally in the main jet. It has a separate slow-running system that operates with the main jet at 'tick-over' speeds. It also incorporates an **anti-dieseling valve** that cuts off the slow-running mixture to prevent running-on when the ignition is turned off. A separate system is used for starting purposes when cold.

Learning tasks

1. What would the effects be of a sticking cold-starting aid. List the tests that should be carried out to identify the problem together with the steps taken to put the fault right.
2. List at least two advantages of the variable-choke carburettor over the fixed-choke carburettor. Give one main disadvantage.

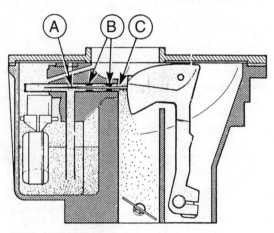

A – Tapered metering rod
B – Main and secondary jets
C – Main fuel outlet

Fig. 3.11 Ford variable venturi carburettor – main jet system

3.9 Petrol injection

One of the problems of the carburettor system of supplying fuel to the engine is that it relies on a depression in the venturi to draw fuel into the air passing into the cylinder. The restriction in the venturi (which causes the depression) can be removed if the petrol is injected into the air stream, thereby ensuring that more is draw into the cylinders. It also means that if a **turbocharger** is fitted the fuel can still be mixed with the pressurized air. Two types of system are commonly fitted: the **single-point** injection and the **multi-point** injection. The latter is shown in Fig. 3.12.

The advantages of the petrol injection system are:

- a cleaner exhaust gas is given off – the injection system supplies precisely the right amount of fuel for all engine speeds and loads, giving the minimum amount of pollutants;
- the minimum amount of maintenance is required – use of electronics means there are very few moving parts and the moving parts in the injector are lubricated by the fuel giving the minimum amount of wear;
- lower fuel consumption, due to the uniform distribution and accurate metering of the fuel.

Single-point injection

Fuel is injected intermittently through a **single injector** fitted centrally on the inlet side of the throttle butterfly. The fuel is mixed with the air in a similar manner to a carburettor and drawn into the cylinders. The system is controlled by an **ECU** (electronic control unit) which receives signals from a number of sensors on the engine. By this means the correct air/fuel ratio can be supplied to suit all engine requirements.

Method of operation

The injector is **solenoid** operated and is held on its seat by a pre-tensioned return spring. The fuel under pressure from the pump enters the valve injector body through the gauze filter. It then passes through the **pressure regulator**, which returns excess fuel back to the tank. This circulation of the fuel helps to prevent the formation of vapour locks which otherwise could occur. The valve is opened once every revolution of the crankshaft by an electrical pulse from the ECU. The frequency of the pulse is related to the speed of the engine. This input to the ECU is from the crank angle and speed sensors. The amount of fuel injected depends on how long the valve is open for; and this depends on inputs from the engine temperature, speed, load, and acceleration sensors feeding data to the ECU.

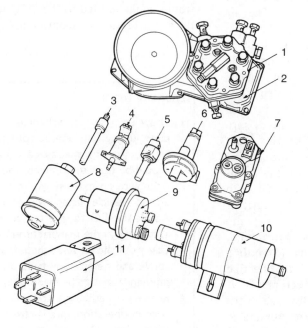

1 – Fuel distributor	5 – Thermo-time switch	8 – Fuel filter
2 – Air sensor	6 – Auxiliary air device	9 – Fuel accumulator
3 – Injection valve	7 – Warm-up regulator	10 – Electric fuel pump
4 – Cold start valve		11 – Impulse module

Fig. 3.12 The components of the multi-point petrol injection system

The dome-shaped injector valve opens and fuel is forced through a number of holes onto an inverted cup-shaped deflector. It then rebounds in the form of a highly atomized conical spray. It is this spray formation which is mainly responsible for the high quality of air/fuel mixture distribution which takes place in the mixing chamber just above the throttle valve.

Fast idle

The fast idle cam only comes on when the engine is cold. It is operated by a capsule filled with wax in which there is a stainless steel pin; when cold the pin is at its innermost (shortest) position. This allows the cam and peg to rotate the throttle valve to the fast idle position. As the engine warms up the wax melts and expands forcing the pin out against the lever attached to the cam spindle which returns the throttle valve to its slow hot-idle (tick-over) position.

Multi-point injection

As the name suggests this system uses one injector for each cylinder, each being fed from a common distribution rail/pipe.

Method of operation

In the Bosch LE Jetronic (Fig. 3.13) the air flows through the **air flow sensor** (6) past the **throttle valve** (12) into the **intake manifold** (10) and on to the individual cylinders. The air flow **sensor flap** (6a) is deflected and the angle is converted into an electrical signal by a **potentiometer**. The signal is fed to the ECU (7) which forms one of the input signals required by the fuel management system. The system does not require a device of its own for measuring the engine speed as this is supplied by the ignition system. The two main input variables, quantity of air and engine speed, enable the ECU to calculate the quantity of fuel to be metered and control both timing and opening duration of the injector valves. Fuel is delivered by an electric pump (2), which draws fuel from the petrol tank (1), feeds it through a fine filter (3) into a distribution pipe (4). It is from this line that fuel is fed to the individual injectors (9). A pressure regulator (5) at the end of the distribution pipe maintains a constant pressure in the system and excess fuel is returned back to the fuel tank.

Cold starting

During starting, the **start valve** (11) injects more fuel into the intake manifold. The length of operation of this valve is governed by the **thermo-time switch** (14) which senses engine temperature.

Warm-up

After a cold start the engine requires up to three times as much fuel to 'warm up' as when at normal operating temperatures. The **temperature sensor** (8) measures the engine temperature and converts it into an electrical signal which is fed to the ECU as a correction variable. Using the output signal, the electronics control enrichment of the air/fuel mixture.

Idling

In bypassing the throttle valve, the **auxiliary air device** (13) supplies the engine with an extra quantity of air. This increases the idle speed when the engine is cold. The auxiliary air device is controlled by an electrically heated bi-metallic strip which varies the gap depending on engine temperature.

Full load

Engines which run very lean at part load require mixture enrichment at full load. The position of full load is detected by the **throttle valve switch** (12a); this is converted into an electronic signal and fed to the ECU which adjusts the air/fuel ratio to the optimum full load value.

Learning tasks

1. Draw up a service schedule for the complete fuel system of a petrol injection vehicle. Itemize any specialized equipment that should be used to complete the task.
2. Complete an exhaust gas test on a petrol engine vehicle fitted with fuel injection. Adjust the CO to give the correct reading according to the manufacturer's data.
3. Carry out the service schedule shown at (1) above and itemize any faults found or recommendations to be made on the job sheet.
4. Remove a petrol injector unit and test for correct operation, spray pattern and dribble from nozzle. Pressure-test the distribution circuit and check results against manufacturer's data.

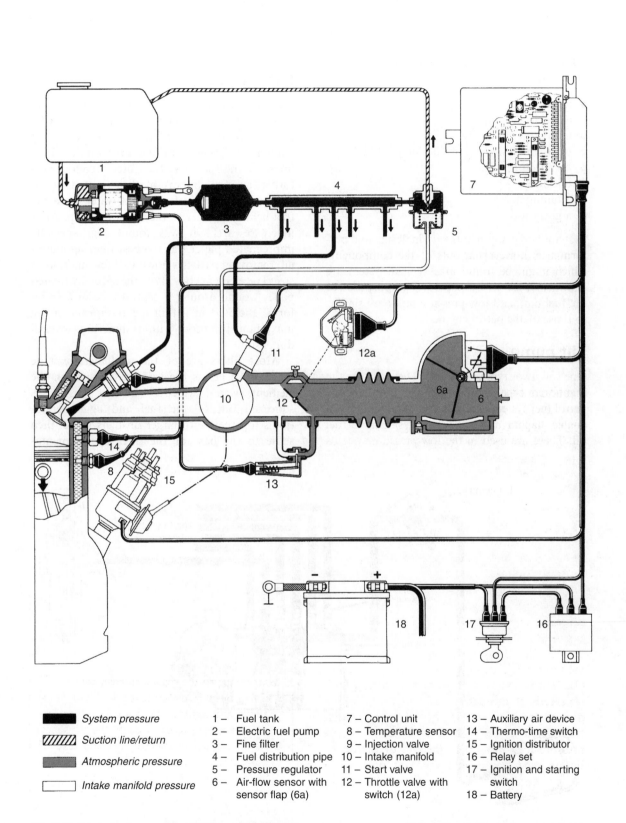

![System pressure] System pressure	1 –	Fuel tank	7 –	Control unit

System pressure

Suction line/return

Atmospheric pressure

Intake manifold pressure

1 – Fuel tank
2 – Electric fuel pump
3 – Fine filter
4 – Fuel distribution pipe
5 – Pressure regulator
6 – Air-flow sensor with
    sensor flap (6a)

7 – Control unit
8 – Temperature sensor
9 – Injection valve
10 – Intake manifold
11 – Start valve
12 – Throttle valve with
     switch (12a)

13 – Auxiliary air device
14 – Thermo-time switch
15 – Ignition distributor
16 – Relay set
17 – Ignition and starting
     switch
18 – Battery

Fig. 3.13 Schematic diagram of Bosch LE-Jectronic fuel injection

3.10 Diesel fuel systems

The purpose of the injection equipment in a diesel fuel system is to supply quantities of fuel oil into the combustion chamber in the form of a very fine spray at precisely timed intervals. To achieve this the following components are usually employed:

- a fuel tank or tanks
- a fuel feed pump
- a fuel filter or filters
- high- and low-pressure fuel supply lines
- an injector pump
- injectors
- a timing device
- a governor

Systems and components vary in design and performance; however, layouts of the components which might be found in a typical system are shown in Figs 3.14 and 3.15. The purposes of the fuel tank and low-pressure pipes are similar to those of the petrol engine.

Lift pump

One of two types is used. The first is the diaphragm-type, similar in operation to the petrol fuel system except that it commonly has a **double diaphragm** fitted that is resistant to fuel oil. These are used in the low-pressure systems

and deliver fuel at a pressure of approximately $34.5 \, \text{kN/m}^2$. The other type used is the **plunger operated** pump where higher delivery pressures are required. The plunger is backed up by a diaphragm to prevent fuel leakage. These deliver at approximately $104 \, \text{kN/m}^2$.

Fuel filters

Working clearances in the injector pump are very small, approximately 0.0001 mm (0.000 04 inch); therefore the efficiency and life of the equipment depends almost entirely on the cleanliness of the fuel. The fuel filter therefore performs a very important function, that of removing particles of dirt and water from the fuel before they get to the injector pump. After much research, it was found that specially impregnated paper was the best filtering material, removing particles down to a few microns in size. The element consists of the specially treated paper wound around a central core in a spiral form, enclosed in a thin metal canister giving maximum filtration within minimum overall dimension.

Most filters are of the **agglomerator** type (Fig. 3.16), i.e. as the fuel passes through the element, water, which is always present, is squeezed out of the fuel and agglomerates (joins together) into larger droplets which then settle to the base of the filter by sedimenta-

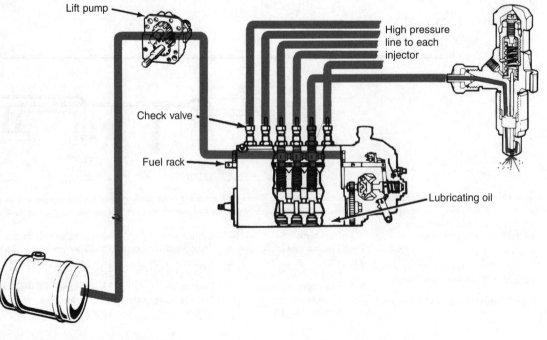

Fig. 3.14 In-line fuel-injection-pump system

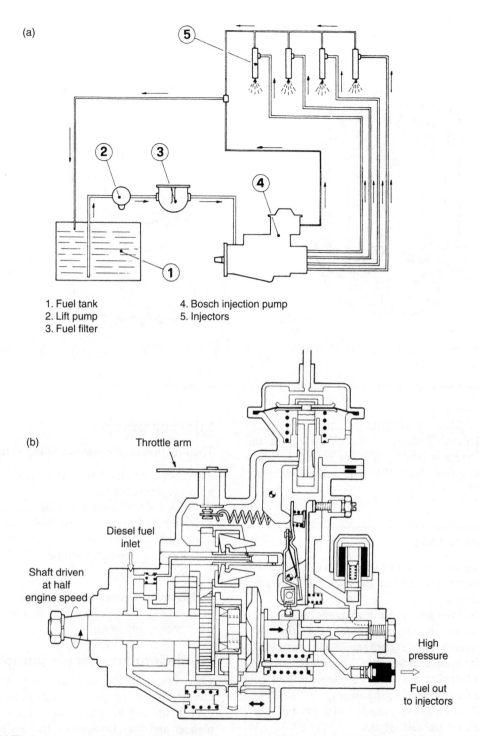

(a)

1. Fuel tank
2. Lift pump
3. Fuel filter
4. Bosch injection pump
5. Injectors

(b)

Throttle arm

Diesel fuel inlet

Shaft driven at half engine speed

High pressure

Fuel out to injectors

Fig. 3.15 (a) The basic components of a diesel fuel system are a fuel tank, lift pump with priming lever, fuel filter, injection pump, injector pipes and injectors. Additonal pipes connected to the injection pump and injectors return excess fuel to the fuel tank. (b) Distributor-type fuel injection pump

tion. Choking of the filters is caused not only by the solid matter held back by the element but also by the sludge and wax in the fuel which, under very cold conditions, form a coating on the surfaces of the fuel filter element thus reducing the rate of fuel flow. Where this becomes too much of a problem a simple sedimenter-type filter, i.e. one which does not incorporate an element, is fitted between the fuel tank and the lift pump. The object of a simple sedimenter is to separate the larger particles of dirt, wax and water from the fuel; they are then periodically drained off. Provision is made for the venting

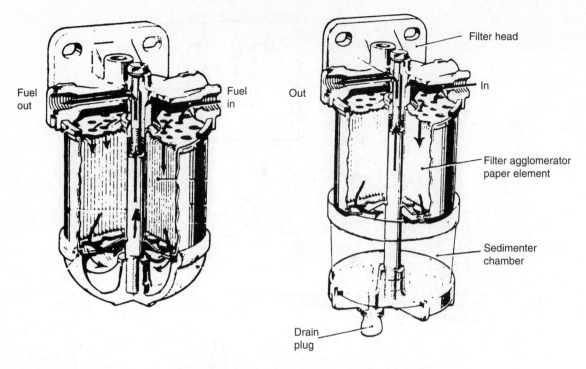

Fig. 3.16 Bowless-type filter-agglomerator-sedimenter showing agglomerator flow through element

of the filter of air (this is commonly called **bleeding** the system, where all the air in the fuel system is removed). If air enters the high-pressure fuel lines then the engine will not run.

Learning tasks

1. Remove and refit the fuel filter on a diesel engine vehicle, bleed the system and run the engine.
2. Remove and refit the lift pump of a diesel system, test the operation of the pressure/vacuum valves, record results and check with the manufacturer's data. Give reasons for any differences and make recommendations to the customer on serviceability.
3. Draw up a simple check list for tracing leaks on a diesel fuel system.
4. Make a list of personal safety/hygiene precautions that a mechanic should consider when working on a diesel fuel system.
5. What are the symptoms of a blocked fuel filter?
6. What are the service intervals for the diesel fuel system and what would it involve?

Injector pump

The function of the injector pump is to:

- deliver the correct amount of fuel;
- at the correct time;
- at sufficiently high a pressure to enable the injector to break up the fuel into very fine droplets to ensure complete combustion (that is complete burning of all the fuel injected).

The **multi-element** or the **DPA** (distributor pump application) injector pumps are the ones most commonly used.

Multi-element injector pump

This consists of a casing containing the same number of pumping elements as there are cylinders in the engine. Each element consists of a **plunger and barrel** machined to very fine tolerances, and specially lapped together to form a mated pair. A **helix** (similar to a spiral) is formed on the outside of the plunger which communicates with the plunger crown, either by a drilling in the centre of the plunger or a slot machined in the side. There are two ports in the barrel, both of which connect to a common fuel gallery feeding all the elements. The plunger is operated by a cam and follower tappet and returned by a spring. This system is shown in Fig. 3.17.

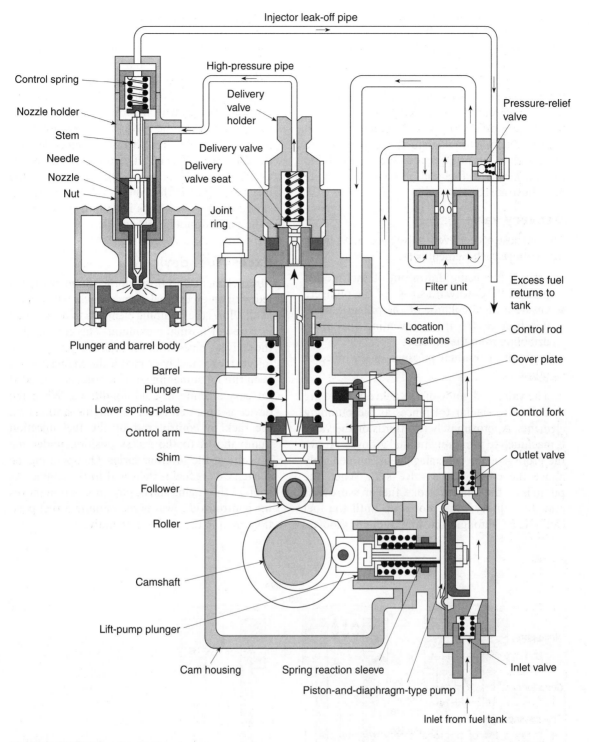

Fig. 3.17 CAV ('Minimec') in-line injection pump

When the plunger is at BDC, fuel enters through the barrel ports filling the chamber above, and also the machined portion forming the helix of the plunger. As the plunger rises, it will reach a point when both ports are effectively cut off (this is known as **spill cut-off** point and is the theoretical start of injection). Further

upward movement of the plunger forces the fuel through the **delivery valve**, injector pipes and injectors into the combustion chamber. With the plunger stroke being constant, any variation in the amount of fuel being delivered is adjusted by rotating the plunger causing the helix to uncover the spill port sooner or later depending on rotation. Immediately the helix uncovers the spill port, the fuel at high pressure above the plunger spills back to the common gallery, the delivery valve resumes its seat and injection stops without any fuel dribbling from the injector. Each injector is rotated simultaneously by a rack or **control rod**. No fuel or engine stop position is obtained by rotating the plunger so that the helix is always in alignment with the ports in the barrel, in this position, pressure cannot build up and hence no fuel will be delivered. Figure 3.18 illustrates this.

Delivery valve

The purpose of a delivery valve (Fig. 3.19) being fitted above each element is to:

● prevent fuel being drawn out of the injector pipe on the downward stroke of the plunger;
● ensure a rapid collapse of the pressure when injection ceases, thus preventing fuel from dribbling from the injector;
● maintain a residual pressure in the injector pipes.

The valve and guide of the delivery valve are machined to similar tolerances as the pumping elements. Approximately two thirds of the valve is machined to form longitudinal grooves. Above the grooves is the **unloading collar**; immediately above the collar is the valve seat. When the pump is on the delivery stroke, fuel pressure rises and the delivery valve moves up until the fuel can escape through the longitudinal grooves.

Immediately the plunger releases the fuel pressure in the barrel, the delivery valve starts to resume its seat under the influence of the spring and the difference in the pressure above and below the valve. As the unloading collar enters the guides dividing the element from the delivery pipe, further downwards movement increases the volume above the valve (by an amount equal to the volume between the unloading collar and the valve seat). The effect of this increase in volume is to suddenly reduce the pressure in the injection pipe so that the nozzle valve 'snaps' closed onto its seat thus instantaneously terminating injection without dribble.

Excess fuel device

Multi-element injection pumps are normally fitted with an excess fuel device which, when operated, allows the pumping elements to deliver fuel in excess of normal maximum. This ensures that the delivery pipes from the injection pump to the injectors are quickly primed if the engine has not been run for some time or if assistance is needed for easy starting in cold conditions. When the device is operated (with the engine stationary), the rack or control rod of the fuel injection pump moves to the excess position under the pressure of the **governor spring**. On operating the starter, excess fuel is delivered to the engine. As soon as the engine starts, governor action moves the control rod towards the minimum fuel position making the device inoperative.

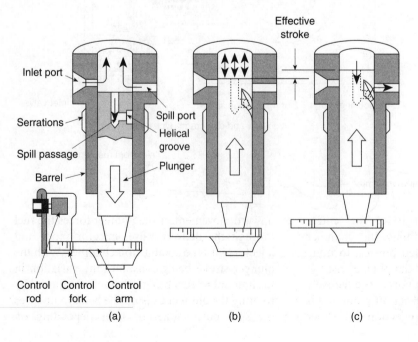

Fig. 3.18 Plunger and barrel. (a) Pumping element filling. (b) Injection. (c) Spill: no fuel out

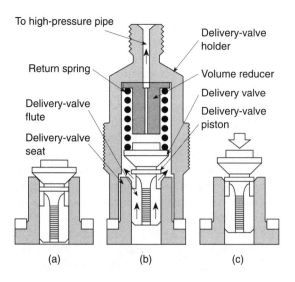

Fig. 3.19 Delivery-valve action

Cam shapes

To prevent the possibility of reverse running, it is normal practice to fit a camshaft with profiles designed so that the plunger is at TDC for approximately two-thirds of a revolution. In the event of a back-fire the engine will not run. Certain CAV pumps are fitted with reversible type camshafts. In order to prevent reverse running, a spring-loaded coupling, similar to the **pawl-type free-wheel** is fitted between the pump and the engine. Figure 3.20 shows a cam profile.

Phasing and calibration

Phasing is a term used when adjustment is made to ensure injection occurs at the correct time, i.e. on four-cylinder engines each element injects at 90° intervals while on a six-cylinder engine each element injects at 60° intervals. This adjustment is carried out by raising or lowering the plunger so the spill cut-off point is reached at the correct time. Simms pumps have spacers in the tappet blocks (Fig. 3.19). CAV pumps have normal tappet adjustment. Phasing should not be confused with spill timing (this is when the injection pump is timed to the engine).

Calibration refers to the amount of fuel that is injected. Correct calibration ensures that the

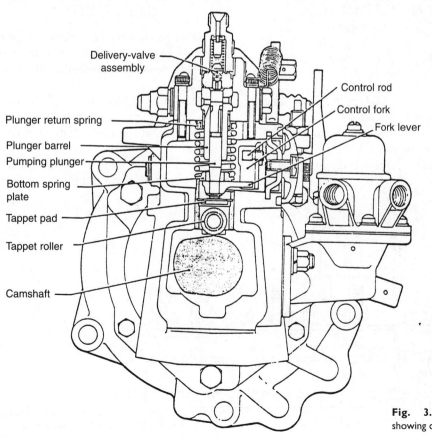

Fig. 3.20 Sectioned view showing cam profile

same amount of fuel is injected by each element at a given control rod setting. It is effected by rotating the plunger independently of the control rod. Both phasing and calibration can only be carried out on proper equipment and using data sheets to obtain speed and fuel delivery settings for any given injection pump. When settings are adjusted correctly the maximum fuel stop screw is sealed and must not be adjusted under any circumstances.

Lubrication

The delivery valves and pumping elements are lubricated by the fuel oil, a small quantity of which leaks past the plunger and barrel into the cambox. The camshaft, bearings, tappets, etc. are lubricated by engine oil contained in the cambox. To prevent a build-up of oil due to the fuel leaking past the elements, the level plug incorporates a leak-off pipe.

Spill timing the multi-element pump to the engine

After mounting the injection pump to the engine and checking that the alignment and drive coupling clearance are correct, it is necessary to adjust the pump to ensure that number one cylinder is on compression. Refer to the workshop manual for the correct static timing (e.g. it may read 28° BTDC). The correct method would be as follows.

1. Set the engine to 28° BTDC with number one cylinder on compression stroke.
2. Remove the delivery valve from number one cylinder pump element.
3. Replace the delivery valve body and fit the spill pipe.
4. Loosen the pump coupling and fully retard the pump.
5. Ensure that the stop control is in the run position.
6. Operate the lift pump; fuel will now flow from the spill pipe.
7. Whilst maintaining pressure on the lift pump, slowly advance the injection pump when a reduction in the flow of fuel from the spill pipe will be noticed as the plunger approaches the spill cut-off point. Continue advancement until approximately one drop every ten to fifteen seconds issues from the spill pipe.
8. Tighten the coupling bolts, remove the spill pipe and refit the delivery valve. The pump is now correctly timed in relation to the engine.

Spill timing is shown in Fig. 3.21.

Bleeding the fuel system

Bleeding the fuel system refers to removing all the air from the pipes, lift pump, filters, injection pump and injectors. This operation must be carried out if the fuel system is allowed to run out of fuel, any part of the system is disconnected or the filter elements are changed. Assuming the system has been disconnected for some reason the correct method is as follows.

1. Disconnect the pressure side of the lift pump, operate the lift pump until fuel, free from air bubbles, flows from the outlet. Reconnect the fuel line.
2. Slacken off the bleed screw of the fuel filter and operate the lift pump until all the air is expelled from the filter Re-tighten the bleed screw.
3. Open the bleed screw (sometimes called the vent screw) on the injection pump and oper-

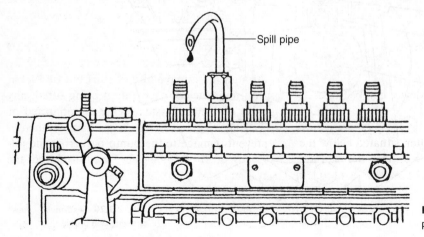

Fig. 3.21 Spill timing no 1 pumping element to no 1 cylinder

ate the lift pump again. When fuel free from air bubbles comes out re-tighten the screw.

4. It may also be necessary to bleed the high-pressure pipes to the injectors by slackening the union at the injector and operating the starter until small amounts of fuel can be seen to be coming from the union. Re-tighten the unions and operate the starter to run the engine. Small amounts of air in the fuel system, though not necessarily enough to prevent the engine starting, may cause loss of power and erratic running. It is therefore necessary to carry out this operation methodically and with care.

Learning tasks

1. Explain in your own words the difference between phasing, calibration and spill timing. When would each term be used in the course of servicing the diesel fuel system?
2. Remove a multi-element injection pump from a diesel engine, turn both the pump and engine over, re-time the pump to the engine, bleed the fuel system and run the engine.

The DPA or rotary fuel injection pump

The DPA fuel injection pump (Fig. 3.22) serves the same purpose as the multi-element type and offers the following advantages:

- it is smaller, more compact and can be fitted in any position not just horizontal;
- it is an oil-tight unit, lubricated throughout by fuel oil;
- only one pumping element is used, regardless of the number of cylinders to be supplied;
- no ball or roller bearings are required and no highly stressed springs are used;
- no phasing is required; calibration once set is equal for all cylinders;
- an automatic advance device can be fitted.

In this pump the fuel at lift pump pressure passes through a nylon filter, situated below the inlet union, to the **transfer pump**. Fuel pressure is increased by the transfer pump, depending on the speed of rotation of the pump and controlled by the **regulating valve**. The regulating valve maintains a relationship between pump speed and transfer pressure, which at low revolutions is between 0.8 and 1.4 kg/cm^2 (11–20 lbs/inch^2) increasing to between 4.2 and 7.0 kg/cm^2 (60–100 lbs/inch^2) at high revolutions. From the transfer pump, fuel flows through a gallery to the **metering valve**. The metering valve, which is controlled by the **governor**, meters the fuel passing to the rotor depending on engine requirements. The fuel is now at metering pressure, this being lower than transfer pressure. As the rotor rotates, the inlet ports come into alignment and fuel enters the rotor displacing the plungers of the pumping elements outwards until the ports move out of alignment. Further rotation brings the outlet ports of the rotor into alignment with one of the outlet ports which are spaced equally around the hydraulic head. At the same time, contact between the plunger rollers and the cam ring lobes forces the pumping elements inwards. Fuel pressure between the plungers increases to injection level and fuel is forced along the control gallery, through the outlet port to the injector pipe and injector. As the next charge port in the rotor aligns with the metering valve port, the cycle begins again. Figure 3.23 illustrates this.

The inside of the cam ring has as many equally spaced lobes as there are cylinders in the engine. Each lobe consists of **two peaks**, the recess between being known as the retraction curve. As the pumping element rollers strike the first peak, injection takes place. On reaching the retraction curve, a sudden drop in pressure occurs and injection stops without fuel dribbling from the injector. Further movement of the rotor brings the rollers into contact with the second peak which maintains residual line pressure until the outlet port moves out of alignment. The cam ring rotates within the pump housing varying the commencement of injection. Movement is controlled by the advance/retard device.

It should be remembered that this type of pump is lubricated by the fuel oil flowing through the pump and if it runs out of fuel at any time, due to a new pump being fitted, any parts of the fuel system being disconnected or the filter elements having been changed, then to prevent damage to the pump occurring the following method should be used to bleed the system of air.

1. Slacken the vent screw on the fuel filter. This may be a banjo union of the 'leak-off' pipe.

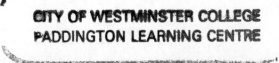

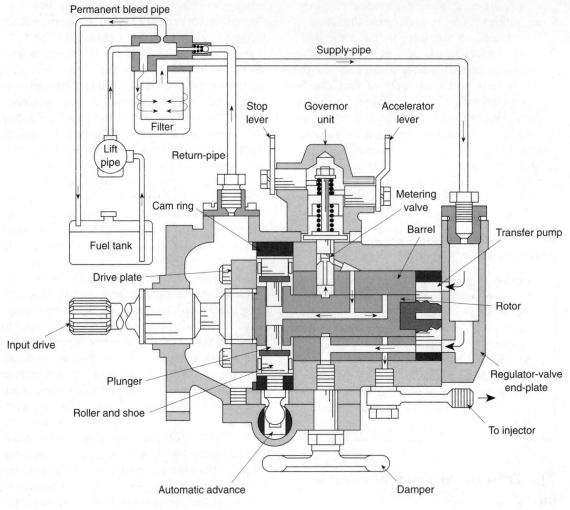

Fig. 3.22 CAV ('DPA') distributor-type injection pump

Operate the lift pump until fuel free from air flows from the filter. Tighten the vent screw.

2. Slacken the main feed pipe union nut at the pump end and operate the lift pump until fuel free from air flows from the union. Tighten the union.

3. Slacken the vent screw of the governor control housing and the vent screw in the hydraulic head. Operate the lift pump until fuel free from air flows from the vent screws. Tighten the hydraulic head vent screw and governor control housing vent screw.

4. Crank the engine by hand one revolution and repeat the operations listed at 3.

5. Slacken all high-pressure injection pipes at the injector end and turn the engine over with the starter until fuel free from air flows from unions. Tighten unions and start engine.

Note: Always ensure that the stop control is in the start position and the throttle is wide open when bleeding the pump.

Figure 3.24 shows one type of injector pump. This is fitted with a mechanical means of governing the maximum and minimum revs of the engine. The automatic advance operates when the engine is stationary, enabling injection to take place earlier than normal when starting the engine. This gives easier starting and reduces the amount of smoke being passed through to the atmosphere.

Injectors

The injector can be considered as an **automatic valve** which performs a number of tasks. It may vary in design but all conform to the following requirements:

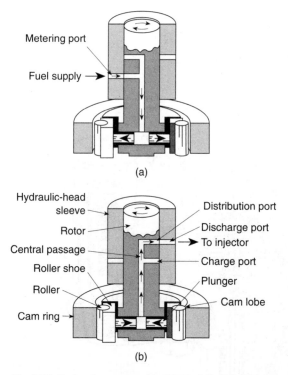

(a)

(b)

Fig. 3.23 Cycle of operation (a) charge phase, (b) injection phase

Labels for figure (a):
Metering port
Fuel supply →

Labels for figure (b):
Hydraulic-head sleeve
Rotor
Central passage
Roller shoe
Roller
Cam ring →
Distribution port
Discharge port
→ To injector
Charge port
Plunger
Cam lobe

- it ensures that injection occurs at the correct pressure;
- it breaks up the fuel into very fine droplets in the form of a spray which is of the correct pattern to give thorough mixing of the fuel with the air;
- it stops injecting immediately the injection pump pressure drops.

The **nozzle** is the main functional part of the injector. It consists of a **needle valve** and **nozzle body** machined to fine tolerances and lapped together to form a mated pair. Extreme care must be exercised when handling this component.

Lubrication is achieved by allowing a controlled amount of fuel to leak past the needle valve. Provision is made for this **back-leakage** to return either to the filter or fuel tank, it also circulates heated fuel to help overcome the problem of the fuel freezing in very cold weather.

Adequate cooling of the injector is most important and is catered for by careful design and positioning in the cylinder head. To prevent over-heating, it is essential that the correct injector is fitted and that any joint washers are replaced each time the injector is removed (do make sure the old joint washer is removed before fitting a new one). No joint washer is required on those engines fitted with copper sleeves which

form part of the injector housing. In addition to the normal copper sealing washer, a corrugated type steel washer is sometimes located between the nozzle and the heat shield. It is essential that the outside edge faces *away* from the nozzle, otherwise serious overheating of the injector will occur. To prevent the washer turning over whilst fitting it should be fed down a long bladed instrument such as a screwdriver or a suitable length of welding rod.

Method of operation

The needle is held on its seat by spring pressure acting through the spindle. Fuel, when delivered at high pressure from the injector pump, acts on the shoulder at the lower end of the needle. When the fuel pressure exceeds the spring tension the needle lifts off its seat and fuel is forced through the hole(s) in a finely atomized spray. The spring returns the needle valve back onto its seat at the end of each injection. The spring tension is adjustable by releasing the lock nut and screwing the spring cap nut in or out as required. This determines at what pressure injection commences. The pressures at which the injector operates are very high, typically between 125 and 175 atmospheres. It should be noted that the spring tension only determines at what pressure injection starts. Pressure may momentarily increase up to a maximum of approximately 420 atmospheres (to start the needle moving), depending on engine speed and load. At these high pressures it is very important that the testing is done with the proper equipment and in the correct way. If the hand was placed in front of the injector whilst it was being tested then it is possible for the fuel to be injected directly into the blood stream with serious consequences and possible death. Use of safety equipment such as gloves and goggles is essential to reduce any possible risks of injury to a minimum.

Types of injector

These are classified by the type of nozzle fitted and fall into four main groups

- single-hole
- multi-hole
- pintle
- pintaux

Single- and multi-hole injectors

The **single-hole** nozzle has one hole drilled centrally in its body which is closed by the needle

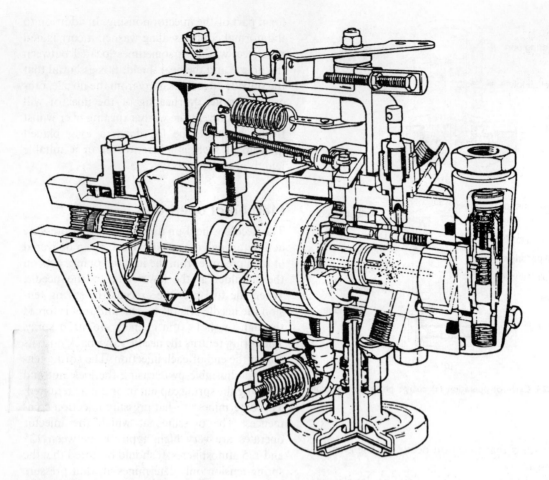

Fig. 3.24 DPA pump with mechanical governor and automatic advance

valve. The hole can be of any diameter from 0.2 mm (0.008 in) upwards. This type is now rarely used in motor vehicle engines. **Multi-hole** injectors (Fig. 3.25) have a varying number of holes drilled in the bulbous end of the nozzle beneath the needle valve seating. The actual number, size and position depends on the requirements of the engine concerned. There are usually three or four. This is the type that is fitted to the **direct injection** engine which, due to the larger combustion chamber, requires the fuel to be injected in a number of sprays at high pressure to ensure even distribution and good penetration of fuel into the rapidly moving air stream. They are often of the long stem type to give good cooling of the injector.

Pintle

This nozzle is designed for use with **indirect injection** combustion chambers. The needle valve stem is extended to form a pintle which protrudes beyond the mouth of the nozzle body. By modifying the size and shape of this pintle the spray angle can be altered from parallel to a 60° angle or more. A modified pintle nozzle, known as the **delay** type, gives a reduced rate of injection at the beginning of delivery. This gives quieter running at idling speed on certain engines.

Pintaux nozzles

A development of the pintle-type nozzle, these have an auxiliary hole to assist starting in cold conditions. At cranking speeds, the pressure rise is slow and the needle valve is not lifted high enough for the pintle to clear the main discharge port. The fuel passing the seat is sprayed from the auxiliary hole towards the hottest part of the combustion chamber (that is within the area of the heater plug). At normal running speeds, the rapid pressure rise lifts the pintle clear of the main discharge port allowing the fuel to form the appropriate spray pattern. Approximately 10% of the fuel continues to pass through the auxiliary hole at normal running speeds to keep it free from carbon.

The efficiency of the injector deteriorates

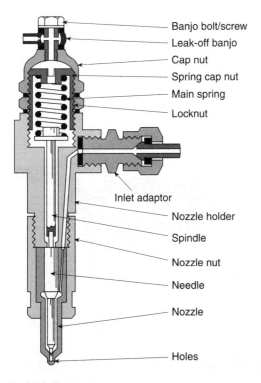

Fig. 3.25 Multi-hole injector

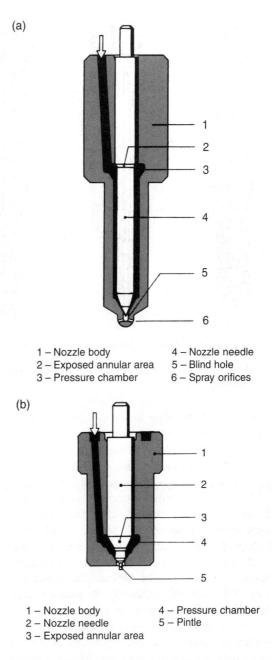

1 – Nozzle body   4 – Nozzle needle
2 – Exposed annular area   5 – Blind hole
3 – Pressure chamber   6 – Spray orifices

1 – Nozzle body   4 – Pressure chamber
2 – Nozzle needle   5 – Pintle
3 – Exposed annular area

Fig. 3.26 (a) Hole-type nozzles, (b) pintle-type nozzles

with prolonged use making it necessary to service the nozzles at periodic intervals. The frequency of maintenance depends on factors such as operating conditions, engine condition, cleanliness of fuel, etc.

Examples of nozzles are shown in Figs 3.26(a) and (b).

Cold starting aids

Some form of cold starting aid is usually fitted to CI engines to assist starting in cold conditions. There are numerous types the two most common being:

- heater plugs
- thermo-start unit

Heater plugs

These are located in the cylinder head, the heating element of the plug being located just inside the combustion chamber. When an electrical current is supplied to the plug, the element heats up thus heating the air trapped in the chamber. Typical heater plugs are shown in Fig. 3.27.

The **'pencil'**-type heater plug is similar in design to the **'coil'**-type except that the heating coil is contained in a tube which when heated

glows red. The plugs are wired in **parallel** and operate at 12 V with a loading of approximately 60 W. This gives a maximum element temperature of 950–1050 °C. When the heater plug has been in service some time the small air gap between the element sheath and the cylinder head becomes filled with carbon. This reduces the efficiency making starting more difficult in very cold weather. There is also a risk of the element burning out through over-heating. This can be avoided by removing the heater plugs and

(a)   (b)

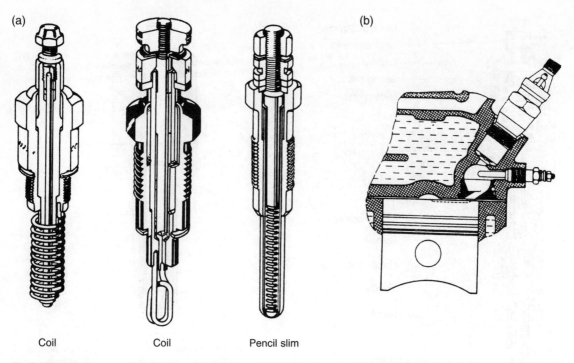

Coil   Coil   Pencil slim

Fig. 3.27 (a) Three types of heater plugs used on indirect injection diesel engines, (b) sectional view showing the position of the plug in the cylinder head

cleaning out the plug hole from time to time. Before refitting the plug remove any particles of carbon which may have lodged in the conical seating in the cylinder head. A faulty plug may be located by removing each feed wire in turn and fitting a test lamp or ammeter in the circuit. If the plug is in working order, the lamp will light or the ammeter will show a reading of approximately five amps when the heater circuit is in operation. A quick test can be carried out when the engine is cold. Operate the heater circuit and after approximately 30 seconds each plug should feel warm to the touch.

In the double-coil type the plugs are connected in **series**, each one operating at 2 V. A resistance unit is wired into the circuit to reduce battery voltage to plug requirements. Apart from keeping the exterior of the plug and electrical connections tight, no other servicing or maintenance is required.

Thermo-start unit

The unit, shown in Fig. 3.28, is screwed into the inlet manifold below the butterfly valve. Fuel is supplied to the unit from a small reservoir fed from the injector leak-off pipe. The thermo-start comprises a valve surrounded by a heater coil, an extension of which forms the igniter. The valve body houses a spindle which holds a ball valve in position against a seat, preventing

fuel entering the device. When an electric current is supplied to the unit, the valve body is heated by the coil and expands. This releases the ball valve from its seat, allowing fuel to enter the manifold where it is vaporized by the heat. When the engine is cranked, air is drawn into the manifold and the vapour is ignited by the coil extension thus heating the air being drawn into the engine. On switching off the current to the unit, the valve body contracts and the spindle returns the valve to its seat cutting off the fuel supply. The reservoir must be positioned 10–25 cm above the thermo-start unit to provide a positive fuel supply. This unit gives very little trouble in service provided the preheat time before operating the starter does not exceed that recommended (approximately 15 seconds).

Electrical connections

The heater plugs are connected so that when the ignition is switched on the warning lamp on the dashboard is illuminated; this warns the driver that the heater plugs are operating (warming up). The starter should not be operated until the warning lamp goes out which happens automatically after approximately 10–20 seconds. The heater plugs will now be at their correct temperature for cold starting. This is shown in Fig. 3.29.

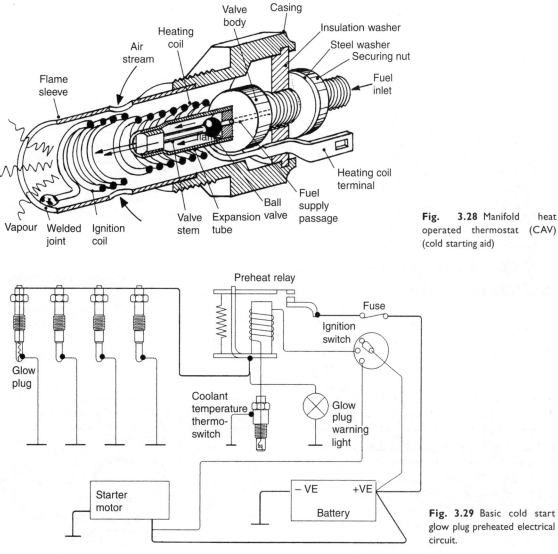

Fig. **3.28** Manifold heat operated thermostat (CAV) (cold starting aid)

Fig. 3.29 Basic cold start glow plug preheated electrical circuit.

Learning tasks

1. Remove a DPA fuel injection pump from a diesel engine. Turn both the pump and engine, time the pump to the engine, bleed the fuel system and run the engine.

2. Draw up a service schedule for a diesel system fitted with a DPA fuel pump. Base the schedule on either mileage or time.

3. State how the timing of a DPA fuel injection pump is adjusted. When would it be necessary to carry out this adjustment?

4. Remove the heater plugs, clean and check their resistance. Record your results and compare them with the manufacturer's recommendations. How would the driver notice if the heater plugs were not operating correctly?

5. Write out a logical test procedure for identifying the fault of a diesel engine producing black smoke when operating under load.

6. Complete the above test and produce a report to show the minimum and maximum engine revs, static timing, amount of advance on acceleration and amount of smoke allowable from the exhaust for a diesel engine. Compare your results with the manufacturer's data and produce a set of recommendations for the customer's report sheet. Name any specialized equipment used together with printouts that were produced in the test.

7. Remove a set of injectors from both direct injection and indirect injection engines.

Using the correct equipment, test for correct opening pressure, back leakage and spray pattern. Refit the injectors and run the engine.

8. Dismantle both types of injectors and identify the main differences. After cleaning all the components reassemble the injectors, set the pressure and check back leakage and spray pattern.

9. On undertaking a smoke meter test on a diesel engine, it was found that the smoke produced was excessive. Draw up a simple logical test procedure for tracing and rectifying the fault.

Practical assignment – SU carburettor

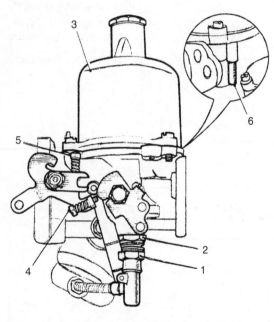

The type HS carburettor

I – Jet adjusting nut	4 – Fast-idle adjusting screw
2 – Jet locking nut	5 – Throttle adjusting screw
3 – Piston/suction chamber	6 – Piston lifting pin

Activity – tuning single carburettors

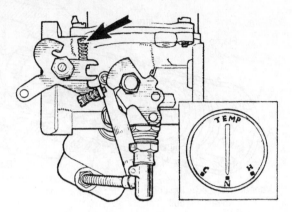

I. (a) Warm engine up to normal temperature.
   (b) Switch off engine.
   (c) Unscrew the throttle ajusting screw until it is just clear of its stop and the throttle is closed.
   (d) Set throttle adjusting screw I$\frac{1}{2}$ turns open.

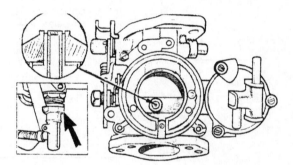

2. (a) Mark for reassembly and remove piston/suction chamber unit.
   (b) Disconnect mixture control wire.
   (c) Screw the jet adjusting nut until the jet is flush with the bridge of the carburettor or fully up if this position cannot be obtained.

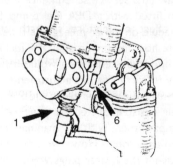

3. (a) Replace the piston/suction chamber unit as marked.
   (b) Check that the piston falls freely onto the bridge when the lifting pin (6) is released.
   (c) Turn down the jet adjusting nut (1) two complete turns.

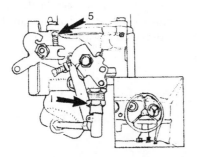

4. (a) Restart the engine and adjust the throttle adjusting screw (5) to give desired idling as indicated by the glow of the ignition warning light.
   (b) Turn the jet adjusting nut (1) up to weaken or down to richen until the fastest idling speed consistent with even running is obtained.
   (c) Readjust the throttle adjusting screw (5) to give correct idling if necessary.

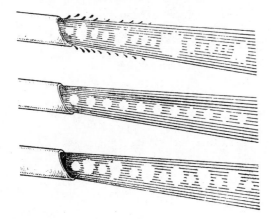

5. The effect of mixture strength on exhaust smoke
   (a) Too weak: Irregular note, splashy misfire, and colourless.
   (b) Correct: Regular and even note.
   (c) Too rich: Regular or rhythmical misfire, blackish.

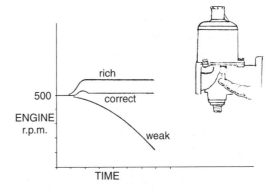

6. (a) Check for correct mixture by gently pushing the lifting pin up about $\frac{1}{32}$ in (0.8 mm) after free movement has been taken up.
   (b) The graph illustrates the effect on engine r.p.m. when the lifting pin raises the piston, indicating the mixture strength:

rich mixture	RPM increase considerably
correct mixture	RPM increase very slightly
weak mixture	RPM immediately decrease

   (c) Readjust the mixture strength if necessary.

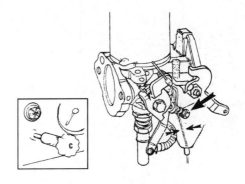

7. (a) Reconnect the mixture control wire with about $\frac{1}{16}$ in (16 mm) free movement before it starts to pull on the jet lever.
   (b) Pull the mixture control knob until the linkage is about to move the carburettor jet and adjust the fast-idle screw to give an engine speed of about 1000 RPM when hot.

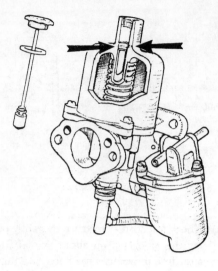

8. Finally top up the piston damper with the recommended engine oil until the level is $\frac{1}{2}$ in (13 mm) *above* the top of the hollow piston rod.

Note: On dust-proofed carburetters, identified by a transverse hole drilled in the neck of the suction chambers and no vent in the damper cap, the oil level should be $\frac{1}{2}$ in (13 mm) below the top of the hollow piston rod.

4

Engine air supply and exhaust systems

Liquid fuels such as petrol and diesel oil contain the energy that powers the engine. **Hydrogen** and **carbon** are the main constituents of these fuels and they need **oxygen** to make them burn and release the energy that they contain. The oxygen that is used for combustion comes from the atmosphere. Atmospheric air contains approximately 77% nitrogen and 23% oxygen by weight. For proper combustion, vehicle fuels require approximately 15 kg of air for every 1 kg of fuel. When the fuel and air are mixed and burned in the engine, chemical changes take place and a mixture of gases is produced. These gases are the exhaust. The principal exhaust gases are **carbon dioxide**, **nitrogen** and **water** (steam).

Safety note

You should be aware that combustion is often not complete and carbon monoxide is produced in the exhaust. Carbon monoxide is deadly if inhaled. For this reason, engines should never be run in confined spaces. Workshops where engines are operated inside must be equipped with adequate exhaust extraction equipment.

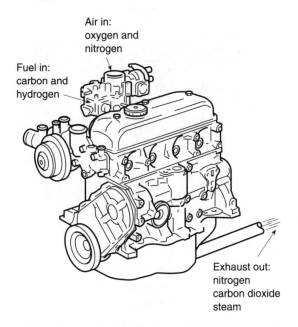

Fig. 4.1 Engine showing fuel/air in and exhaust out

(labels on figure:)
Fuel in: carbon and hydrogen

Air in: oxygen and nitrogen

Exhaust out: nitrogen carbon dioxide steam

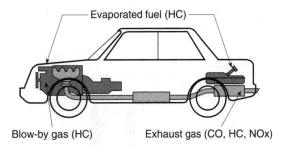

(labels on figure:)
Evaporated fuel (HC)

Blow-by gas (HC)

Exhaust gas (CO, HC, NOx)

Fig. 4.2 Various bad emissions from engine and fuel system

If all conditions were perfect the fuel and air would burn to produce carbon dioxide, superheated steam, and nitrogen (Fig. 4.1). Unfortunately these 'perfect' conditions are rarely achieved and significant amounts of other harmful gases, namely **carbon monoxide CO**, **hydrocarbons HC**, **oxides of nitrogen NOx** and **solids** (particulates like soot and tiny metallic particles) are produced (Fig. 4.2).

Most countries have laws that control the amounts of the harmful gases (emissions) that are permitted and engine air and exhaust systems are designed to comply with these laws.

4.1 Engine air supply systems (carburettor)

Figure 4.3 shows the main features of a petrol (spark ignition) engine **air supply system**. Our main concern, at the moment, is the **air cleaner** and the **intake pipe** (induction tract) leading to the combustion chamber. The **blow-by filter** and the **positive crankcase ventilation** (PCV) system are part of the **emission control system**.

Air filter

The purpose of the air filter (Fig. 4.4) is to remove dust and other particles so that the air reaching the combustion chamber is clean. Pulsations in the air intake generate quite a lot of noise and the air cleaner is designed so that it also acts as an **intake silencer**.

The porous paper element is commonly used as the main filtering medium. Intake air is drawn through the paper and this traps dirt on the surface. In time this trapped dirt can block the filter and the air filter element is replaced at regular service intervals. Failure to keep the air filter clean can lead to problems of restricted air supply which, in turn, affects combustion and exhaust emissions.

Temperature control of the engine air supply

To improve engine 'warm up' and to provide as near constant air temperature as possible, the air cleaner may be fitted with a device that heats up the incoming air as and when required. Figure 4.5 shows the layout of a temperature controlled air intake

It shows that the **manifold vacuum** has lifted the **intake control door** off its seat and air is drawn into the air cleaner over the surface of the

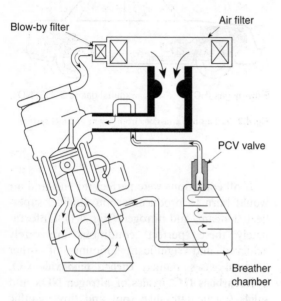

Fig. 4.3 An engine air supply system

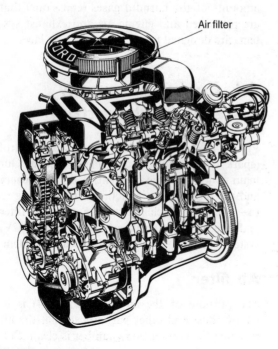

Fig. 4.4 An air cleaner

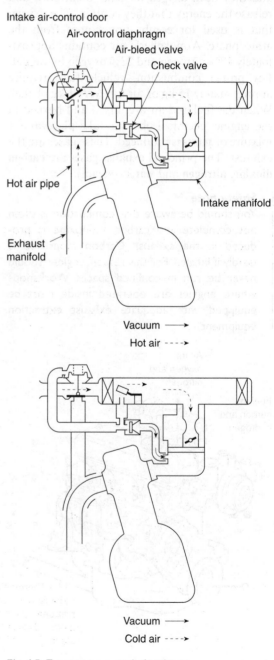

Vacuum ⟶
Hot air ----⟶

Vacuum ⟶
Cold air ----⟶

Fig. 4.5 Temperature control of intake air

exhaust manifold. The **bi-metallic spring** has pushed the **air bleed valve** on to its seat. When the air in the **air cleaner** reaches a temperature of 25–30 °C, the bi-metal spring lifts the air bleed valve from its seat. This removes the vacuum from above the **air control door** diaphragm, thus closing the intake control door. The intake air now enters direct from the atmosphere. During cold weather the temperature-control system will be in constant operation.

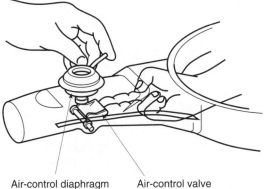

Air-control diaphragm   Air-control valve

Fig. 4.6 Checking the air control valve

Checking the operation of the air control valve

Figure 4.6 shows the type of practical test that can be applied to check the operation of the air control diaphragm and the air door. The flap is raised against the spring and a finger is placed over the vacuum pipe connection. The air door valve is then released and the valve should remain up off its seat.

Fuel injected engine air intake system

Figure 4.7 shows an air intake system for a modern engine fitted with electronic controls. This system has several components that we need to consider briefly.

Air flow meter

The air intake for a fuel injected petrol engine includes an **air flow meter** (Fig. 4.8). The purpose of the air flow meter is to generate an electrical signal that 'tells' the electronic controller how much air is flowing into the combustion

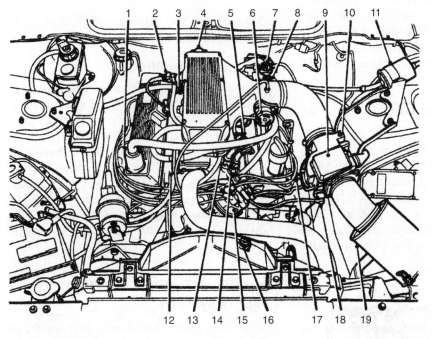

1 – Breather flame trap
2 – Cold start injector
3 – Fuel pressure regulator
4 – Overrun valve
5 – Throttle potentiometer connection
6 – Throttle potentiometer
7 – Engine air breather
8 – Idle speed adjustment screw
9 – Air flow meter
10 – Idle mixture adjustment screw

11 – Fuel filter
12 – Extra air valve
13 – Coolant temperature switch
14 – Thermo-time switch
15 – Distributor
16 – Diagnostic plug
17 – Spark plug – No.1 cylinder
18 – Ignition coil
19 – Air cleaner

Fig. 4.7 Air supply system – petrol injection engine

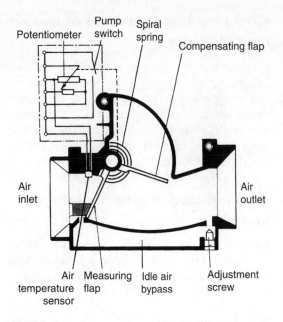

Fig. 4.8 An air flow meter

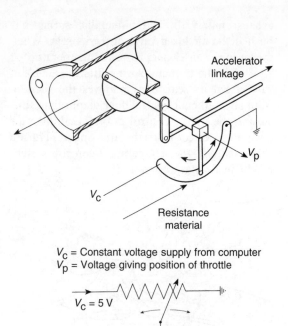

V_c = Constant voltage supply from computer
V_p = Voltage giving position of throttle

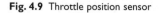

V_p varies with throttle angle

Fig. 4.9 Throttle position sensor

chambers. It is also known as an 'air flow sensor'.

The intake air stream causes a rotating action on the sensor flap, about its pivot. The angular movement of the flap produces a voltage at the sensor that is an accurate representation of the amount of air entering the engine. This voltage signal is conducted to the electronic control unit (**ECU**), where it is used in 'working out' the amount of fuel to be injected.

Throttle position sensor (potentiometer)

This is the sensor (shown as 6 on Fig. 4.7) that 'tells' the ECU the angular position of the throttle butterfly valve. The principle of a throttle position sensor is shown in Fig. 4.9. The voltage from the throttle position sensor is also conducted to the ECU for use in the process of determining the amount of fuel to be injected.

Idle air control

When the driver's foot is removed from the accelerator pedal, the throttle butterfly valve is virtually closed. In order that the engine will continue to run properly (idle) the intake system is provided with a separate system that provides an air supply for idling purposes. Figure 4.10 shows an electronically controlled air valve.

Air valves of the type shown in Fig. 4.10 are controlled by the ECU. The ECU will admit extra air to provide fast-idle speed so that the engine keeps running even when extra load is

imposed with the throttle closed, such as by switching on the headlights.

Air intake manifold

On many engines the intake air is supplied to a central point on the intake manifold as shown in Fig. 4.11. The manifold is provided with ports that connect to the individual cylinders of the engine. The seal, often a gasket, between the intake manifold and the cylinder head must be secure and it is advisable to check the tightness of the securing nuts and bolts periodically. These nuts and bolts must be tightened in the proper sequence, shown for a particular engine in Fig. 4.12.

Service attention to the air supply system

A normal service requirement is to renew the air filter element at regular intervals. Should the **filter element** become 'clogged' it will restrict the flow of air to the engine and cause the engine to 'run rich'. This will obviously affect the engine performance and it will also cause the emission control system to malfunction. To guard against problems in this area, all vehicles should be properly serviced before they are tested for

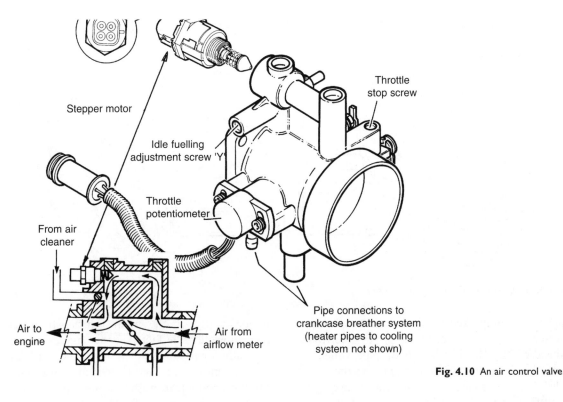

Stepper motor

Idle fuelling
adjustment screw 'Y'

Throttle
stop screw

Throttle
potentiometer

From air
cleaner

Air to
engine

Air from
airflow meter

Pipe connections to
crankcase breather system
(heater pipes to cooling
system not shown)

Fig. 4.10 An air control valve

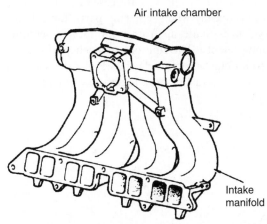

Air intake chamber

Intake
manifold

Fig. 4.11 An air intake manifold

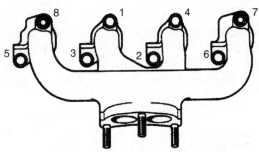

Fig. 4.12 Tightening sequence for exhaust manifold retaining
hardware (nuts)

compliance with the emissions regulations, e.g. a
pre-MOT service and check-over.

Other items that should receive regular attention include: sensor connections, condition of
flexible hoses and tightness of joints and securing brackets. Air flow meters, throttle position
sensors, etc. are normally quite reliable. In the
event of problems with these items, it will normally be necessary to 'read out' fault codes,
either through the 'on-board' diagnostic system
or by the use of diagnostic code readers and
other tools.

4.2 Exhaust system

A fundamental purpose of the **exhaust system** is
to convey exhaust gas away from the engine and
to expel it into the surrounding atmosphere at
some point that is convenient to vehicle occu-
pants. On motor cars this usually means through
the tail pipe at the rear of the vehicle. On trucks
it is often at some other point, often just behind
the driver's compartment. Another function of
the exhaust system is to deaden the exhaust
sound to an acceptable level. This sound level is
regulated by law.

The exhaust system shown in Fig. 4.13 has a
number of sections. Starting at the front of the
vehicle the sections are: the **down pipe**, or **front**

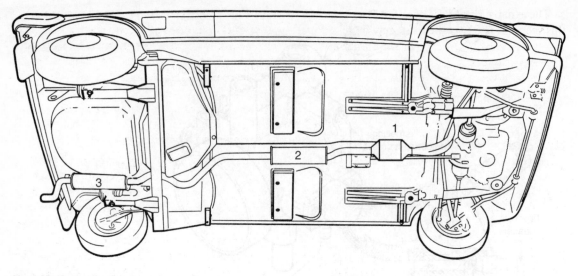

Fig. 4.13 Underside view of an exhaust system

pipe; the unit marked 1, this is the **catalytic convertor**, an interconnecting pipe to the **first silencer** (2); a further length of pipe which is curved to take it round other units on the vehicle; this pipe connects to the **rear silencer** (3); and the gas finally leaves through the **tail pipe**.

The exhaust system is mounted firmly to the exhaust manifold at the front end, but it is flexibly mounted to the underside of the vehicle for the remainder of its length. The flexible mountings are required to allow the system to move independently of the main vehicle structure. This allows for the fact that the engine itself is normally flexibly mounted, and the type of exhaust mountings used prevent noise and vibration being transmitted to the vehicle structure. In order to provide for ease of maintenance and economy when replacing parts, the exhaust system is made up from a number of separate components. The number of such parts varies from vehicle to vehicle, but Fig. 4.14 shows a typical exhaust system, together with its fixings.

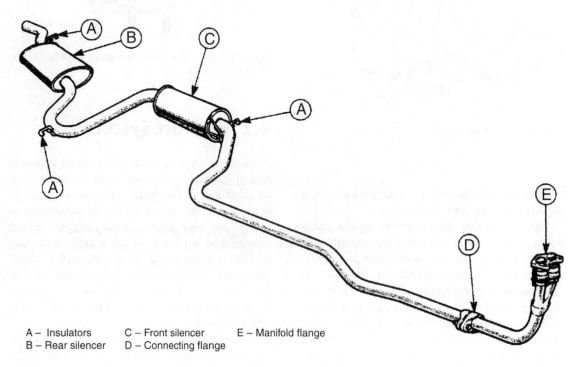

A – Insulators   C – Front silencer   E – Manifold flange
B – Rear silencer   D – Connecting flange

Fig. 4.14 Component parts of an exhaust system

The exhaust catalyst is dealt with at the end of this section. The two silencers may be of different types, **expansion**-type and **absorption**-type. The expansion-type is sometimes called a resonator because of the way that it works. Figure 4.15. shows the basic principles of the two types of silencer commonly used.

Broken or damaged exhaust systems

In addition to the noise factor, which is often the most evident sign of a broken exhaust system, there is also the danger of leaking exhaust gas finding its way into the passenger compartment. Broken exhaust systems should be repaired as a matter of urgency and, when an exhaust has been repaired, it should be thoroughly checked to ensure that there are no leaks. In order to prevent leaks, all pipe joints, flanges and their gaskets and other fixings must be made secure, using sealant where it is recommended.

Catalytic convertor

Function

The purpose of the catalytic convertor is to enable the vehicle to comply with emissions regulations. The principal emissions of concern are oxides of nitrogen (NOx), hydrocarbons (HC), carbon monoxide (CO) plus particulates (pieces of soot and metallic particles). Figure 4.16

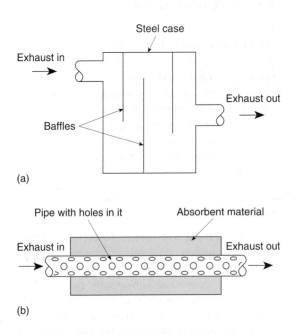

(a)

(b)

Fig. 4.15 Silencers (a) expansion-type, (b) absorption-type

shows a catalytic convertor in the exhaust system. It is mounted near to the engine. This helps to maintain it above its minimum working temperature of approximately 300 °C. Further up the front pipe, near the engine, is an **oxygen sensor**. The oxygen sensor plays an important part is the successful operation of the catalyst.

Method of operation

A catalyst is a material that produces chemical changes in substances that come into contact with it, but is not itself affected by the chemical changes. In the exhaust catalyst the three harmful pollutants, NOx, HC and CO, are changed (by **oxidation** or **reduction**) into nitrogen, carbon dioxide and water. A catalytic convertor that deals with these three pollutants is called a three-way catalyst (TWC). The catalytic convertor will only function correctly when the engine is supplied with a chemically correct (stoichiometric) air/fuel ratio.

For petrol engines this air/fuel ratio is approximately 15:1 by weight. This ratio is given the name **LAMBDA** which has a value of 1. If the air/fuel ratio is 12:1 (a rich mixture) LAMBDA is about 0.9. If the air/fuel ratio is 17:1 LAMBDA is about 1.1. The **exhaust oxygen sensor** (EGO) 'measures' the oxygen content of the exhaust gas and this gives an accurate measure of the air/fuel ratio of the mixture entering the engine, and that is why it is sometimes known as a LAMBDA sensor.

The commonly used catalyzing agents are the rare metals **platinum**, **rhodium** and **palladium**. These metals are spread thinly over a large surface area so that the exhaust gas can be made to come into contact with them. This large surface area is achieved by the use of **pellets** covered with the metals, or a **ceramic honeycomb** covered with catalysts. The two different methods are shown in Fig. 4.17. In order to function correctly, the catalyst must reach approximately 300 °C and it is becoming common practice to fit catalysts with a **pre-heating element** which makes them more effective during cold starts. A note of warning too. Leaded fuel will 'poison' a catalyst and prevent it from working. Leaded fuel must never be used in an engine fitted with a catalytic convertor.

Oxygen sensor

The exhaust oxygen sensor is a critical part of the engine emissions control system. The oxygen sensor transmits an electrical signal to the

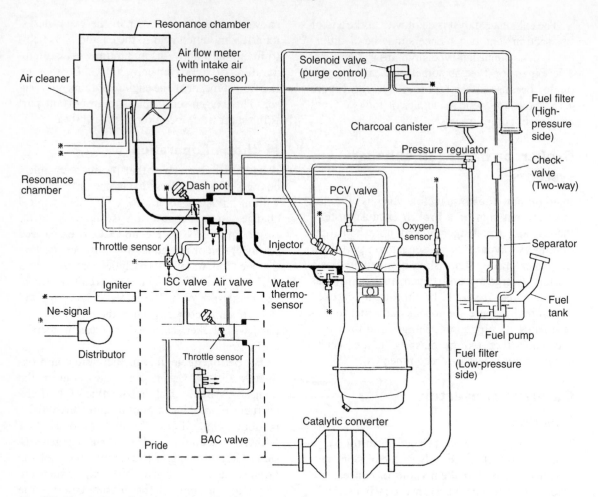

Fig. 4.16 The catalyst and the oxygen sensor in the exhaust system

ECU and the ECU then makes the necessary adjustments to the amount of fuel injected so that LAMBDA is maintained within the design limits. The active element (a ceramic) of the oxygen sensor is sensitive to temperature and it must be hot for it to work properly. For this reason, oxygen sensors are often fitted with an electric heating element. This type of sensor is then known as a **heated exhaust gas oxygen sensor** (HEGO).

At the time of writing, there are two different types of exhaust oxygen sensors in common use. One type uses **zirconium oxide**; this produces a small voltage at its terminals. The other type uses **titanium oxide**; this relies on changes of conductivity for its operation and is supplied with voltage. It is important to recognize this because the test procedures for the sensors involve different procedures. Exhaust oxygen sensors are shown in Fig. 4.18.

Exhaust emissions test

Exhaust emissions are tested by means of an **exhaust gas analyser**. Failure to 'pass' the test does not necessarily mean that the catalyst has failed. As mentioned in the section on air supply, a choked air filter can upset the whole system. Exhaust catalysts are expensive items and it is important to make sure that all other parts of the engine emissions system are in good working order before condemning the catalyst.

Maintenance

Exhaust systems are subject to corrosive attack from the outside and the inside environment. The outside corrosion arises from water, salt and other corrosive substances that may be present on the running surface. The internal corrosion arises, in part, from the water that is produced by combustion of the fuel. Each litre

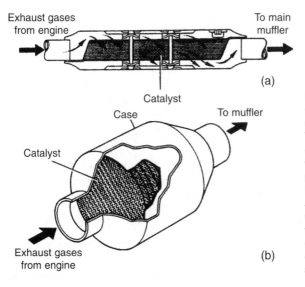

Catalyst

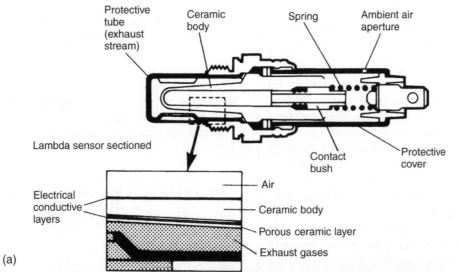

Case

To muffler

Catalyst

Exhaust gases
from engine

(b)

Fig. 4.17 Exhaust catalysts. (a) Pellet-type catalytic converter. Catalysts supported on aluminas, carbons and other speciality materials are produced for use in many chemical processes. The cost-effectiveness and catalytic selectivity of finely dispersed platinum group metal catalysts greatly exceeds those of alternative processes: indeed, many modern processes depend exclusively on these catalysts. (b) Honeycomb- or monolithic-type catalytic converter. Autocatalysts utilize honeycomb supports to assure the maximum reactive surface within the smallest possible volume, with consequent high catalytic activity and minimum engine power loss. Whilst the majority of catalysts use a ceramic support, some specialized applications demand the added durability of steel supports.

(a)

(b)

Fig. 4.18 Exhaust oxygen sensor (a) construction of zirconia-type oxygen sensor, (b) the oxygen sensor in the exhaust pipe

of petrol burned produces almost a litre of water. When the exhaust system is hot, the water leaves the tail pipe as super-heated steam but, when the exhaust system is cold and the atmospheric conditions are right, some of the steam condenses to water inside the exhaust. To extend the life of exhaust silencers they are sometimes coated, internally and externally, with a thin layer of aluminium. The exterior of the whole exhaust system should be checked for signs of holes and all pipe clamps and joints should checked for leaks. The flexible mountings should also be checked from time to time and any that are found to be in danger of breaking should be replaced, in order to prevent more expensive work at some later date.

Learning tasks

1. Draw up a list of the equipment that you have used to perform an emissions test for an MOT. Describe the procedure and give details of the acceptable MOT emissions levels for any modern vehicle.

2. Draw up a test procedure for checking the oxygen sensor. Itemize any precautions that should be observed, e.g. corrosion of terminals and care when removing and refitting.

3. Remove a complete exhaust system from a vehicle, including the exhaust manifold. Replace the manifold gasket and any other components that are corroded and mountings that are separating. Replace/refit the exhaust system. How should the system be checked for leaks after refitting?

4. Remove the inlet manifold complete with carburettor. Check the operation of the one-way valve to the brake servo cylinder. Refit the manifold using a new gasket. State the purpose of using water to heat/cool the inlet manifold.

5. Remove the air cleaner and check the operation of the air control valve. Replace the filter element and air cleaner.

6. What are the symptoms of a leaking inlet manifold gasket? What tests would you use to identify this fault?

7. Describe the procedure that you have used to fit a replacement air filter to an engine. Explain how a blocked air filter may affect the exhaust emissions from an engine.

8. Examine an engine inlet manifold and note down the type of material that it is made from. State why it is necessary to follow a sequence when tightening an inlet manifold when refitting it to an engine.

9. Examine an exhaust oxygen sensor installation. Note down the number of wires that lead into the sensor and state whether or not it is a type that carries its own heating element.

10. After fitting a new exhaust system it is necessary to check that there are no leaks in the system. Describe the practical methods that you use, in your workplace, to carry out this check.

11. Exhaust fumes are very dangerous. Write down the precautions that must be observed when working on running engines, in a confined space. Make a list of the exhaust extraction equipment fitted in your workshop

---

Practical assignment – air supply and exhaust systems

Objective

The purpose of this assignment is to allow you to develop your knowledge and skill in this important area of motor vehicle work and to help you to build up your file of evidence for NVQ.

Activity

The nature of this assignment is such that you will need to work under supervision, unless you have previously been trained and are proficient. The assignment is intended to be undertaken during a routine service and MOT test on a petrol engined vehicle that is equipped with electronically controlled petrol injection.

The assignment is in two parts.

Part 1

1. Locate the idle control valve. Describe the purpose of this valve and describe any adjustments that can be made to it.
2. Specify the effects on engine performance and exhaust emissions that may arise if this valve is not working correctly.

Part 2

1. Perform the emissions test part of the MOT test.
2. Record the results and compare them with the legal limits.
3. Write short notes on the test procedure and describe any work that should be carried out before starting the emissions test.
4. Give details of remedial work that can be performed if a vehicle should fail the emissions test.
5. Make a list of the tools and equipment used.

5
Transmission systems

5.1 The clutch

Most clutches used in the modern motor car are called **friction clutches**. This means that they rely on the friction created between two surfaces to transmit the drive from the engine to the gearbox. The clutch fulfils a number of different tasks. The three main ones are:

- it connects/disconnects the drive between the engine and the gearbox;
- it enables the drive to be taken up gradually and smoothly;
- it provides the vehicle with a temporary neutral.

The three main component parts of a clutch are:

- the **driven plate**, sometimes referred to as the **clutch**, **centre** or **friction plate**;
- the **pressure plate** which comes complete with the clutch cover, springs or diaphragm to provide the force to press the surfaces together;
- the **release bearing** which provides the bearing surface which, when the driver operates the clutch pedal, disconnects the drive between the engine and the gearbox.

Through the centre of the pressure plate the **input shaft** of the gearbox (sometimes called the **spigot**, **first motion** or **clutch shaft**) is splined to the middle of the driven plate. On the conventional vehicle layout it is located on a bearing (called the **spigot bearing**) in the flywheel.

Multi-spring clutch

The driving members of the multi-spring clutch consist of a **flywheel** and pressure plate (both made of cast iron) with the driven plate trapped between. The pressure plate rotates with the flywheel, by means of projections on it locating with slots in the clutch cover which is bolted to the flywheel. A series of springs located between the cover and the pressure plate force the plate towards the flywheel trapping the clutch plate between the two driving surfaces. The **primary** (or input) shaft of the gearbox is splined to the hub of the clutch disc and transmits the drive (called **torque** which means turning force) to the gearbox. The drive is disconnected by withdrawing the pressure plate and this is achieved by the operation of the release levers. Figure 5.1 shows a multi-spring clutch.

Diaphragm-spring clutch

The diaphragm-spring clutch (shown in Fig. 5.2) is similar in many ways to the coil spring type. The **spring pressure** is provided by the **diaphragm** which also acts as the lever to move the pressure plate. On depressing the clutch pedal the release lever is forced towards the flywheel thus pulling the pressure plate away from the flywheel. This type has a number of advantages over the coil spring type.

- It is much simpler and lighter in construction with fewer parts.
- It has a lighter hold-down pressure and is therefore easier to operate thus reducing driver fatigue.
- The clutch assembly is smaller and more compact.
- It provides almost constant pressure throughout the life of the driven plate.
- Unlike the coil spring the diaphragm spring is not affected by centrifugal force at high engine speeds. It is also easier to balance. One type of diaphragm spring, the strap drive, gives almost frictionless movement of the pressure plate inside the clutch cover.

Friction plate construction

The important features incorporated in the design of a driven plate can best be seen by considering the disadvantages of using a plane steel plate with a lining riveted to each side. A number of serious problems would very soon be encountered.

- Buckling of the plate can occur due to the heat that is generated when the drive is taken up.

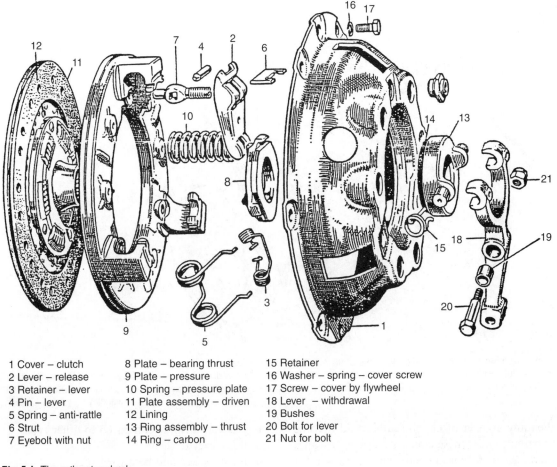

1 Cover – clutch
2 Lever – release
3 Retainer – lever
4 Pin – lever
5 Spring – anti-rattle
6 Strut
7 Eyebolt with nut

8 Plate – bearing thrust
9 Plate – pressure
10 Spring – pressure plate
11 Plate assembly – driven
12 Lining
13 Ring assembly – thrust
14 Ring – carbon

15 Retainer
16 Washer – spring – cover screw
17 Screw – cover by flywheel
18 Lever – withdrawal
19 Bushes
20 Bolt for lever
21 Nut for bolt

Fig. 5.1 The coil spring clutch

- The drive may not be disconnected completely (called **clutch drag**), caused by the plate rubbing against the flywheel when the clutch should be disconnected.
- Very small movement of the clutch pedal. The clutch is of the 'in or out' type, with very little control over these two points. This may cause a sudden take up of the drive (called **clutch judder**).

To overcome these problems the plate is normally **slotted** or **'set'** in such a way as to produce a flexing action. Whilst disengaging, the driven plate will tend to jump away from the flywheel and pressure plate to give a clean break. Whilst in this position the linings will be held apart and air will flow between them to take away the heat. During engagement, spring pressure is spread over a greater range of pedal movement as the linings are squeezed together. This gives easier control and smoother engagement. In most cases the hub is mounted independently in the centre of the clutch plate, allowing it to twist independently from the plate. To transmit the drive to the plate either springs or rubber, bonded to the hub and plate, are used. This flexible drive absorbs the torsional (twisting) shocks due to the engine vibrations on clutch take-up, which could otherwise cause transmission noise or rattle. These features can be seen in the clutch drive (H) in Fig. 5.2.

Friction plate materials

Coefficient of friction

This is the relationship between two surfaces rubbing together. On a clutch both static and sliding friction are necessary. Sliding friction occurs when the drive is being taken up and static friction when the clutch is fully engaged.

Wear properties

This relates to the ability of a material to withstand wear. The surfaces of the flywheel and pressure plate should not become scored or damaged due to friction as the surfaces slide over each other. If they do become damaged

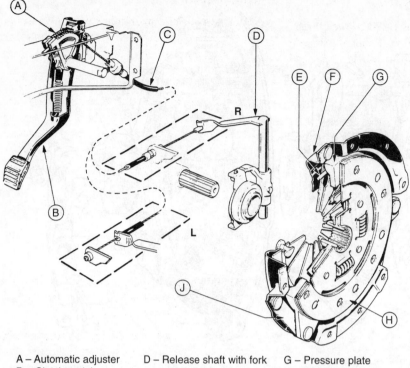

A – Automatic adjuster
B – Clutch pedal
C – Clutch cable

D – Release shaft with fork
       and thrust bearing
E – Fulcrum ring
F – Clutch cover

G – Pressure plate
H – Clutch disc
J – Spring steel straps

Fig. 5.2 Diaphragm spring clutch components (L = LHD, R = RHD)

then any number of clutch faults could become apparent; under these circumstances they would be replaced. A typical coefficient of friction for a motor car would be approximately 0.3.

Linings

These should have a high and stable coefficient of friction against the flywheel and pressure plate surfaces over a wide a range of temperatures and speeds. They should also have good wear resistance and not score or cause thermal damage to any of the surfaces with which they are in contact (e.g. flywheel or pressure plate). The material used for the linings is normally an **asbestos resin** mix which gives the best compromise to meet the above demands. A thermo-setting resin reinforced by **asbestos fibres** and small amounts of **copper**, **brass** or **aluminium** is added to improve the wear properties. Two types of linings are in use, woven linings and moulded linings.

Woven linings

These are formed from a roll of loosely woven asbestos containing brass or zinc wires which is soaked in resin and other ingredients. The resin is then polymerized (which hardens the resin mixture). This has the following advantages:

- it is very flexible compared to other types;
- it is easier to drill;
- it can be cut and bent to shape.

They also have a high coefficient of friction when used in conjunction with cast iron surfaces. They are not suitable for heavy duty use where the temperature is much above 200 °C, (this gives a loss of friction and a high wear rate).

Moulded linings

These are more popular now. In this type the various components are mixed together and cured in dies at high temperatures and pressures to form a very hard material. These can withstand high temperatures and pressures when in use. Different types of linings can be made having widely different coefficients of friction and wear properties because of the much wider range of **polymers** that can be used in their manufacture. They require more careful handling during drilling and riveting as the material is more brittle than the woven type. They must also be formed to the required radius as they cannot be cut or bent. Heavy duty clutches often use **ceramic materials** as these can withstand higher operating temperatures and pressures. Since the end of November 1999, asbestos has been banned by law in the manufacture of new clutch linings.

Operating mechanisms

The clutch release bearing is fitted to the clutch release fork. When the clutch pedal is pressed down by the driver, pressure is exerted against the diaphragm spring fingers by the release bearing forcing them towards the flywheel, this action disengages the drive from the engine.

The pedal linkage may be either **mechanical** or **hydraulic**. It must be flexibly mounted as the engine (which is mounted on rubbers) may move independently of the body/chassis.

Hydraulic linkage

In this arrangement, shown in Fig. 5.3, oil is displaced by the movement of the piston in the **master cylinder** to the **slave cylinder** to operate the release fork. The reservoir on the master cylinder tops up the system as wear in the clutch takes place.

Mechanical linkage

This operates on the principle of levers and rods or cable. The movement ratio and force ratio can be arranged to give a large force acting on the clutch with a small force acting on the pedal. Figures 5.2 and 5.4 shows this system.

Adjustment

Adjustment of the hydraulic operating mechanism is automatic. As wear of the linings takes place the piston in the slave cylinder takes up that amount of wear.

The mechanical system is usually a flexible cable and may have an automatic self-adjusting mechanism as in Fig. 5.2 or else it may need to be checked and adjusted at regular service intervals.

Clutch faults

These are the most common faults found on the clutch.

Clutch slip

This occurs when the clutch fails to transmit the power delivered by the engine. It may be caused by one of the following faults:

- insufficient 'free' movement on the clutch pedal or at the withdrawal (release) lever;
- oil or grease on the friction linings;
- friction linings worn out;
- scored faces on the flywheel or pressure plate.

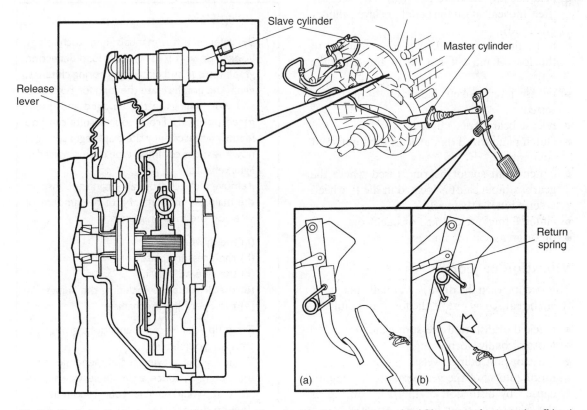

Fig. 5.3 The hydraulic clutch release mechanism. (a) Position of spring with pedal depressed and (b) position of spring in the off (rest) position

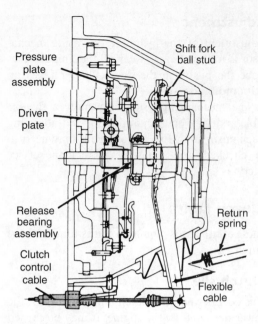

Fig. 5.4 Cable-operated clutch arrangement

Clutch drag

This produces some difficulty in engaging and changing gear. It may be cause by one of the following faults:

- insufficiently effective pedal travel (excessive 'free' movement on the pedal or slave cylinder push rod);
- hydraulic system defective (due usually to the loss of most if not all of the hydraulic oil);
- release lever broken, incorrectly adjusted or seized;
- release bearing defective;
- clutch plate seized on the gearbox input shaft splines;
- clutch shaft spigot bearing (used where the gearbox input shaft is located in the flywheel) is seized in the flywheel;
- clutch linings are cracked or buckled;
- oil or grease on the linings.

Vibration or judder

This occurs when the drive is gradually taken up. It can be caused by one of the following faults:

- cracked or distorted pressure plate;
- loose or badly worn linings;
- loose or protruding rivets;
- misalignment of the gearbox with the engine, caused by distortion of the bell housing or the dowels not being located correctly;
- engine or gearbox mountings defective;

- excessive backlash (play) in the universal joints (UJs) of the drive/prop shafts, (bolts may be loose on the UJ flange);
- flywheel bolts loose on the crankshaft flange;
- defective release mechanism.

Other types of clutches

Multi-plate clutches

Used in certain specialized applications, e.g. agricultural tractors, where a continuous drive is required at the power take-off (PTO); heavy-duty vehicles such as those used by the armed forces; and earth moving and large plant vehicles. The most common application that the motor mechanic is likely to see is that of the motor bike where a small multi-plate clutch can transmit a large amount of power due to the large surface area of all the clutch plates added together.

Fluid clutches

These are commonly used in **fluid flywheels** which are found in some semi-automatic gearboxes and in **torque converters** used in automatic gearboxes.

Learning tasks

1. By reference to manuals and technology books, draw up a typical load/deflection graph for coil and diaphragm spring clutches. From the graphs state the load for both new and worn linings in the engaged and disengaged positions. From your results can you identify a reason why the diaphragm spring is now the most common type of clutch used in light vehicles?

2. Remove a clutch from an engine and inspect the main components. Note the amount of wear on the following units:

   (a) the flywheel
   (b) the pressure plate
   (c) the release bearing
   (d) the driven plate, including the linings
   (e) the operating mechanism.

   Draw up your recommendations giving reasons for your findings.

3. What are the service recommendations for the clutch? Produce a simple service schedule that would enable your recommendations to be recorded.

4. Describe the *symptom* (how would the driver notice) and the *cause* (what caused the problem to occur) of the following:

   (a) clutch slip
   (b) clutch drag
   (c) clutch judder

5.2 The gearbox

The purpose of the gearbox is:

- to multiply the torque being transmitted by the engine;
- to provide a means of reversing the vehicle;
- to provide a permanent position for neutral.

The gearbox can be described as a collection of levers (the gears) that are arranged so as to multiply the turning effort (the torque) of the engine to suit the needs of the vehicle.

Transmission layouts

The position of the engine in relation to the rest of the transmission is shown in Fig. 5.5. The advantages of each layout are taken into consideration by the manufacturer when designing the vehicle.

Types of gears used in the gearbox

Several types of gear teeth shape are used in the modern gearbox depending on the application. All are called **spur** teeth.

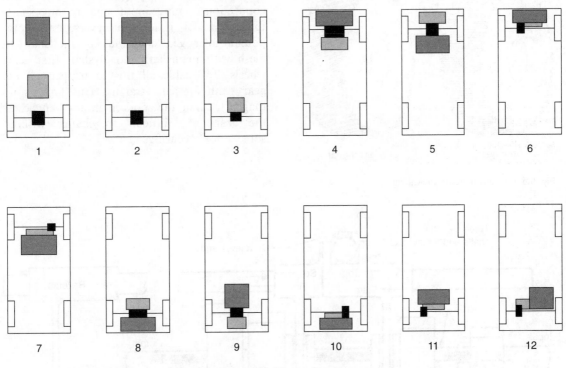

1. A centrally mounted gearbox, used on the Morgan Plus Four
2. The most common layout for RWD vehicles with the gearbox mounted directly on the engine
3. For better weight distribution, the gearbox is mounted with the differential; this arrangement is used on the Alfretta and Ferrari Daytona
4. This layout has been used by Citroen with the engine at the extreme front thus allowing ample passenger space
5. This rather unusual layout has been used by Renault
6. This is the layout of Issigonis in the Mini. This also gives lots of passenger space
7. This variation of the FWD is used by Peugeot
8. This rear engine layout is used on the famous VW air-cooled engine cars
9. This mid-engined layout is used on all Formula One cars and also the Tomaso Pantera
10. No cars now use this rear transverse mounted engine
11. This is the arrangement used by the Ferrari Dino and Boxer
12. Another unusual layout this time employed on the Lamborghini Urraco

Fig. 5.5 Transmission arrangements showing the position of the engine, gearbox and final drive

Straight cut teeth

Shown in Fig. 5.6 these have a rolling/sliding action as they mesh together. They are rather noisy when running together and generate high forces and temperatures between the gear teeth which tends to force them apart when high loads are transmitted. They are almost always used for reverse gear. They can also be found in the gearboxes of some racing cars.

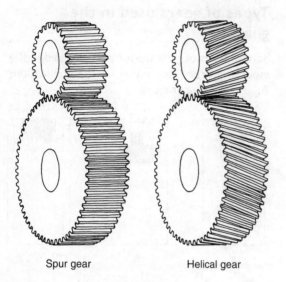

Spur gear   Helical gear

Fig. 5.6 Gear teeth profile straight cut

Helical cut teeth

These have the teeth cut at an angle across the gear producing a sideways force which is normally taken by thrust washers on the shaft. The helical shape is used on the forward gears as they are quieter running, have more than one tooth in mesh at any one time and can therefore carry a greater load. **Double helical** gears are sometimes used to overcome the side force and can transmit even greater loads but they are more expensive to produce.

Sliding mesh gearbox

In this type of gearbox, shown in Fig. 5.7, the **mainshaft gearwheels** slide on splines in the direction of the arrows to mesh with the appropriate layshaft gear for first, second and third gears. Top gear is a **dog clutch** connection joining input and output shafts to give a 1:1 ratio. For reverse the 'compound' idler gear slides along the shaft to mesh with mainshaft and layshaft first gearwheels. To enable all this to happen all the gear teeth are cut straight. This type is no longer used in the modern motor vehicle, as the gears are difficult to change without some noise occuring.

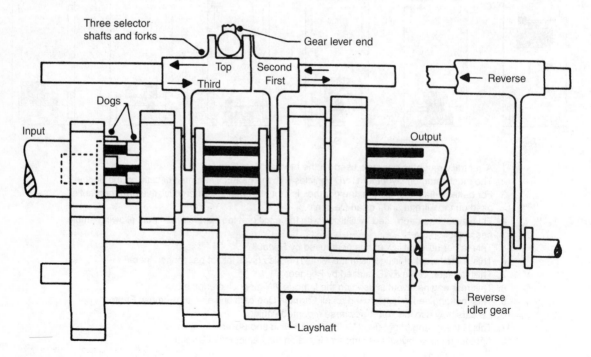

Fig. 5.7 Three speed sliding mesh gearbox

Constant mesh gearbox

In a constant mesh gearbox (Fig. 5.8) the mainshaft gearwheels rotate on bushes and are in constant mesh with the **layshaft gears**. The appropriate gearwheel may then be locked to the output shaft and made to revolve with it by a dog clutch splined to the shaft and slid along it by the same sort of selector fork and collar as was used in the sliding mesh gearbox. This has the following advantages:

- it allows the use of helical gears;
- it is quieter in operation than spur-type teeth;
- it is stronger than the spur type as there is more than one tooth in engagement at any one time;
- it makes gear changing easier as the gearwheels have to be rotating at the same speed before engagement can take place (this is achieved through the use of a **synchromesh** device).

Synchromesh gearboxes

If the dog clutches could be replaced by some kind of friction clutch, perfect synchronization of the output shaft and the selected gearwheel could be achieved rapidly and smoothly. A friction clutch strong enough to transmit full torque would be far too big and heavy, but a small clutch that had to do no more than overcome the inertia of a freely rotating gearwheel and layshaft assembly could be quite small. The two synchromesh devices used in the gearbox are the **constant load** (Fig. 5.9) and the **baulk ring** (Fig. 5.10).

Constant load synchromesh

The **female cone** of the clutch is formed in the hub, which has internal and external splines. A series of spring loaded balls are carried in radial holes in the hub, and these push outwards into a groove machined in the sleeve. Movement of the selector fork carries the sleeve and hub on splines along the mainshaft towards the gear selected and allows the cones to contact. At this point, the friction between the cones adjusts the speed of the gearwheel to suit the hub and mainshaft. Extra pressure on the lever will allow the sleeve to over-ride the spring loaded balls and positively engage with the dogs on the gear. If the gear change is rushed there will not be enough time for the gearwheels to synchronize their speeds and the change will be noisy. The time taken for the speeds to equalize is governed by the frictional force at the cone faces, which in turn is governed by:

- the total spring strength;
- the depth of the groove in the sleeve;
- the angle of the cones;

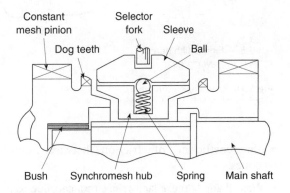

Fig. 5.9 Constant load synchromesh gearbox

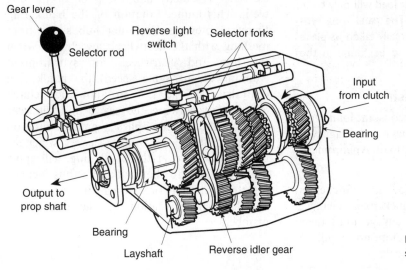

Fig. 5.8 The constant mesh four speed gearbox

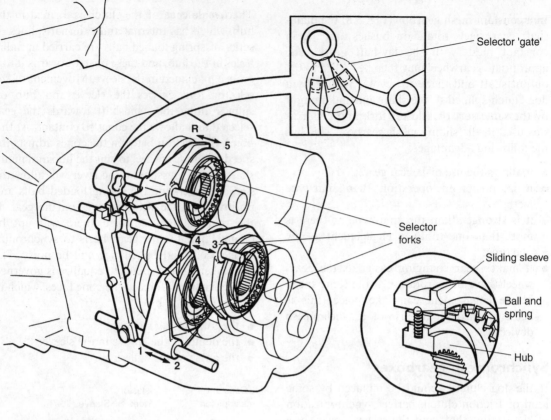

1–5 – First to fifth gears
R – Reverse gear

Fig. 5.10 Baulk ring synchromesh

● the coefficient of friction between the cones.

Note: If any of these factors are reduced, due to mechanical defects, synchronization will take longer and noise will probably be heard. Because of this the constant load will only be in older types of gearboxes. The baulk ring synchromesh has almost universally taken its place and is the most common to be found in the modern gearbox.

Baulk ring synchromesh

This is a development of the constant load type. The main advantages of the baulk ring synchromesh over the constant load synchromesh are:

● the synchronization of the dog clutches is quicker, thus allowing a quicker gear change;
● the dog clutches cannot engage until their speeds are equal and therefore noise will be eliminated.

When the gear selector moves the outer sleeve the baulk ring cone contacts the gearwheel cone. Rotation of the baulk ring is limited to the clearance between the shifting plate and the slot in the baulk ring; this clearance is exactly half the pitch of the dog teeth. This limited rotation of the baulk ring therefore prevents the outer hub sleeve from meshing with the gearwheel dog clutch. When the hub and gearwheels are synchronized (running at the same speed) the baulk ring centralizes in the slot to allow dog clutch engagement between the sleeve and the gear dogs. If the driver applies a greater force on the gear lever the outer sleeve, which is unable to slide over the baulk ring, will apply a greater force to the baulk ring thus increasing the frictional force which, in turn, speeds up the synchronization of the dog clutch members.

Path of the drive through the gearbox

Figure 5.11 shows the path taken by the drive through the four forward gears and reverse of a trans-axle (front engine FWD) gearbox.

Gear selection mechanism

This allows the driver to select and engage a gear. It is achieved by the use of a gear lever which engages in the **selector gate**, and a number of **selector rods** with forks. The rods slide in the gearbox housing and the forks attached to the rods locate in grooves in the outer part of the sliding gear hub (the **sleeve**). A means of locking the gear in position and also preventing the selection of more than one gear at once is provided in the selector arrangement.

Interlocking mechanism

One type of locking mechanism is shown in Fig. 5.12. The shift locking plate rotates with the guide shaft to prevent the movement of the other gear shift rods, ensuring that only one gear is engaged at any one time.

Another arrangement uses plungers between the selector rods (Fig. 5.13). The caliper plate interlock operates in a similar way to the shift locking plate, preventing movement of the selector rods when a gear is engaged.

Direct acting gear lever

In the direct acting arrangement, the gear lever is mounted directly in the top of the gearbox. As the lever is operated by the driver, it pivots on a ball and socket near the base of the lever and acts directly on the selector gate.

Fig. 5.12 Locking mechanism, A guide spring, B shift locking plate

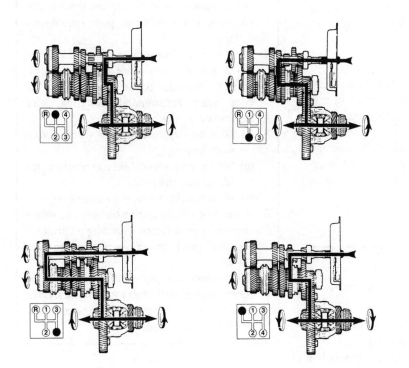

Fig. 5.11 Path of the drive through a five speed gearbox

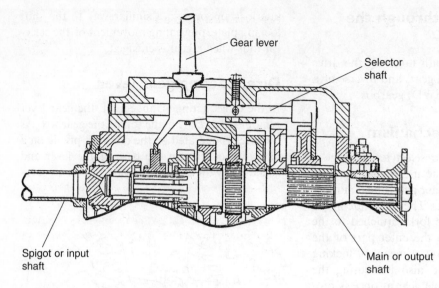

Gear lever

Selector shaft

Spigot or input shaft

Main or output shaft

Fig. 5.13 Direct acting gear lever

Remote acting gear lever

In the remote control type, the gear lever operates through a number of rods and levers before it moves the selector in the gearbox. This is shown in Fig. 5.8. The gear lever may be mounted on the steering column (**column gear change**) or positioned between the driver's seat and passenger's seat, for convenience. This type is the most commonly used as most vehicles are of the transverse engine, trans-axle layout. Its main advantage is that it allows the gearbox to be positioned in what is the most advantageous position for weight distribution and drive line layout, as well as being the most comfortable position for the driver.

Trans-axle

This is an American term used where the transmission and axle are mounted together in one unit, as can be seen in most front engine FWD vehicles. The trans-axle may also be used where the vehicle is a front engine with RWD and the gearbox is located with the rear axle to give better weight distribution together with more room in the passenger compartment.

Learning tasks

1. Draw up a service schedule for the gearbox. In it identify the following:

   (a) type of oil used and the quantity required
   (b) position of drain and level plugs
   (c) security and soundness of gearbox mountings

   (d) oil leaks and remedial work required
   (e) noise coming from gearbox when in operation
   (f) ease of gear engagement and play in gear linkage.

2. Draw up a simple checklist/worksheet for the inspection of a dismantled gearbox. Include the inspection of gear teeth, shafts, bearings, selector mechanism, operation of interlocking mechanism, oil seals and impurities in the gear oil. Ensure that you have space to write your recommendations.

3. Remove and dismantle either a FWD or RWD gearbox and complete your worksheet as you inspect the components. Produce your recommendations for your supervisor or the customer.

4. (a) Give two symptoms of a worn output shaft bearing.
   (b) Name one simple test procedure for identifying the fault.
   (c) How should the fault be put right?

5. Name one simple test to identify the difference between a clutch with drag (difficulty in engaging gear) and a worn synchromesh device.

6. On checking the gear oil it was found to be contaminated with silvery looking bits. What would you suspect the fault to be and how should it be rectified?

5.3 Epicyclic gear train

Purpose

This is used to produce different gear ratios within the **overdrive** and **automatic** transmissions. The output from the engine or gearbox is now the input into the **planetary set** of gears. The four main components in the simple epicyclic gear train are:

- the **sun** gear
- the **annulus**
- the **planet** gears
- the **planet gear carrier**

These are shown in Fig. 5.14.

All the gears are helical in design and are always in **constant mesh**. To select different gear ratios the sun, annulus or planet carrier is held. This will give a number of forward as well as reverse gears.

Method of operation

A simple epicyclic gear train can perform the following functions in a motor vehicle gearbox.

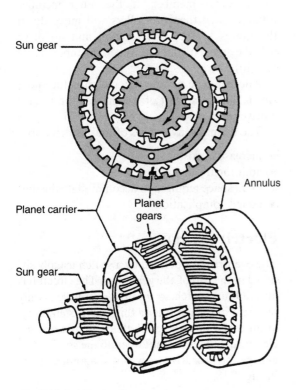

Fig. 5.14 Simple epicyclic gear train

Neutral condition

If any one member is rotated and the remaining two members are allowed to run free, no drive will be transmitted through the gear train and the whole unit will merely idle in neutral.

Direct drive

If any two of the three members are locked together, the third member will be carried round by the teeth of the two locked members at the same speed and in the same direction. The gear train has in effect become solid, and therefore acts in the same manner as a direct mechanical coupling with no increase in torque.

Forwards reduction

If the annulus gear is held stationary and the sun gear is rotated, the planet pinions will be compelled to 'walk' in the annulus. The planet carrier will therefore rotate in the same direction as the sun gear, but at a much reduced speed and with a corresponding increase in torque. Conversely, if the sun gear is held stationary and the annulus is rotated, the planet pinions will be compelled to walk round the sun gear. The planet carrier will therefore rotate in the same direction as the annulus gear, but at a less reduced speed and with not so great an increase in torque.

Reverse reduction

If the planet carrier is held stationary and the sun gear is rotated, the 'idling' planet pinions will rotate the annulus gear in the opposite direction. The speed of the annulus gear will be reduced and its torque increased.

It is not possible to have two forward with one reverse in a single epicyclic gear train as one member must always be connected to the output and one to the input. This gives one forward gear and one reverse gear. But when two simple epicyclic gear trains are connected together in series it is possible to gain more gear ratios and this is the arrangement used in the automatic gearbox.

5.4 Overdrives

An overdrive (means to drive faster) exists when the input shaft or gear rotates more slowly than the output shaft or gear. A typical overdrive arrangement is shown in Fig. 5.15.

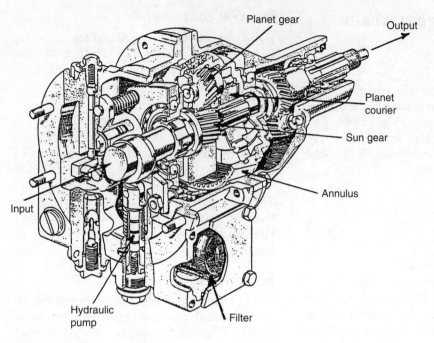

Planet gear

Output

Planet courier

Sun gear

Annulus

Input

Hydraulic pump

Filter

Fig. 5.15 The Laycock-de-Normanville overdrive unit as fitted to the main output shaft of the gearbox

Purpose

It allows the engine speed to be reduced for a given road speed. This has the effect of reducing fuel consumption, wear and engine noise.

The main units in an overdrive are a simple epicyclic gear train, a hydraulically operated friction clutch and a uni-directional (one way) clutch.

Method by operation

When **direct drive** is selected (overdrive not operating) the springs move the cone clutch along the splined sun gear into contact with the annulus thus locking the epicyclic gear train. The drive is transmitted through the one-way clutch and the cone friction clutch transmits the drive on over-run and in reverse.

When overdrive is engaged (Fig. 5.16), oil under pressure from a pump driven by the input shaft acts on pistons which force the **cone clutch** against spring pressure into contact with the casing. This prevents the sun from rotating. The planet carrier, which is the drive input, causes the planet wheels to rotate around the locked sun gear. This action will drive the annulus faster than the input shaft (planet carrier) to give overdrive. During this condition the one-way clutch is free-wheeling. The overdrive may be engaged without the use of the main clutch, thus making the operation quick and easy.

The uni-directional clutch will transmit a drive when rotated in one direction and will 'freewheel' when turned in the opposite direction. The one-way clutch shown in Fig. 5.17(a) has rollers that move up the ramps and the wedging action provides a drive from the inner to the outer member. If the outer member rotates faster, then the rollers will move down the ramps to the wider section and no drive will be passed to the inner member (Fig. 5.17(b)).

Another type of one-way clutch is the **sprag clutch**. The same sort of wedging action to give a drive takes place.

The main disadvantages of an overdrive are:

- increase in cost
- additional weight carried
- extra space required to accommodate the unit
- added complication

Electrical circuit

The overdrive is operated by a switch usually situated in the top of the gear lever. The circuit has an inhibitor switch so that the overdrive is only in operation when top or third gear is engaged; at all other times, even if the switch is on, the electrical system will not operate the solenoid to engage the overdrive. A wiring diagram is given in Fig. 5.18.

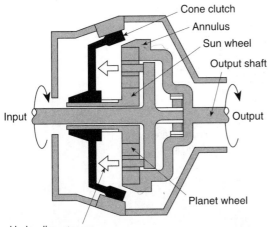

Fig. 5.16 Overdrive engaged

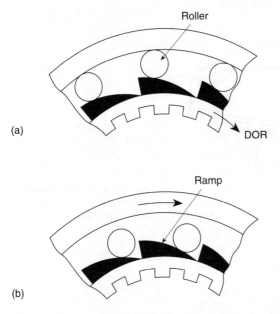

Fig. 5.17 The one-way clutch (a) drive – inner rotates faster than outer, (b) free-wheel – outer rotates faster than inner

---

Learning tasks

1. What type of oil should be used to lubricate the overdrive unit and why?
2. Draw up a simple service schedule for the overdrive unit. Include checks that should be made on the electrical circuit.
3. How should the overdrive be checked for correct operation? Name any test equipment that you would use.
4. How would the driver notice if the one-way clutch was slipping? What test would you undertake to identify the fault from a slipping engine clutch?

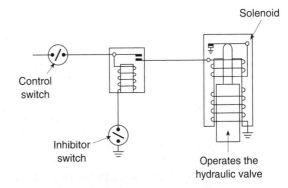

Fig. 5.18 Wiring diagram for an overdrive unit

5.5 Propeller shafts and drive shafts

Prop shafts

On a vehicle of conventional layout (front engine RWD), the purpose of the **prop shaft** is to allow a drive to be transmitted through a varying angle from the gearbox to the final drive at the rear axle. The usual type of layout used is the **Hotchkiss open shaft drive** arrangement as in Fig. 5.19.

Universal joints (UJs) are used to allow for the variation in the drive angle as the road wheels rise and fall. As the rear axle swings up and down the distance between the axle and the gearbox changes. It is therefore necessary to allow for this change in length by the use of a **sliding joint** in the prop shaft assembly.

Figure 5.20 shows how the prop shaft varies in length and that either the sliding joint can be positioned on the shaft (Fig. 5.19) or the shaft may slide in and out of the gearbox on the main output shaft. The shaft will also vary in length as the drive is taken up and the suspension twists clockwise, or as the brakes are applied and the suspension twists anti-clockwise as can be seen in Fig. 5.20.

The prop shaft is made **tubular** to:

- reduce weight;
- reduce out-of-balance which would cause **whirling** as the shaft rotates;
- make it similar in strength to a solid shaft and easier to balance.

Because of the problems of weight and 'whirling' the shaft is often divided into two and a centre bearing is fitted. This arrangement is called a **two-piece prop shaft** (Fig. 5.21). The centre

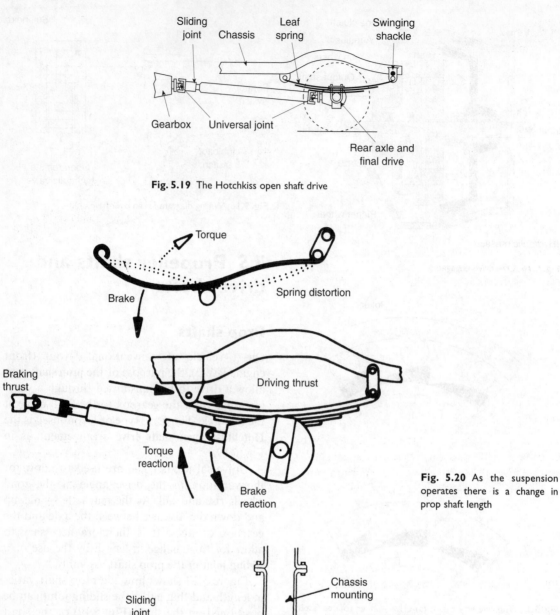

Fig. 5.19 The Hotchkiss open shaft drive

Fig. 5.20 As the suspension operates there is a change in prop shaft length

Fig. 5.21 Two-piece prop shaft with centre bearing

bearing is chassis mounted and provides support for the shaft thus effectively reducing its length. The advantages of this are:

- vibration is reduced
- smaller diameter shafts can be used
- it is more suitable for high prop shaft speeds
- the rear axle can be mounted further back from the engine

Drive shafts

In the front engine FWD, drive shafts are used instead of a prop shaft. These are normally fitted with constant-velocity (CV) joints to enable the drive to pass through a greater angle without the problems associated with universal joints. Figure 5.22 illustrates this.

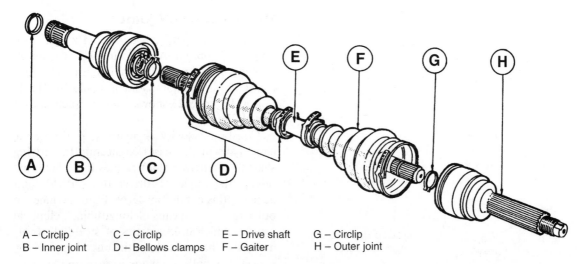

A – Circlip   C – Circlip   E – Drive shaft   G – Circlip
B – Inner joint   D – Bellows clamps   F – Gaiter   H – Outer joint

Fig. 5.22 Drive shaft assembly and CV joints as used on front engine FWD

5.6 Constant-velocity universal joints

Variation in speed

When a single Hooke-type joint is used to transmit a drive through an angle, you will find that the output shaft does not rotate at a constant speed. During the first 90° of its motion, the shaft will travel faster, and on the second 90° slower. Correction of this speed variation is normally done by a second coupling, which must be set so that when the front coupling increases the speed the rear coupling decreases the speed (Fig. 5.23). When the two Hooke-type couplings are aligned correctly, the yoke at each end of the propeller shaft is fitted in the same plane. When fitted to a vehicle, the two or more joints cannot always be operated such that the two angles remain equal. To allow for angle variation and shaft wind-up, especially on larger vehicles such as LGVs, the joints are sometimes set slightly out of phase.

Apart from the Hooke joint a number of other types are used. The doughnut and the Layrub coupling are similar in that they are made from steel and rubber bonded together. So long as the angle of drive is not too large these will give satisfactory service with the added advantage of not requiring any lubrication.

Constant-velocity (CV) joints

A single Hooke-type joint driving through a comparatively large angle would give severe vibration due to the inertia effect produced by the speed variation. This variation increases as the drive angle enlarges, e.g. the percentage variation in speed is about nine times greater at 30 mph than at 10 mph. Any drive shaft subjected to speed changes during one revolution will cause vibration, but provided the drive angle is small and the shaft is light in weight, then drive-line elasticity will normally overcome the problem. Large drive angles, as used in FWD vehicles, need special compact joints which maintain a constant speed when driving through an angle – these joints are called CV joints.

Tracta CV joints

The need for CV joints was discovered in 1926 when the first FWD vehicle was made in France by Fenallie and Gregoire – the Tracta (traction-avant) car. When the second car was made, the drive-line incorporated CV joints, and the type used on that car is now known as a Tracta joint. This type is now made by Girling and details are shown in Fig. 5.24.

Input
Speed constant

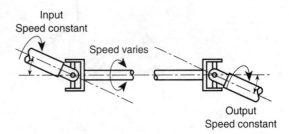

Speed varies

Output
Speed constant

Fig. 5.23 Driving through an angle. Both angles are equal giving no variation between input and output

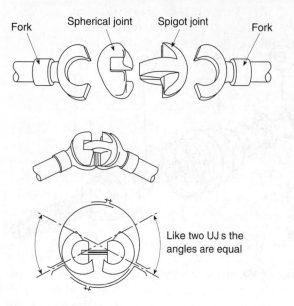

Fig. 5.24 The Tracta joint

Reference to the figure shows that the operating principle is similar to two Hooke-type joints: the angles are always kept constant and the yokes are set in the same place.

The joint is capable of transmitting a drive through a maximum angle of about 40° and its strong construction makes it suitable for agricultural and military vehicles, but the friction of the sliding surfaces makes it rather inefficient. The joint is also too large to be accommodated in a small FWD vehicle with wheel diameters of less than approximately 15 inches (38 cm).

Rzeppa-type CV joint

This joint was patented by A H Rzeppa (pronounced Zeppa) in America in 1935. The development of this type is in common use today; it is called a Birfield joint and is made by Hardy Spicer. Figure 5.25 shows the construction of a Birfield joint.

Constant velocity is achieved if the device (**steel balls** in this case) connecting the driving shaft to the driven shaft rotates in a plane that bisects the angle of drive: the Birfield joint achieves this condition. Drive from the inner to outer race is by means of longitudinal, elliptical grooves which hold a series of steel balls (normally six) that are held in the bisecting plane by a cage. The balls are made to take up their correct positions by offsetting the centres of the radii for inner and outer grooves.

A Birfield joint has a maximum angle of about 45°, but this angle is far too large for continuous operation because of the heat generated by the balls. Lubrication is by grease – the appropriate quantity is packed in the joint 'for life' and a synthetic rubber boot seals the unit.

Plunge joints

These universal joints allow a shaft to alter its length due to the up and down movement of the suspension. A Birfield joint has been developed to give a plunge action (in and out) as required. It will be seen that the grooves holding the balls in place are straight instead of curved; this allows the shaft length to vary. Positioning of the balls in the bisecting plane is performed by

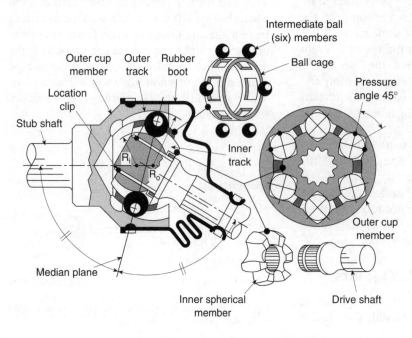

Fig. 5.25 Birfield Rzeppa-type constant-velocity joint

the cage. Since about 20° is about the maximum drive angle, this type of joint is positioned at the engine end of the drive shaft used for FWD vehicles.

Weiss CV joint

This type was patented in America in 1923 by Weiss and later developed by Bendix. it is now known as the Bendix–Weiss and produced in this country by Dunlop. The two forks have grooves cut in their sides to form tracks for the steel balls; there are four tracks so four balls are used to transmit rotary motion. A fifth ball is placed in the centre of and locates the forks, resisting any inward force placed on the drive shaft. The driving balls work in compression, so two balls take the forward drive and the other two operate when reverse drive is engaged. The complete joint is contained in a housing filled with grease. The maximum angle of drive is approximately 35°. Constant velocity is achieved in a manner similar to the Rzeppa joint – the balls always take up a position in a plane that bisects the angle of drive.

Learning tasks

1. How would the driver notice if there was severe wear in the UJ of the prop shaft?
2. Draw up a schedule for removing and refitting the CV joint on a front engine FWD vehicle. Make a special note of any safety precautions that should be observed.
3. What checks would be made on the drive-line of a front engine RWD or FWD vehicle when undertaking an MOT?
4. What should you look out for when reassembling a divided-type prop shaft. What would be the result if these were ignored?
5. If the vehicle on being driven round a corner made a regular clicking noise, what component in the drive-line would you suspect as being worn and why? How would you put the fault right?

5.7 Axles and axle casings

Axles

Axles may be divided into two types, the **live axle** and the **dead axle**. The difference is that a dead axle only supports the vehicle and its load, whereas a live axle not only supports the vehicle and its load but also contains the drive.

Axle casings

Three main types of casings are in use.

- **Banjo**   normally built up from steel pressings and welded together. The crown wheel assembly is mounted in a malleable housing which is bolted to the axle. This is the most common type fitted to light vehicles and is shown in Fig. 5.26.
- **Split casing**   these are formed in two halves and bolted together to contain the final drive and differential (see Fig. 5.27). They are used more in heavy vehicle applications as they are more rigid in construction and can withstand heavy loads.
- **Carrier**   this is more rigid than the banjo casing. The final drive assembly is mounted directly into the axle and the axle tubes are pressed into the central housing and welded into place. A cover is fitted to the rear of the housing to allow for access and repair. It is used in off-road 4 × 4 and LGVs and is shown in Fig. 5.28.

5.8 Final drive

The purpose of the final drive is two-fold: first to transmit the drive through an angle of 90°, and second to provide a permanent gear reduction and therefore a torque increase, usually about 4:1 in most light vehicles. Several types of bevel gearing have been used in the drive between the pinion and the crown wheel. These are the straight bevel, the spiral bevel, the hypoid and the worm and wheel.

Straight bevel

The straight bevel (Fig. 5.29(a)) is not designed for continuous heavy-duty high-speed use as in the normal crown wheel and pinion. This is because only one tooth is in mesh at any one time. The gearing is noisy and suffers from a high rate of wear, but the design is the basis from which the final drives are formed.

Spiral bevel

Shown in Fig. 5.29(b) this has more than one tooth in mesh at a time. It is quieter, smoother, can operate at much higher loadings and is used

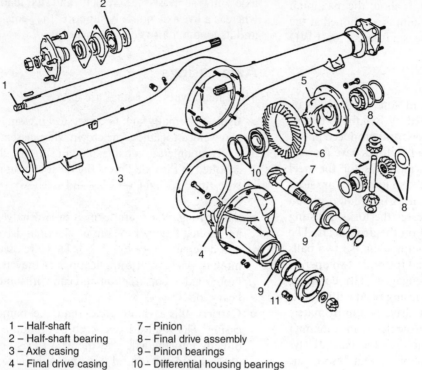

1 – Half-shaft
2 – Half-shaft bearing
3 – Axle casing
4 – Final drive casing
5 – Differential housing
6 – Crown wheel

7 – Pinion
8 – Final drive assembly
9 – Pinion bearings
10 – Differential housing bearings
11 – Pinion oil seal

Fig. 5.26 Banjo axle casing

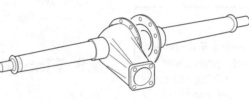

Fig. 5.27 Split axle casing

where the shaft operates centre-line as the crown wheel.

Hypoid bevel

This is similar to the spiral bevel in action but the shaft operates at a lower level than the crown wheel. This has the advantage of the prop shaft being lower and not intruding into the floor space of the passenger compartment. It is stronger and is the quietest in operation. Extreme pressure (EP) oil must be used as a lubricant because of the frictional forces and high loadings generated between the gear teeth (a disadvantage of this arrangement). The materials used in their manufacture are a nickel–chrome alloy which is carburized after machining and case-hardened to give long life. Figure 5.29(c) shows a hypoid bevel.

Worm and wheel

The worm in this arrangement, shown in Fig. 5.29(d), is driven by the prop shaft and looks like a very coarse screw thread. The wheel has a toothed outer edge with which the screw thread of the worm meshes. There are a number of advantages with the worm and wheel the two main ones being: first it provides a very large gear reduction and therefore a large torque increase in one gear set; and second it gives a high prop shaft, this is especially useful for off-road vehicles and LGVs.

Servicing and adjustments

Excessive wear will result on the gear teeth if the backlash between the crown wheel and pinion is set incorrectly.

To adjust the backlash, shims must be added or removed to obtain the correct readings. The

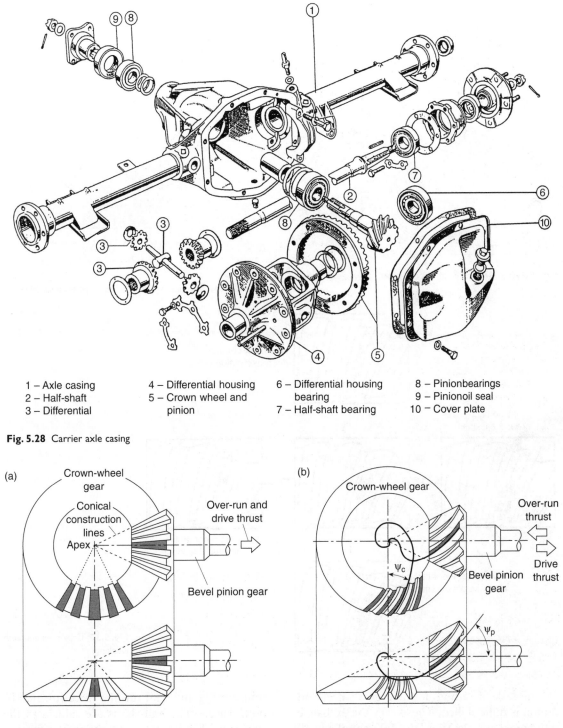

1 – Axle casing
2 – Half-shaft
3 – Differential

4 – Differential housing
5 – Crown wheel and
   pinion

6 – Differential housing
   bearing
7 – Half-shaft bearing

8 – Pinionbearings
9 – Pinionoil seal
10 – Cover plate

Fig. 5.28 Carrier axle casing

(a)

Crown-wheel gear

Conical construction lines

Apex

Over-run and drive thrust

Bevel pinion gear

Fig. 5.29(a) Geometry of straight-tooth bevel-gear crown wheel and pinion

(b)

Crown-wheel gear

Over-run thrust

Drive thrust

ψ_c

Bevel pinion gear

ψ_p

Fig. 5.29(b) Geometry of spiral-tooth bevel-gear crown wheel and pinion

crown wheel teeth shown in Fig. 5.30 give the different markings, the centre diagram showing where the marks should occur. To obtain the markings on the gear teeth a little engineers' blue is placed on the pinion teeth and the pinion

rotated until the crown wheel has completed one revolution.

A dial test indicator (DTI) should be used to check the crown wheel and pinion backlash (this is the amount of play between the gear teeth). It should be positioned as shown in Fig. 5.31.

(c)

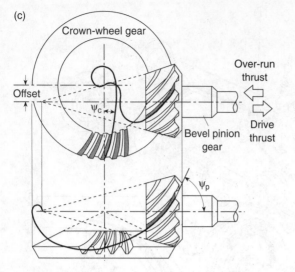

Fig. 5.29(c) Geometry of hypoid-tooth bevel-gear crown wheel and pinion

(d)

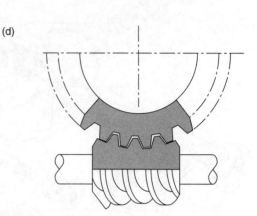

Fig. 5.29(d) Hourglass worm and worm-wheel final drive

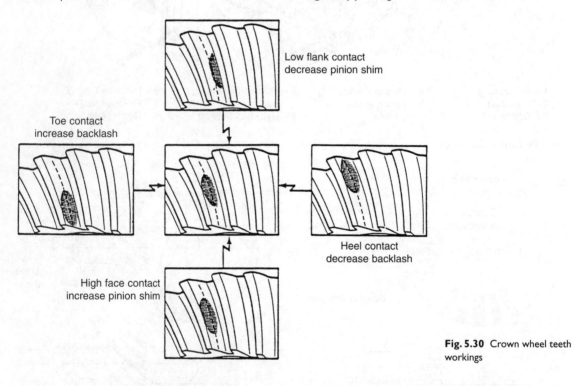

Low flank contact
decrease pinion shim

Toe contact
increase backlash

Heel contact
decrease backlash

High face contact
increase pinion shim

Fig. 5.30 Crown wheel teeth workings

The task of setting up the crown wheel and pinion is quite skilled. This is why the exchange unit comes complete with the differential and all the settings are done by the manufacturer. All the mechanic has to do when changing the final drive is fit the unit to the axle.

5.9 Differential

The purpose of the differential is to allow the wheels to rotate at different speeds, whilst still transmitting an equal turning force (torque) to both wheels. The half-shafts are splined to the sun gear, the planets transmitting the motion from one sun gear to the other when the vehicle is turning a corner. This is shown in Fig. 5.32.

When both drive shafts are travelling at the same speed the planet gears orbit (rotate) with the sun gears but do not rotate on their shafts. The whole unit acts as a solid drive. See Fig. 5.33.

If one shaft is stopped the planet gears turn on their shafts, orbiting round the stationary sun

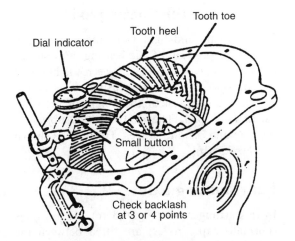

Fig. 5.31 Position of the DTI

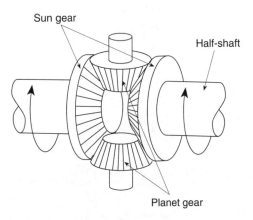

Fig. 5.33 Operation of the differential when the vehicle is travelling in a straight line

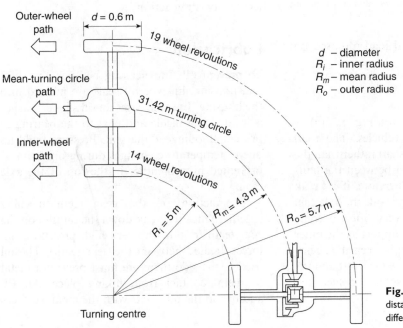

d – diameter
R_i – inner radius
R_m – mean radius
R_o – outer radius

Fig. 5.32 Illustration to show the distance travelled by each wheel. The differential allows for this difference

gear and driving the other sun gear but twice as fast.

In the final drive the differential is in a housing (sometimes called a cage) to which the crown wheel is bolted. When the car is travelling in a straight line the planet gears orbit, but do not rotate on their shafts, and the unit drives both half-shafts at the same speed as the crown wheel and with the same turning force.

When turning a corner, the sun gear on the inner half-shaft turns more slowly than the crown wheel, the outer half-shaft, driven by the other sun gear, turns correspondingly faster. The crown wheel turns at the average of the half-shaft speeds.

A sectioned view of the complete final drive and differential arrangement is shown in Fig. 5.34. Both the crown wheel and pinion are held in the housing by taper roller bearings. The cross pin acts as the drive for and the shaft on which the planet gears rotate.

5.10 Rear hub bearing and axle shaft arrangements

Three layouts are now commonly used and are subjected to various forces acting on the axle shaft, e.g. **twisting** when accelerating or braking, **bending** due to cornering and some of the load

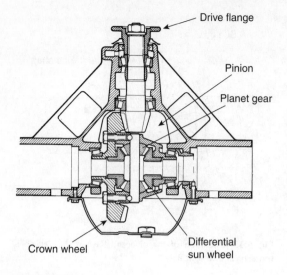

Fig. 5.34 Final drive gear. Crown wheel and pinion and differential

and **shear** due to the vertical load imposed on the axle shaft.

Semi-floating axle

This hub arrangement, shown in Fig. 5.35(a), is used on many small light vehicles. The road wheel is attached to the **half-shaft** rather than the hub and the bearing is fitted between the half-shaft and the **axle casing**. Therefore, if a break should occur in the half-shaft inside the axle casing the wheel will tilt and very often become detached due to the lack of support at the inner end of the half-shaft. As can be seen the shearing point is positioned between the shaft and the axle casing, and the shaft is subject to shearing, bending and twisting forces.

Three-quarter floating axle

Used on cars and light vans, the main difference is the position of the bearing, now shown on the outside of the axle between the hub and the outside of the axle casing. The casing therefore takes most of the weight of the vehicle and its load. The shaft is still subject to twisting and bending forces. This type is shown in Fig. 5.35(b).

Fully floating axle

In this arrangement (Fig. 5.35(c)) the bearings (normally taper roller) are fitted between the hub and the outside of the axle casing. In this way the only force to which the axle shaft is subject is a twisting action.

Lubrication

To prevent oil from leaking between the shaft and housing, lip-type oil seals are pressed into the housing. In some cases an oil slinger washer is located just inside and next to the bearing to prevent flooding of the seal. Pressure build-up due to temperature changes during operation is prevented by a breather in the top of the axle casing.

The action of the gear teeth meshing together tends to break down the oil film on the gear teeth (due to the very high pressures and forces created between the gear teeth). The oil used in the axle therefore must prevent a metal to metal contact from taking place. An EP additive in the oil reacts with the metal surfaces

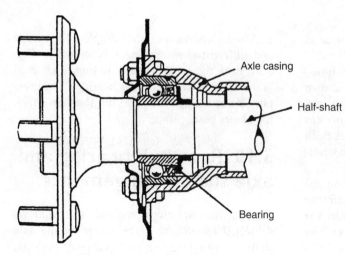

Fig. 5.35(a) Semi-floating axle

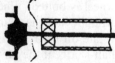

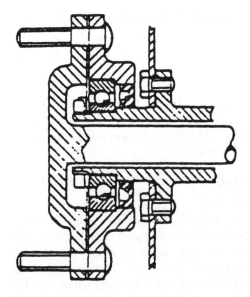

Fig. 5.35(b) Three-quarter floating axle

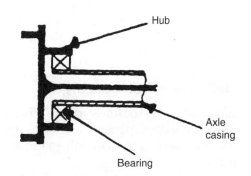

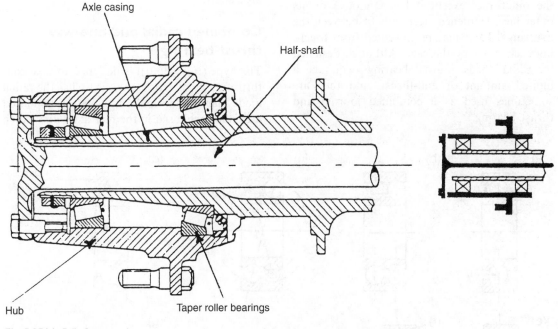

Fig. 5.35(c) Fully floating axle

at high temperatures to produce a low-friction film or coating on the teeth. This prevents scuffing and rapid wear from taking place; in effect the additive becomes the oil. It is essential that no other type of oil is used as this could cause rapid wear and early failure of the final drive to take place.

5.11 Types of bearings used in the transmission system

Plain bearings

A plain bearing can be described as a round hole lined with bearing metal or fitted with a bearing bush. These metals reduce friction in the bearing and also enable easy replacement as wear takes place. Typical examples of where these are used are in the engine (big-end and main bearings), in the gearbox (main shaft and lay shaft bearings) and in the flywheel (spigot shaft bearing).

Ball and roller bearings

Ball and roller bearings reduce friction by replacing sliding friction with rolling friction. There are several types of ball and roller bearings in use.

Single-row deep groove radial or journal bearing

In this bearing (Fig. 5.36(a)) the outer 'race' is a ring of hardened steel with a groove formed on its inner face. The inner race is similar to the outer race except it has a groove on its outer face. Hardened steel balls fit between the two rings. The balls are prevented from touching each other by the cage. Although designed for radial loads, journal bearings will take a limited amount of end-thrust, and they are sometimes used as a combined journal and thrust bearing.

Double-row journal bearing

This bearing is similar to the single-row journal bearing and is shown in Fig. 5.36(b). There are two grooves formed in each race together with a set of balls and cages. These are able to take larger loads and are often used where space is limited. A typical example would be in the wheel bearing or hub bearing. Some axle shafts are fitted with this type.

Double-row self-aligning journal bearing

This bearing (Fig 5.36(c)) has a double row of grooves and balls. The groove of the outer race is ground to form part of a sphere whose centre is on an axis with the shaft. This allows the shaft to run slightly out of alignment which could be caused by shaft deflection. This is commonly used as the centre bearing in the two/three piece prop shaft.

Combined radial and one-way thrust bearing

This type (Fig 5.36(d)) is designed to take end-thrust in one direction only, as well as the radial load. They are normally mounted in pairs and are commonly used in the rear axles and clutch

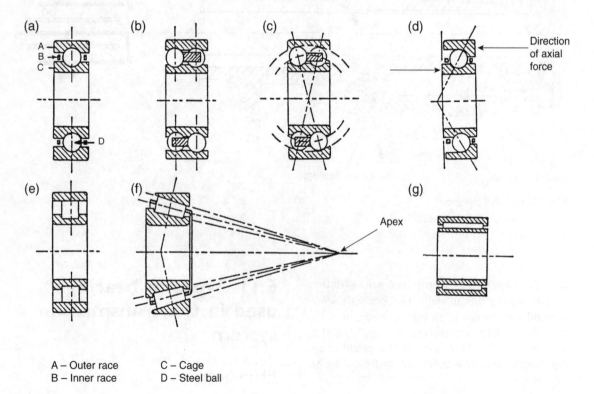

A – Outer race   C – Cage
B – Inner race   D – Steel ball

Fig. 5.36 (a) Single-row deep groove radial or journal bearing, (b) double-row radial or journal bearing, (c) double-row self-aligning bearing, (d) radial and one-way thrust bearing, (e) parallel-roller journal bearing, (f) taper roller bearing, (g) needle roller bearing

withdrawl thrust bearings. It is very important that these are fitted correctly otherwise the bearing will fall to pieces. They are also used as wheel bearings fitted back to back to enable them to take the side-thrust imposed on the wheel.

Parallel-roller journal bearing

This bearing (Fig. 5.36(e)) consists of cylindrical rollers having a length equal to the diameter of the roller. These can withstand a heavier radial load than the corresponding ball bearing, but cannot withstand any side-thrust. They are used in large gearboxes and in some cases have replaced the plain bearing.

Taper roller bearing

The rollers and race of this bearing (Fig. 5.36(f)) are conical (tapered) in shape with a common apex (centre) crossing at a single point on the centre line of the shaft. This ensures that the rollers do not slip. The rollers are kept in position by flanges on the inner race. This type of bearing can withstand larger side-thrusts than radial loads and they are normally used in pairs facing each other. They are most often used in the final drive, rear and front wheel hub assemblies. Some form of adjustment is normally used to reduce movement to a minimum or to provide some pre-load to the bearing.

Needle roller bearing

In this bearing (Fig. 5.36(g)) the rollers have a length of at least three roller diameters, packed in cages between inner and outer sleeves. The bearings can be found in universal joints and gearboxes especially where space is limited.

Learning tasks

1. Draw up a simple service schedule for checking the axle and final drive for correct operation. Include such things as type, grade and amount of oil used, and time/mileage base for changing/checking oil level.
2. How should the differential be checked for abnormal wear? What would be the main signs of early failure?
3. If a steady whining noise was heard as the vehicle was driven at a constant speed along a level road what would you suspect as being the fault and what would your recommendations be to put it right?

---

4. What main safety precautions would you observe when removing a live axle from a vehicle?
5. Why is it that most vehicles now use the hypoid type of gearing on the final drive?
6. Draw up the procedure for replacing the half-shaft on a live axle, assume the vehicle has been brought into the workshop, and the half-shaft has sheared between the final drive and the hub bearing.
7. Investigate the differences between a front engine FWD and a front engine RWD final drive and differential. Itemize the differences in servicing and adjustments that may be necessary when removing, stripping, rebuilding and refitting.
8. An axle requires a new crown and pinion fitting. Remove and dismantle an assembly using the procedure illustrated in Figs 5.30 and 5.31 to give the correct markings on the gear teeth.

Practical assignment – removing a clutch

When completing the task of removing and refitting the clutch, complete the following worksheet.

Questions

1. Why are the splines of the gearbox input shaft left clean and dry and not lubricated with engine oil?
2. State the type of clutch spring fitted to the vehicle.
3. Make a simple sketch of the clutch release mechanism. Label your sketch with the main components.
4. Inspect a diaphragm spring clutch assembly when attached and removed from the flywheel. Sketch the shape (a side view will do) of the diaphragm spring in the normal run position and in the removed position.
5. State the method used to adjust the clutch and the manufacturer's recommended clearance.
6. Record the condition of the following components:

   (a) the driven plate
   (b) the pressure plate assembly
   (c) the release bearing and mechanism

(d) the oil seals of both the engine and the gearbox

7. Make your recommendations to the customer to give adequate operation of the clutch for say the next 50 000 miles.

Practical assignment – removing and refitting a gearbox

Complete this when undertaking the removal and refitting of the gearbox.

Questions

1. Dismantle a front engine FWD gearbox. Identify wear on moving components such as bearings, shafts, gear teeth, thrust washers and oil seals. List the equipment used to measure this wear.
2. Identify the type of synchromesh unit fitted to the gearbox. From what material is it made?
3. Make a simple sketch of the method used to prevent the engagement of two gears at the same time. When does this unit operate?
4. Sketch and label the position of the selector forks, rails and location devices. Describe how the gear, once it is engaged, is held in position.
5. Identify first, second, third, fourth and where necessary fifth gear positions. State the gear ratios for each gear. The formula for calculating gear ratios is:

$$\frac{\text{driven gear}}{\text{driver gear}} \times \frac{\text{driven gear}}{\text{driver gear}}$$

6. Reassemble the gearbox and state any special precautions to be observed during reassembly and safety points to look out for.

Practical assignment – axles and final drives

Remove and dismantle the final drive and differential unit from a front engine RWD vehicle.

Questions

1. The type of final drive is:

   (a) straight bevel
   (b) spiral bevel
   (c) hypoid
   (d) worm and wheel

2. The bearings used to support the crown wheel are:

   (a) ball bearing taking axial thrust only
   (b) taper roller bearings taking axial thrust only
   (c) ball bearings taking axial and radial thrust
   (d) taper roller bearings taking axial and radial thrust

3. Why should the pinion be pre-loaded?
4. The type of bearing arrangement supporting the half shafts is:

   (a) semi-floating
   (b) three-quarter floating
   (c) fully floating
   (d) a combination of (a), (b) and (c).

5. The axle half-shaft is splined to the:

   (a) sun gear
   (b) planet gear
   (c) crown wheel
   (d) pinion gear

6. The type of axle is:

   (a) split axle
   (b) live axle
   (c) dead axle
   (d) trans-axle

7. Describe the procedure for reassembling the final drive and differential, state the following information:

   (a) the pre-load on the pinion bearing
   (b) the tolerance for backlash
   (c) the torque setting for the pinion nut
   (d) the final drive ratio
   (e) the type of oil seal used on the pinion
   (f) the type of oil seal used on the axle half-shaft
   (g) the type and grade of oil used in the axle
   (h) the service interval when the oil should be changed

6

Suspension systems

The suspension of a vehicle is present to prevent the variations in the road surface encountered by the wheels from being transmitted to the vehicle body. There are two main categories of suspension systems: **independent** and **non-independent**. An independent type has each wheel moving up and down without affecting the wheel on the opposite side of the vehicle. On non-independent systems movement of one wheel will affect the wheel on the opposite side of the vehicle. A typical system consists of:

- a wheel and pneumatic tyre;
- a spring and damper unit together with arms and links that attach the wheel or axle to the vehicle.

Many different types are used on light vehicles.

6.1 Non-independent suspension systems

Leaf spring

The laminated 'semi-elliptic' **leaf spring** is used mainly on LGV's and the rear suspensions on cars. A spring when loaded will deflect and release the energy acquired as a rebound. The friction between the leaves reduces the bouncing effect although it also reduces flexibility. Bushes are fitted in the spring eyes to prevent the shackle bolts from being in direct contact with the spring. A **swinging shackle** is fitted to the rear of the spring between the spring eye and the chassis to allow for the change in length between the spring eyes as the spring deflects. The advantages of the leaf spring are:

- it is cheap;
- it locates the axle;
- it is robust;
- it is simply connected.

The disadvantages are:

- a harsh ride is given;

- it requires two pivot points on the chassis;
- it requires more room;
- it is not as flexible as the coil spring type;
- the amount of deflection is limited;
- it has a high unsprung weight (this is the weight under the spring).

A rear axle and suspension assembly is shown in Fig. 6.1.

Coil spring

This type of spring gives a smoother ride than the multi-leaf due to the absence of **interleaf friction**. It can be used on front and rear systems. The helical spring is normally used in conjunction with independent suspension and is now often used with beam-axle rear suspensions. Figure 6.2 illustrates this type.

The **coil spring** and the **torsion bar** suspension are alike and are superior to the leaf spring as

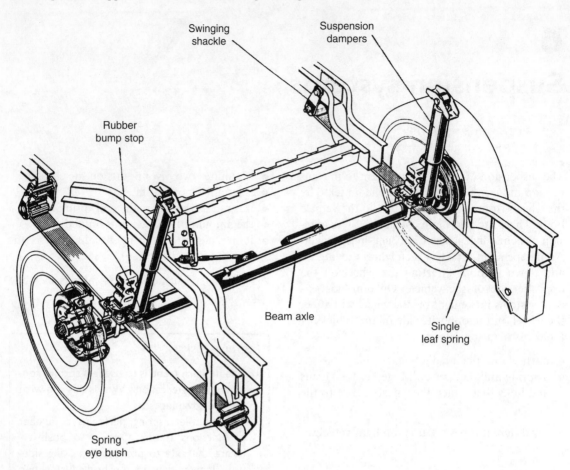

Fig. 6.1 Rear axle and suspension assembly

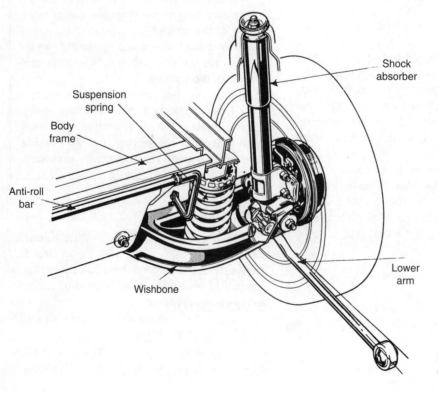

Fig. 6.2 Near side independent rear suspension

regards the energy stored but <u>unlike</u> the leaf spring extra members to locate it are required which adds to the basic weight. The advantages of the coil spring are:

- a reduction in unsprung weight
- energy storage is high
- it can provide a softer ride
- it allows for a greater movement of suspension
- it is more compact

Its main disadvantage is the location of the spring (the axle requires links and struts to hold it in place). This is shown in Fig. 6.3.

Learning tasks

1. What method would you adopt to check a suspected weak spring?
2. Write out a work schedule for removing a coil spring from a MacPherson strut. Itemize the safety points that *must* be observed.
3. Using your schedule remove a MacPherson strut from a vehicle. Remove the spring from the strut. Check: the operation of the damper; oil leaks from the seals; the upper bearing for wear; rubber bump stop and damage or severe rust to the spring mountings. Reassemble the spring to the strut and the suspension assembly to the vehicle.
4. What other checks do you think should be carried out after reassembling the strut to the vehicle?
5. How could the stiffness of a coil spring suspension be increased to enable the driver to tow a caravan? What other improvements might be required?

Torsion bar

This is a straight bar which can either be round or square section and fixed at one end to the chassis. The other end is connected by a lever to the axle. At each end of the bar the section is increased and serrated or splined to connect with the lever or chassis. Adjustment is provided for at the chassis end to give the correct **ride height** for the vehicle. This type of suspension is shown in Fig. 6.4 and is used on the front of vehicles. Figure 6.5 shows the arrangement used on the rear suspension.

Since the coil spring is a form of torsion bar

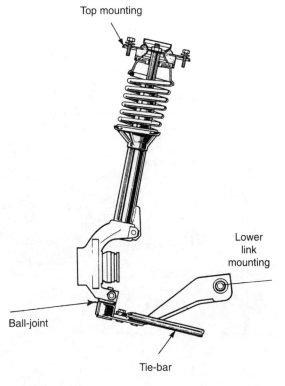

Fig. 6.3 MacPherson strut off side front suspension

suspension, the rate of both types of spring is governed by the same factors.

- The length of the bar.
- The diameter of the bar. If the length is increased or the diameter decreased, the rate of the spring will decrease, i.e. the spring will become softer.
- The material it is made from.

Learning tasks

1. How is the 'ride height' adjusted on a vehicle fitted with a torsion bar front suspension? Where on the vehicle is the measurement taken?
2. List the main advantages and disadvantages of torsion bar suspension over the leaf and coil spring types?

6.2 Independent suspension

Cars and many of the lighter commercial vehicles are now fitted with some form of **independent front suspension** (IFS) and/or **independent**

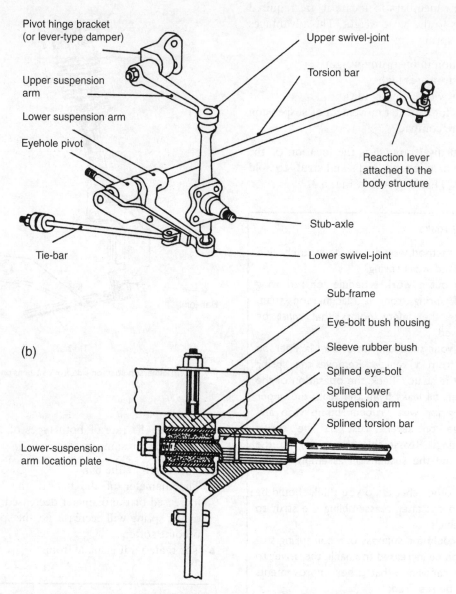

(a)

Pivot hinge bracket
(or lever-type damper)

Upper swivel-joint

Upper suspension
arm

Torsion bar

Lower suspension arm

Eyehole pivot

Reaction lever
attached to the
body structure

Stub-axle

Tie-bar

Lower swivel-joint

(b)

Sub-frame

Eye-bolt bush housing

Sleeve rubber bush

Splined eye-bolt

Splined lower
suspension arm

Splined torsion bar

Lower-suspension
arm location plate

Fig. 6.4 Torsion-bar double-transverse-arm independent front suspension (a) pictorial view, (b) section view – lower-suspension-arm pivot asembly

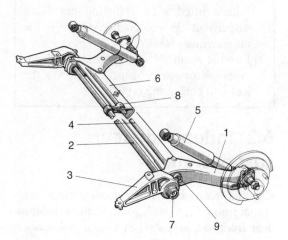

1 – Trailing link
2 – Torsion bar (N/S)
3 – Mounting bracket
4 – Torsion bar (O/S)
5 – Shock absorber
6 – Cross member

7 – Torsion bar mounting
   in bracket
8 – Connector
9 – Serated profile mounting
   torsion bar in trailing link

Fig. 6.5 Transverse torsion bar rear suspension

rear suspension (IRS). These have the following advantages over the earlier beam axle and leaf spring arrangements.

- Reduced unsprung weight.
- The steering is not affected by the 'gyroscopic' effect of a deflected wheel being transmitted to the other wheel.
- Better steering stability due to the wider spacing of the springs.
- Better road holding as the centre of gravity is lower – due to the engine being mounted nearer the ground. This is because there is no front beam axle in the way.
- More space in the body due to the engine being lower and possible further forward.
- More comfortable ride due to the use of lower rate springs.

Where a beam axle and parallel leaf spring arrangement is used the springs are subjected to the following forces:

- suspension loads due to vehicle weight;
- driving and braking thrusts due respectively to the forward movement of the chassis and its retardation when braking;
- braking torque reaction – the spring distorting but preventing the rotating of the back plate and axle;
- twisting due to the deflection of one wheel only.

When the springs are strong enough to resist all these forces they are too stiff and heavy to provide a comfortable ride and good road holding. Independent suspension designs must provide for the control or limitation of these same forces, and their action must not interfere with the steering geometry or the operation of the braking system.

As we have already mentioned with the independent suspension when one wheel moves up or down it has little or no effect on the opposite wheel. In the case of the beam axle suspension, when one wheel rises over a bump the other wheel on the same axle is also affected. Because of this neither wheel is vertical to the road surface and so the road holding ability of the vehicle is affected. In a truly independent system each wheel is able to move without affecting any of the others. This has a number of obvious advantages:

1. a softer ride giving greater comfort for the passengers
2. better road holding especially on rough or uneven road surfaces
3. the engine can normally be mounted lower in the vehicle
4. because of (1) (2) and (3) the vehicle will corner better
5. it allows for a greater rise and fall of the wheel

Because of the expense, greater complication and difficulty of mounting, many vehicle manufacturers of smaller cars fit independent suspension to the front and beam axle on the rear especially where the engine drives the front wheels. This arrangement gives a light, simple layout for the rear suspension using coil springs and links to support the axle to the body.

The effects of uneven road surfaces and body roll on the suspension can be seen in Fig. 6.6. From the illustrations it will be seen that the **MacPherson strut** arrangement gives the most stable body and wheel alignment. This is one reason why the MacPherson strut is the most common type of suspension fitted to light vehicles.

Learning tasks

1. Explain what is meant by 'brake torque reaction'. Illustrate where necessary your answer with a simple sketch.
2. List a typical sequence of checks that should be made to find a reported knocking noise coming from the front off side suspension.
3. What effect would the lowering of the front suspension have on the steering geometry of the vehicle? Give reasons for your answer.

Axle location

As already mentioned the leaf spring locates the axle, but the coil, torsion bar, **rubber** and **air spring** suspension support the vehicle and its load and remove the unevenness of the road surface. They do not locate the wheel assembly or axle in any way. Extra arms (**radius arms**) or links are fitted to locate the wheels for both fore and aft movement and to resist the turning forces of both driving and braking. A **Panhard rod** gives sideways location between the axle and the body (see Fig. 6.7).

A number of other methods are in use that locate the axle. These include the use of **tie rods**, **wishbone** and **semi-trailing links** (Fig. 6.8). When an IRS is fitted (as on some of the more expen-

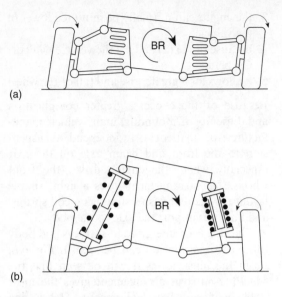

(a)

(b)

Fig. 6.6 Effects of (a) body roll and (b) irregular road surfaces on suspension geometry

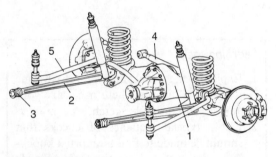

1 – Axle casing
2 – Longitudinal (down the length of the car) control arms
3 – Rubber mountings
4 – Panhard rod
5 – Anti-roll bar

Fig. 6.7 Layout of rigid line axle using coil springs and Panhard rod

sive vehicles) then the arrangement for location of the wheel assembly can become more complicated.

The method used to attach the links and arms to the body is by the use of **rubber bushes**. There is always a certain amount of 'give' in these rubber joints and this is termed compliance. This is generally allowed for in the specifications given by the manufacturer when checking the suspension for alignment.

> *Learning tasks*
>
> 1. To which types of suspension arrangements is the Panhard rod fitted and why to this particular type?

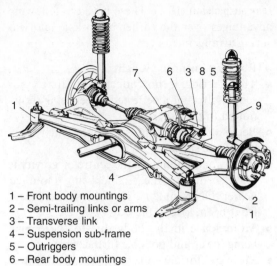

1 – Front body mountings
2 – Semi-trailing links or arms
3 – Transverse link
4 – Suspension sub-frame
5 – Outriggers
6 – Rear body mountings
7 – Final drive
8 – Rubber mountings
9 – McPhearson strut suspension

Fig. 6.8 Independent rear suspension and final drive using semi-trailing links

> 2. How should the rubber bushes in the suspension be checked for wear?
> 3. If a driver complained of vehicle instability especially when cornering or driving over rough and uneven road surfaces what would you suspect the fault to be? Give reasons for your answer.
> 4. Remove and refit a suspension link, inspect the bushes for wear and soundness, the link for signs of accident damage and rust and the mounting point for signs of wear or rust.

Rubber suspensions

Rubber can be used as the suspension medium as well as for mountings and pivots. Its main advantage is that for small wheel movements the ride is fairly soft but it becomes harder as wheel movement increases. It has the advantage of being small, light and compact and will absorb some of the energy passed to it, unlike a coil spring which gives out almost as much energy as it receives. The rubber spring is also commonly used on LGVs and trailers. A rubber suspension unit is shown in Fig. 6.9.

Hydrolastic suspension

This is a combination of rubber and fluid (which is under pressure). Each wheel is fitted with a **hydrolastic unit** which consists of a steel cylinder mounted on the body of the car. A tapered piston, complete with a rubber and nylon

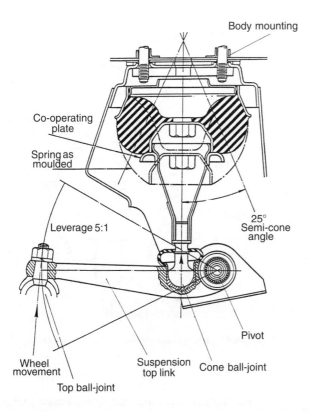

Body mounting

Co-operating plate

Spring as moulded

Leverage 5:1

25° Semi-cone angle

Wheel movement

Suspension top link

Top ball-joint

Cone ball-joint

Pivot

Fig. 6.9 Rubber suspension unit

diaphragm which is connected to the upper suspension arm, fits in the bottom of the unit. When the wheel moves upwards the piston is also moved up and via fluid action compresses the rubber spring. The units are connected together on the same side by large bore pipes and some of the fluid is displaced down the pipe to the other unit. In this way the tendency for the vehicle to pitch (this is the movement of the body fore and aft, that is front to back) is reduced. A hydroelastic system is shown in Fig. 6.10.

Hydrogas suspension

Sometimes called **hydropneumatic** this system, shown in Fig. 6.11, is a development of the hydrolastic system. The main difference is that the rubber is replaced by a gas (usually nitrogen), hence the term 'pneumatic'. With this type the gas remains constant irrespective of the load carried. Gas pressure will increase as volume is reduced. This means that the suspension stiffens as the load increases. The units are connected together in a similar manner to the hydrolastic suspension and the fluid used is a mixture of water, alcohol and an anti-corrosive agent.

The ride height in both these systems can be raised or lowered by the use of a hydrolastic suspension pump to give the correct ride height and ground clearance.

Learning tasks

1. What safety precautions must be observed when working on pressurized suspension systems?
2. State the method used for adjusting the 'ride height' on the hydropneumatic suspension system. Identify any specialized equipment and fluid type that must be used. Adjust the ride height to the upper limit specified by the manufacturer in the repair manual.
3. Identify *four* units in the suspension that use rubber bushes to mount the suspension to the body or chassis.
4. Remove a suspension unit from a vehicle with hydrolastic or hydrogas suspension. Identify any worn or defective components. Replace the unit and adjust the ride height as necessary.

Active or 'live' hydropneumatic suspension

This system, shown in Fig. 6.12, allows the driver to adjust the ride height (sometimes inaccurately referred to as ground clearance) of the vehicle. It also maintains this clearance irrespective of the load being carried. First developed by

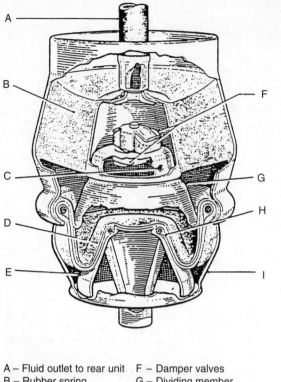

A – Fluid outlet to rear unit   F – Damper valves
B – Rubber spring   G – Dividing member
C – Fluid bleed hole   H – Reinforcing in diaphragm
D – Rubber diaphragm   I – Tapered outer cylinder
E – Tapered piston

Fig. 6.10 Hydrolastic spring displacer unit

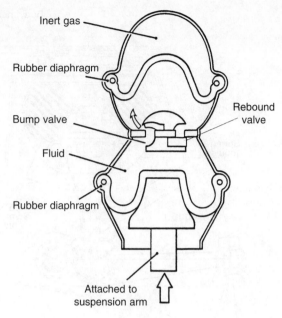

Fig. 6.11 Hydrogas suspension

Citroen it has recently been taken up by a number of other manufacturers. On the Citroen arrangement each **suspension arm** is supported by a **pneumatic spring**.

Connected between the suspension arms at both front and rear are **anti-roll bars**. These are linked to **height correctors** by means of control rods. An engine driven pump supplies oil under pressure to a **hydraulic accumulator** and this is connected to the height control or **levelling valves**.

As the vehicle is loaded, the downward movement of the body causes the rotation of the anti-roll bar. This moves the slide valve in the height correctors and uncovers the port to supply oil under pressure from the accumulator to the suspension cylinders. When the body reaches the predetermined height, (which can be varied by the driver moving a lever inside the vehicle), the valve moves to the 'neutral' position. Removal of the load causes the valve to vent oil from the cylinder back to the reservoir.

A delay device is incorporated to prevent rapid oil flow past the valve when the wheel contacts a bump. This prevents the valve from continuously working and giving unsatisfactory operation.

In some systems a third spring unit is fitted between the two spring units on the front axle and between the two spring units on the rear axle. This gives a variable spring rate and roll stiffness, i.e. the suspension is active. The system is controlled by an ECU (electronic control unit) which senses steering wheel movement, acceleration, speed and body movement and reacts accordingly via control valves to regulate the flow of oil to and from the suspension units. Under normal driving conditions the ECU operates the solenoid valve which directs fluid to open the regulator valves. This allows fluid to flow between the two outer spring units and the third spring units via the damper units to give a soft ride. During harder driving the solenoid valve is switched off automatically relieving the regulator valves which close, preventing fluid flow between the spring units. The third spring unit being isolated and not in use gives a firmer ride.

There are a number of benefits of this system:

- it automatically adjusts the spring and damper rate to suit road conditions and driving styles;
- it can provide a soft and comfortable ride under normal driving conditions;
- it will stiffen to give better road holding during hard driving;
- a near constant ride height can be achieved irrespective of the load on the vehicle.

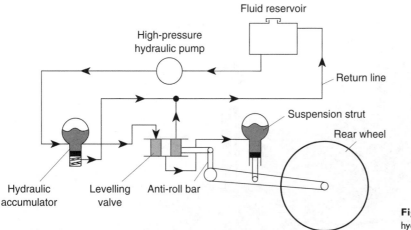

Fig. 6.12 Simplified layout of hydropneumatic suspension system

Rear wheel 'suspension steer'

In some systems the rear suspension is arranged to produce a steering effect when cornering. As the suspension is deflected the road wheel **toes-in** due to the arc of movement of the semi-trailing link. This produces **understeer** on cornering (it gives a small degree of same direction rear-steer). Figure 6.13 shows one example that will give:

- toe-in when braking
- understeer when cornering
- stability in straight line running and when changing lanes

A simpler suspension arrangement is shown in Fig. 6.14 that produces toe-in under similar operating conditions.

Air suspension

Some vehicle manufacturers fit air suspension units in place of the conventional coil springs. A typical example with electronically controlled air suspension is shown in Fig. 6.15. Three switches, positioned near the steering column, control the ride height: the upper switch raises the vehicle by approximately 40 mm for driving through deep water or over rough ground; the middle switch gives a similar ride height to the coil-sprung model; the lower switch lowers the vehicle approximately 60 mm below the standard setting to enable easier loading and for getting in and out. A number of automatic adjustments such as lowering the vehicle when driving over 50 mph to reduce wind resistance and raising the vehicle if it should become grounded are programmed into the ECU and operate independently of the driver.

Another system uses a digital controller (ECU) which reacts to suspension acceleration and ride height by varying the oil pressure. It will also adjust damper action by reference to body movement.

Some manufacturers make **ride height levellers** (Fig. 6.16), which are shock absorbers that will raise the rear of the vehicle to its normal ride height when loaded. The system is operated through a switch, electric motor and compressor; the dampers are pumped up via air pipes connecting the units together.

The **suspension damper** has to perform a number of functions. These are:

- absorb road surface variations;

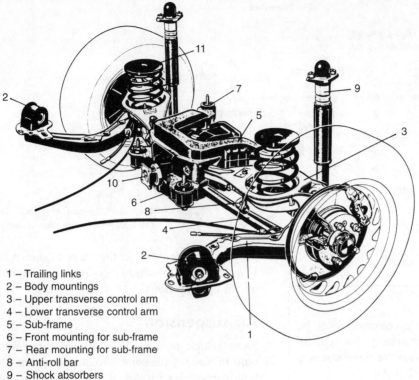

1 – Trailing links
2 – Body mountings
3 – Upper transverse control arm
4 – Lower transverse control arm
5 – Sub-frame
6 – Front mounting for sub-frame
7 – Rear mounting for sub-frame
8 – Anti-roll bar
9 – Shock absorbers
10 – Differential unit
11 – Minibloc springs

Fig. 6.13 Multi-link rear suspension

- insulate the noise from the vehicle body;
- give resistance to vehicle body pitch under braking and acceleration;
- offer resistance to roll when cornering.

A passive mechanical system to tackle each of these tasks is impossible as the rate of the damper must be varied to suit differing circumstances and handling characteristics. Shock absorber manufacturers have made provision for some control over the damping rate by making them adjustable, but once set even these are not suitable for all applications and uses.

With this in mind many of the new suspension systems are **active**; in other words they will operate continuously adjusting to pre-set limits the suspension spring rate. One system uses an ECU which receives information on cruising, suspension condition, body roll and pitch. It then directs air from the compressor to the suspension units to give the correct spring rate and ride height for the load carried.

Learning tasks

1. What is the purpose of the ECU and electronic sensors in an active suspension system? What attention do these units require and at what intervals should checks be carried out?
2. On some models the system is connected to the anti-lock braking system. Explain in simple terms the reason for this and how it operates.
3. List the maintenance requirements for one of the 'active' suspension systems with which you are familiar.
4. Draw up a work schedule for removing a suspension unit from a vehicle. Special note should be made of the safety aspects of the task.
5. Remove an ECU from an active suspension system, check the terminals for corrosion or damage and clean with appropriate spray cleaner where necessary. Ensure that the mounting surface is clean and free from rust. Refit the ECU taking special care when refitting the terminal connector.

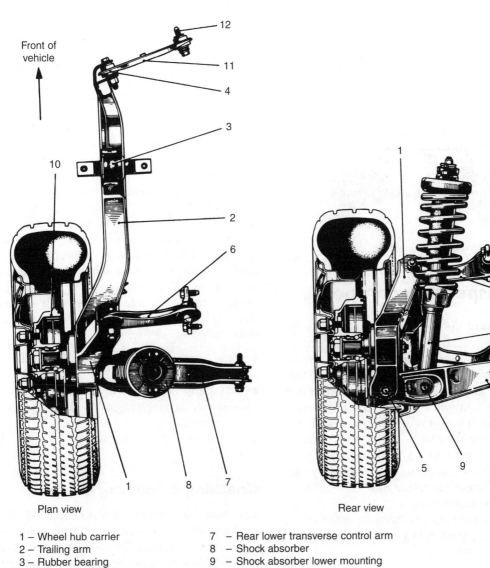

Front of
vehicle

12

11

4

3

10

2

6

1

8

7

Plan view

1

8

7

6

8

7

5

9

Rear view

1 – Wheel hub carrier
2 – Trailing arm
3 – Rubber bearing
4 – Trailing arm front mounting
5 – Trailing arm rear mounting
6 – Upper transverse control arm

7 – Rear lower transverse control arm
8 – Shock absorber
9 – Shock absorber lower mounting
10 – Brake drum
11 – Front lower transverse control arm
12 – Inner mounting

Fig. 6.14 Multi-link rear suspension giving toe-in during braking and cornering

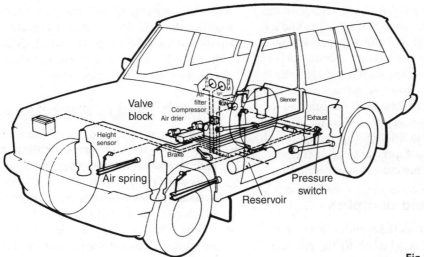

Valve
block

Air
filter
Compressor
Air drier

IGN

Silencer

Exhaust

Height
sensor

Brake

Air spring

Reservoir

Pressure
switch

Fig. 6.15 Air suspension

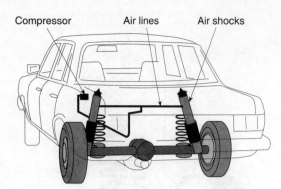

Fig. 6.16 Height levellers in the rear axle

6.3 Suspension dampers

The function of the suspension damper is not to increase the resistance to the spring deflecting but to control the **oscillation** of the spring (this is the continuing up and down movement of the spring after going over a bump or hollow in the road surface). In other words it absorbs energy given to the spring, hence the more common name of **shock absorber**. It does this by forcing oil in the damper to do work by passing it through holes in the piston and converting the energy of the moving spring into heat which is passed to the atmosphere.

Two main categories of dampers are in common use: the **direct-acting** (usually telescopic) and the **lever arm**.

The twin-tube telescopic damper

This type is usually located between the chassis and the axle so that on both bump and rebound oil is forced through the holes in the piston. The reservoir is used to accommodate the excess oil that is displaced as a result of the volume in the upper cylinder being smaller. If oil is lost and air enters the damper it will affect its performance and it will become 'spongy' in operation. This will have an effect on the stability of the vehicle especially when cornering, travelling over rough ground, uneven surfaces and on braking or accelerating. When checking for correct operation disconnect one end of the damper and check the amount of resistance to movement. Figure 6.17 shows a telescopic shock absorber.

Gas-pressurized dampers

A **single tube** is used as the cylinder in which the piston operates. It is attached to the car body and suspension by rubber bushes to reduce noise and vibration and to allow for slight sideways movements as the suspension operates. A chamber in the unit, sealed by a free piston, contains an inert gas that is under pressure when the damper is filled with oil. As the suspension operates the piston moves down the cylinder and oil is forced through the 'bump' valve to the upper chamber; excess oil that cannot be accommodated in the upper chamber because of the rod moves the free piston to compress the gas. On rebound the oil is made to pass through the 'rebound' valve in the piston; by varying the size of the holes in the valves the resistance of each stroke can be altered to suit different vehicle applications. This arrangement is most commonly fitted to the MacPherson strut suspension systems. The main advantages of the single-tube damper are:

- it can displace a large volume of fluid without noise or fluid aeration;
- it is fairly consistent in service even when operating at large angles to the suspension movement;
- it has good dissipation of heat to the air flow.

Checking damper operation

Two tests are normally used to check whether the dampers are serviceable without removing them from the vehicle. The **bounce test** involves pushing down on each corner of the vehicle and observing the up and down movement of the body as it comes to its rest position. The second method involves the use of some form of **tester** of which there are several types available. One type uses an eccentric roller arrangement that the vehicle is driven onto to produce the required movement of the suspension. In another the vehicle is driven up a collapsible ramp; when set the ramp is dropped. Both types give a graphical printout of the test that shows the oscillations of the suspension.

Materials used in suspensions

- **Road springs** These are made from a silicon manganese steel as they must withstand very high stresses and fatigue yet still retain elasticity and strength.
- **Suspension links** Here a nickel steel is used which gives elasticity together with toughness.
- **Bushes** These are usually made from rubber to reduce vibration, noise and the need for lubrication.

(a)

(b)

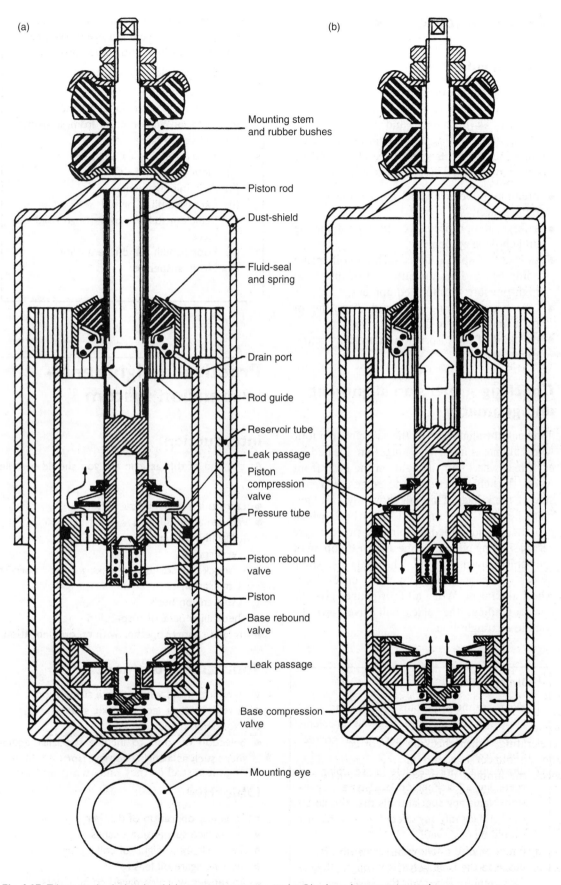

Mounting stem
and rubber bushes

Piston rod

Dust-shield

Fluid-seal
and spring

Drain port

Rod guide

Reservoir tube

Leak passage

Piston
compression
valve

Pressure tube

Piston rebound
valve

Piston

Base rebound
valve

Leak passage

Base compression
valve

Mounting eye

Fig. 6.17 Telescopic shock absorber (a) bump or compression stroke, (b) rebound or extension stroke

Maintenance checks

General rules

There are a number of general rules that should be observed when carrying out maintenance checks and adjustments; and there are also methods of protecting the system against accidental damage during repair operations on the suspension system. These are listed below:

- preliminary vehicle checks – see the vehicle report sheet;
- safety – the proper use of lifting supporting and choking equipment;
- safe use of special tools such as coil spring compressor, high-pressure lubricants and high-pressure hydraulic equipment;
- care when working with and disposing of toxic and corrosive fluids;
- checking of the suspension thoroughly before road testing.

Checking suspension alignment and geometry

To check the alignment of the suspension a four wheel aligner is used. The gauges are located on each rear wheel and the light on the each front wheel; the light shines onto the gauge down each side of the vehicle. This will show any misalignment between the front and rear wheels which can then be identified, helping to prevent tyre scrub, steering pulling to one side or crabbing of the vehicle down the road. The lights also shine across the front of the vehicle to check front wheel alignment. When all four gauges give the correct readings, the vehicle will drive down the road in a straight line.

Learning tasks

1. What are the symptoms of faulty dampers? How will the driver notice this problem? How should they be checked for correct operation?
2. Draw up a work schedule for stripping and rebuilding a MacPherson strut-type suspension. Name any special tools that should be used and identify any safety precautions that should be observed?
3. For each of the following suspension faults: describe the fault (what is wrong?); identify the symptom (how will the driver notice?);

---

state the probable cause (what has caused the fault?); and give the preventative or corrective action that should be taken.

- (a) Excessive uneven tyre wear
- (b) Excessive component wear
- (c) Premature failure of component
- (d) Vibration and/or noise from suspension
- (e) Uneven braking
- (f) Steering pulling to one side
- (g) Incorrect trim height
- (h) Axle misalignment
- (i) Excessive pitch or roll
- (j) Vehicle instability over rough road surfaces
- (k) Poor handling and ride quality
- (l) Noisy suspension

Practical assignment – suspension system

Introduction

At the end of this assignment you should be able to:

- carry out a visual inspection
- remove and replace a
  - MacPherson strut
  - coil spring
  - shock absorber, checking for correct operation
  - suspension bush
- check alignment of suspension
- make a report together with recommendations

Tools and equipment

- A vehicle fitted with suitable suspension
- A vehicle lift or jack and axle stands
- Workshop manual
- Selection of tools to include specialist equipment such as a spring compressor

Objective

- To check operation of damper
- To replace suspension bushes
- To check 'free height' of coil spring
- To investigate oil leaks
- To replace worn/damaged components

Activity

1. After suitably raising and supporting the vehicle remove the wheels (*do not* support the vehicle under the suspension to be removed).
2. Observe and note the type of suspension, e.g. coil spring, leaf spring, torsion bar, rubber, etc.
3. Make a simple sketch of the layout.
4. Before cleaning around the mounting points look for signs of:

   (a) insecure or loose components
   (b) places where dirt may be rubbed off by something catching
   (c) bright or rusty streak marks where body or chassis may be cracked
   (d) rust where thickness of material may be reduced to a failure level
   (e) excessively worn components
   (f) accident damage to body or components

5. Remove suspension and dismantle where necessary.
6. Check operation of damper.
7. Reassemble suspension (replacing any worn/broken components) according to manufacturer's manual.
8. Check for correct assembly and tightness of all mounting bolts before fitting wheel.
9. Complete an inspection report and recommendations for the customer.

Checklist

Vehicle

Removal and refitting
MacPherson strut
Coil spring
Leaf spring
Shock absorber
Rubber suspension bush

Dismantle and reassemble
MacPherson strut
Shock absorber

Checking and adjusting
Castor angle
Camber angle
King pin inclination
Toe-out on turns
Wheel alignment
Axle alignment
Body alignment
Ride height

Investigating and reporting
Rubber
Hydrogas
Hydrolastic
Hydropneumatic
Coil spring
Leaf spring
Air

Student's signature

Supervisor's signature

7
Braking systems

The purpose of the braking system is to slow down or stop the vehicle and, when it is stationary, to hold it in the chosen position. When a vehicle is moving it contains energy of motion (**kinetic energy**) and the function of the braking system is to convert this kinetic energy into **heat energy**. It does so through the friction at the brake linings and the brake drum, or the brake pads and the disc.

Some large vehicles are fitted with secondary braking systems that are known as retarders. Examples of **retarders** are exhaust brakes and electric brakes. In all cases the factor that ultimately determines how much braking can be applied is the grip of the tyres on the driving surface.

7.1 Types of brakes

Two basic types of **friction brakes** are in common use on vehicles. These are:

- the **drum brake**
- the **disc brake**

Drum brake

Figure 7.1 shows a drum brake as used on a large vehicle. This cut-away view shows that the linings on the shoes are pressed into contact with the inside of the drum by the action of the cam. In this case the cam is partially rotated by the action of a compressed air cylinder. The road wheel is attached to the brake drum by means of the wheel studs and nuts.

A brake of this type has a **leading shoe** and a **trailing shoe**. The leading shoe is the one whose leading edge comes into contact with the drum first, in the direction of rotation. A leading shoe is more powerful than a trailing shoe and this shows up in the wear pattern because a leading shoe generally wears more than a trailing shoe owing to the extra work that it does.

Disc brake

Figure 7.2 shows the principle of the disc brake. The road wheel is attached to the disc and the slowing down or stopping action is achieved by the clamping action of the brake pads on the disc.

In this brake the disc is gripped by the two friction pads. When **hydraulic pressure** is applied to the hydraulic cylinder in the caliper body, the pressure acts on the piston and pushes the brake pad into contact with the disc. This creates a reaction force which causes the pins to slide in the carrier bracket and this action pulls the other pad into contact with the disc so that the disc is tightly clamped by both pads.

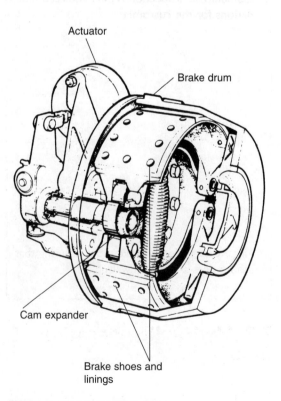

Actuator

Brake drum

Cam expander

Brake shoes and linings

Fig. 7.1 A cam operated drum brake

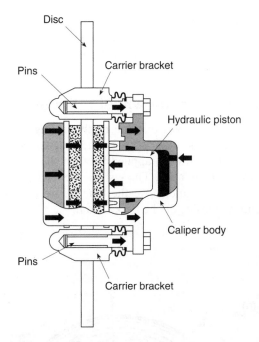

Fig. 7.2 A disc brake

Learning tasks

1. List the main safety hazards when working on the braking system. How should brake dust, fluid and worn friction materials be disposed of?

2. Remove a set of pads from a disc brake. Check pad friction material for thickness and even wear rate. Check disc for scoring and thickness. Check piston and caliper for correct and smooth operation. Observe any safety precautions when working on the braking system, e.g. removing brake dust, use of locking agent on bolts, use of type of grease on sliding components, etc. Reassemble brake pads, operate the brake pedal and check brake fluid level in master cylinder reservoirs.

3. Dismantle a drum brake. Name the type of layout of shoes, the type of cylinder fitted and the method of adjustment. Give one advantage of using a bonded lining rather than a riveted lining. Reassemble the brake shoes ensuring that the springs are correctly fitted.

7.2 Hydraulic operation of brakes

The main braking systems on cars and most light commercial vehicles are operated by **hydraulic systems**. At the heart of a hydraulic braking system is the **master cylinder** for it is here that the pressure that operates the brakes is generated.

Principle of the hydraulic system

The small diameter master cylinder is connected to the large diameter actuating cylinder by a strong metal pipe.

The cylinders and the pipe are filled with hydraulic fluid. When a force is applied to the master cylinder piston a pressure is created and this pressure is the same at all parts of the interior of the system. Because pressure is the amount of force acting on each square millimetre of surface the force exerted on the larger piston will be greater than the force applied to the small piston. In the example shown in Fig. 7.3 the force of 100 newtons (N) on an area of $400\,mm^2$ of the master cylinder piston creates a pressure of $0.25\,N$ per square millimetre. The piston of the actuating cylinder has an area of $800\,mm^2$ and this gives a force of $200\,N$ at this cylinder.

Master cylinder

The part of the hydraulic braking system where the hydraulic operating pressure is generated is the master cylinder. Force is applied to the master cylinder piston by the action of the driver's foot on the brake pedal. In the example shown in Fig. 7.4 the action is as follows. When force is applied to the push rod the piston moves along the bore of the master cylinder to take up slack.

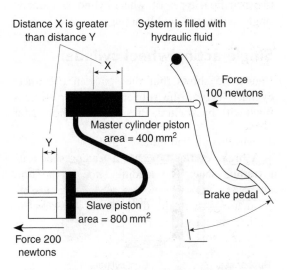

Fig. 7.3 The principle of a hydraulic braking system. The hydraulic pressure is equal at all parts of the system

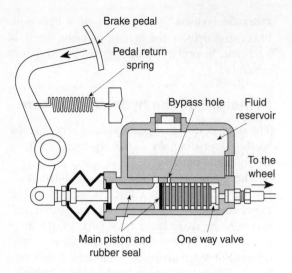

Fig. 7.4 A simple type of hydraulic master cylinder

As soon as the lip of the main rubber seal has covered the bypass hole the fluid in the cylinder, and the system to which it is connected, is pressurized.

When the force on the brake pedal and the master cylinder push rod is released, the return spring pushes the piston back and the hydraulic operating pressure is removed. The action of the main piston seal ensures that the master cylinder remains filled with fluid.

7.3 Wheel cylinders

The hydraulic cylinders that push the drum brake shoes apart, or apply the clamping force in the disc brake, are the wheel cylinders. There are two principal types of wheel cylinders namely: **single-acting** and **double-acting**.

Single-acting wheel cylinder

Figure 7.5 shows that the space in the **wheel cylinder**, behind the rubber seal and piston, is filled with brake fluid. Pressure from the master cylinder is applied to the wheel cylinders through pipes. Increased fluid pressure pushes the piston out and this force is applied to the brake shoe or brake pad.

Double-acting wheel cylinder

Figure 7.6 shows that the double-acting wheel cylinder has two pistons and rubber seals. Hydraulic pressure applied between the pistons pushes them apart. The pistons then act on the brake shoes and move the linings into contact with the inside of the brake drum.

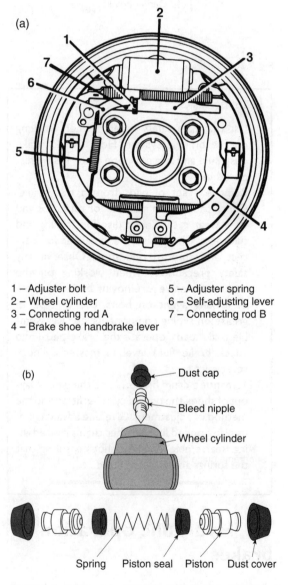

1 – Adjuster bolt   5 – Adjuster spring
2 – Wheel cylinder   6 – Self-adjusting lever
3 – Connecting rod A   7 – Connecting rod B
4 – Brake shoe handbrake lever

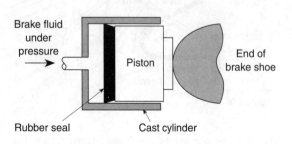

Fig. 7.5 A single acting hydraulic wheel cylinder

Fig. 7.6 A double acting hydraulic wheel cylinder (a) Rover 200 Series drum brake, (b) a double acting wheel cylinder

7.4 Handbrake

The **handbrake (parking brake)** is required to hold the vehicle in any chosen position when the vehicle is stationary. In addition to its function as a parking brake, the handbrake is also used when making hill starts and similar manoeuvres. The handbrake also serves as an **emergency brake** in the event of failure of the main braking system. Figure 7.7 shows the layout and main features of a handbrake for a car or light van. The vehicle has trailing arm rear suspension and the swivel sector pivots (4) are needed to guide the cable on these suspension arms. The purpose of the **compensator** (3) is to ensure that equal braking force is applied to each side of the vehicle. The handbrake normally operates through the normal brakes at the rear of the vehicle.

In normal use, the brake linings will wear and it is also possible that the handbrake cable may stretch a little. In order to keep the handbrake working properly it is provided with an adjustment, as shown in Fig. 7.8. The nut (2) is the adjusting nut and the nut (1) is the lock nut. In order to adjust the handbrake the rear of the vehicle must be lifted so that the wheels are clear of the ground. The normal safety precautions must be observed and the wheels should be checked for freedom of rotation after the cable has been adjusted.

Learning tasks

1. Dismantle a brake caliper and check the following:

   (a) piston for corrosion, scoring or damage
   (b) housing for rust and scoring
   (c) sliding mechanism for smooth operation
   (d) rubber seals for damage and wear
   (e) dust covers for cracks, wear and damage
   (f) signs of brake fluid leaks
   (g) reassemble the brake caliper and make out a report sheet together with your recommendations.

2. Remove the handbrake mechanism complete. Identify any faults such as worn pivots and cables. Reassemble the mechanism and grease all cables, pivots and slides. Adjust the cables to give the correct operation. Ensure that the foot brake mechanism is fully adjusted before adjusting the hand brake.

3. Dismantle the hand brake mechanism from a disc brake, clean and lubricate as necessary on reassembly. Readjust the hand brake as required.

7.5 Split braking systems

The **split braking circuit** provides for emergencies such as a leak in one area of the braking system. There are various methods of providing split

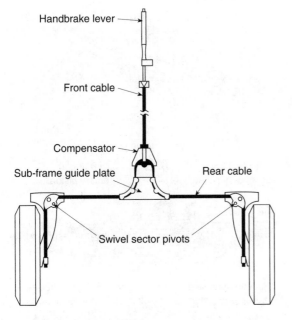

Fig. 7.7 A handbrake system

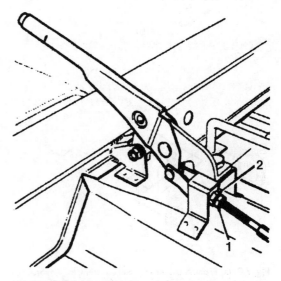

Fig. 7.8 Handbrake cable adjustment

braking circuits, some of which are shown in Fig. 7.9 (a), (b) and (c).

Front/rear split

Figure 7.9(a) shows how the front brakes are operated by one part of the master cylinder and the rear brakes by the other part. This system is used for rear wheel drive cars.

Diagonal split

One part of the **tandem master cylinder** is con-

nected to the offside front and the nearside rear brakes and the other part of the master cylinder is connected to the nearside front and the offside rear, as shown in Fig. 7.9(b).

Front axle and one rear wheel split

This is known as the **'L' split**. One part of the master cylinder is connected to the front brakes and the offside rear wheel brake and the other part of the master cylinder is also connected to the front brakes and the nearside rear wheel brake. This arrangement requires four **piston calipers** for the front disc brakes or two pistons if they are **floating calipers**.

7.6 Tandem master cylinder

In each split system a tandem master cylinder is used. Figure 7.10 shows a tandem master cylinder.

The master cylinder is designed to ensure that the brakes are applied evenly. There are two pistons: a primary piston and a secondary piston. The spring (1) is part of the primary piston and it is stronger than the spring (2) that is fitted to

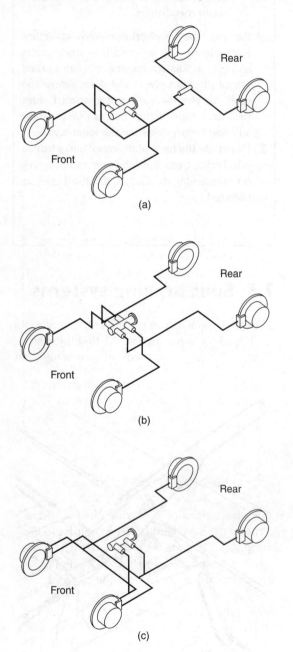

(a)

(b)

(c)

Fig. 7.9 (a) Front/rear split of braking system, (b) diagonal split of braking system, (c) front axle and one rear wheel split

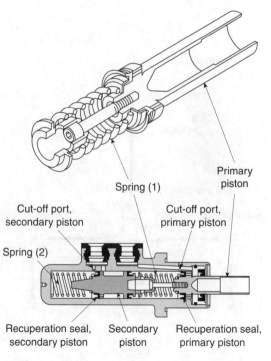

Fig. 7.10 A tandem master cylinder

Spring (1)

Primary piston

Cut-off port, secondary piston

Cut-off port, primary piston

Spring (2)

Recuperation seal, secondary piston

Secondary piston

Recuperation seal, primary piston

the secondary piston. Application of force to the piston causes the spring (1) to apply force to the secondary piston so that both pistons move along the cylinder together. The two piston seals cover their respective cut-off ports at the same time and this ensures simultaneous build up of pressure in the primary and secondary circuits.

When the brake pedal force is released, the primary and secondary pistons are pushed back by the secondary spring and both cut-off ports are opened at the same time, thus releasing the brakes simultaneously.

In the event of leakage from one part of the master cylinder, the other cylinder remains operative. This is achieved through the design of the stops and other features of the master cylinder.

7.7 The brake fluid reservoir

The fluid reservoir is usually mounted direct onto the master cylinder. Figure 7.11 shows a

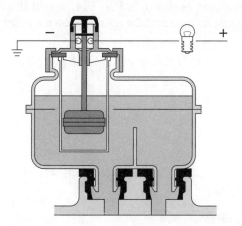

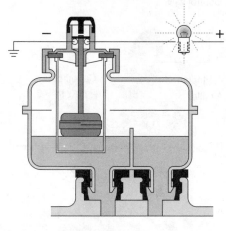

Fig. 7.11 The fluid level indicator

fluid reservoir equipped with a fluid level indicator. The fluid reservoir is normally made from translucent plastic and, provided it is kept clean, it is possible to view the fluid level by under bonnet inspection. The reservoir is fitted with an internal dividing panel and this ensures that one section remains operative should the other section develop a loss of fluid. The fluid level indicator operates a warning light. Should the fluid level drop below the required level, the switch contacts will close and the warning light on the dash panel will be illuminated.

7.8 Brake pipes and hoses

The hydraulic pressure created at the master cylinder can be conveyed to the wheel brakes in two possible ways. Strong metal pipes are used where they can be clipped firmly to the vehicle and flexible hoses where there is relative movement between the parts, e.g. axles and steered wheels and the vehicle frame.

Learning tasks

1. Change the brake fluid in the braking system and bleed the system. Ensure that the correct bleeding sequence is used according to the layout of the system.
2. Dismantle a single-acting master cylinder and check for faults similar to the wheel cylinders. Reassemble the master cylinder observing the correct procedure and check operation.
3. Dismantle a dual master cylinder, check for faults and reassemble. Make out a report sheet together with your recommendations on serviceability.

7.9 Brake servo

It is common practice to provide some means of increasing the force that the driver applies to the brake pedal. The **servo** is the device which allows the driver to apply a large braking force by the application of relatively light force from the foot. The amount of increased force that is produced by the servo is dependent on the driver's effort in pressing the brake pedal. This ensures that the braking effort is proportional to the force applied to the brake pedal.

On petrol engined vehicles, **manifold vacuum**

is used to provide the boost that the servo generates. On diesel engined vehicles there is often no appreciable manifold vacuum, owing to the way in which the engine is governed; in these cases the engine is equipped with a vacuum pump that is known as an **exhauster**. As shown in Fig. 7.12

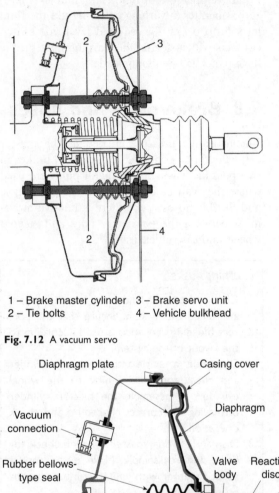

1 – Brake master cylinder   3 – Brake servo unit
2 – Tie bolts   4 – Vehicle bulkhead

Fig. 7.12 A vacuum servo

the master cylinder (1) is firmly bolted to the servo unit on one side and, on the other side, the servo unit is firmly bolted to the vehicle bulkhead (4). The brake pedal effort is applied to the servo input shaft and this in turn pushes directly on the master cylinder input piston.

Figure 7.13 shows the servo in greater detail. At this stage you should concentrate on the flexible diaphragm, the sealed container, the two chambers (A) and (B) and the vacuum connection. The valve body and the control piston are designed so that, when the brakes are off, the manifold vacuum will draw out air and create a partial vacuum in chambers (A) and (B), on both sides of the **diaphragm** (7).

When force is applied to the brake pedal, the **control piston** closes the **vacuum port** and effectively shuts off chamber (B) from chamber (A). At this stage the control piston moves away from the **control valve** and atmospheric pressure air is admitted into chamber (B). The greater pressure in chamber (B), compared with the partial vacuum in chamber (A), creates a force that adds to the pedal effort applied by the driver. The servo output rod pushes direct on to the master cylinder piston as shown in Fig. 7.14, so that there is no lost motion and the resulting force applied to

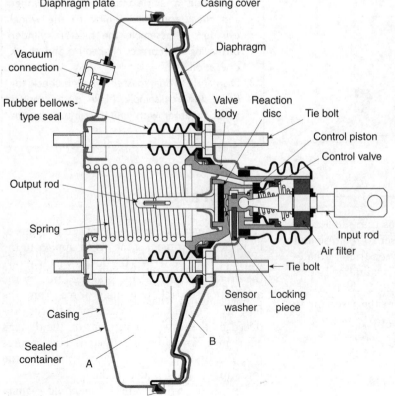

Fig. 7.13 Details of a vacuum servo

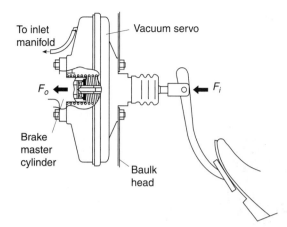

Fig. 7.14 Vacuum servo and master cylinder

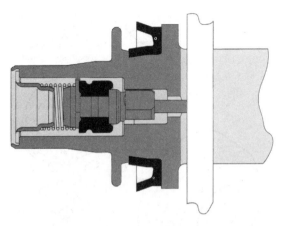

Fig. 7.15 The non-return valve in the vacuum pipe

the master cylinder is proportional to the effort that the driver applies to the brake pedal.

It is common practice to fit a non-return valve in the flexible pipe between the manifold and the servo unit as shown in Fig. 7.15. This valve serves to retain vacuum in the servo after the engine is stopped and it also prevents petrol engine vapours and 'backfire' gases from entering the servo.

Learning tasks

1. Check the servo for operation. Apply the brakes without the engine running. Start the engine; the brake pedal will move down further if the servo is operating.
2. Check the operation of the one-way valve in the pipe from the inlet manifold or exhauster.

7.10 Brake adjustment

During normal usage, the brake friction surfaces wear. In disc brakes this means that the actuating pistons push the pads closer to the disc and the light rubbing contact between friction material (pads) and the discs is maintained; disc brakes are thus **self-adjusting**. There is some displacement of brake fluid, from the reservoir to the wheel cylinders, and this will be noticed by the lowering of fluid level in the reservoir. When new brake pads are fitted there may be an excess of fluid in the system if the fluid was topped up when the brakes were in a worn condition.

When the friction linings on brake shoes wear, the gap between the lining and the inside of the brake drum increases. To compensate for this wear drum brakes are provided with **adjusters**. Adjusters take two forms:

- manual adjusters
- automatic adjusters

Manual brake adjuster

Figure 7.16 shows a type of manual brake adjuster that has been in use for many years. The threaded portion is provided with a slotted part that permits it to be rotated by means of a lever. The adjuster is accessed through a hole in the brake drum and the lever, probably a screwdriver, is applied through this hole. The two ends of the adjuster are located onto the brake shoes and screwing out the threaded portion pushes the shoes apart until the correct **lining to drum clearance** is obtained.

Automatic brake adjuster

This adjustment mechanism relies on the movement of the operating mechanism to operate a ratchet and pawl. The mechanism together with part of the two brake shoes is shown in Fig. 7.17. The ratchet is a small toothed wheel that is fixed to the adjusting bolt. The pawl is on the end of the adjusting lever and it engages with the ratchet. The connecting rod which is in two parts, (A) and (B), fits between the two brake shoes. The pawl is pulled lightly into contact with the ratchet by the spring. Operation of the brake shoes pushes the shoes apart and this creates a clearance at the end of the **connecting rod**.

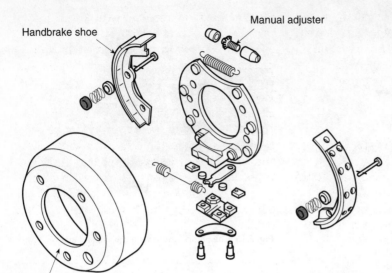

Handbrake shoe

Manual adjuster

Brake drum

Fig. 7.16 A manual brake adjuster

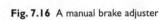

Clearance

Connecting rod B

Adjuster bolt

Adjusting layer

Connecting rod A

Fig. 7.17 An automatic brake adjuster

When there is sufficient clearance the **ratchet** will rotate by one notch. This increases the length of the connecting rod and takes up the excess clearance between the shoes and the drum.

These mechanisms work well when they are properly maintained and service schedules must be properly observed to ensure that the brakes are maintained in good order.

Learning tasks

1. Dismantle a drum brake with manual adjusters. Dismantle the adjusters, clean and regrease on reassembly. Reassemble and adjust the brake drums.
2. Dismantle a self-adjusting drum brake, clean, lubricate and reassemble.

7.11 Wear indicators

The purpose of the **friction pad wear indicator** is to alert the driver to the fact that the pads have worn thin. The warning light on the dash panel is illuminated when the pads have worn by a certain amount. Figure 7.18 shows a pair of brake pads. One of the pads is equipped with a pair of

Anti-rattle retaining spring

Brake pads

Electrical sensor connection

Fig. 7.18 Pad wear indicator light

wires whose ends are embedded in the friction material of the pad. When the pad wears down to the level of the ends of the wires, the wires are bridged electrically by the metal of the brake disc. This completes a circuit and illuminates the warning light.

7.12 Stop lamp switch

The purpose of the stop lamp switch is to alert following road users to the fact that the driver of the vehicle in front of them is applying the brakes. Figure 7.19 shows an arrangement that is frequently used to operate the brake light switch. As the foot is applied to the pedal, a spring inside the switch closes the switch contacts to switch on the brake lights.

7.13 Brake pressure-control valve

A **pressure-control valve** is fitted between the front and rear brakes to prevent the rear wheels from **locking up** before the front wheels. This arrangement contributes to safer braking in emergency stops. Figure 7.20 shows how such a valve is mounted on a vehicle. The internal details of the valve are shown in Fig. 7.21.

Under 'normal' braking fluid under pressure passes through the valve from port (B) to port (E) and the rear brakes. If the deceleration of the vehicle reaches the critical level, the ball (D) will move and seal off the fluid path to the bore of the valve (F). At this point the rear brakes are effectively 'cut off' from the front brakes and the pressure on the rear brakes is held at its original level. Further pressure on the brake pedal increases the front brake pressure without increasing the rear brake pressure. Dependent on the design of the valve, further brake pedal pressure will cause the piston (G–H) to move and increase the pressure in the rear brake line. When the deceleration falls, the ball will 'roll' back to its seat on the diffuser (C) and the pressure throughout the braking system will be stabilized.

> ### Learning task
>
> 1. Remove a pressure-limiting valve. Refit it, bleed the brakes and check for correct operation.
> 2. Dismantle a pressure-limiting valve, identify any faults, reassemble and report on serviceability.
> 3. Check the operation of a brake light switch. Complete a continuity check on a faulty switch and brake light circuit.

7.14 Brake fluid

Brake fluid must have a boiling temperature of not less than 190 °C, and a freezing temperature not higher than −40 °C. Brake fluid is **hygroscopic**, which means that it absorbs water from

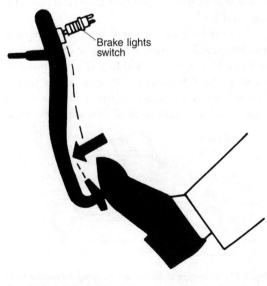

Fig. 7.19 A brake light switch

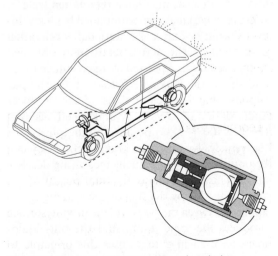

Fig. 7.20 The pressure limiting valve on the vehicle

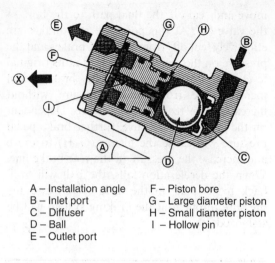

A – Installation angle   F – Piston bore
B – Inlet port   G – Large diameter piston
C – Diffuser   H – Small diameter piston
D – Ball   I – Hollow pin
E – Outlet port

Fig. 7.21 Internal detail (cross-sectional view) of inertia-type limiting brake pressure control valve – diagram simplified to show schematic flow of fluid

the atmosphere. Water in brake fluid affects its boiling and freezing temperature which is one of the reasons why brake fluid needs to be changed at the recommended intervals.

Brake fluid is normally based on vegetable oil and its composition is carefully controlled to ensure that it is compatible with the rubber seals and not corrosive to the metal parts. Some manufacturers use mineral oil as a base for brake fluid and their systems are designed to work with this fluid. It is important always to use only the type of fluid that a vehicle manufacturer recommends for use in their vehicles.

7.15 Braking efficiency

The concept of braking efficiency is based on the 'idea' that the maximum **retardation** (rate of slowing down) that can be obtained from a vehicle braking system is **gravitational acceleration** $g = 9.8 \, \text{m/s}^2$. The actual retardation obtained from a vehicle is expressed as a percentage of '*g*' and this is the *braking efficiency*. For example, suppose that a vehicle braking system produces a retardation of $7 \, \text{m/s}^2$. The braking efficiency = $(7/9.8) \times 100 = 71\%$. Because of the physics of the vehicle dynamics the braking efficiency can be obtained without actually measuring deceleration. This is so because the total weight of the vehicle divided by the sum of the braking forces applied between the tyres and the driving surface produces the same result. Brake testing equipment as used in garages uses this principle to measure braking efficiency.

In Fig. 7.22 the left (F1) and right (F2) front braking forces are measured and recorded. The vehicle is moved forward so the that the rear wheels are on the rollers. The test procedure is repeated and the two rear wheel braking forces (F3) and (F4) are recorded. The four forces are added together and divided by the weight of the vehicle. For example, in a certain brake test on a vehicle weighing 1500 kg the four braking forces add up to 1050 kg. This gives a braking efficiency of $(1050/1500) \times 100 = 70\%$. Often the data relating to a particular vehicle is contained on a chart which is kept near the test bay.

The regulations about braking efficiency and the permitted differences in braking, from side to side of the vehicle, together with other data are contained in the tester's manual. Any technician carrying out brake tests must familiarize themselves with the current regulations.

> *Learning task*
>
> Complete a brake test on a vehicle with both disc and drum brakes. Complete a report sheet on the results.

7.16 Anti-lock braking system (ABS)

The term **ABS** covers a range of electronically controlled systems that are designed to provide optimum braking in difficult conditions. These systems are used on many cars, commercial vehicles and trailers.

The purpose of anti-skid braking systems is to provide safer vehicle handling in difficult conditions. If wheels are skidding it is not possible to steer the vehicle correctly and a tyre that is still rolling, not sliding, on the surface will provide a better braking performance. ABS does

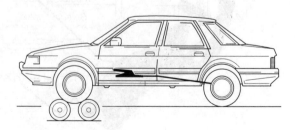

Fig. 7.22 Roller-type brake tester measuring the braking force at each wheel

not normally operate under normal braking. It comes into play in poor road surface conditions, ice, snow, water etc., or during emergency stops. Figure 7.23 shows a simplified diagram of an ABS which gives an insight into the way that such systems operate. The master cylinder (1) is operated via the brake pedal. During normal braking manually developed hydraulic pressure operates the brakes and, should an ABS defect develop, the system reverts to normal pedal operated braking. The solenoid operated shuttle valve (2) contains two valves, A and B. When the **wheel sensor** (5) signals the ABS computer (ECU) (7) that driving conditions require ABS control, a procedure is initiated which energizes the **shuttle valve solenoid**. The valve (A) blocks off the fluid inlet from the master cylinder and the valve (B) opens to release brake line pressure at the wheel cylinder (6) into the reservoir (3) and the pump (4) where it is returned to the master cylinder.

In this simplified diagram the shuttle valve is enlarged in relation to the other components. In practice, the movement of the shuttle valve is small and movements of the valve occur in fractions of a second.

In practical systems the solenoids, pump and valves, etc. are incorporated into a single unit as shown in Fig 7.24. This unit is known as a **modulator**.

This brief overview shows that an anti-lock braking system has: sensors, an **actuator**, an ECU and **interconnecting circuits**. In order that the whole system functions correctly each of the separate elements needs to be working correctly.

In order to decide whether or not a vehicle wheel is skidding, or on the point of doing so, it is necessary to compare the rotational movement of the wheel and brake disc, or drum, with some part such as the brake back plate which is fixed to the vehicle. This task is performed by the wheel speed sensing system and the procedure for doing this is reasonably similar in all ABS systems, so the wheel speed sensor is a good point at which to delve a little deeper into the operating principles of ABS.

Wheel speed sensor

Figure 7.25 shows a typical wheel sensor and reluctor ring installation. The sensor contains a **coil** and a **permanent magnet**. The **reluctor ring** has teeth and when the ring rotates past the sensor pick-up the lines of magnetic force in the sensor coil vary. This variation of magnetic force causes a varying voltage (**emf**) to be induced in the coil and it is this varying voltage that is used as the basic signal for the wheel sensor. The particular application is for a Toyota but its principle of operation is typical of most ABS wheel speed sensors (see Fig. 7.26).

The raw output voltage waveform from the sensor is approximately of the form shown in Fig. 7.27. It will be seen that the voltage and frequency increase as the wheel speed, relative to the brake back plate, increases. This property means that the sensor output is a good representation of the wheel behaviour relative to the back plate and is thus able to provide a signal that indicates whether or not the wheel is about to skid. In most cases this raw curved waveform is not used directly in the controlling process and it has first to be shaped to a rectangular waveform and tidied up before being encoded for control purposes.

If the brake is applied and the **reluctor** (rotor) starts to decelerate rapidly, relative to the sensor pick-up, it is an indication that the wheel rotation is slowing down. If the road surface is dry and the tyre is gripping well the retardation of the wheel will match that of the vehicle and normal braking will occur.

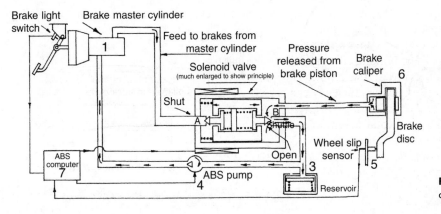
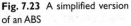

Fig. 7.23 A simplified version of an ABS

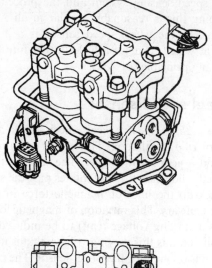

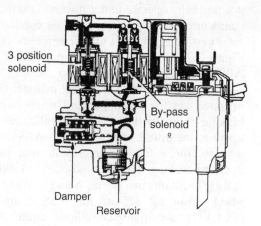

3 position
solenoid

By-pass
solenoid

Damper

Reservoir

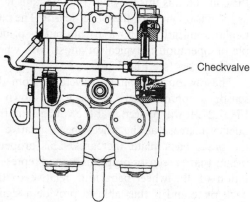

Checkvalve

Fig. 7.24 ABS modulator

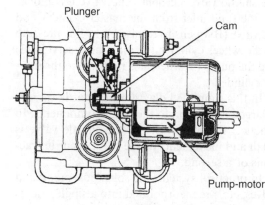

Plunger

Cam

Pump-motor

However, if the road surface is slippery a sudden braking application will cause the reluctor and road wheel to decelerate at a greater rate than the vehicle, indicating that a skid is about to happen. This condition is interpreted by the ECU. Comparisons are made with the signals from the other wheel sensors and the **brake line**

pressure will be released, automatically, for sufficient time (a fraction of a second) to prevent the wheel from locking.

In hydraulic brakes on cars the pressure release and re-application is achieved by solenoid valves, a pump and a **hydraulic accumulator** and these are normally incorporated into one unit called the modulator. The frequency of 'pulsing' of the brakes is a few times per second, depending on conditions, and the pressure

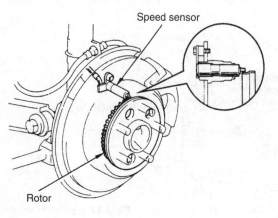

Speed sensor

Rotor

Fig. 7.25 ABS wheel sensor

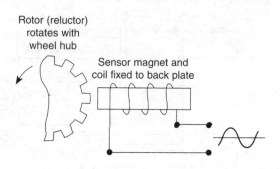

Rotor (reluctor)
rotates with
wheel hub

Sensor magnet and
coil fixed to back plate

Fig. 7.26 The basic principle of the ABS sensor

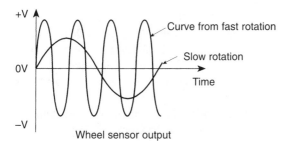

Fig. 7.27 The voltage waveform of the ABS sensor output

pulsations can normally be felt at the brake pedal.

With air brakes on heavy vehicles, the principle is much the same except that the pressure is derived from the air braking system and the actuator is called a modulator. The valves that release the brakes during anti-lock operation are solenoid operated on the basis of ECU signals and the wheel sensors operate on the same principle as those on cars.

As for the strategy that is deployed to determine when to initiate ABS operation there appears to be some debate. Some systems operate what is known as **select low**, which means that brake release is initiated by the signal from the wheel with the least grip, irrespective of what the grip is at other wheels. An alternative strategy is to use individual wheel control. Whichever strategy is deployed, the aim is to provide better vehicle control in difficult driving conditions and it may be that the stopping distance is greater than it would be with expert manual braking.

Learning tasks

1. Using the appropriate equipment check the output from a wheel speed sensor. Adjust the air gap and recheck the output.
2. Draw up a maintenance check sheet for the ABS. Using your check sheet complete a service check and draw up your recommendations for the customer.

ABS warning light

ABS systems are equipped with a warning light. This lamp is illuminated when the system is not operating. When the vehicle is first started the ABS warning light is illuminated and the system runs through a self check procedure. As the

vehicle moves away the ABS warning lamp will remain on until a speed of 3 mph (5 km/h) is reached. If the ABS is functioning properly the warning lamp will not come on again until the vehicle stops. The system is constantly monitoring itself when the vehicle is in motion. Should a fault occur, the warning light will again come on. Should this happen, the system reverts to normal braking operation and the vehicle should receive urgent attention to ascertain the cause of the problem.

7.17 Bleeding the brakes

During repair work such as replacing hoses and wheel cylinders, air will probably enter the hydraulic system. This air must be removed before the vehicle is returned to use and the process of removing the air is called 'bleeding the brakes'.

Practical assignment – braking systems

With the aid of sketches, describe the equipment and procedures for bleeding brakes on the types of vehicle that you work on.

Braking system check

This check should be completed in a logical manner and in the correct sequence. Make up a tick sheet to indicate pass/fail for each item.

Inside the vehicle

1. *Check the operation of the brake pedal*

   (a) brake pedal travel
   (b) pedal feel, e.g. soft or spongy
   (c) pedal security
   (d) operation of brake light switch
   (e) security of switch and cables

2. *Check the operation of the handbrake*

   (a) distance travelled when applied (no more than three to five clicks)
   (b) handbrake resistance (does it feel right?)
   (c) security of handbrake lever
   (d) operation of ratchet and release button
   (e) operation of warning lamp switch
   (f) security of switch and cables

Under the bonnet

3. *Master cylinder*

   (a) check the fluid level in the reservoir
   (b) check operation of fluid level warning device
   (c) inspect for security of mounting bolts, brackets etc.
   (d) check operation of the servo unit
   (e) look for evidence of hydraulic fluid leaks

4. *Pipes and hoses*

   (a) inspect brake pipes for signs of corrosion,
   (b) check security of pipes (are the retaining clips in position?)
   (c) look for evidence of leaks and check the security of connections and unions
   (d) test flexible hoses for signs of aging and damage
   (e) check the condition of the servo vacuum hose

5. *Front brakes*

   (a) check operation of calipers/brakes
   (b) measure thickness of brake pads
   (c) measure thickness of brake discs and check the condition of the disc surfaces
   (d) check for movement of caliper on the slide (where fitted)
   (e) check for splits and cracks in flexible hoses
   (f) check for corrosion and damage in metal pipes and check the unions for security and tightness
   (g) check the security and operation of the pad wear indicator light and cables
   (h) check security and condition of anti-rattle devices
   (i) check for evidence of leaks
   (j) check for movement and excessive free play in wheel bearings

6. *Rear brakes*

   (a) check condition of brake drums and look for evidence of scoring (ensure that dust removal is done with a vacuum cleaner whilst wearing a mask)
   (b) measure thickness of brake shoe linings
   (c) check operation of wheel cylinders (will require an assistant)
   (d) check to see that all parts are in place and that brakes are correctly assembled
   (e) check for fluid leaks
   (f) check security and condition of brake pipes and unions

Under the car

1. Check the security of pipes and flexible hoses. Check that all retaining clips are properly fitted.
2. Look for any evidence of fluid leaks.
3. Check the operation of handbrake cables, compensator, etc.
4. Check lubrication of cables and clevis pins.
5. Check security of handbrake linkages.

Checklist

Vehicle

Remove and refit
Brake shoes
Brake pads
Wheel cylinder
Caliper
Hand brake mechanism
Single-acting master cylinder
Dual-acting master cylinder
Servo cylinder

Bleeding brake system
Basic system
Diagonal split
Front/rear split
Front and one rear split
Changing brake fluid

Dismantle and reassemble
Wheel cylinder
Caliper
Hand brake
Single-acting master cylinder
Dual-acting master cylinder
Servo cylinder
Manual brake adjuster
Automatic brake adjuster
Non-return valve
Pressure limiting valve

Brake testing
Basic braking system
Split braking system
ABS

Student's signature

Supervisor's signature

8

Steering, wheels and tyres

The steering mechanism has two main purposes. It must enable the driver to: easily maintain the straight ahead direction of the vehicle even when bumps are encountered at high speeds; and to change the direction of the vehicle with the minimum amount of effort at the steering wheel. One of the simplest layouts is the **beam axle** arrangement (Fig. 8.1) as used on large commercial vehicles. This is where the hub pivots or swivels on a king pin (in the case of a car a top and bottom ball-joint) to give the steering action.

As can be seen the two stub axles are connected together by two steering arms and a track rod with ball-joints at each end. The **steering gearbox** converts the rotary movement of the steering wheel into a straight line movement of the steering linkage; it also makes it easier for the driver to steer by giving a **gear reduction**. The drop arm and drag link connect the steering gear box to the stub axle. The steering arms, track rod and ball joints connect the stub axles together and allow the movement to be transferred from one side of the vehicle to the other as well as providing for the movement of the linkage as the suspension operates.

8.1 Light vehicle steering layouts

To provide means of turning the front wheels of a vehicle left or right would not be too difficult were it not also necessary to make provision for their movement up and down with the suspension. Most modern cars now have a fully independent front suspension. This creates serious problems when one wheel moves upwards or downwards independent of the opposite wheel. If a single track rod were used the tracking would alter every time the wheels moved causing the vehicle to wander from the straight ahead position. This problem has been overcome by the use of two or three part track rods. As can be seen from Fig. 8.2 on a vehicle fitted with a rack and pinion type steering the centre track rod has been replaced by the rack.

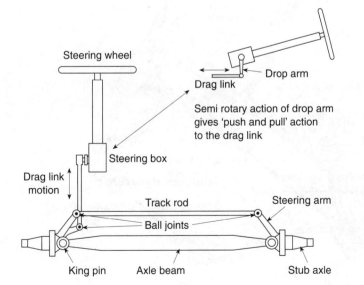

Fig. 8.1 Layout for beam axle steering system

Learning tasks

1. Inspect several different types of vehicles and make a simple line diagram of the layout of the steering system identifying the following components: steering wheel and column, gearbox, linkage and ball-joints, stub axles and swivel joints.

2. Identify how the tracking is adjusted, check the manufacturer's setting for the tracking and state the tolerance given (the difference between the upper and lower readings). What equipment is used to check the measurements and how should it be set up on the vehicle?

3. When undertaking an MOT the steering system should be checked. Look in the MOT tester's manual and list the areas that are subject to testing. What in particular is the tester looking for? Your list should include the following areas:

(a) inside the vehicle

- security of steering column mountings
- play in upper steering column bush
- amount of rotary movement in steering wheel before movement of the steered wheels
- amount of lift in steering column
- security of steering wheel to column
- any undue noise or stiffness when operating the steering from lock to lock

(b) under the vehicle

- security of steering box to chassis
- signs of rust in the chassis around steering box mounting
- excessive wear in steering column universal joints (these may be fitted inside the vehicle)
- excessive play in steering box
- amount of play in inner and outer track rod ends
- splits or holes in rubber boots (steering rack arrangement)
- loss of oil from steering box
- play in suspension mountings and pivots that may affect the operation of the steering
- signs of uneven tread pattern wear that may indicate a fault in the steering mechanism

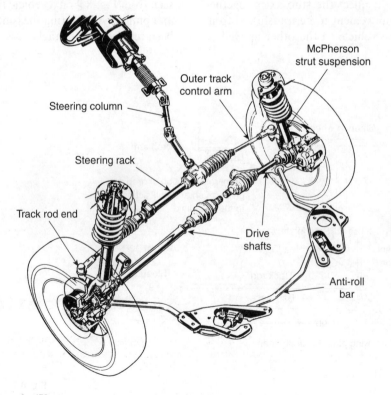

Fig. 8.2 Steering layout for IFS system

8.2 Steering geometry

The subject of steering geometry is a very complex one in its own right and because of this many manufacturers import the knowledge and skills of specialists. However, the basic principles are relatively simple to understand and apply to most vehicles. The development of the steering and suspension (to which it is very closely linked) is based on past experience; much of the work has been through an evolutionary process learning from mistakes and modifying systems to suit varying applications. Many of the terms used are applied only to the steering and have no alternative; hopefully most of these are explained in the text.

The geometry of steering may best be understood by looking at Fig. 8.3. A swinging beam mounted on a turntable frame turns the wheels. This keeps all the wheels at right angles to the centre of the turn which reduces tyre wear especially when turning a corner.

Rudolph Ackermann took out a patent in 1818 in England which is now widely used and is known as the **Ackermann layout**. The angles of the front wheels about the turning point depend upon the wheel base (W) and the width of the track (T). In 1878 Jeantaud showed that the layout should conform to Fig. 8.4. In this arrangement the inner wheel (A) turns through a larger angle than the outer wheel (B) to give true rolling motion. The Ackermann layout does not fully achieve these conditions in all wheel positions; normally it is only accurate when the wheels are straight ahead and in one position on each left and right turn wheel setting. This sys-

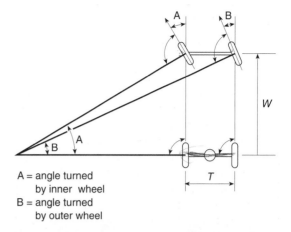

A = angle turned
   by inner wheel
B = angle turned
   by outer wheel

Fig. 8.4 Differing angles of front wheels about centre of turn

tem gives as near true rolling motion as possible together with simplicity.

8.3 Ackermann principle

The Ackermann layout is obtained by arranging for the stub axles to swivel on king pins or ball-joints to give the steering action of the wheels. The track rod ball-joints are positioned on an imaginary line drawn between the king pins and the centre line of the vehicle. When the track rod is positioned behind the swivel pins it is made shorter and has the protection of the axle, but the rod must be made stronger as it is in compression when the vehicle is being driven. This is shown in Fig. 8.5(a). When it is positioned in front of the swivel pins (Fig. 8.5(b)), it is made longer and can be out of the way of the engine and is made thinner as it is in tension when the vehicle is being driven.

Figure 8.6 shows the arrangements for an independent front suspension where the top and bottom ball-joints are placed in a line which forms the king pin inclination and also allows for the movement of the steered wheels both up and down over the irregularities of the road surface and as the driver turns the wheels to negotiate corners.

8.4 Centre-point steering

The stub axle arrangement shown in Fig. 8.7 has certain disadvantages due to the **off-set** (x). These are:

- there is a large force generated, due to the resistance at the wheel (R) from the road

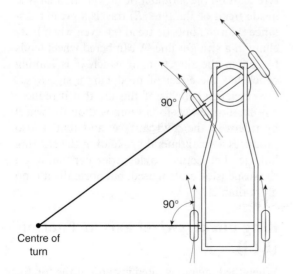

Fig. 8.3 Swing beam steering

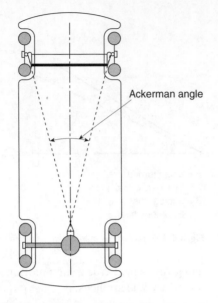

Fig. 8.5(a) Track rod behind swivel pins still conform to Ackerman principle

Fig. 8.5(b) Track rod in front of swivel pins still conform to Ackerman principle

surface trying to turn the steering about the swivel pin (F) especially when the brakes are applied;

- the forces generated produce large bending stresses in the stub axle and steering linkages;
- heavy steering as the steered wheel has to rotate around the king pin. When this off-set is eliminated and the centre line of the wheel and the centre line of the king pin coincide at

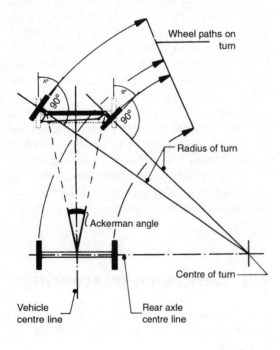

Fig. 8.6 Operation of Ackerman principle right hand wheel turns more than left hand wheel

the road surface then **centre-point steering** is produced. This condition is achieved by the use of **camber**, swivel axis inclination (often referred to as **king pin inclination** or KPI for short) and **dishing** of the wheel.

Camber

Camber (Fig. 8.8) is the amount the wheel slopes in or out at the top relative to the imaginary vertical line when viewed from the front of the vehicle. This reduces the **bending** and **'splaying out' stresses** on the stub axle and steering linkages. The amount of camber angle is usually quite small as large angles will produce rapid tyre wear on the shoulder of the tyre tread as the inside tread of the tyre (*R*) travels a greater distance than the outside tread (*r*), even when travelling in a straight line. A cambered wheel tends to roll in the direction in which it is leaning which has the effect of producing a side force. Two beneficial effects of this are that it reduces any small sideways forces imposed on the wheel by ridges in the road surface, and that it also produces a small lateral pre-load in the steering linkage. The actual angle varies depending on the suspension system used, but normally it is no more than 2°.

King pin or swivel axis inclination (KPI)

When the king pin is tilted inwards at the top the resulting angle between the vertical line and the

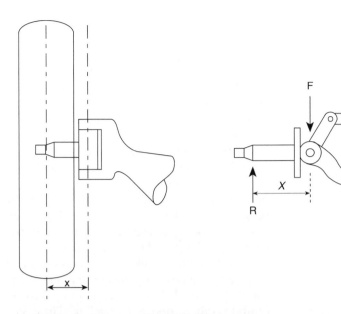

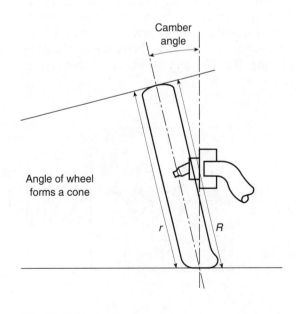

Fig. 8.7 Diagram shows the forces acting on the steering without centre point

king pin centre line is called the king pin inclination (Fig. 8.9). Normally this will be between 5° and 15° to produce **positive off-set** and to accommodate the brake, wheel bearings and drive shaft joint. When the king pin is set outwards at the bottom then **negative off-set** is produced.

As the wheel is steered through an angle it will pivot around the king pin. This will have the effect of lifting the front of the vehicle helping to give a self-centring action to the steering.

8.5 Steering roll radius

If the steering wheel is turned, the front wheels move along an arc around (a) in Fig. 8.10; this is where the extension of the king pin centre line meets the ground. The point (b) is where the tyre centre line meets the ground; radius (a–b) is the steering roll radius.

Whether the steering roll radius is positive or negative depends on the position of the KPI. It is positive if the extension of the KPI axis meets the ground on the inside of the **tyre contact centre**. It is negative if the extension of the KPI meets the ground outside the tyre contact centre. The advantage of having **negative steering roll radius** is increased directional stability in the case of uneven braking forces on the front wheels, or if a tyre is suddenly deflated.

As can be seen in Fig. 8.11 if the brake force on the right hand front wheel is greater, then the vehicle tends to slide in an arc around that wheel, which means that the rear of the vehicle veers out to the left. In a vehicle with negative steering roll radius, the force of the car in

motion will turn the wheel with the stronger braking force around the lower arm formed by the steering roll radius.

8.6 Castor

The action of the castor may best be understood by looking at the castor wheel on a shopping trolley. When the trolley is pushed forwards the castor wheels always follow behind the **pivot points** where they are attached to the trolley. The same action applies to the front wheels of the motor vehicle. When the pivot point is in front of the

Fig. 8.8 Camber angle

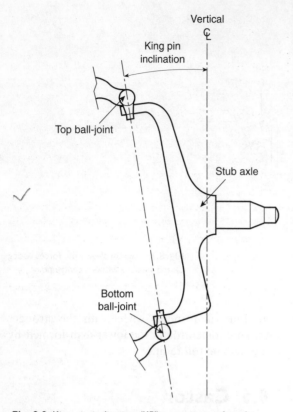

Fig. 8.9 King pin inclination (KPI) sometimes referred to as swivel axis

steered wheel the wheel will always follow behind. This is called **positive castor** and is used on rear wheel drive vehicles; most front wheel drive and four wheel drive vehicles have **negative castor**.

This angle viewed from the side of the vehicle gives some 'driver feel' to the steering. It enables the steering to **self-centre** and a force must be exerted on the steering wheel to overcome the castor action of the steered wheels. It is produced by tilting the king pin forwards at the bottom

approximately 2° to 5° so that when the line of the swivel axis of the king pin is extended it lies in front of the tyre contact point on the road surface; too much castor gives heavy steering and too little causes the vehicle to 'wander'. Castor angle steering geometry is shown in Fig. 8.12.

Tolerances may vary for all the steering angles so it is important to make reference to the manufacturer's specification as even small variations from this can lead to rapid tyre wear and poor handling characteristics. The checking of camber, king pin inclination and castor is done by using a set of gauges such as the Dunlop castor, camber and king pin inclination gauges together with a set of turn tables. The vehicle is driven onto the turn tables and the camber is measured by placing the camber gauge on the side of the wheel. The bubble in the level is adjusted to the central position to give the reading. The castor and KPI gauges are attached to the wheel and set approximately horizontal and the turn tables are adjusted to zero. Steer the wheel to be checked 20° in (i.e. the right hand wheel steered to the left and the left hand wheel steered to the right). Set castor and KPI dials to zero at the pointer and centre the bubbles in the spirit levels by turning the lower knurled screws. Steer the wheel to be checked 20° out and centre the bubbles in the spirit levels by turning the castor and KPI dials and take the readings off the dials.

8.7 Wheel alignment

Adjusting the track

Often referred to as **toe-in/toe-out** or **tracking**, wheel alignment is a plan view of the wheels and means 'are the wheels correctly aligned with

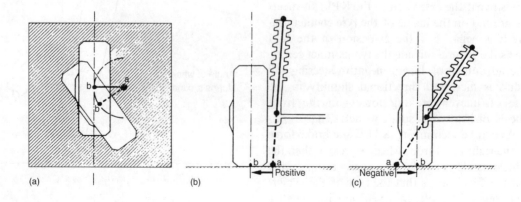

Fig. 8.10 Steering roll radius (a) no steering roll radius, (b) positive roll radius, (c) negative roll radius

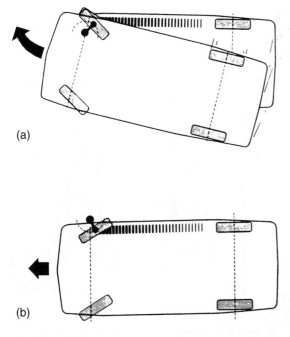

(a)

(b)

Fig. 8.11 (a) With positive steering roll and uneven braking on one front wheel, (b) with negative roll radius extra braking effort equals direction of steered wheels giving greater stability

each other?' When the vehicle is travelling in a straight line all the wheels must be parallel, especially the steered wheels.

Arrangement for changing or adjusting the track is made in the track rod or outer track control arms and, when correctly aligned for toe-in, the distance across the front of the steered wheels measures less than the distance across the rear. These measurements are taken using very accurate measuring gauges of which several types are available (e.g. the **Dunlop optical alignment gauge** (Fig. 8.13)). The gauges are set to zero and are positioned on the wheels. The alignment is adjusted to give a reading on the scale, which is then checked against the manufacturer's specifications.

A more accurate method would be to use four **wheel alignment gauges**. This would give the mechanic more precise information as to which wheel needs adjusting, whether the front axle lines up with the rear axle and if the vehicle suspension has been misaligned in an accident.

Toe-out on turns

When turning a corner, the inner wheel turns through a greater angle than the outer wheel. This difference in angles is called 'toe-out on turns' (Fig. 8.14). To check these angles the wheels are placed on turn tables and the outer wheel is turned on its axis through 20°. The inner wheel should now read a larger angle (typically approximately 22°). This is because it is rolling around a smaller radius.

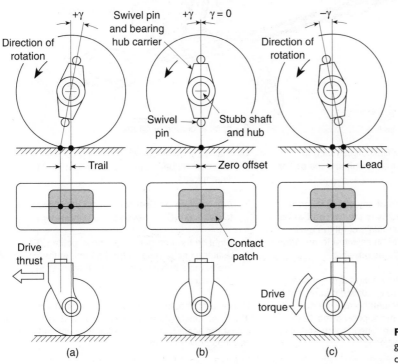

Fig. 8.12 Castor angle steering geometry (a) positive castor, (b) zero castor, (c) negative castor

Fig. 8.13 (a) Toe in. (b) Dunlop AGO/40 optical alignment gauge

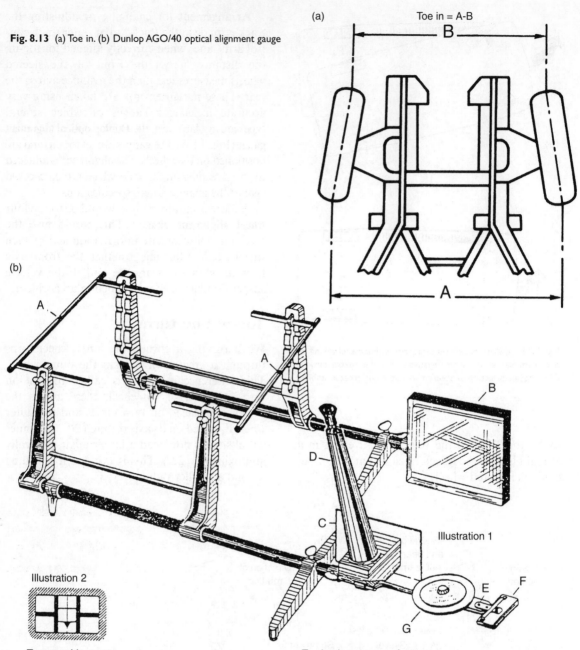

(a)

Toe in = A-B

To assemble gauge

Assemble gauge as shown in illustration 1 with the periscope (D) fixed on the left hand unit and the mirror (B) on the right hand unit.

The contact bars may be fitted at any of five different height positions to suit the radius of the tyre and wheel assembly being checked. The height of all the bars must be the same and should be selected to bring the bars as near hub centre height as possible.

Each bar may be fitted into the support arms in either of two directions providing a range of width sufficient to cover all tyres on 9" to 24" diameter rims. The contact bars may be both inboard of the support arms, both outboard of the support arms, or one inboard and one outboard according to need.

To check accuracy of gauge

1. Stand the complete gauge on a level, clean floor with contact bars touching as shown in (A) illustration 1.

2. Adjust mirror and periscope until the reflection of target plate (C) is visible through periscope.

3. Sighting through periscope move pointer (E) until the image reflects the hair-line in the centre of the triangle between the vertical lines as in illustration 2.

The pointer should now be at zero on graduated scale (F). If not, slacken the two wing nuts holding the scale, adjust the scale to zero and retighten wing nuts, The gauge is now ready for use.

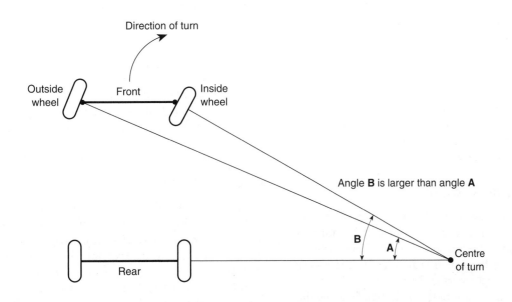

Fig. 8.14 Toe-out angle on turns. Inner wheel turns through a greater angle

Learning tasks

1. Draw a simple diagram of the steering layout to conform to the Ackermann principle. Show the position of the front and rear wheels, point of turn, approximate angles of the front wheels and the position of the track rod. Indicate on your diagram where adjustments may be made

2. Make a list of reasons why the steering mechanism would require adjusting.

3. Draw up a workshop schedule that you could use when checking a steering system for signs of wear and serviceability.

4. What important safety factors would you consider when working under a vehicle on the steering system.

5. Name two steering faults that would cause uneven tyre wear. How would these faults be put right?

6. If a customer came into the workshop complaining that his vehicle was 'pulling to one side' when being driven in a straight line, what would you suspect the fault to be? Describe the tests you would undertake to confirm your diagnosis.

7. Check the tracking on a vehicle using both optical and four wheel alignment gauges. Adjust the steering to the middle of the limits set by the manufacturer.

8.8 Steering gearboxes

The steering gearbox is incorporated into the steering mechanism for two main reasons:

- to change the rotary movement of the steering wheel into the straight line movement of the **drag link**;
- to provide a gear reduction and therefore a torque increase, thus reducing the effort required by the driver at the steering wheel.

Quite a number of different types of steering gearboxes have been used over the years, the most common ones being:

- worm and roller
- cam and peg
- recirculating ball (half nut)
- rack and pinion

The gearbox should have a degree of reversibility to provide some driver 'feel' and at the same time keep the transmission of road shocks through to the steering wheel to a minimum. The arrangement should be positive, i.e. it should have a minimum amount of backlash. Most steering gearboxes are designed with the following adjustments:

- end float of the steering column, usually by shims;
- end float of the rocker shaft, either by shims or adjusting screw and lock nut;

- backlash between the gears – these can be moved closer together, again by the use of shims or adjusting screw and lock nut.

It is essential to keep the 'backlash' to a minimum to provide a positive operation of the steering mechanism and to give directional stability to the path of the vehicle. The components inside the gearbox are lubricated by gear oil and the level plug serves as the topping up and level position for the oil.

Worm and roller

In this arrangement, shown in Fig. 8.15, the **worm** (in the shape of an hour glass) is formed on the inner steering column. Meshing with the worm is a **roller** which is attached to the **rocker shaft**. As the steering is operated the roller rotates in an arc about the rocker shaft giving the minimum amount of backlash together with a large gear reduction. This means that for a large number of turns on the steering wheel there is a very small number of turns on the rocker shaft, with very little free play. Because of the specialized machining geometry and shape, the hour glass worm is really in the form of a cam rather than a gear. This is why the arrangement is sometimes known as a cam-and-roller steering gearbox. It will mainly be found on LGVs as it provides a large gear reduction and can transmit heavy loads.

Cam and peg

In the cam and peg steering box a **tapered** peg is used in place of the roller. This engages with a special **cam** formed on the end of the inner steering column. The peg may be made to rotate on needle roller bearings in the rocker arm to reduce friction as the steering column is rotated and the peg moves up and down the cam.

Recirculating ball

In this arrangement the worm is in the form of a thread machined on the inner steering column. A nut with **steel ball bearings** acting as the thread operates inside the nut; as the worm rotates the balls reduce the friction to a minimum. In many cases a half nut is used and a transfer tube returns the balls back to the other side of the nut. A peg on the nut locates in the rocker arm which transfers a rocking motion to the rocker shaft. In Fig. 8.16 a sector gear is used to transfer the movement to the rocker shaft.

Rack and pinion

This type, shown in Fig. 8.17, is now probably the most common type in use on cars and light vehicles. It has a rack which takes the place of the middle track rod and outer track rods

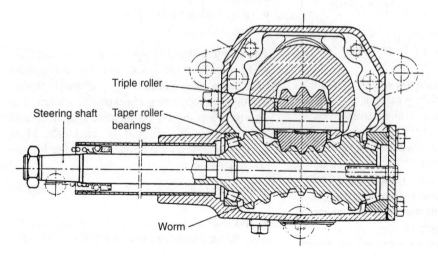

Triple roller

Steering shaft

Taper roller bearings

Worm

Fig. 8.15 Worm and roller steering gearbox

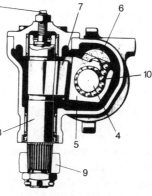

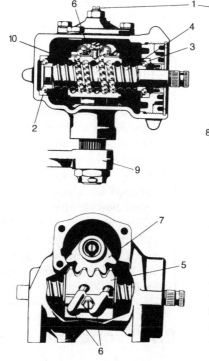

1. Sector shaft alignment
   adjustment screw
2. Worm-shaft ball race
3. Worm-shaft support ball
   race bearing
4. Worm shaft
5. Rack nut
6. Return ball cage
7. Sector gear
8. Sector shaft
9. Drop-arm
10. Recirculating balls

Fig. 8.16 Recirculating ball rack and sector steering box

(sometimes called tie rods) which connect to the steering arms at the hub. The pinion is mounted to the steering column by a universal joint as often the steering column is not in line with the input to the steering rack. This gives ease of mounting and operation of the gearbox. On each end of the rack is a ball joint to which the track rod is mounted; these are spring loaded to allow for movement together with the minimum of play in the joint. The system is arranged so that in the event of an accident the column, because it is out of alignment (not a solid straight shaft) will tend to bend at the joints. This helps to prevent the steering wheel from hitting the driver's chest and causing serious injury. A spring loaded rubbing pad (called a slipper, Fig. 8.18) presses on the underside of the rack to reduce backlash to a minimum and also to act as a damper absorbing road shocks that are passed back through the steering mechanism from the road surface.

Adjustment of the steering rack

The inner ball-joints of the outer track rod are adjusted to give the correct pre-load and the locking ring of the ball-joint housing is tightened. In some cases it is locked to the rack by

locking pins which must be drilled out to dismantle the joint as shown in Fig. 8.19.

Shims are used to adjust the slipper/rubbing block to give the correct torque on rotating the

Fig. 8.17 The complete layout of a rack and pinion steering system showing the steering column, with universal joints (UJs)

pinion (Fig. 8.20). Shims are also used to adjust the bearings on the pinion. It is important that the correct data is obtained and used as these may vary from model to model.

Ball-joints

There are a number of requirements that must be fulfilled by steering ball-joints. These are:

- they must be free from excess movement (backlash) to give accurate control of the steering over the service life of the vehicle;
- they must be able to accommodate the angular movement of the suspension and the rotational movement of the steering levers;
- they must have some degree of damping on the steering to give better control of the wobble of the wheels especially at low speeds;
- where possible eliminate the need for lubrication at regular intervals – this is achieved through the use of good bearing materials and sealing the bearing with a good quality grease at manufacture.

Ball-joints that are used on modern cars do not need lubricating as they are sealed for life, although on some medium to heavy vehicles they may require greasing at regular service intervals. Track rod and ball-joint assemblies are shown in Fig. 8.21.

Learning tasks

1. What is the difference between angular movement and rotational movement? Which component in the steering mechanism uses angular movement and which uses rotational movement?
2. Using workshop manuals identify the method for adjusting the types of steering gearboxes identified in this chapter.
3. Dismantle each of the different types of steering gearboxes. Fill in a job sheet for each type. Note any faults or defects and make recommendations for their serviceability.

8.9 Front hub assemblies

Non-driving hubs

Figure 8.22 shows one type of front hub assembly used on a front engine rear wheel drive vehi-

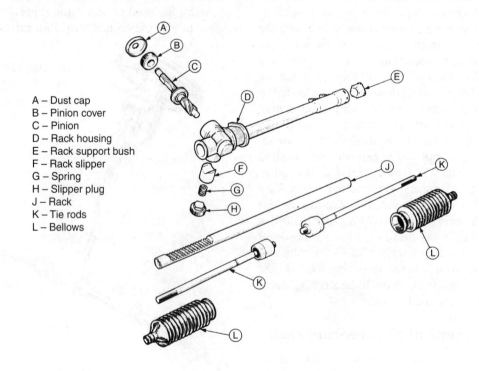

A – Dust cap
B – Pinion cover
C – Pinion
D – Rack housing
E – Rack support bush
F – Rack slipper
G – Spring
H – Slipper plug
J – Rack
K – Tie rods
L – Bellows

Fig. 8.18 Exploded view of steering gear

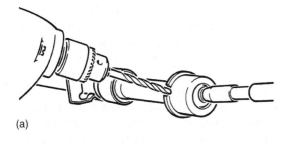

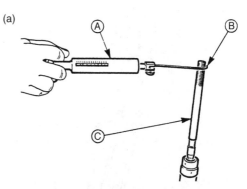

A – Piston pull side or spring balance
B – Wire hook 6mm (0.25") from end of tie rod
C – Tie rod

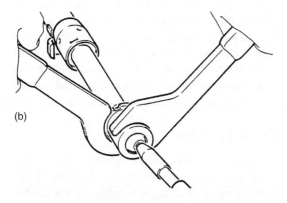

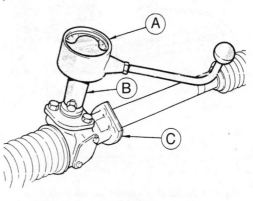

Fig. 8.19 (a) Drilling out tie rod inner ball-joint housing locking pins, (b) unscrewing tie rod inner ball-joint housings

A – Torque gauge, tool number 15-041
B – Adaptor, tool number 13-008
C – Steering gear

Fig. 8.20 (a) Checking tie rod articulation, (b) checking pinion turning torque

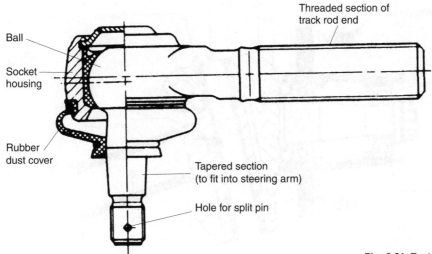

Ball

Socket housing

Rubber dust cover

Threaded section of track rod end

Tapered section (to fit into steering arm)

Hole for split pin

Fig. 8.21 Track rod end ball-joint assembly

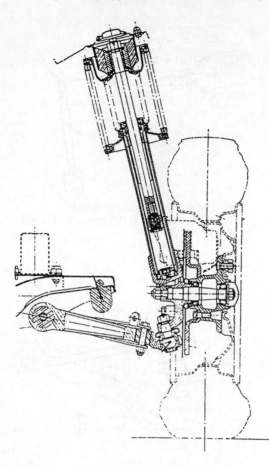

Fig. 8.22 Layout of non-driving hub assembly

cle. As can be seen the hub rotates on a pair of bearings that are either taper roller or angular-

contact ball bearings. The inner bearing is usually slightly bigger in diameter than the outer, as this carries a larger part of the load. Various methods of adjustment are used depending on the type of bearing and the load to be carried. Some manufacturers specify a torque setting for the hub nut (usually where a spacer or shims are positioned between the bearings); others provide a castellated nut that has to be tightened to a specified torque and then released before the split pin is located. The hubs are lubricated with a grease that has a high melting point; this is because the heat from the brakes can be transferred to the hub, melt the grease and cause it to leak out onto the brakes. A synthetic lip-type seal is fitted on the inside of the hub to prevent the grease escaping. It also prevents water, dust and dirt from entering into the bearing. The arrangement in Fig. 8.23 is used mainly on larger vehicles where a beam axle is fitted instead of independent suspension.

Driving hubs

Figure 8.24 shows one arrangement of hub and drive shaft location using thrust-type ball bearings, in this case a single bearing with a double row of ball bearings. When the nut is tensioned/tightened to the correct torque it also adjusts the bearing to the correct clearance.

On a front wheel drive vehicle the drive shaft passes through the hub to engage with the flange that drives the wheel. In this way the hub

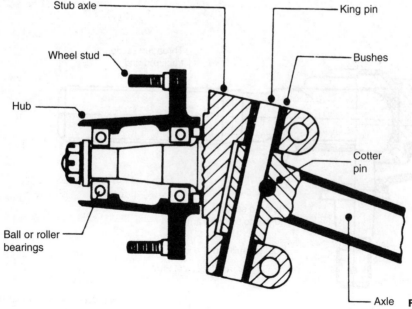

Fig. 8.23 Axle-beam and stub-axle assembly

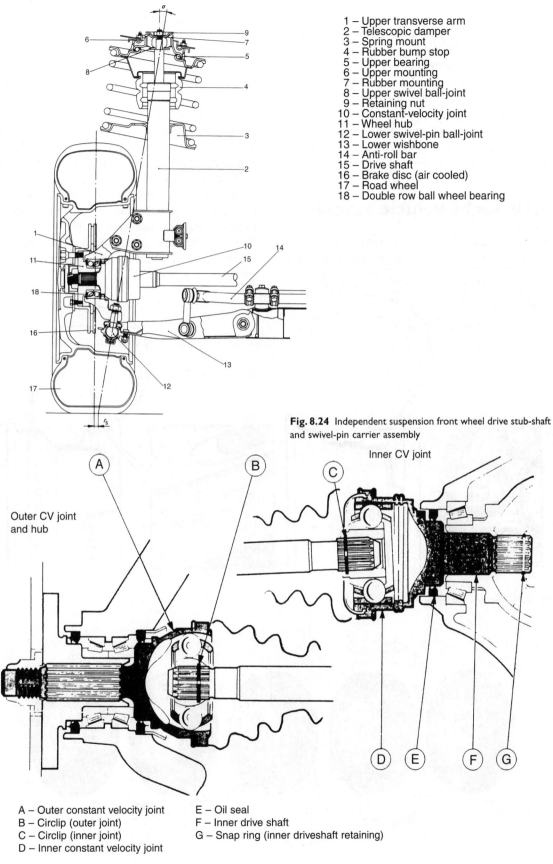

1 – Upper transverse arm
2 – Telescopic damper
3 – Spring mount
4 – Rubber bump stop
5 – Upper bearing
6 – Upper mounting
7 – Rubber mounting
8 – Upper swivel ball-joint
9 – Retaining nut
10 – Constant-velocity joint
11 – Wheel hub
12 – Lower swivel-pin ball-joint
13 – Lower wishbone
14 – Anti-roll bar
15 – Drive shaft
16 – Brake disc (air cooled)
17 – Road wheel
18 – Double row ball wheel bearing

Fig. 8.24 Independent suspension front wheel drive stub-shaft and swivel-pin carrier assembly

Inner CV joint

Outer CV joint
and hub

A – Outer constant velocity joint
B – Circlip (outer joint)
C – Circlip (inner joint)
D – Inner constant velocity joint
E – Oil seal
F – Inner drive shaft
G – Snap ring (inner driveshaft retaining)

Fig. 8.25 Layout of a driving hub arrangement

becomes a carrier for the bearings (normally taper roller – Fig. 8.25) which are mounted close together. Where angular-contact bearings are used they are of the double-row type which have a split inner ring, in this way large-diameter balls can be used to give greater load carrying capacities; they also have the added advantage that they require no adjustment and the torque setting for the drive nut can be high to give good hub-to-shaft security.

8.10 Light vehicle wheels

Most cars use wheels with a well base rim of the types shown in Fig. 8.26. The standard type of rim has the form shown in Fig. 8.26(a). The rim has a slight taper and the internal pressure in the tyre forces the bead of the tyre into tight frictional contact with the wheel. This tight contact is required so as to maintain an air-tight seal and also to provide the grip that will transmit driving and braking forces between the tyre and the wheel. The grip is dependent on the correct tyre pressure being maintained and, in the event of a puncture, the tyre bead is likely to break away from the wheel rim. The double hump rim shown in Fig. 8.26(b) is intended to provide a more secure fixing for the tyre in the sense that, should a puncture occur, the bead of the tyre will be held in place by the humps and this

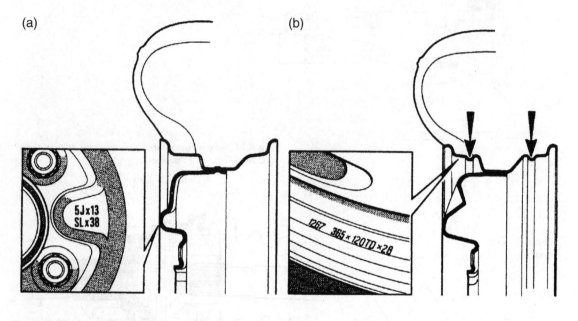

Fig. 8.26 Two types of wheel rim in common use

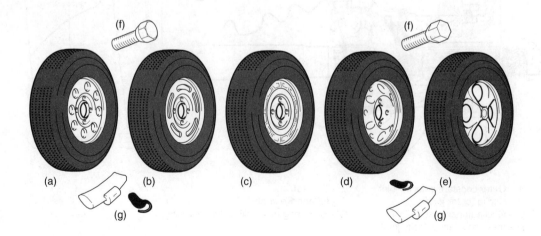

Fig. 8.27 A range of wheels

should provide a degree of control in the event of a sudden, rapid puncture.

8.11 Types of car wheels

Most car wheels are fabricated from **steel pressings** and their appearance is often altered by the addition of an **embellisher**. Figures 8.27 and 8.28 show a range of wheels and wheel trims as used on Ford Escort vehicles. When weight and possibly 'sporty' appearance is a consideration **cast alloy wheels** are used. The metals used are normally **aluminium** alloy, or **magnesium** based alloy, and the wheels are constructed by casting. An alloy wheel is shown in Fig. 8.27(e).

Figure 8.27 (f) and (g) shows the different types of wheel bolts and balance weights that are required. The steel wheel uses a bolt with a taper under the head. This taper screws into a corresponding taper on the wheel and, when the correct torque is applied, the wheel is secured to the vehicle hub. In order to prevent damage to the alloy wheel its bolts are provided with a tapered washer. The taper on the washer sits in the taper on the wheel and the bolt can be tightened without 'tearing' the alloy of the wheel. Figure 8.27 also shows the two different types of wheel balancing weights that are required. The obvious point to make here is that the steel wheel weight is not suitable for use on the alloy wheel, and vice versa.

8.12 Wire wheels

These are wheels that are built up in a similar way to spoked bicycle wheels. Figure 8.29 shows a typical wire wheel. They are normally to be found on sports cars.

8.13 Wheel nut torque

In order to ensure that wheels are properly secure it is advisable to use a torque wrench for

Fig. 8.29 A wire (spoked) wheel

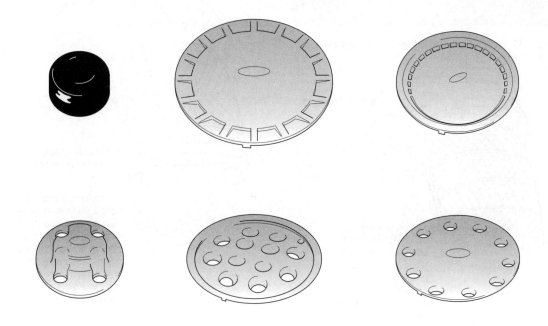

Fig. 8.28 A range of wheel trims (embellishers)

the final tightening of the wheel nuts. This is shown in Fig. 8.30.

8.14 Tyres

Tyres play an important part in the steering, braking, traction, suspension and general control of the vehicle. Two types of tyre construction are in use. These are:

● **cross-ply** tyres
● **radial-ply** tyres.

The term **ply** refers to the layers of material from which the tyre casing is constructed.

Cross-ply tyre

Figure 8.31 shows part of a cross-ply tyre. The plies are placed one upon the other and each adjoining ply has the bias angle of the cords run-ning in opposite directions. The angle between the cords is approximately 100° and the cords in each ply make an angle of approximately 40° with the tyre bead and wheel rim.

Radial-ply tyre

Figure 8.32 shows part of a radial-ply tyre. The plies are constructed so that the cords of the tyre wall run at right angles to the tyre bead and wheel rim.

Cross-ply versus radial-ply tyre

Radial-ply tyres have a more flexible side wall and this, together with the **braced tread**, ensures that a greater area of tread remains in contact with the road when the vehicle is cornering. Figure 8.33 shows the difference between cross-ply and radial-ply tyres when the vehicle is corner-ing. In effect, radial-ply tyres produce a better grip.

It is this remarkable difference between the performance of cross-ply and radial-ply tyres that leads to the rules about mixing of cross-ply and radial-ply tyres on a vehicle. Cross-ply tyres on the front axle and radial-ply tyres on the rear axle are the only combination that can be used.

Fig. 8.30 Using a torque wrench for the final tightening

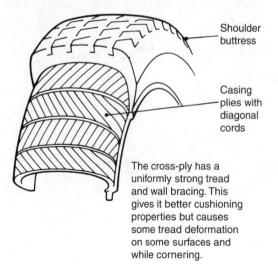

Shoulder buttress

Casing plies with diagonal cords

The cross-ply has a uniformly strong tread and wall bracing. This gives it better cushioning properties but causes some tread deformation on some surfaces and while cornering.

Fig. 8.31 Cross-ply tyre construction

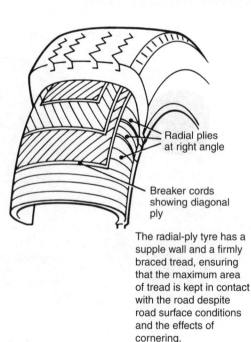

Radial plies at right angle

Breaker cords showing diagonal ply

The radial-ply tyre has a supple wall and a firmly braced tread, ensuring that the maximum area of tread is kept in contact with the road despite road surface conditions and the effects of cornering.

Fig. 8.32 Radial-ply tyre construction

The radial-ply tyre has a great number of advantages over the cross-ply tyre. Cornering stability is greatly improved; as you can see in the Figure the flexible side walls of the radial together with the braced tread ensure that the contact area is held firmly on the road when cornering. For this reason also, tyre life is extended.

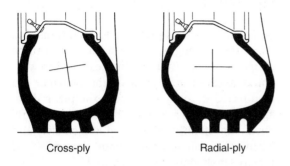

Cross-ply   Radial-ply

Fig. 8.33 Cross-ply and radial-ply tyres under cornering conditions

Tyre sizes

In general tyres have two size markings, one indicating the width of the tyre and other giving the diameter of the wheel rim on which the tyre

fits. Thus, a 5.20 by 10 marking indicates a tyre which is normally 5.20 inches wide which fits a 10 inch diameter wheel rim. Radial-ply tyres have a marking which gives the nominal width in millimetres and a wheel rim diameter in inches; for example, a 145–14 tyre is a tyre with a nominal width of 145 mm with a wheel rim diameter of 14 inches.

Originally vehicle tyres were of circular cross-section and the width of the tyre section was equal to its height. Over the years, developments have led to a considerable change in the shape of the tyre cross-section and it is now common to see tyres where the width of the cross-section is greater than its height. These tyres are known as 'low-profile' tyres. Modern tyres now have an additional number in the size; for example, 185/70–13. The 185 is the tyre width in millimetres, the 13 is the rim diameter in inches, and the 70 refers to the fact that the height of the tyre section is 70% of the width. This 70% figure is also known as the **aspect ratio**. The aspect ratio = (tyre section height/tyre section width) × 100 per cent. Tyre size and other information is carried on the side wall and Fig. 8.34 shows how they appear on a typical tyre.

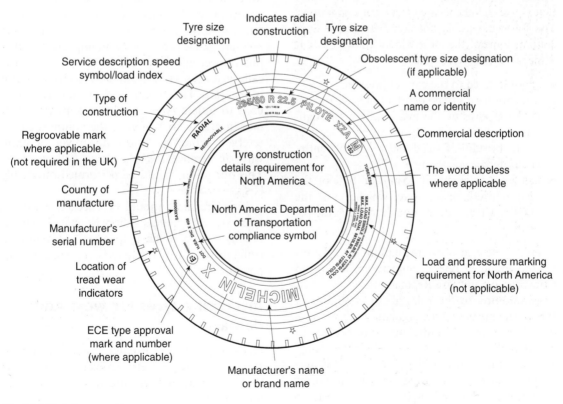

Fig. 8.34 Typical tyre markings

Load and speed ratings

The tyre load and speed ratings are the figures and letters that refer to the maximum load and speed rating of a tyre. For example 82S marked on a tyre means a load index of 82 and a speed index of S. In this case the 82 means a load capacity of 475 kg per tyre and the S relates to a maximum speed of 180 km/h or 113 mph. One of the main points about these markings is that they assist in ensuring that only tyres of the correct specification are fitted to a vehicle.

Tread wear indicators (TWI)

Tyres carry lateral ridges (bars) 1.6 mm high in the grooves between the treads at intervals around the tyre. The purpose of these **tread wear indicators** is to show when the tyre tread is reaching its minimum depth. Their position on the tyre is marked by the letters **TWI** on the tyre wall, near the tread.

Tyre regulations

Tyres must be free from any defect which might cause damage to any person or to the surface of the road. There are strict laws about worn tyres. They vary from time to time and it is important that you should be aware of current regulations. The following list is not complete but it does contain some of the more widely known ones. It is illegal to use a tyre which:

- is not inflated to the correct pressure;
- does not have a tread depth of at least 1.6 mm in the grooves of the tread pattern throughout a continuous band measuring at least ¾ of the breadth of tread and round the entire circumference of the tyre;
- has a cut in excess of 25 mm or 10% of the section width of the tyre, whichever is the greater, which is deep enough to reach the ply or the cord.

There are several other regulations and details can be found in tyre manufacturers' data and Construction and Use Regulations.

In addition to the rules about condition of tyres there are also strict regulations about mixing of cross-ply and radial-ply tyres. For example, it is illegal to have a mixture of cross-ply and radial-ply tyres on the same axle. It is also illegal to have cross-ply tyres on the rear axle of a vehicle that has radial-ply tyres on the front axle. If radial-ply and cross-ply tyres are to be used on the same car, the rule is *radials on the rear*.

8.15 Wheel and tyre balance

Unbalanced wheels give rise to vibrations that affect the steering and suspension, they can be dangerous and, if not rectified, can lead to wear and damage to components. Wheel balance can be affected in many ways; for example, a damaged wheel or tyre caused by hitting the kerb. Such damage must be rectified immediately and when the repair has been made the wheel and tyre assembly must be re-balanced.

A **wheel balancer** is a standard item of garage equipment. When new tyres are fitted, or if wheels are being moved around on the vehicle to balance tyre wear, the wheel and tyre assembly should be checked and, if necessary, rebalanced.

8.16 Tyre maintenance

Tyre pressures

Modern vehicle steering and ride comfort are greatly affected by tyre pressures and it is important to check tyre pressures regularly. The tyre pressure gauge is obviously an important tool in this respect and it should be checked, periodically, against a known standard to ensure that it is accurate. The compressed air supply that is used to inflate tyres should be kept free from moisture and, to this end, the compressed air reservoir should be 'blown down' via the drain valve to remove the water that collects there. This operation should be performed on a daily basis.

Tyre pressures should be checked when the tyres are cold, unless otherwise stated. This is because the tyres heat up when the vehicle is being driven. Hot air expands and increases the pressure.

Inspecting tyres for wear and damage

Uneven tyre wear is usually a sign of a suspension or steering geometry problem. Tyres should thus be examined at intervals to check for uneven wear.

Tyre walls and tread areas should be examined for damage. This applies to the inner wall as well as the outer wall of the tyre.

Learning tasks

1. Remove the wheels and tyres complete from a vehicle. Check the following and record your results on the job sheet for the customer:
   (a) tread depth
   (b) cuts and bulges
   (c) tyre pressures
   (d) signs of abnormal wear
   Complete you report with a set of recommendations.
2. Remove a tyre from a wheel, remove all the balance weights, clean the rim and inspect the tyre bead for damage. Check the inside of the tyre for intrusions and signs of entry of any foreign body such as a nail. Lubricate the bead of the tyre and replace on the wheel, inflate to the correct pressure, rebalance the wheel and refit to vehicle.
3. Produce a list of the current MOT requirements for wheels and tyres.
4. Describe a procedure that you have used for fitting a new tyre.
5. Make a list of the precautions that must be taken when removing a wheel in order to do some work on the vehicle. Make special note of the steps taken to prevent the vehicle from moving and also the steps taken to ensure that the vehicle cannot slip on the jack.
6. Examine a selection of wheel nuts. State why the conical part of the nut, or set bolt, is necessary. State why some vehicles, especially trucks, have left-hand threaded wheel nuts, on the near side. (Left-hand side of the vehicle when sitting in the driving seat).
7. Make a note of the type of wheel-balancing machine that is used in your workshop. State the safety precautions that must be taken when using it and make a list of the major points that you need to know about when balancing a wheel and tyre assembly.
8. State the type of tyre-thread depth gauge that you use. Describe how to use it and state the minimum legal tread depth in the UK.
9. Examine a number of tyres and locate the tyre-wear indicator bars. State which mark on the tyre wall helps you to locate these wear indicators.

Practical assignment – steering worksheet

Introduction

After this practical exercise you should be able to:

- check and adjust steering alignment
- assess for wear in steering components
- remove and replace track rod ends
- check tyres for misalignment
- make a written report on your findings

Tools and equipment

- vehicle with appropriate steering mechanism
- appropriate workshop manual
- selection of tools and specialist equipment, e.g. alignment gauges
- vehicle lift or jacks and stands

Activity

1. Inspect the steering for wear and security, e.g.
   (a) uneven wear on tyres
   (b) play in track-rod ends, steering rack and column
   (c) play in wheel bearings
   (d) security of shock absorbers/dampers, check for leaks
   (e) wear/play in suspension joints
   (f) security/wear in anti-roll bar mountings
2. Remove and refit at least one track rod end.
3. Using appropriate equipment check tracking of vehicle's steered wheels.
4. Check steering angles – castor, camber, king pin inclination, toe-out on turns.
5. Make any adjustments necessary.
6. Investigate where possible the following types of steering gearboxes:
   (a) worm and roller
   (b) cam and peg
   (c) recirculating ball
   (d) rack and pinion
7. Make any adjustments on the above types of steering gearboxes after stripping and rebuilding them.
8. Produce a report on the condition of the steering including the gearboxes, indicating wear and serviceability.
9. State the meaning of the following terms:
   (a) tracking
   (b) toe-out on turns
   (c) steering angles – castor, camber, KPI, Ackerman angle
   (d) roll radius

Checklist

Vehicle

Exercise	Date started	Date finished	Serviceable	Unserviceable
Rack and pinion				
Recirculating ball				
Worm and peg				
Worm and roller (hour glass)				
Castor				
Camber				
KPI				
Toe-out on turns				
Optical alignment gauge				
Four wheel aignment				
Body alignment				

Student's signature

Supervisor's signature

Section Two

9

Electrical and electronic systems

Modern vehicles are equipped with a good deal of electrical and electronic equipment. It is estimated that some vehicles contain several kilometres of wire. The amount of wire (cable) used, and the amount of electric current that passes through it, causes designers to use other solutions, one of which is called **multiplexing**. Multiplexing is used in computer controlled systems where it is possible to use a **data (control) bus**, which is a cable that carries electronic messages to switch equipment on and off, and a **power bus** which is a cable that carries the main electric current to operate the equipment. The system most widely used for computer controlled equipment is known as **CAN** (controller area network). Ordinary and multiplex wiring are shown in Fig. 9.1.

Modern vehicle technicians are, therefore, required to have a good knowledge of electrical and electronic systems in addition to the conventional mechanical skills. However, at this stage we must start at the beginning and learn some basic technology. We can return to some of the more advanced ideas when we have put the foundations in place.

We should start with the **battery**. This is where the energy is stored that operates the **starter motor** and, as vehicle journeys usually start by starting up the vehicle engine, this seems like a good point at which to start our journey through the electrical parts of the vehicle.

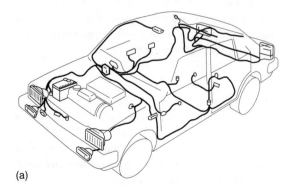

(a)

Units 1 to 6 are remote electronic switching devices.
The data bus carries digital messages from the ECU (computer).
The power bus carries the battery current for the various units.

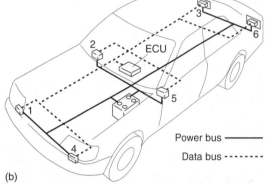

(b)

Power bus ———
Data bus - - - - - - -

Fig. 9.1 (a) Ordinary wiring, (b) multiplex wiring

9.1 Vehicle batteries

Chemical effect of electric current

If two suitably supported **lead plates** are placed in a weak solution of sulphuric acid in water (**electrolyte**) and the plates connected to a suitable low voltage electricity supply as shown in Fig. 9.2, an electric current will flow through the electrolyte from one plate to the other. After a few minutes the lead plate P will appear a brownish colour and the plate Q will appear unchanged. The cell has caused the electric current to have a chemical effect.

This electrochemical effect can be reversed, i.e. removing the DC supply and replacing it with a lamp (bulb) will allow electricity to flow out of the cell and 'light up' the lamp. Electric current will continue to flow out of the cell until it has returned to its original state, or until the lamp is disconnected.

As a result of the electrochemical action, the two lead plates develop a difference in electrical potential. One plate becomes electrically positive

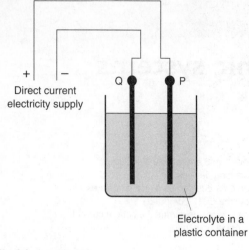

+　−
Direct current
electricity supply

Q　P

Electrolyte in a
plastic container

Fig. 9.2 A simple cell

and the other becomes electrically negative. The difference in electrical potential causes an electric force. This force is known as an **electromotive force** (EMF). EMFs are measured in volts and the EMF generated by the two plates in Fig. 9.2 can be measured by connecting a **voltmeter** across the metal plates. This simple cell is known as a **secondary cell**. It can be charged and recharged.

Dry batteries, similar to those used in a hand torch, exhaust their active materials in the process of making an electric current and they cannot be recharged. Such dry batteries are **primary cells**. These are not to be confused with modern secondary cells of similar appearance.

Because secondary cells can be charged and recharged they are used to make vehicle batteries. There are two types of vehicle batteries: one is **lead acid** and the other is **nickel–iron alkaline**. The lead acid battery is the one that is most widely used and it is this type that we propose to concentrate on.

Lead acid vehicle battery

Safety note

Before we proceed with this work on batteries, there are several points that need to be emphasized.

- Batteries are heavy. Proper lifting practices must be used when lifting them.
- Sulphuric acid is corrosive and it can cause serious injury to the person and damage to materials. It must be handled correctly. You must be aware of the actions to take in case of contact with acid. Every workshop must have proper

safety provision and the rules that are set must be observed. In the event of spillage of acid on to a person, the area affected should be washed off with plenty of clean water. Any contaminated clothing should be removed. If acid comes into contact with eyes, they should be carefully washed out with clean water and urgent medical attention obtained.

- Batteries give off explosive gases, e.g. hydrogen. There should be no smoking or use of naked flame near a battery. Sparks must be avoided when connecting or disconnecting batteries. This applies to work on the battery when it is on the vehicle and also when the battery has been removed from the vehicle for recharging.
- When disconnecting the battery on the vehicle. Make sure everything is switched off. Remove the earth terminal *first*.
- When reconnecting the battery. Make sure everything is switched off. Connect the earth terminal *last*.
- In the case of batteries 'on charge' the battery charger must be switched off before disconnecting the battery from the charger leads.

Typical vehicle battery

Figure 9.3 shows a battery in the engine compartment of a light vehicle. The notes on the diagram indicate factors that require attention. The type of battery shown in Fig. 9.3 is typical of batteries used on modern vehicles. Most light vehicles use 12 V batteries. The 12 V is obtained by connecting six cells in **series**. Each single lead acid cell produces 2 V.

Some larger trucks and buses use a 24 V electrical system. In this case two 12 V batteries are connected in series to give the 24 V.

Battery construction

Case

The **battery casing** needs to be acid resistant and as light and as strong as possible. Plastic material such as **polypropylene** is often used for the purpose. Figure 9.4 shows the construction of a fairly typical battery case.

Cells

Each cell of the battery is housed in a separate container and there are **ribs** at the bottom of the **cell compartment** which support the plates so that they are clear of the container bottom. **Sediment** can accumulate in this bottom space without short circuiting the plates.

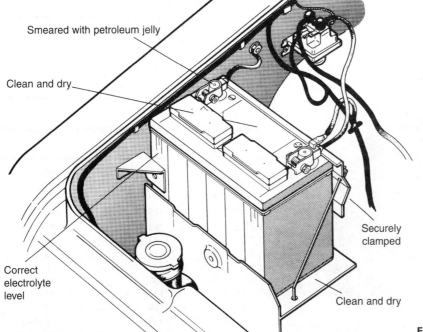

Smeared with petroleum jelly

Clean and dry

Securely clamped

Correct electrolyte level

Clean and dry

Fig. 9.3 The battery installation

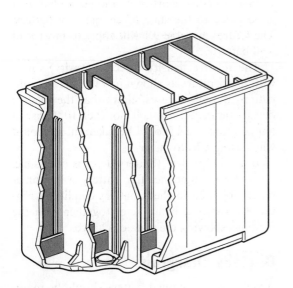

Fig. 9.4 The polypropylene battery case

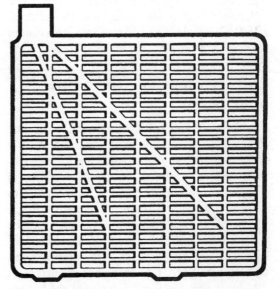

Fig. 9.5 A battery plate

Plates

The plates are made in the form of a grid which is cast in **lead**. In order to facilitate the casting process a small amount of **antimony** is added to the lead. In **maintenance-free batteries calcium** is added to the lead because this reduces losses caused by **gassing**. Figure 9.5 shows a battery plate.

During the manufacturing process other materials are pressed into the plate grid. On the positive plate the material added is **lead peroxide** (a browny red substance) and on the negative plate it is **spongy lead**, which is grey. The completed plates are assembled as shown in Fig. 9.6.

The positive plates are connected together with a space in between. The negative plates are also joined together with a space in between. The negative plates are placed in the gaps between the positive plates and the plates are prevented from touching each other by the

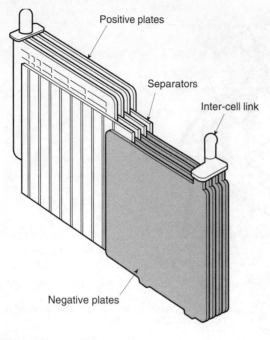

Positive plates

Separators

Inter-cell link

Negative plates

Fig. 9.6 Battery plates

Table 9.1 State of charge vs relative density

State of charge	Relative density
Fully charged	1.280
Half charged	1.200
Completely discharged	1.100

Table 9.2 Variation of electrolyte relative density with temperature

SG (corrected to 15 °C)	Density (kg/m³) (corrected to 25 °C)	State of charge %
1.273	1280	100
1.253	1260	90
1.233	1240	80
1.213	1220	70
1.193	1200	60
1.173	1180	50
1.133	1140	30
1.093	1100	10
1.073	1080	0 (flat)

separators which slide in between them. The separators are made from porous material which allows the electrolyte to make maximum contact with the surfaces of the plates.

Battery capacity – the ampere-hour (A-H)

The unit of quantity of electricity is the **coulomb**. One coulomb is the equivalent of a current of one ampere (A) flowing for one second. This is a very small amount of electricity in comparison with the amount that is required to drive a starter motor. It is usual, therefore, to use a larger unit of quantity of electricity to describe the electrical energy capacity of a vehicle battery. The unit that is used is the **ampere-hour**. One ampere-hour is equivalent to a current of 1 A flowing for one hour. The size of the battery plates and the number of plates per cell are factors that have a bearing on **battery capacity**. In general, a 75 A-H battery will be larger and heavier than a 50 A-H battery.

Relative density of electrolyte (specific gravity)

One of the chemical changes that takes place in the battery during charging and discharging is that the **relative density** of the electrolyte (dilute sulphuric acid) changes. There is a link between relative density of the electrolyte and the cell voltage. Relative density of the electrolyte is a good guide to the state of charge of a battery. The figures in Table 9.1 will apply to most lead acid batteries.

The relative density (**specific gravity**) varies with temperature as shown in Table 9.2. Examination of these figures shows that the relative density figure falls by 0.007 for each 10 °C rise in temperature. This should be taken into account when using a **hydrometer**.

If the electrolyte (battery acid) is accessible, e.g. not a maintenance-free battery, a hydrometer can be used to check battery condition. Figure 9.7 shows a hydrometer together with the readings showing the state of charge.

Battery charging

A properly maintained battery should be maintained in a charged condition by the **vehicle alternator** during normal operation of the vehicle. If it becomes necessary to remove the battery from the vehicle to recharge it, from a **battery charger**, the ampere-hour capacity of the battery gives a good guide to the current that should be used and the length of time that the battery should stay on charge.

Battery charging rate

The test for battery capacity can be a 10 hour test or a 20 hour test. If, as a guide, we take the

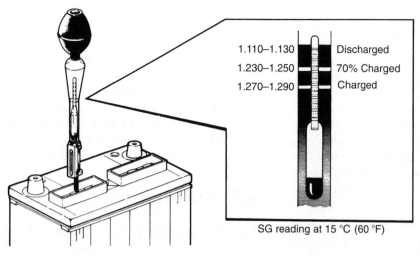

1.110–1.130	Discharged
1.230–1.250	70% Charged
1.270–1.290	Charged

SG reading at 15 °C (60 °F)

Fig. 9.7 The hydrometer

10 hour rating of a 50 A-H battery, in theory this means that the battery will give 5 A for 10 hours, i.e. 5 × 10 = 50. It does not work quite like that, but it is a guide. If this 50 A-H battery was being completely recharged, it would require a charging current of 5 A to be applied for 10 hours.

Reserve capacity

In recent years it has become the practice to give the **reserve capacity** of a battery rather than the A-H capacity, because reserve capacity is considered to be a better guide to how long the battery will provide sufficient current to operate vehicle systems. Reserve capacity is the time in minutes that it will take a current of 25 A to cause the cell voltage to fall to 1.75 V. That is to say, the number of minutes that it takes for a six cell 12 V battery voltage to drop to 10.5 V, when it is supplying a current of 25 A.

Battery suppliers will provide the data for the batteries that they supply. Manufacturers' charging rates must be used.

Testing batteries

Batteries are normally reliable for quite a number of years. However, batteries do sometimes fail to provide sufficient voltage to operate the vehicle starting system. Such failure can arise for reasons such as:

1. the lights, or some other system, have been left switched on and the battery has become discharged;
2. the battery is no longer capable of 'holding' a charge;
3. the battery is discharged because the alternator charging rate is too low.

If it is (1) and the lights have been left on and caused the battery to 'run down' a quick check of switch positions, i.e. are they in the on position? will reveal the most likely cause. A hydrometer test, or a voltage check at the battery terminals, will confirm that the battery is discharged. The remedy will be to recharge the battery, probably by removing it and replacing it, temporarily, with a **'service' battery**.

If it is (2) or (3) it will be necessary to check the battery more thoroughly. A **high rate discharge tester** (Fig. 9.8) that tests the battery's ability to provide a high current for a short period is very effective, but it can only be used if the battery is at least 70% charged. The state of

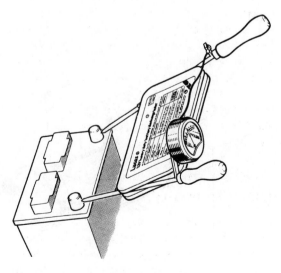

Fig. 9.8 High rate discharge tester

charge of the battery can be determined by using a hydrometer. If the specific gravity (relative density) reading shows that the battery is less than 70% charged, the battery should be recharged at the recommended rate. After charging, and leaving time for the battery to settle and the gases to disperse, the high rate discharge test can be applied. Many different forms of high rate discharge testers are available and it is important to carefully read the instructions for use. Checking the alternator charging rate is covered in the next section on alternators.

Learning tasks

1. Ask your supervisor or tutor about the workshop rules that apply to the handling of battery charging in your workshop. Write a summary of these rules.
2. On which types of vehicles are you likely to find the 12V batteries connected in series, cars and light commercial vehicles or heavy trucks and buses?
3. On some electronically controlled systems, settings such as idle speed are held in the volatile memory of the ECU. That is to say that the settings are lost when the battery is discharged or disconnected. Write out a brief description of the procedure that is followed to restore such settings.
4. What is a 'rapid' battery charger? What precautions must be observed when using one?

5. Examine a vehicle battery installation and make a simple sketch to show how the battery is secured to the vehicle.
6. Assuming that you are asked to remove the battery that you have examined for question 5, describe the procedure to be followed. State which battery lead to remove first and include any steps taken to observe safety rules and protect the vehicle.

9.2 Alternator

The alternator supplies the electrical energy to recharge the battery and to operate the electrical/electronic systems on the vehicle, while the engine is running. (If you are unsure about electromagnetic principles you are advised to study Section 9.9 on electrical principles.

Basic vehicle alternator (generator of electricity)

In a vehicle alternator, the **magnet** is the rotating member and the **coil** in which current is generated is the stationary part. Figure 9.9 illustrates the general principle. The **rotor shaft** is driven round by the **pulley** and **drive belt** and the **stator** is fixed to the body of the alternator.

Figure 9.10 shows how the EMF (voltage) produced by this simple rotating magnet and stator coil varies during one complete revolution (360°) of the magnetic rotor.

(a)
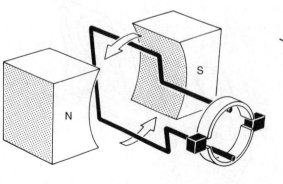

(b)
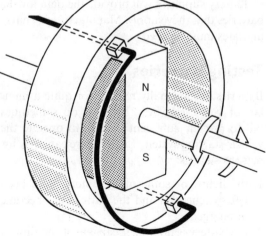

Fig. 9.9 The principle of the generator (a) dynamo stationary field, (b) alternator rotating field

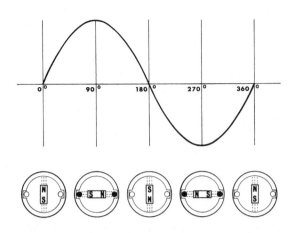

Fig. 9.10 Diagram showing EMF produced in one complete cycle relative to magnet position

Alternating current (AC)

Alternating current, as produced by this simple alternator, is not suitable for charging batteries. The alternating current must be changed into **direct current** (DC). The device that changes AC to DC is the **rectifier**. Vehicle rectifiers make use of electronic devices such as the P-N **junction diode**. The property of the diode that makes it suitable for use in a rectifier is that it will pass current in one direction but not the other. Figure 9.11 demonstrates the principle of the semi-conductor diode. More detail about diodes appears in Section 9.12.

Using a single diode as a simple half-wave rectifier

As a guide to the principle of operation of the actual rectifier as used in a vehicle alternator we think that it is useful to consider, very briefly, the operation of the simple **half-wave rectifier** shown in Fig. 9.12. In this simple rectifier the negative half of the wave is 'blocked' by the diode. The resulting output is a series of positive half waves separated by 180°. In order to get a smooth DC supply it is necessary to use a circuit that contains several diodes. The **bridge circuit rectifier** is the basic approach that is used.

Full-wave rectifier – the bridge circuit

Figure 9.13(a) shows a full-wave rectifier circuit. There are four diodes, A, B, C and D, which are connected in bridge form. There is an AC input and a voltmeter is connected across the output resistor.

Reference to Fig. 9.13(b) shows how the current flows for one half of the AC cycle and Fig. 9.13(c) shows the current flow in the other half of the AC cycle. In both cases the current flows through the load resistor R in the same direction. The output is thus DC and this is achieved by the 'one way' action of the diodes.

Typical vehicle alternator

The following description of the parts shown in Fig. 9.14 should help to develop an understanding that will aid the additional study and training that will build the skills necessary for successful work on electrical/electronic systems.

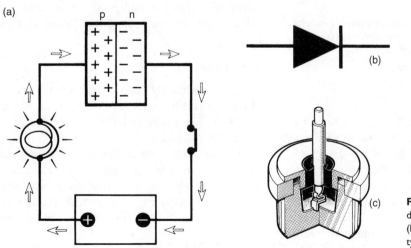

(a)

(b)

(c)

Fig. 9.11 The principle of the diode (a) circuit for diode principle, (b) circuit symbol for a diode, (c) typical heavy duty diode

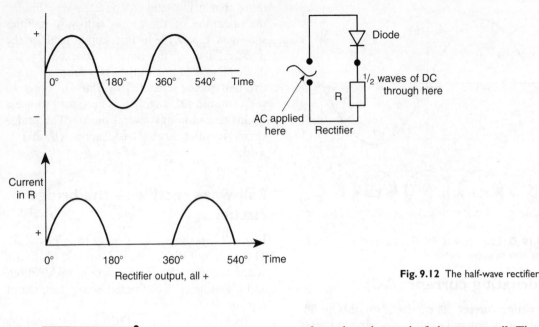

Fig. 9.12 The half-wave rectifier

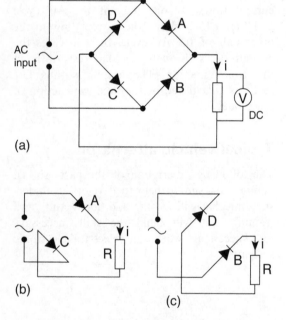

(a)

(b)

(c)

Fig. 9.13 The full-wave rectifier (a) complete bridge circuit, (b) current flow for one half of the voltage waveform, (c) current flow for the other half of the voltage waveform.

Rotor

This is where the **magnetic field** is generated by the current that flows into the **rotor windings** through the **slip rings** and **brushes**. Figure 9.15 shows three types of rotors that are used in Lucas alternators. The rotor is made from an **iron core** around which is wound a coil of wire. The current in this coil of wire creates a **magnetic north pole** at one end and a **magnetic south**

pole at the other end of the **stator coil**. The **iron claws** of the rotor are placed on opposite ends of the **rotor (field) winding**. The 'fingers' of the claws are north or south magnetic poles, according to the end of the field coil that they are attached to. This makes pairs of north and south poles around the circumference of the rotor. The whole assembly is mounted on a **shaft**. This shaft also has the **drive pulley** fixed to it so that the rotor can be driven by the engine.

Stator

These stators (Fig. 9.16) have a **laminated iron core**. (Iron is used because it magnetizes and demagnetizes easily, with a minimum of energy loss.) Three separate coils are wound on to the stator core. A separate AC wave is generated in each winding, as the rotor revolves inside the stator. The stator windings are either **star-**, or **delta-**connected, according to alternator type (Fig. 9.17).

Rectifier

A fairly commonly used bridge circuit of an **alternator rectifier** uses six diodes, as shown in Fig. 9.18. The stator windings are connected to the diodes as shown.

In operation a power loss occurs across the diodes and, in order to dissipate the heat generated, the diodes are mounted on a **heat sink** which conducts the heat away into the atmosphere. Typical diode packs are shown in Fig. 9.19.

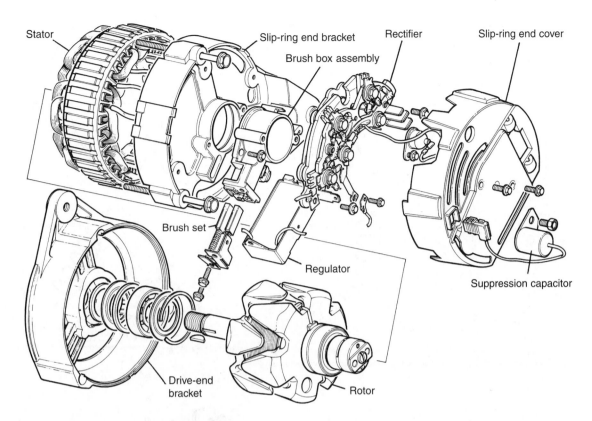

Fig. 9.14 The main component parts of an alternator

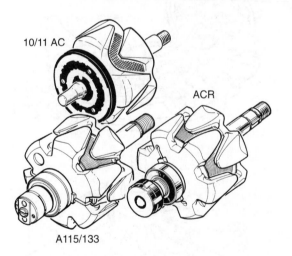

Fig. 9.15 Alternator rotors (electromagnets)

Fig. 9.16 A selection of alternator stators

Voltage regulator

The **voltage regulator** is an electronic circuit that holds the alternator voltage to approximately 14 V on a 12 V system, and approximately 28 V on a 24 V system. It operates by sensing either the voltage at the alternator (**machine sensing**) or at the battery (**battery sensing**). The regulator controls the amount of current that is supplied to the rotor field winding. This alters the strength of the magnetic field and hence the alternator output voltage.

Brushes and brushbox

The **brushes** carry the current to the slip rings and from there to the rotor winding. Alternator brushes are normally made from **soft carbon**

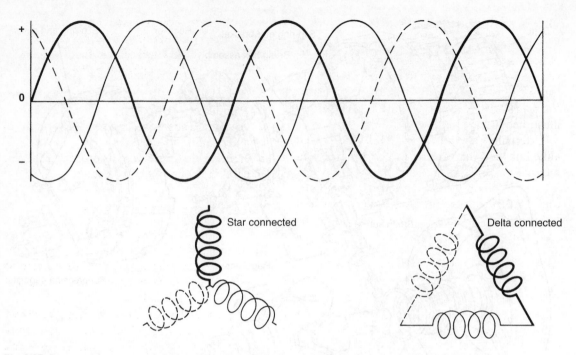

Fig. 9.17 Diagram showing star and delta connected stator windings

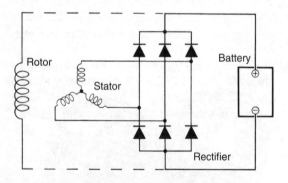

Fig. 9.18 A six-diode rectifier in the alternator circuit

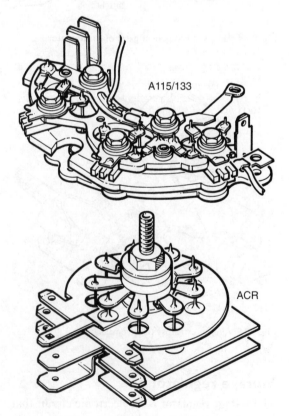

Fig. 9.19 Rectifier diodes and heat sinks

because it has good electrical conducting properties and does not cause too much wear on the brass slip rings. In time, the brushes may wear and the brush box is normally placed so that brush checking and replacement can be performed without major dismantling work.

Bearings

The rotor shaft is mounted on **ball races**, one at the **drive-end**, the other at the **sliprings-end**. These bearings are pre-lubricated and are designed to last for long periods without attention. The drive-end bearing (Fig. 9.14) is mounted in the drive-end bracket and, as you would expect, the slipring-end bearing is mounted in the slipring-end bracket. These two brackets also provide the supports that allow the alternator to be bolted to the vehicle engine.

Drive pulley and cooling fan

The **drive pulley** is usually belt driven by another pulley on the engine. The **alternator cooling fan** is mounted on the **rotor shaft** and is driven round with it. This fan passes air through the alternator to prevent it from over-heating. These are illustrated in Fig. 9.20.

Externally, alternators all look very much alike but they vary greatly in performance and internal construction. The description given here is intended to provide an introduction to the topic. When working on a vehicle it is essential to have access to the information relating to the actual machine being worked on.

Alternator output

Before starting on the alternator test procedure, there are a few general points about care of alternators that need to be made.

- Do not run the engine with the alternator leads disconnected. (Note that in the tests that follow the engine is switched off and the ammeter is connected before restarting the engine.)
- Always disconnect the alternator and battery when using an electric welder on the vehicle. Failure to do this may cause stray currents to harm the alternator electronics. Do not disconnect the alternator when the engine is running.
- Take care not to reverse the battery connections.

With these points made we can turn our attention to the alternator tests. As with any test a thorough visual check should first be made. In the case of the alternator this will include:

- checking the drive belt for tightness and condition;
- checking leads and connectors for tightness and condition;
- ensuring that the battery is properly charged;
- checking any fuses in the circuit.

Alternator output tests

The question of whether to repair or replace an alternator is a subject of debate. However, one thing that is certain is the need to be able to accurately determine whether or not the alternator is charging properly.

The test procedure shown in Fig. 9.21 shows the procedure for checking alternator current output under working conditions. The **test link** will be a cable with suitable **crocodile clips**. This link must be securely attached to ensure proper connections. The **ammeter** connections must also be secure, with the cables and the meter safely positioned to ensure accurate readings and to avoid mishaps.

The **drive belt tension** must also be checked, as shown in Fig. 9.22. The belt tension may also be checked by means of a **torque wrench**, or a **Burroughs-type tension gauge**, as shown in Fig. 9.23.

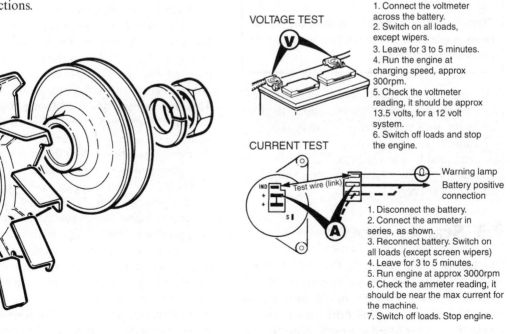

VOLTAGE TEST

1. Connect the voltmeter across the battery.
2. Switch on all loads, except wipers.
3. Leave for 3 to 5 minutes.
4. Run the engine at charging speed, approx 300rpm.
5. Check the voltmeter reading, it should be approx 13.5 volts, for a 12 volt system.
6. Switch off loads and stop the engine.

CURRENT TEST

Warning lamp
Battery positive connection

1. Disconnect the battery.
2. Connect the ammeter in series, as shown.
3. Reconnect battery. Switch on all loads (except screen wipers)
4. Leave for 3 to 5 minutes.
5. Run engine at approx 3000rpm
6. Check the ammeter reading, it should be near the max current for the machine.
7. Switch off loads. Stop engine.

Fig. 9.20 The alternator drive pulley and cooling fan

Fig. 9.21 Alternator output tests

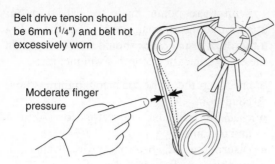

Belt drive tension should be 6mm ($^1/_4$") and belt not excessively worn

Moderate finger pressure

Fig. 9.22 Checking the drive belt tension

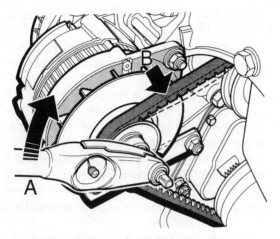

A – Direction of rotation of the gauge
B – Degree of flexure in the drive belt

Fig. 9.23 Using the belt tension gauge

> ### Learning task
>
> Describe, with the aid of diagrams, the equipment needed and the procedure used to test an alternator output.

If the belt is too tight (excessive tension) alternator bearings may be damaged and if the tension is insufficient the drive belt may slip; this will cause a loss of alternator power and, in time, can lead to worn pulleys. This is why it is important to know what the tension should be and set it accurately.

9.3 Starter motor

The **starter motor** shown in Fig. 9.24 is fairly typical of starter motors in modern use. Most modern starter motors are of the **pre-engaged** type. This means that the **drive pinion** on the starter motor is pushed into engagement with the **ring gear** on the engine **flywheel**, before the

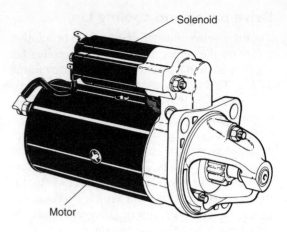

Solenoid

Motor

Fig. 9.24 A starter motor

starter motor begins to rotate and start the engine.

The amount of **torque** (turning effect) that the starter motor can generate is quite small and it has to be multiplied to make it strong enough to rotate the engine crankshaft at about 100 revolutions per minute (RPM). This multiplication of torque is achieved by the ratio of the number of teeth on the flywheel divided by the number of teeth on the starter pinion. In the example shown in Fig. 9.25, the ratio is 10:1.

In the starter motor shown in Fig. 9.24, the pinion is moved into engagement by the action of the **solenoid** on the **operating lever**. The circuit shown in Fig. 9.26 shows that there are two solenoid coils that are energized when the starter switch is closed. The **armature** (plunger) of the solenoid is attached to the operating lever as shown in Fig. 9.27. When the pinion is properly engaged, the heavy current contacts of the solenoid will close and the starter motor will rotate. This action bypasses the **closing coil** and the **holding coil** remains energized until the starter switch is released. The plunger then returns to the normal position taking the starter pinion out of engagement with the flywheel.

The starter motor pinion must be taken out of engagement with the flywheel immediately the engine starts. An engine will normally start at approximately 100 RPM. If the starter motor remains in engagement, the engine will drive the starter motor at high speed (because of the gear ratio) and this will destroy the starter motor. To guard against such damage, pre-engaged starter motors are equipped with a **free-wheeling device**. A common example of such an over-run protection device is the **roller clutch drive assembly**

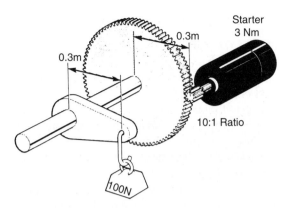

Fig. 9.25 Gear ratio of a starter pinion and flywheel gear

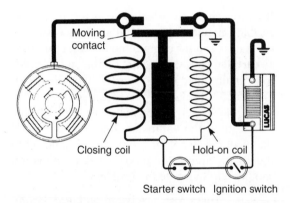

Fig 9.26 The starter solenoid

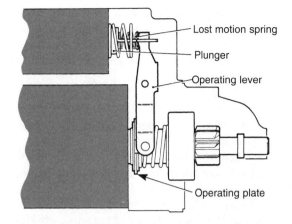

Fig. 9.27 The operating lever

In a book like this it is not realistic to expect to find answers to everything. What we can do is to cover the general approach; beyond that it is a job for the individual to learn more and to know where to find data that provides the information for specific cases.

In the case of a starter motor system and assuming that the starter motor does not operate when the switch is on, step 1 of the six steps will include a visual check to see whether all readily visible parts such as cables, etc. are in place and secure. The next step would be to check the battery. An indication of battery condition can be obtained by switching on the headlights. If the starter switch is operated with the headlights on and the lights go very dim, there is a case for a battery test as described in the section on batteries.

If the battery condition is correct there are some voltmeter tests that can be performed to check various parts of the starter motor circuit. For these tests it is best to use an assistant to operate the starter switch because it is unwise to attempt to make the meter connections, observe the meter readings in the vicinity of the starter

shown in Fig. 9.28. The inner member is fixed to the starter motor shaft and the outer member to the starter motor pinion.

This is as far as we are going on this preliminary trip around the starter motor. If you are able to absorb most of what is covered here you should be well on the way to developing the expertise that will assist you in dealing with repair and maintenance of starter motors.

This is a convenient point at which to have a look at some tests that can be used to trace faults in starter motor circuits.

Testing starter motor circuits

As with all diagnostic work it is advisable to adopt a strategy. One strategy that works quite well is the six step approach. The six steps are:

1. collect evidence
2. analyse evidence
3. locate the fault
4. find the cause of the fault and remedy it
5. rectify the fault (if different from 4)
6. test the system to verify that repair is correct

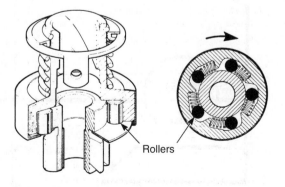

Fig. 9.28 Starter pinion over-run protection

motor and attempt to operate the starter switch simultaneously. The meter must be set to the correct DC range and clips should be used so that secure connections can be made to the various points indicated.

To avoid unwanted start up, the ignition system should be disabled; on a coil ignition system the low tension lead between the coil and distributor should be disconnected. On a **compression ignition** (diesel) engine, the fuel supply should be cut off, probably by operating the stop control. The instructions that relate to the vehicle being worked on must be referred to; this warning is particularly important when working on **engine management systems** because **fault codes** may be generated.

Figure 9.29 shows the test to check voltage at the battery terminals under load. Here the battery voltage is being checked while the starter switch is being operated. For a 12 V system on a petrol engined vehicle the voltmeter should show a reading of approximately 10 V. On a diesel engined vehicle the reading will be lower; approximately 9 V should be obtained.

Starter terminal voltage

The test shown in Fig. 9.30 is to check the heavy current circuit of the starter motor and the condition of the solenoid contacts. When the starter motor switch is in the start position, the voltage recorded between the input terminal and earth should be within 0.5 V of the battery voltage on load. If that voltage was 10.5 V, then the voltage recorded here should be at least 10 V.

Checking the solenoid contacts

Should the starter motor voltage under load be low, it is possible that the heavy current solenoid contacts are defective. The test shown in Fig. 9.31 checks for voltage drop across the solenoid contacts. Good contacts will produce little or no voltage drop. The voltmeter must be connected, as shown, to the two heavy current terminals of the solenoid. When the starter switch is in the off position, the voltmeter should read battery voltage. When the starter switch is in the start position the voltmeter reading should be zero.

Checking the earth circuit

Because vehicle electrical systems rely on a good **earthing circuit** such as metallic contact between the starter and the engine, and other factors such as **earthing straps**, this part of the circuit needs to be maintained in good order. The test shown in Fig. 9.32 checks this part of the starter circuit. When the starter motor switch is turned to the on position, the voltmeter should read zero. If the reading is 0.5 V, or more, there is a defect in the earth circuit. A good visual examination should help to locate the problem.

> *Note* – These tests are based on Lucas recommendations. Lucas sell a range of inexpensive, pocket size **test cards**. These are recommended for use by those who are learning about vehicle maintenance. The one that relates to 12 V starting systems has the reference XRB201. We believe that other equipment manufacturers produce similar aids to fault diagnosis.

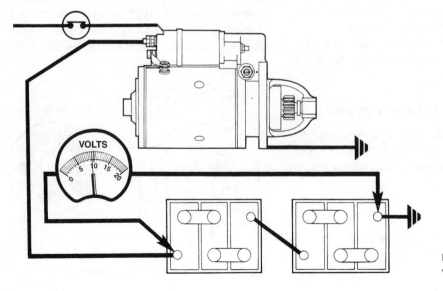

Fig. 9.29 Testing battery voltage under load

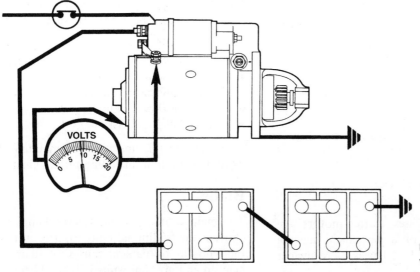

Fig. 9.30 Starter motor voltage under load

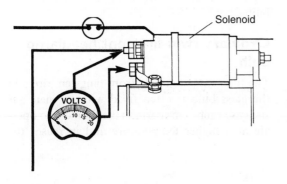

Fig. 9.31 Checking the soleniod contacts

9.4 Other types of electric motors used in vehicle systems

In many vehicle applications the main magnetic field for a motor or generator is provided by an **electromagnet** and the 'coils' that provide this magnetism are known as **field coils** or field windings. An alternative to this is to use a permanent magnet to provide the magnetic field. **Permanent magnet motors** can offer considerable savings in size and weight and they are used in many applications on vehicles, e.g. to drive windscreen wipers, to operate seat adjustments and sliding

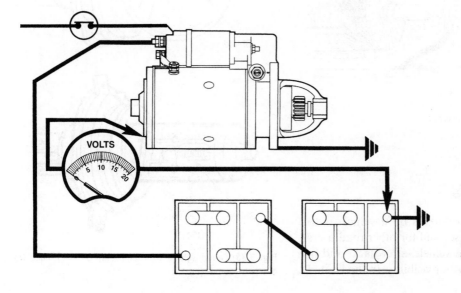

Fig. 9.32 Testing the voltage drop in the earth circuit

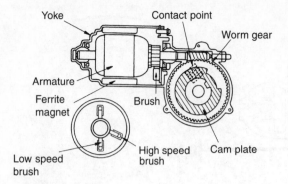

Fig. 9.33 A permanent magnet motor

roofs and, in some cases, starter motors. An example of the use of a permanent magnet motor is shown in Fig. 9.33 This is a screenwiper motor.

Learning tasks

1. Figure 9.34 shows the commutator and brush gear for a typical starter motor. Write out the details of checks that can be made to see if the brushes and commutator are in good condition.
2. Examine a set of starter motor brushes and also a set of alternator brushes. Write down any differences that you observe and state why they are made from different materials.

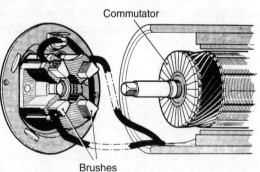

Fig. 9.34 Starter motor brushes

9.5 Lighting

The main purpose of lights on a vehicle is to enable the driver to see and for other road users to be able to see the vehicle, after dark, and in other conditions of poor visibility. In the United Kingdom there are legal requirements for the lights that must be fitted. In summary, these requirements are:

- headlamps (minimum of two, one each side);
- side, rear and number plate lamps;
- direction indicator lamps (flashers);
- stop lamps (brake lights);
- rear fog lamp (at least one).

All of these lamps must be maintained in working condition, including proper alignment.

Bulbs

The main source of light for the lamps listed above is the traditional bulb. Electric current in the bulb (lamp) filament causes the filament to heat up and give out whitish light. Where other colours are required, e.g. for stop and tail lights, the **lamp lens** is made from coloured material. Figure 9.35 shows two commonly used types of bulbs.

Ordinary twin-filament headlamp bulb

The filaments are made from **tungsten wire** and the glass bulb is often filled with an **inert gas** such as **argon**. This permits the filament to operate at a higher temperature and increases the

(a)

Shield

(b)

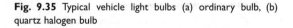

Shield

Fig. 9.35 Typical vehicle light bulbs (a) ordinary bulb, (b) quartz halogen bulb

reliability. One of the filaments provides the **main beam** and the other filament, which is placed a little above centre, provides the **dipped beam**. The effect is shown in Fig. 9.36.

In order to locate the bulb accurately in the lamp **reflector**, the metal base of the bulb is equipped with a **notch**, as shown in Fig. 9.37.

Quartz halogen twin-filament headlamp bulb

A problem with ordinary tungsten lamp bulbs is that, over a long period of time, the filament deteriorates (evaporates) and discolours the glass. The rather more elaborate **quartz halogen bulb** is designed to give brighter light and to prevent the evaporated tungsten from being deposited on the inside of the bulb. **Halogens** are gases such as **iodine**, **chlorine**, etc.; they react chemically inside the bulb to provide the **halogen cycle**. The halogen cycle preserves the life of the tungsten filament.

Oil, grease and salt from perspiration can damage the quartz and it is recommended that these bulbs are handled by the metal part to prevent damage. Figure 9.38 shows a typical method of locating a quartz halogen bulb.

Stop/tail bulb

This has two filaments, which are normally 21 W and 5 W. The 21 W filament is for the stop (brake) lights, and the 5 W filament is for the tail lights. The metal base of the bulb is provided with **off-set pins** so that it cannot be fitted incorrectly.

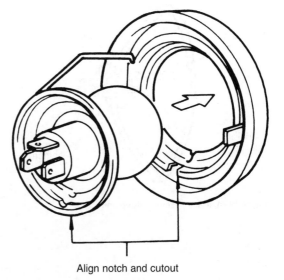

Align notch and cutout

Fig. 9.37 The location notch in the bulb base – regular type

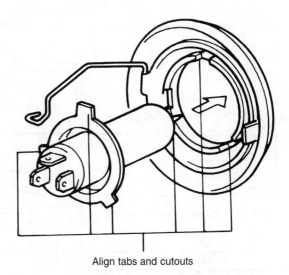

Align tabs and cutouts

Fig. 9.38 Locating a quartz halogen bulb

Sealed beam units

The construction of a **sealed beam unit** is shown in Fig. 9.39. There is no separate bulb. The assembly (lighting filaments, reflector and lamp lens) is a single unit. During manufacture, the inside of the unit is evacuated and filled with inert gas, the unit is then hermetically sealed. The idea is that the dust and other contaminants cannot enter and the accuracy of the setting of the filament in relation to the focal point of the reflector cannot be altered. A disadvantage is that, in the event of filament failure, the whole unit must be replaced. A typical lighting circuit is shown in Fig. 9.40.

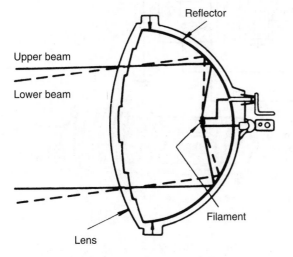

Fig. 9.36 The dipped beam principle

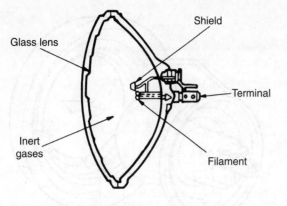

Fig. 9.39 A sealed beam headlamp unit

Headlamp dipping

The **reflector** concentrates the light produced by the bulb and projects it in the required direction. The lens is specially patterned to 'shape' the light beam so that the beam is brighter in the centre and less bright on both sides, the intention being to reduce the risk of 'dazzling' oncoming drivers and pedestrians. Headlamps must also be provided with the means to deflect the beam downwards and, in a two headlamp system, this is achieved by switching the lamps from the main beam filament to the dip beam filament.

Headlamp alignment

To ensure that headlamps are correctly adjusted it is necessary to check the **alignment**. Special

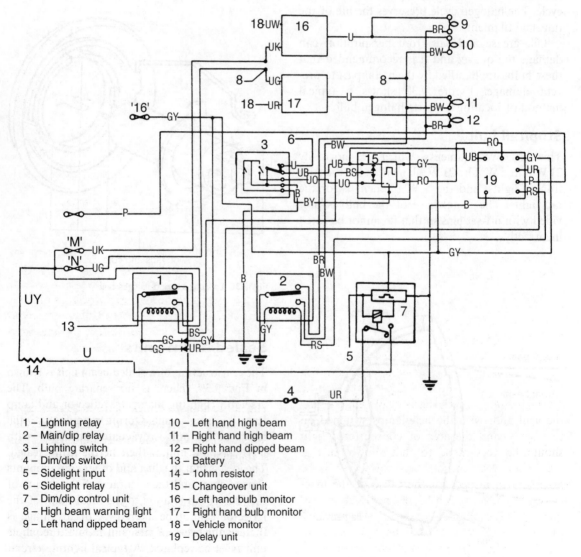

1 – Lighting relay
2 – Main/dip relay
3 – Lighting switch
4 – Dim/dip switch
5 – Sidelight input
6 – Sidelight relay
7 – Dim/dip control unit
8 – High beam warning light
9 – Left hand dipped beam
10 – Left hand high beam
11 – Right hand high beam
12 – Right hand dipped beam
13 – Battery
14 – 1ohm resistor
15 – Changeover unit
16 – Left hand bulb monitor
17 – Right hand bulb monitor
18 – Vehicle monitor
19 – Delay unit

Fig. 9.40 A typical headlamp circuit

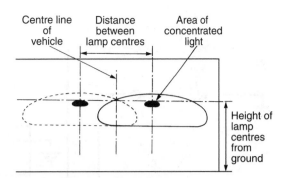

Front of vehicle to be square with screen
Vehicle to be loaded and standing on level ground
Recommended distance for setting is at least 8m
For ease of setting, one headlamp should be covered

Fig. 9.42 Using a marked wall for headlamp alignment

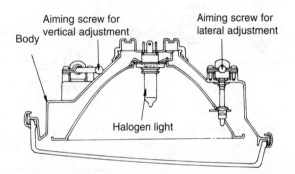

Fig. 9.43 Headlamp alignment screws

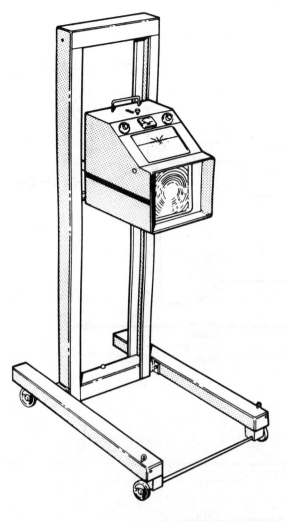

Lucas Beam Tester Mk. II

Fig. 9.41 Lucas headlamp alignment machine

machines of the type shown in Fig. 9.41 are often used for this purpose.

If such a machine is not available it is acceptable to use a flat, vertical surface such as a wall or a door.

The wall should be marked out as shown in Fig. 9.42. The vehicle is placed so that the headlamps are parallel to the wall and 8 m from the wall. The centre line of the vehicle must line up with the centre line marked on the wall and, with the headlamps switched on to main beam, the area of concentrated light should be very close to that shown in Fig. 9.42. Should the settings be incorrect it will be necessary to inspect for the cause of the inaccuracy. It may be a case of incorrect adjustment. If adjustment is required it is probable that the headlamp unit will be equipped with screws to alter the horizontal and vertical settings, as shown in Fig. 9.43.

Headlight and rear fog light circuit

In the circuit shown in Fig. 9.44 the **rear fog lamp** circuit is fed from the main light switch. The purpose of the rear fog lamp is to make the presence of the vehicle more visible in difficult driving conditions. The headlamps are connected in **parallel** so that failure of one lamp does not lead to failure of the others.

Lighting regulations

The law relating to vehicle lights is quite complicated and you are advised to check the regulations to ensure that you understand them. This is particularly important when fitting extra lights to a vehicle.

Direction indicators

Direction indicator lights (flashers) are required so that the driver can indicate any intended manoeuvre. Figure 9.45 shows a typical indicator

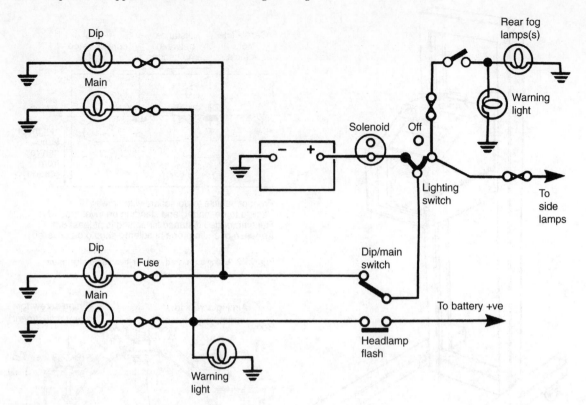

Fig. 9.44 Headlamp and rear fog lamp circuit

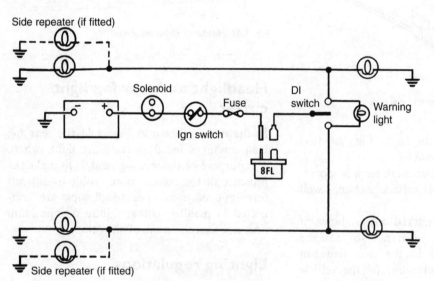

Fig. 9.45 Indicator lamp circuit

lamp circuit. The **flasher** unit is designed so that the frequency of flashes is not less than 60 per minute and not more than 120 per minute. The circuit is also designed so that failure of an indicator lamp will lead to an increased frequency of flashing, warning the driver that a lamp has failed.

Flasher unit

The unit shown in Fig. 9.45 is marked 8FL. This is a Lucas unit that operates on the basis of thermal expansion and contraction of a metal strip. The flasher unit shown in Fig. 9.46 employs a **capacitor** and a **relay** to provide the flashing action. Examination of the circuit diagram shows that the **contact points**

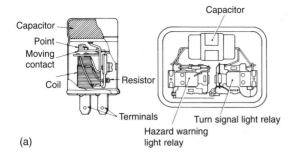

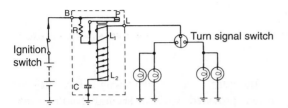

(a)

Current type

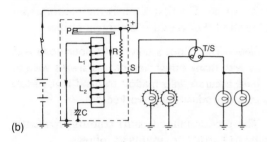

Voltage type

(b)

Fig. 9.46 Capacitor and relay flasher units and circuits (a) construction of the flasher units, (b) circuits for the two types of flasher unit

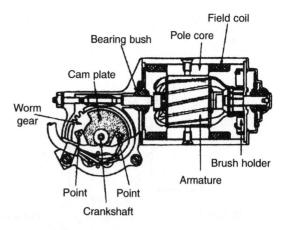

Fig. 9.47 Windscreen wiper motor, structure of compound-wound wiper motor

windscreen wipers because this gives the opportunity to consider an application of a permanent magnet motor.

Wiper motors normally allow for two different speeds of wiping action. The method of obtaining the two speeds varies according to the type of wiper motor used. Two basic types of wiper motor are commonly used. These are:

- a motor with **field windings** to set up the magnetic field;
- a **permanent magnet** motor.

Examples of both types of motor are shown in Figs 9.34 and 9.47.

In the compound-wound motor the speed variation is obtained by varying the field current and hence the strength of the magnetic field. In the permanent (ferrite) magnet motor the field strength remains constant and the speed is changed by switching armature current between the low-speed and high-speed armature brushes, according to the wiper switch position.

9.7 Circuits and circuit principles

Circuit (wiring) diagrams

A complete circuit is needed for the flow of electric current. Figure 9.48 shows two diagrams of a motor in a circuit. Should the fuse be blown, the circuit is incomplete, current will not flow and the motor will not run. In the right hand diagram the fuse has been replaced. The circuit is now complete and the motor will run. Basic electrical principles, such as this, are fundamental

are normally at rest, in the closed position. When the indicator switch is moved to indicate a turn, to left or right, current flows to the indicator lamps, through the upper winding of the relay.

This current energizes the relay and opens the contact points, the current flow is interrupted and the lamps 'go out'. As the lamps 'go out' the contact points close and the lights 'come on' again. This happens at a frequency of approximately 90 flashes per minute and the timing of the flash rate is controlled by the capacitor.

9.6 Windscreen wipers

It is not intended that this book should attempt to cover every item of vehicle electrical equipment. However, we think it desirable to include

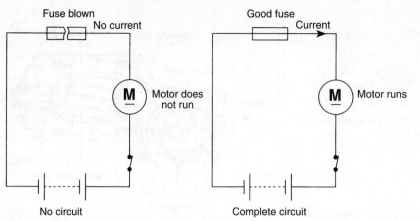

Fig. 9.48 An electric circuit

to good work on electronic systems because much of the testing of electronic systems requires checking of circuits to ensure that they are complete.

It is essential to be able to understand and follow circuit diagrams and this requires a knowledge of circuit symbols.

There is a set of standard circuit symbols, some of which are shown in Fig. 9.49. However, non-standard symbols are sometimes used and this can cause confusion. Figure 9.50 shows an alternative symbol for a lamp (bulb) and one for a fuse.

Fortunately, when alternative symbols are used in a circuit diagram they are usually accompanied by a descriptive list. Figure 9.51 gives an example: the injector resistors are shown as a saw tooth line, number 21 on the list, and on the diagram. This solves the problem of deciphering the diagram.

The **wiring diagram** is an essential aid to **fault tracing**. To help the user to understand a wiring diagram certain codes are used. Two important codes that are used for this purpose are:

- the **colour code**;
- the **code of symbols** that are used to represent devices as shown in Fig. 9.49.

Colour code

A commonly used colour code is given here.

N = brown	Y = yellow
P = purple	K = pink
W = white	R = red
O = orange	LG = light green
U = blue	B = black
G = green	S = slate

In order to assist in tracing cables they are often provided with a second colour tracer stripe. The wiring diagram shows this by means of letters, e.g. a cable on the wiring diagram with GB written on it is a green cable with a black tracer stripe. The first letter is the predominant colour and the second is the tracer stripe.

Note – This is not a universal colour code and, as with many other factors, it is always wise to have accurate information to hand that relates to the product being worked on.

The predominant (main) colours frequently relate to particular circuits as follows:

- brown (N) = main battery feeds
- white (W) = essential ignition circuits (not fused)
- light green and also green (LG) (G) = auxiliary ignition circuits (fused)
- blue (U) = headlamp circuits
- red (R) = side and tail lamp circuits
- black (B) = earth connections
- purple (P) = auxiliary, non-ignition, circuits (probably fused)

A typical wiring diagram is shown in Fig. 9.52.

The wiring loom or harness

It is common practice to bind cables together to facilitate positioning them in the vehicle structure. It used to be the practice to fabricate the **loom**, or **harness**, from a woven fabric. Modern loom sheathing materials are likely to be a PVC-type of material. Figure 9.53 shows the engine compartment part of a typical wiring loom.

As the amount of electrical devices on vehi-

Name of device	Symbol	Name of device	Symbol
Electric cell		Lamp (bulb)	
Battery		Diode	
Resistor		Transistor (npn)	
Variable resistor		Light emitting diode (LED)	
Potentiometer		Switch	
Capacitor		Conductors (wires) crossing	
Inductor (coil)		Conductors (wires) joining	
Transformer		Zener diode	
Fuse		Light dependent resistor (LDR)	

Fig. 9.49 A selection of circuit symbols

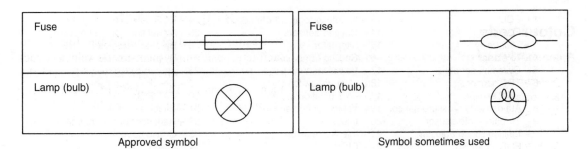

Fuse		Fuse	
Lamp (bulb)		Lamp (bulb)	
Approved symbol		Symbol sometimes used	

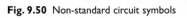

Fig. 9.50 Non-standard circuit symbols

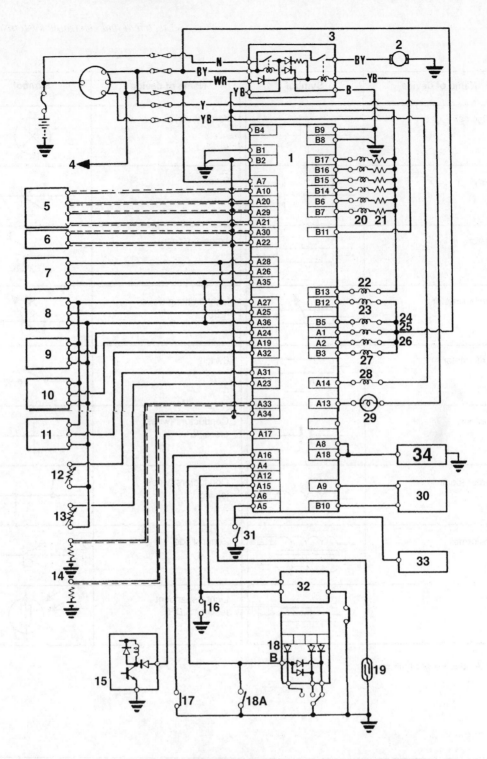

Fig. 9.51 System diagram with list describing circuit elements

1 – ECU	13 – Air intake temperature sensor	24 – EGR solenoid
2 – Fuel pump	14 – Oxygen sensors*	25 – Air suction control solenoid*
3 – Main relay	15 – Alternator	26 – By-pass solenoid B
4 – To starter	16 – Cooling fan switch	27 – By-pass solenoid A
5 – Cyl/crank sensor	17 – Power steering switch	28 – Air-con clutch relay
6 – TDC sensor	18a – Neutral switch (MT)	29 – Check engine light
7 – MAP sensor	18b – A/T position switch	30 – EAT ECU
8 – Atmospheric pressure sensor	19 – Vehicle speed sensor	31 – Clutch switch M/T
9 – Throttle angle sensor	20 – Injectors	32 – Radiator fan control unit
10 – Ignition timing adjuster	21 – Injector resistors	33 – Cruise control
11 – EGR lift sensor	22 – EICV	34 – Igniter unit
12 – Water temperature sensor	23 – Pressure regulator solenoid	*Emission vehicles only

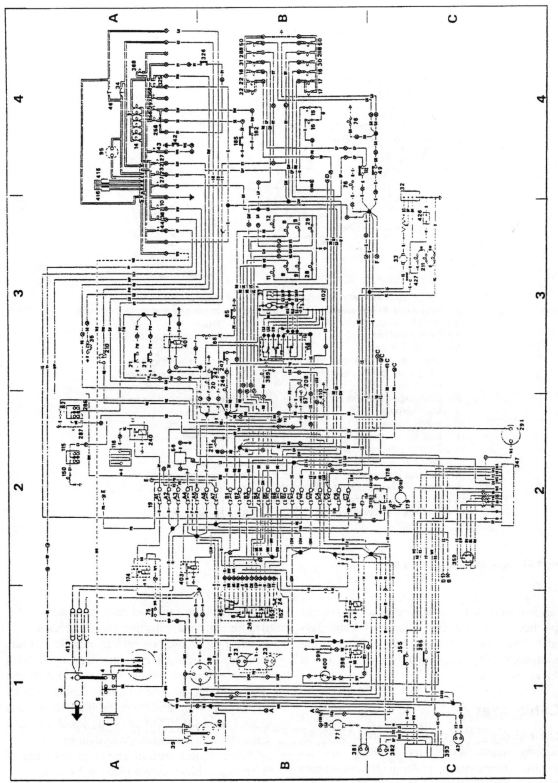

Fig. 9.52 A typical wiring diagram

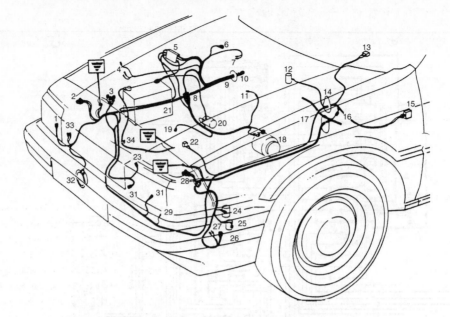

1 – RH direction indicator lamp connector
2 – RH headlamp connector
3 – Relays – air conditioning
4 – Ignition coil connector
5 – Fusible link box
6 – Windscreen wiper motor plug
7 – Handbrake warning lamp switch
    connector
8 – Main/engine harness connector
9 – Main harness
10 – Bulkhead grommet
11 – Fuel cut-off solenoid
12 – Throttle solenoid – air conditioning
13 – Switch – air conditioning
14 – Bulkhead grommets
15 – Relay – air conditioning – 'A' post
16 – Main/air conditioning harness connector
17 – Harness – air conditioning
18 – Alternator

19 – Reverse light switch
20 – Starter solenoid
21 – Battery
22 – Charging pressure switch –
    air conditioning
23 – Cooling fan connector
24 – Headlamp washer motor
25 – Windscreen washer motor
26 – LH direction indicator lamp
    connector
27 – LH side lamp
28 – LH headlamp connector
29 – Compressor clutch –
    air conditioning
30 – Fan – air conditioning
31 – Thermostatic switch
32 – Horn
33 – RH side lamp
34 – Cable clip

Fig. 9.53 Engine compartment wiring loom

cles has increased, the heating effect of current has become a problem. Alternative cable layouts have been devised where cables are grouped, side by side, so that heat can escape to the atmosphere.

Cable sizes

The **resistance** of a cable (wire) is affected by (among other factors) its diameter and its length. For a given material the resistance increases with length and decreases with diameter. Doubling a given length of cable will double its resistance, doubling the diameter of the same length of cable will decrease the resistance to one quarter of the original value. Cable sizes are,

therefore, important and only those sizes specified for a given application should be used.

Most cables used on vehicles need to be quite flexible. This flexibility is provided by making the cable from a number of strands of wire and it is common practice to specify cable sizes by the number of strands and the diameter of each strand, e.g. 14/0.30 means 14 strands of wire and each strand has a diameter of 0.30 mm.

Some typical current carrying capacities of cables for vehicle use are given in Table 9.3.

The choice of cable is a factor that is decided at the design stage of a vehicle. However, it sometimes affects vehicle repair work when, for example, an extra accessory is being fitted to a vehicle or a new cable is being fitted to replace a

Table 9.3 A sample of cable sizes, their current ratings and typical uses

Size of cable	Current rating	Typical use
14/0.30	8.75 A	Side and tail lamps
28/0.30	17.5 A	Headlamps
120/0.30	60 A	Alternator to battery

damaged one. In such cases, the manufacturer's instructions must be observed.

Wiring diagrams

Figure 9.52 shows a full wiring diagram for a vehicle. In order to make it more intelligible Rover uses a grid system with numbers 1 to 4 across the page, and letters A, B and C at the sides. This means that an area of diagram can be located . For example, the vehicle battery is in the grid area 1A.

As a further aid to the user, wiring diagrams are often broken down into circuits that relate to a specific system. An example is shown in Fig. 9.51. Should the diagnostics report an injector circuit fault, reference to the code shows that the injectors are at 20, 21 and they are connected to the main relay by a YB (yellow with black tracer) cable. As shown in the description of the ohm-meter test for the resistance of the injector coil, and the separate resistor, this diagram directs the technician to the precise part of the circuit where the tests are conducted.

9.8 Circuit protection

Fuses

The purpose of the **fuse** is to provide a 'weak' link in the circuit which will fail (blow) if the current exceeds a certain value and, in so doing, protect the circuit elements and the vehicle from the damage that could result from excess current. The fuse is probably the best known **circuit protection device.** There are several different types of fuses and some of these are shown in Fig. 9.54.

Fuses have different **current ratings** and this accounts for the range of types available. Care must be taken to select a correct replacement; larger rated fuses must never be used in an attempt to 'get round' a problem. Many modern vehicles are equipped with a **fusible link** which is fitted in the main battery lead as an added safety precaution.

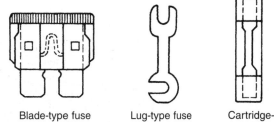

Blade-type fuse   Lug-type fuse   Cartridge-type fuse

Fig. 9.54 Fuse types

It is common practice to place fuses together in a reasonably accessible place on the vehicle. Another feature of the increased use of electrical/electronic circuits on vehicles is an increase in the number of fuses to be found on a vehicle. Figure 9.55 shows an **engine compartment fusebox** that carries fusible links in addition to 'normal' fuses. The same vehicle also has a **dashboard fusebox**. This also carries 'spare' fuses which appear to the right of the other fuses as shown in Fig. 9.56.

Whilst in the event of circuit failure it is common practice to check fuses and replace any 'blown' ones, it should be remembered that something caused the fuse to blow. Recurrent fuse 'blowing' requires that circuits be checked to ascertain the cause of the excess current that is causing the failure.

Some circuits are protected by **thermal circuit breakers**, as shown in Fig. 9.57. This is a convenient point at which to introduce the circuit breaker. The thermal circuit breaker relies for its operation on the principle of the **bi-metallic strip**. In Fig. 9.57 the bi-metal strip carries the current between the terminals of the circuit breaker. Excess current, above that for which the circuit is designed, will cause the temperature of the bi-metal strip to rise to a level where the strip will curve and cause the contacts to separate. This will open the circuit and current will cease to flow. When the temperature of the bi-metal strip falls the circuit will be re-made. This action leads to intermittent functioning of the circuit, which will continue until the fault is rectified. An application may be of a 7.5 A circuit breaker to protect a door lock circuit. The advantage of the circuit breaker over a fuse is that the circuit breaker can be re-used.

Other circuit protection

Vehicle circuits are subject to **transient voltages** which arise from several sources. Those which

No.	Rating	Function
G	50 amp	Radio, power amplifier, electric seats
H	50 amp	Ignition switch circuit
I	80 amp	Battery output
J	50 amp	Window lift
K	50 amp	ABS brake system
L	50 amp	Supply to fuses 4, 5 and 6 and sidelight relay

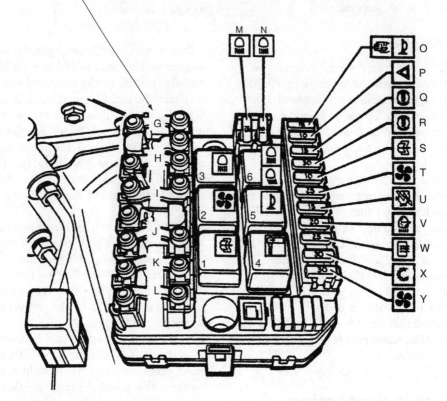

Relays
1 – Cooling fan changeover or manifold heater
2 – Cooling fan
3 – Lighting
4 – Starter
5 – Horns
6 – Main/dip beams
7 – Air conditioning changeover

Fig. 9.55 Engine compartment fusebox (Rover 800)

interest us here are **load dump**, **alternator field decay voltage**, switching of an **inductive device** (coil, relay, etc.) and over voltage arising from incorrect use of batteries when **jump starting**.

Load dump occurs when an alternator becomes disconnected from the vehicle battery while the alternator is charging, i.e. when the engine is running. Figure 9.58 shows a **Zener diode** as used for surge protection in an alternator circuit. The breakdown (Zener) voltage of

the diode is 10–15 V above the normal system voltage. Such voltages can occur if an open circuit occurs in the main alternator output lead when the engine is running. Other vehicle circuits, such as **coil ignition**, can also create **inductive surges**. Should such voltage surges occur they could damage the alternator circuits but, with the Zener diode connected as shown, the excess voltage is 'dumped' to earth via the Zener diode. Should such a voltage surge occur it may

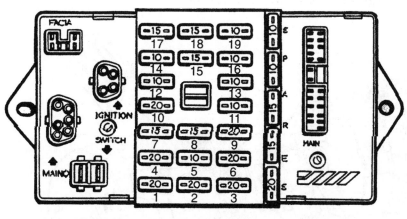

Fuse functions

Fuse No.	Rating	Wire colour	Function
1	20 amp	N/O	Sunroof, driver's seat heater
2	20 amp	S/U	RH front door window lift
3	20 amp	S/R	LH front door window lift
4	20 amp	P/N	Front and rear cigar lighters Footwell lamps
5	10 amp	P	Interior lights, boot light, interior light delay unit, map light, door open lights, trip computer memory, radio station memory, clock memory, headlight delay unit
6	20 amp	P/O	Burglar alarm ECU (optional) Central locking ECU
7	15 amp	R/O	RH number plate lamp RH side, tail and marker lights Trailer plug
8	10 amp	R/B	Cigar lighter illumination, LH licence plate lamp, sidelight warning light, glovebox light, trailer plug, dashboard illumination, LH side tail lights
9	20 amp	S/O	LH rear window lift
10	20 amp	S/G	RH rear window lift

Fig. 9.56 Dashboard fusebox (Rover 800)

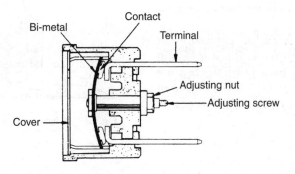

Fig. 9.57 A circuit breaker (Toyota)

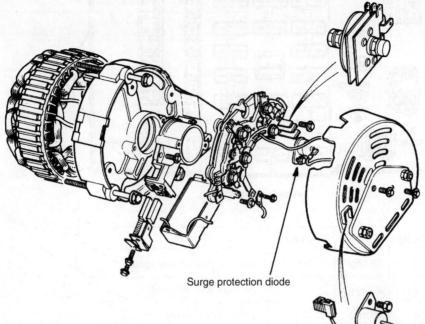

Surge protection diode

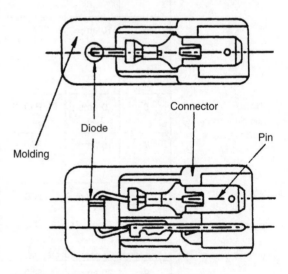

Fig. 9.58 Voltage surge protection by Zener diode

destroy the protection diode. The alternator would then cease charging. In such a case the surge protection diode would need to be replaced, after the cause of the surge had been remedied.

Figure 9.59 shows another form of circuit protection where a diode is built into a cable connector. This reduces the risk of damage from reversed connections and it is evident that one should be aware of such uses because a continuity test on such a connector will require correct polarity at the meter leads.

Connectors

Increased use of electrical/electronic circuits has led to an increase in the number of electrical connections. These connections may consist of **multiple pins** (Fig. 9.60), as in the case of the main wiring harness at the ECU, or a single connection (Fig. 9.61), as in the case of an ignition coil.

Comprehensive coverage of connectors is beyond the scope of this book. But it is helpful to consider some of the basic principles because connectors are thought to be a major source of problems if they are incorrectly fitted or poorly maintained.

Molding   Diode   Connector   Pin

Fig. 9.59 A protection diode in a cable connector

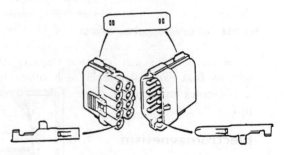

Fig. 9.60 Multiple pin connector

Fig. 9.61 Single cable connectors

9.9 Electrical principles

Electricity and magnetism

For our purposes we need to consider two types of magnet: permanent magnets and electromagnets.

Permanent magnets

Permanent magnets are found in nature; magnetite which is also known as lodestone is naturally magnetic and ancient mariners used it as an aid to navigation. Modern permanent magnets are made from **alloys**. One particular permanent (hard) magnetic material named **alnico** is an alloy of iron, aluminium, nickel, cobalt and a small amount of copper. The magnetism that it contains arises from the structure of the atoms of the metals that are alloyed together.

Magnetic force is a natural phenomenon. To deal with magnetism, rules about its behaviour have been established. The rules that are important to our study are related to the behaviour of magnets and the main rules that concern us are:

- magnets have **north** and **south poles**;
- magnets have **magnetic fields**;
- magnetic fields are made up from **lines of magnetic force**;
- magnetic fields flow from north to south.

If two bar magnets are placed close to each other, so that the north pole of one is close to the south pole of the other, the magnets will be drawn together. If the north pole of one magnet is placed next to the north pole of the other the magnets will be pushed apart. This tells us that like poles repel each other and unlike poles attract each other. This is shown in Fig. 9.62.

Electromagnetism

The magnetic effect of an electric current

Figure 9.63 shows how a circular magnetic field is set up around a wire (conductor) which is carrying electric current.

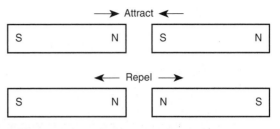

Fig. 9.62 Attraction and repulsion of magnets

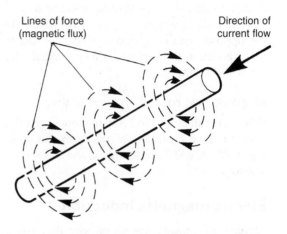

Fig. 9.63 Magnetic field around a straight conductor

Direction of the magnetic field due to an electric current in a straight conductor

Think of screwing a right hand threaded bolt into a nut or a screw into a piece of wood. The screw is rotated clockwise (this corresponds to the direction, north to south, of the magnetic field). The screw enters into the wood and this corresponds to the direction of the electric current in the conductor. The field runs in a clockwise direction and the current flows in towards the wood, as shown in Fig. 9.64.

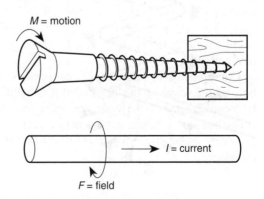

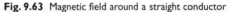

Fig. 9.64 Direction of magnetic field

Current in   Current out

Fig. 9.65 Convention for representing current flow and magnetic field

This leads to a convention for representing current flowing into a conductor and current flowing out (Fig. 9.65). At the end of the conductor where current is flowing into the wire, a + is placed; this represents an arrow head. At the opposite end of the wire, where current is flowing out, a dot is placed; this represents the tip of the arrow.

Magnetic field caused by a coil of wire

When a conductor (wire) is made into a coil the magnetic field created is of the form shown in Fig. 9.66. A coil such as this is the basis of a solenoid.

Electromagnetic induction

Figure 9.67 shows a length of wire that has a voltmeter connected to its ends. The small arrows pointing from the north pole to the south

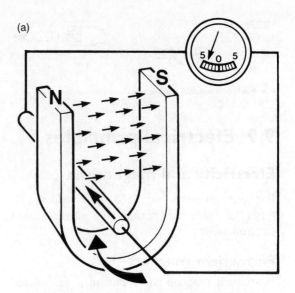

(a)

An EMF (electromotive force) is produced in the wire whenever it moves across the lines of magnetic flux.

Note: The reversal of current takes place when direction of movement is reversed.

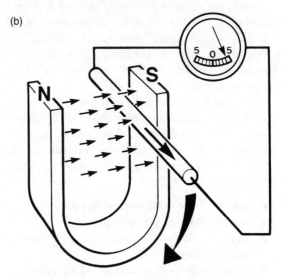

(b)

Fig. 9.67 Current flow, magnetic field and motion

pole of the magnet represent lines of magnetic force (flux) that make a magnetic field. The arrow in the wire (conductor) shows the direction of current flow and the larger arrow, with the curved tail, shows the direction in which the wire is being moved.

Movement of the wire through the magnetic field, so that it cuts across the lines of magnetic force, causes an electromotive force (EMF – voltage) to be produced in the wire. In Fig. 9.67(a) where the wire is being moved upwards the electric current flows in towards the page. In Fig. 9.67(b) the direction of motion of the wire

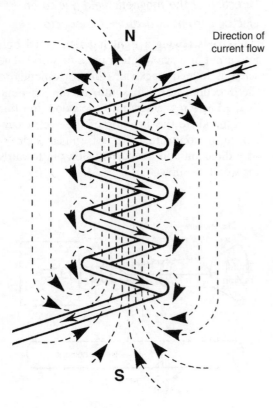

N

Direction of current flow

S

Fig. 9.66 Magnetic field of a coil

is downwards, across the lines of magnetic force, and the current in the wire is in the opposite direction. Current is also produced in the wire if the magnet is moved, up and down, while the wire is held stationary. Mechanical energy is being converted into electrical energy; this is the principle that is used in generators such as alternators and dynamos.

Electric motor effect

If the length of wire, shown in Fig. 9.67(a), is made into a loop, as shown in Fig. 9.68, and electric current is fed into the loop, **opposing magnetic fields** are set up. In Fig. 9.68, the current is fed into the loop via brushes and a split ring. This split ring is a simple commutator. One half of the split ring is connected to one end of the loop and the other half is connected to the other end. The effect of this is that the current in the loop flows in one direction. The coil of wire that is mounted on the pole pieces, marked N and S, creates the magnetic field.

These opposing fields create forces. These forces 'push' against each other, as shown in Fig. 9.69, and they cause the loop to rotate. In Fig. 9.69 the ends of the loop are marked A and B. B is the end that the current is flowing into and A is the end of the loop where the current is leaving the loop.

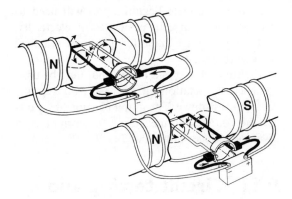

Fig. 9.68 Current flowing through the loop

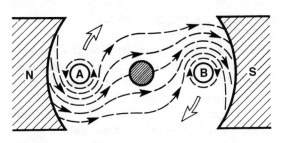

Fig. 9.69 Opposing magnetic fields

By these processes, electrical energy is converted into mechanical energy and this is the principle of operation of electric motors, such as the starter motor. Just to convince yourself, try using **Fleming's rule** to work out the direction of the current, the field and the motion.

Fleming's rule

Consider the thumb and first two fingers on each hand. Hold them in the manner shown in Fig. 9.70.

- **Motion** this is represented by the direction that the thumb (M for motion) is pointing.
- **Field** the direction (north to south) of the magnetic field is represented by the first finger (F for field).
- **Current** think of the hard c in second. The second finger represents the direction of the electric current.

Note – We think that it is helpful for vehicle technicians to think of the MG car badge. If you imagine yourself standing in front of an MG, looking towards the front of the vehicle, the badge will present you with an M on your left, and a G on your right. So you can remember *M for motors* and *G for generators*, left hand rule for motors, right hand rule for generators.

Electric circuit principles

Materials can usefully be divided into three categories:

- **conductors**
- **semi-conductors**
- **insulators**

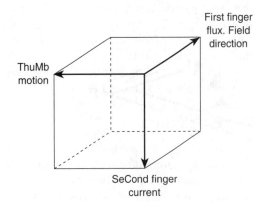

Fig. 9.70 Fleming's rule

Electrical conductance and resistance

The ability of a material to conduct electricity is known as its **conductivity**. The opposite (inverse) of conductivity is **resistivity**. Examples of commonly used conductors are **copper**, **aluminium** and, in electronics, **silver** and **gold**.

Semi-conductors

Materials such as **silicon** do not have good insulating properties and they are not good conductors. Silicon is a semi-conductor material that is widely used in electronics and its conductivity can be varied by **doping**.

Insulators

These are materials where large electrical potential (applied voltage) causes only very small current to flow. **Rubber**, most **plastics** and **ceramics** like **porcelain** are commonly used insulators.

Temperature coefficient of resistance

The resistance of most materials changes with temperature. In the case of conductors the resistance of the material increases as the temperature increases. The relationship between resistance and temperature is affected by a factor known as the **temperature coefficient of resistance**.

When the temperature of a semi-conductor rises, the resistance falls and it is said to have a **negative temperature coefficient** (NTC).

Electric current

All materials are made up from **atoms**. Each atom is made up of smaller particles. An atom has a **nucleus** and, for our purposes, the nucleus can be thought of as being surrounded by **electrons** rotating (orbiting) around it. Electrons carry a charge of electricity. In solid materials, such as metals, the atoms are bonded tightly but some of their electrons are not held tightly to the nucleus. At room temperature these **free electrons** move randomly about the material.

Electric circuits

Up to this point we have shown that there are two principal sources of electricity on a vehicle, namely the battery and the alternator. Electricity will only perform its task if it has circuits to flow in. It is, therefore, necessary to have an appreci-

ation of electric circuits. To begin with, we need to consider three electrical units. These are:

- the **volt**   this is the unit of electrical pressure;
- the **ampere** or amp   this is the unit of electric current;
- the **ohm**   this is the unit of electrical resistance.

9.10 Ohm's law

Voltage, current and resistance are related by **Ohm's law**. Ohm's law is often taken to mean that if a voltage is applied to a circuit that contains resistance, the current that flows in the circuit will be proportional to the voltage, provided that the temperature remains constant. Ohm's law is normally expressed mathematically as:

voltage = current $\times$ resistance

The symbol V is used for voltage in volts. $I =$ current in amperes. $R =$ resistance in ohms. Ohm's law is expressed algebraically as:

$V = IR$

A common practice in teaching is to build circuits and, by using low voltage (2 V), DC supplies and resistors of known value, to take meter readings of current and voltage. These readings are noted down and compared with those that are calculated by using Ohm's law. The examples shown here should make the point adequately. If you are a complete beginner you will need to take a short course in principles of electricity, preferably a course that offers plenty of practical work with circuits.

Figure 9.71 shows a circuit that may be used to check the relationship between voltage, current and resistance. The graph obtained by varying the voltage and measuring the current for a given resistance shows that $V = I \times R$.

9.11 Circuit testing and meters

Circuit testing

Electrical systems are designed so that each element of a circuit will have a known **resistance value**. These resistance values must be maintained throughout the life of the system.

The operation of vehicle electrical/electronic systems can be upset if resistance values, for any part of a circuit, are incorrect. Checking of elec-

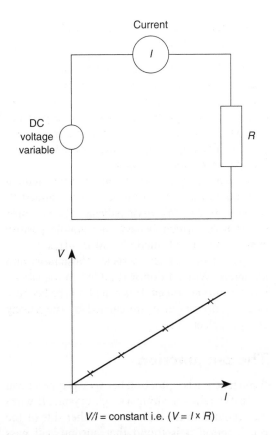

(a)

(b)

Fig. 9.71 Demonstrating Ohm's law

V/I = constant i.e. $(V = I \times R)$

Fig. 9.72 Two types of test meters (a) moving coil, (b) digital

trical resistance in vehicle circuits is therefore an important part of a vehicle technician's skill. Whilst it is possible to perform resistance checks on vehicle circuits without a great deal of background knowledge, it is beneficial to have some understanding of principles because a little deeper understanding often assists technicians in working out why some device is not working correctly.

Meters

The instrument panel on most vehicles carries a great deal of driver information, e.g. vehicle speed (speedometer), coolant temperature, oil pressure and so on. **Meters** are also used for fault diagnosis and we think it useful to have an insight into the operating principles of two test meters because this will assist you in understanding how other meters work. Figure 9.72 shows two meters that can be used for circuit testing: (a) is a **moving coil meter** and (b) is a **digital meter**. Figures 9.73(a) and (b) show these in more detail.

Moving coil meter

The moving coil meter takes the sample current into the moving coil. This causes the moving coil magnetic field to react with the field of the permanent magnet. Partial rotation of the coil and its pointer then occurs, against the force of the control spring. The amount of movement is related to the size of the variable being measured, e.g. volts, amperes or ohms. A good quality moving coil meter with a resistance of 20 000 ohms per volt is suitable for most circuit testing on vehicles.

Digital meter

A digital meter samples the variable being measured, e.g. volts, amperes or ohms, and processes them in the **electronic circuits** of the

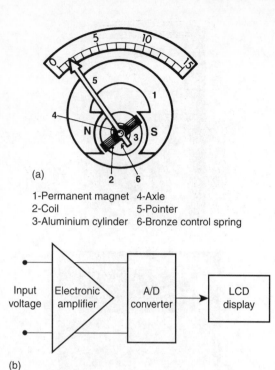

(a)

1-Permanent magnet   4-Axle
2-Coil   5-Pointer
3-Aluminium cylinder 6-Bronze control spring

Input voltage → Electronic amplifier → A/D converter → LCD display

(b)

Fig. 9.73 Detail of the test meters (a) moving coil, (b) digital voltmeter circuit

meter. The resulting reading is displayed on a **liquid crystal (LCD) panel**. Digital meters have a very high input impedance (resistance) which makes them suitable for diagnostic checks on electronic systems.

9.12 Electronics

Electronics is the branch of electrical engineering concerned with the 'the science and technology of the conduction of electricity in a vacuum, a gas or a semi-conductor'. It is the semi-conductor that concerns us most, at this stage, so it is necessary to explain what the term means.

Semi-conductors

Metals such as copper, aluminium and gold are good conductors of electricity; other materials like rubber and PVC are bad conductors and they are known as insulators. Materials such as silicon and **germanium** have conductivity which lies between that of good conductors and insulators. These materials are semi-conductors. Semi-conductors allow an electric current to flow only under certain circumstances.

Doping

Pure silicon, when treated (doped) with substances such as aluminium or **gallium**, is widely used in the manufacture of electronic components. The **doping agents** which are added in tiny concentrations, probably less than one part per million, cause the silicon to become more conductive. The doping agents are divided into two groups: **acceptors** and **donors**.

Typical acceptors are **boron**, gallium, **indium** and aluminium. When an acceptor is added to the silicon it forms **p-type silicon**. The acceptor forms holes which behave like **mobile positive charge** and so this silicon is called p-type.

Typical donors are **arsenic**, **phosphorus** and **antimony**. When a donor is added to the silicon it forms **n-type silicon**. It is called n-type because electric currents in it are carried by (negatively charged) electrons.

The p-n junction

A **p-n junction** is a junction between p-type silicon and n-type silicon within a single crystal. If wires are attached to the material on either side of the p-n junction it is found that current will pass through the device in one direction, but hardly at all in the opposite direction. Such a device is a junction rectifier which is commonly known as a **junction diode** or just **diode**. We thus have a device that acts like a one-way valve; it will pass current in one direction but not the other.

Figure 9.74 shows a representation of a p-n junction in silicon, connected to a source of electricity. When it is connected in the way shown, with the positive battery terminal connected to the p-type material, the junction is said to be **forward biased**. When the forward voltage reaches approximately 0.7 V a continuous cur-

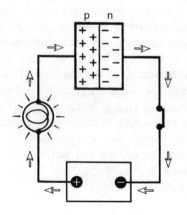

Fig. 9.74 A p-n junction

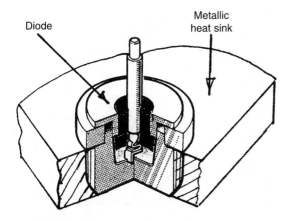

Fig. 9.75 A diode

rent will flow in the forward direction. Figure 9.75 shows a diode in a **metallic heat sink**. The second terminal of the diode is formed from the metal case into which it is built and the heat sink conducts heat away from the diode.

Figure 9.76 shows the symbol for a diode. The arrow indicates the direction in which current will flow. Diodes are used in circuits to permit current flow in one direction only. A common use of a diode is in the conversion (rectifying) of alternating current (AC) to direct current (DC), as shown in Section 9.2 on alternators.

Testing a junction diode

The fact that a diode conducts freely in the forward direction and, virtually, not at all in the reverse direction means that an **ohm-meter** can be used to check it for correct operation. This is shown in Fig. 9.77.

Other types of diodes

In addition to the junction diode extensive use is made in vehicle technology of other types of diodes. We shall have a brief look at two of these, namely the Zener diode and a **light emitting diode** (LED).

Zener diode

The **Zener effect** occurs when a heavily doped diode is **reverse biased**. The Zener effect permits a low reverse voltage to produce breakdown and the diode conducts in the reverse direction.

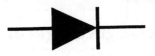

Fig. 9.76 Circuit symbol for a diode

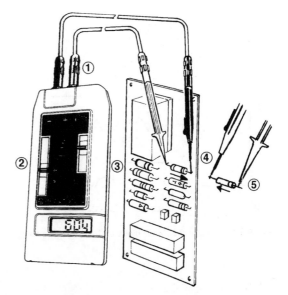

1 – Test leads
2 – Multimeter scale setting (continuity)
3 – Electronic components on a circuit board
4–5 – Test probes placed on the diode to check for correct operation

Fig. 9.77 Diode test using Avo 2002 (Thorn EMI)

Diodes that are made to work in this way are called 'Zener' diodes. The Zener diode may be thought of as a **voltage conscious switch** and it is often used as a voltage reference in devices such as **voltage regulators**.

Figure 9.78 shows a simple circuit with a Zener diode in series with a bulb. If the potential divider slider is placed in the zero volts position and then moved towards the right, the Zener diode will conduct; when the Zener voltage is reached the bulb will light up. Note the direction of current flow through the Zener diode.

Light emitting diode (LED)

Silicon is an opaque material which blocks the passage of light and the energy which derives from the action of the diode is given off as heat. LEDs are different because they use other semiconductor materials such as gallium, arsenic and phosphorus and the energy deriving from their operation is given out as light. The material from which the LED is made determines the colour of the light given out. Figure 9.79 shows an LED and its circuit symbol.

It may be considered that the LED is a semiconductor device which gives out light when current flows through it. LEDs are used as **indicator lights** and for **fault indicator codes** on

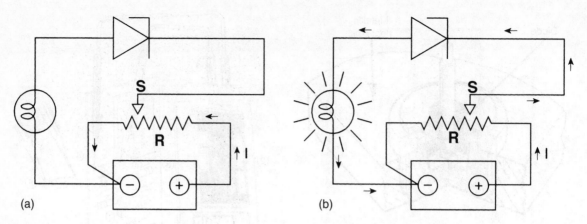

Fig. 9.78 Action of the Zener diode (a) low voltage – no light, (b) higher voltage – lamp lights

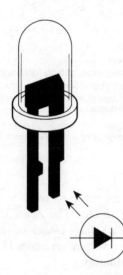

Fig. 9.79 An LED and its circuit symbol

1 – Electronic control unit   3 – Yellow LED
2 – LED display   4 – Red LED

Fig. 9.80 LEDs for fault code display

some electronic systems, for example. This is illustrated in Fig. 9.80.

Transistors

The **transistor** is another basic building block of electronic circuits. It may be thought of as two p-n junction diodes connected back to back, as shown in Fig. 9.81. (This makes a bi-polar transistor.) Transistors are used as **switches** or **current–voltage amplifiers** and in many other applications.

Transistors have three connections shown in Fig. 9.82 and named as follows;

- base – (B)
- collector – (C)
- emitter – (E)

Transistors are non-conductive until a very small current flows through the **base–emitter**

circuit. This very small current in the base–emitter circuit 'turns on' the **collector–emitter circuit** and permits a larger current to flow through it. When the base–emitter current is switched off the collector–emitter immediately ceases to conduct and the transistor is effectively switched off. This happens in a fraction of a second (a few nano-seconds usually) and makes the transistor suitable for **high-speed switching operations**, as required in many vehicle applications. The use of switching transistors is covered in Chapter 10 on ignition systems.

Integrated circuits (I/Cs)

Many diodes, resistors and transistors can be made on a single piece of silicon (a **chip**). When

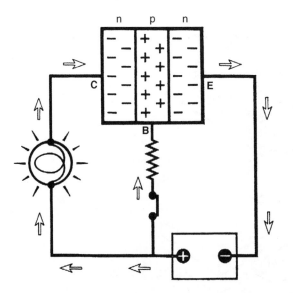

Fig. 9.81 Two p-n junctions back to back

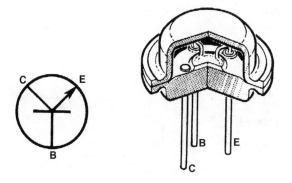

Fig. 9.82 A transistor

Fig. 9.83 A typical I/C

the diodes, resistors and transistors are connected together in specific ways to make circuits on one piece of silicon, the resulting device is known as an **integrated circuit** (I/C). When a small number of diodes, transistors and resistors are connected together (about 12) the result is called **small scale integration** (SSI); when the number is greater than 100 it is called **large scale integration** (LSI).

From the outside an I/C looks like Fig. 9.83. The 'legs' along the sides are metal tags which are used to connect the I/C to other components. The number of tags is related to the complexity of the I/C. When I/Cs are packaged as shown they are known as **DIL type**, which means that the 'legs' are dual in line. Figure 9.84 shows an I/C built into an ECU.

Field effect transistors (FETs)

This type of transistor is faster in operation and uses less power than a bi-polar transistor. They are used in integrated circuits and many other applications.

The **FET** shown in Fig. 9.85 is a **CMOS device**. The CMOS stands for complementary metal-oxide semi-conductor. These words relate to the way that the transistor works and the various layers of material that make up the transistor. When the **gate voltage** reaches a certain level the channel becomes conductive and an electrical connection is made between the **source** and the **drain**. The source and drain can thus be connected and disconnected, electrically, by the application and removal of the gate voltage. There are several different types of FETs and the circuit symbol shown in Fig. 9.86 is typical of the type of symbol used to represent them on circuit diagrams.

9.13 Logic devices

A common use of transistors is to make **logic devices**, such as the **NOR gate**. Figure 9.87 shows how a 'logic' gate is built up from an arrangement of resistors and a transistor. There are three inputs A, B, and C. If one or more of these inputs is high (logic 1), the output will be low (logic 0). The output is shown as A + B + C with a line, or bar, over the top; the + sign means OR. Thus the A + B + C with the line above means 'not A or B or C' (NOR : NOT OR).

The base resistors R_b have a value that ensures that the base current, even when only one input is high (logic 1), will drive the transistor into saturation to make the output low (logic 0). (RTL stands for resistor transistor logic.)

Truth tables

Logic circuits operate on the basis of **Boolean logic** and terms like **NOT, NOR, NAND**, etc.

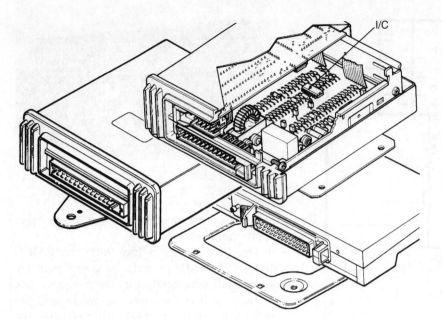

Fig. 9.84 An I/C in an ECU

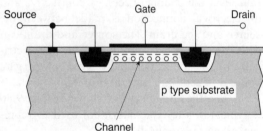

Fig. 9.85 A CMOS field effect transistor

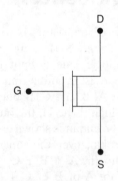

Fig. 9.86 Circuit symbol for FET

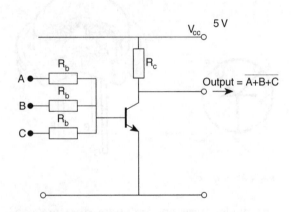

Fig. 9.87 The RTL NOR gate

In the NOR truth table, when the inputs A and B are both 0 the gate output, C, is 1. The other three input combinations each give an output C = 0. A range of other commonly used logic gates and their truth tables is given in Fig. 9.89.

Electronic control unit (ECU)

In this section the intention is to provide an insight into the way in which an **electronic control unit**, shown in Fig. 9.90, works. Seldom, if ever, would a vehicle technician in a garage have to attempt to repair a control unit. The normal process of diagnosis and repair requires the **black box** treatment. That is to say that the defective unit must be accurately located, the cause of its failure rectified and then a *correct* replacement unit fitted. Most test equipment is made on the assumption that this is the case. The word *correct* is emphasized because the ECU for

derive from Boolean algebra. This need not concern us here, but it is necessary to know that the input–output behaviour of logic devices is expressed in the form of a **truth table**. The truth table for the NOR gate is given in Fig. 9.88.

In computing and control systems, a system known as TTL (**transistor to transistor logic**) is used. In TTL logic 0 is a voltage between 0 and 0.8 V. Logic 1 is a voltage between 2.0 and 5.0 V.

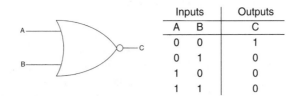

Inputs		Outputs
A	B	C
0	0	1
0	1	0
1	0	0
1	1	0

Fig. 9.88 NOR gate symbol and truth table

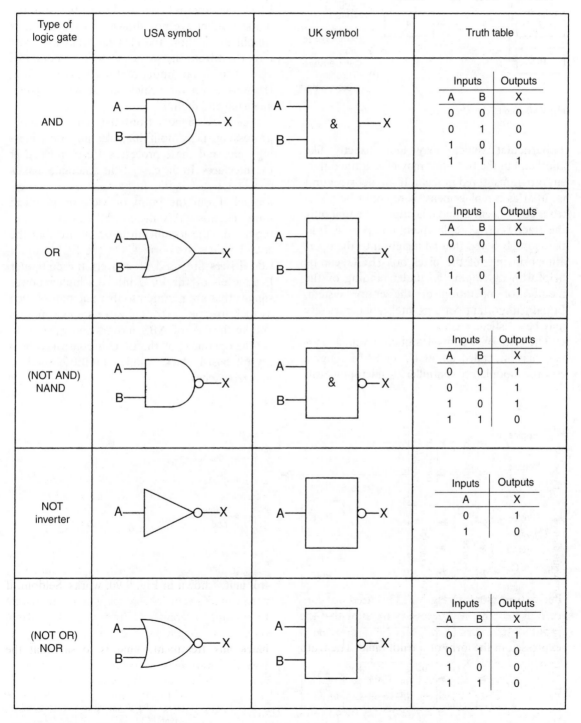

Type of logic gate	USA symbol	UK symbol	Truth table
AND			Inputs: A B, Outputs: X 0 0 | 0 0 1 | 0 1 0 | 0 1 1 | 1
OR			Inputs: A B, Outputs: X 0 0 | 0 0 1 | 1 1 0 | 1 1 1 | 1
(NOT AND) NAND			Inputs: A B, Outputs: X 0 0 | 1 0 1 | 1 1 0 | 1 1 1 | 0
NOT inverter			Inputs: A, Outputs: X 0 | 1 1 | 0
(NOT OR) NOR			Inputs: A B, Outputs: X 0 0 | 1 0 1 | 0 1 0 | 0 1 1 | 0

Fig. 9.89 A table of logic gates and symbols

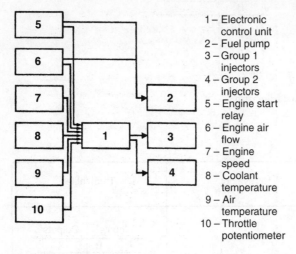

1 – Electronic control unit
2 – Fuel pump
3 – Group 1 injectors
4 – Group 2 injectors
5 – Engine start relay
6 – Engine air flow
7 – Engine speed
8 – Coolant temperature
9 – Air temperature
10 – Throttle potentiometer

Fig. 9.90 The ECU in the system

a particular vehicle may look exactly like another, but the two units may have quite different programs stored in them. If an incorrect unit is fitted as a replacement there could be disastrous consequences and it is imperative that only the exactly correct replacement unit is used. It is, therefore, believed that an insight into the operating principles of the 'black box' (ECU) can be helpful in developing an understanding of the method of operation of the entire system. Equally important perhaps intellectual curiosity may be satisfied.

The electronic control unit in a vehicle system may be called an ECU, an **ECM** (engine control module), a **controller**, a **microprocessor**

or some other name. To a large extent it depends on the system in which the device is used as a controller and the make and age of the vehicle to which it is fitted. However, for the current purpose we will use the term electronic control unit and work on the principle that it contains a microprocessor (or equivalent) and that the microprocessor operates on computing (digital) principles.

Figure 9.91 shows a simplified diagram of an ECU. The internal circuits (buses) that link the units together are not shown and the device is simplified to show the elements that are most important from the service technician's point of view. The signal inputs that are obtained from the sensors on the vehicle are shown as **pulse**, **analogue** and **digital**.

The 'raw' signals from the sensors require processing, i.e. amplifying, cleaning up (filtering), etc. and these processes are performed at the **interfaces**. In the case of the analogue signals conversion to digital form must also be performed. From the point of view of practical fault diagnosis this means that, on the ECU input side, the technician must ensure that the sensor values are correct. On the ECU output side **drivers** are used to convert the computer logic levels of the ECU into the higher power signals that are required to drive actuators such as fuel injectors, extra air valve stepper motors and, in the case of ABS, motors and valves.

The operation of the ECU is controlled by a **crystal based clock**, similar to those used in quartz watches.

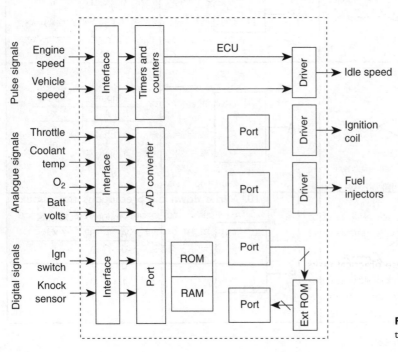

Fig. 9.91 A simplified microcontroller-type ECU

Modern ECUs usually include an **external diagnostic (serial) port** through which **diagnostic equipment** can direct the processor to perform functional checks of the input and output circuits. To aid this process, a section of **durable memory** may be set aside to store fault codes that have been generated while the vehicle has been operating. The electronic memory used for this purpose may be an **EEPROM** (electrically erasable programmable read only memory) which stores fault codes until they are removed by a specially generated voltage pulse; or it may be a **semi-permanent KAM** (keep alive memory) which is energized direct from the battery, not via the ignition switch. The information stored in such a memory can be read out through the self diagnostics on the vehicle or by an instrument connected to the diagnostic port of the ECU.

Because it is impracticable for the average garage to test an ECU it is vitally important that all sensors and the ECU inputs that they generate, and all actuators that operate on ECU outputs, are properly verified before an ECU is changed. And, as stated earlier, it is also important to ensure that the defect is not caused by something simple like a fouled spark plug or a disconnected cable. This is why it is so important to employ an orderly strategy, such as the six steps, for work on electronically controlled systems.

Learning tasks

In most cases the procedure for performing the practical tasks is detailed in the text; however, you should always seek the advice of your supervisor before you start.

Working on vehicles can be dangerous so you must not attempt work that you have not been trained for, and when you are in training you must always seek the permission of your supervisor before attempting any of the practical work.

In the case of the first task you will need to have been trained before you can read out the fault codes.

Part of the purpose of these practical tasks is to assist you in building up a portfolio of evidence for your NVQ. You should, therefore, keep the notes and diagrams that you make, neatly in a folder.

---

1. With the aid of diagrams, where necessary, describe the procedure for obtaining fault codes from an ECU on a vehicle system that you are familiar with.
2. Write down the procedure for removing a battery from a vehicle. Make careful note of the safety precautions and specify which battery terminal should be disconnected.
3. Describe the tools and procedures for checking the state of charge of a battery.
4. Carry out a check of the charging rate of an alternator. Make a list of the tools and equipment used and give details of the way in which you connected the test meter. Make a note of the voltage values recorded.
5. Make a sketch of the provision made for tensioning the alternator drive belt on any vehicle that you have worked on. Explain why the drive belt tension is important. State the types of problems that may arise if an alternator belt is not correctly adjusted.
6. With the aid of diagrams, explain how to check for voltage at the starter motor terminal when the engine is being cranked.
7. Examine the leads that are connected to the headlights on a vehicle. Make a note of the colours of the cable insulation. Obtain a wiring diagram for the same vehicle and, by reference to the wiring daigram and the colours of the cables, locate the headlamp cables on the wiring diagram.
8. Make a note of the headlamp alignment equipment that is used in your workshop. Describe the procedure for carrying out a headlamp alignment check. Make a sketch of the method used to adjust headlamp alignment on any vehicle that you have worked on.
9. Give details of the fuseboxes on any vehicle that you are familiar with. State the type and current rating of the side- and tail-lamp fuse.
10. Write down the precautions that should be taken to protect vehicle electrical equipment before attempting any electric arc welding on the vehicle.

Practical assignment – electrical and electronic systems

Objective

The purpose of this assignment is to allow you to develop your knowledge and skills in this area of work and to allow you to demonstrate your competence to your supervisor, or other persons involved in the NVQ. The notes that you make will assist you to build up your file of evidence.

Tools and equipment required

- A digital multi-meter
- Suitable tool kit
- Instruction manual
- Clear bench space
- A defective alternator
- A container in which to place components
- A note pad and pencil

Activity

With the aid of the instruction manual, dismantle the alternator. Make careful note of the positioning of the parts so that you know how to reassemble the machine.

Do the following:

(a) check the condition of the drive pulley;
(b) check the condition of the bearings;
(c) check the condition of the slip rings and brushes;
(d) check the electrical resistance between the slip rings and the rotor elements;
(e) carry out resistance checks on the stator windings;
(f) conduct a continuity test on the diodes in the diode pack.

Make notes of your findings as you proceed, and discuss the results with your supervisor. Carry out any necessary repairs, and then re-assemble the machine.

10

Ignition systems

The purpose of the **ignition system** is to provide a spark to ignite the **compressed air–fuel mixture** in the **combustion chamber**. The spark must be of sufficient strength to cause ignition and it must occur at the correct time in the cycle of operations.

The ignition system is the means by which the 12 V supply from the **vehicle battery** is converted into the many thousands of volts that are required to produce the spark at the sparking plug, as illustrated by Figs 10.1 and 10.2.

10.1 Producing the high voltage required to cause ignition

Electromagnetism was discussed under electrical principles (Section 9.9). It is these electromagnetic principles that are employed in the **induction coil-type** of ignition system (Fig. 10.3).

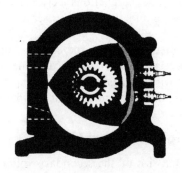

Fig. 10.2 Position of the spark in a rotary engine

In this coil there are two windings, **primary** and **secondary**. The primary winding consists of a few hundred turns of **lacquered copper wire**. The secondary winding consists of several thousand turns of **thin**, lacquered copper wire. The primary winding is wound around the outside of

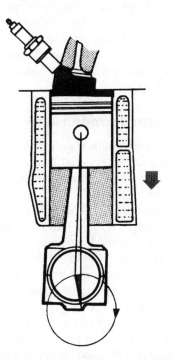

Fig. 10.1 Position of the spark in a reciprocating (piston) engine

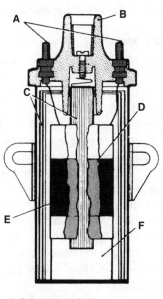

A-Primary terminals
B-High tension terminals
C-Laminations
D-Secondary winding
E-Primary winding
F-Porcelain insulator

Fig. 10.3 The type of ignition coil that has been commonly used on vehicles

the secondary winding because the heavier current that it carries generates heat which needs to be dissipated. The layers of windings are normally electrically insulated from each other by a layer of insulating material.

In the centre of the secondary winding there is a **laminated soft iron core**. The purpose of this laminated core is to concentrate the magnetic field that is produced by the current in the coil windings. The laminations between the coil's outer casing and the windings serves a similar purpose.

The interior parts of the coil are supported on a **porcelain** base. In some cases the coil may be filled with a **transformer oil** to improve electrical insulation and to aid heat dissipation.

Principle of operation

The actual size of the secondary voltage (high tension (HT) voltage) is related to the **turns ratio** of the coil, e.g. several thousand turns in the secondary winding and a few hundred turns in the primary winding.

In order for the ignition system to operate, the primary winding current must be switched on and off and this is done by the **contact breaker**. Before getting into details of contact breaker operation it is useful to consider the method of operation of the primary winding.

Primary winding

Figure 10.4. shows a simple ignition coil primary circuit. Current from the vehicle battery flows through the primary winding via the **ignition switch** and the closed contact breaker points to earth. The current of about 3 A in the primary winding causes a strong **magnetic field** which is concentrated by the soft iron laminations at the coil centre and the outer sheath of iron. It should be remembered that the secondary winding is inside the primary winding so the magnetic field from the primary winding also affects the secondary winding. A primary purpose of the primary winding is to create the strong magnetic field that will induce the high voltage in the secondary circuit.

Inducing the HT secondary voltage

Switching off the primary current by opening the contact breaker points has two major effects which are caused by the collapsing inwards of the magnetic field.

● **Self induction**   a voltage of approximately

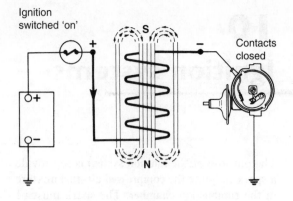

Ignition switched 'on'

Fig. 10.4 A basic primary circuit of an ignition coil with contacts closed

250 V is generated across the ends of the primary winding. The direction of this induced voltage in the primary winding is such that it opposes the change which produced it, i.e. it attempts to maintain the same direction of current flow.

● **Mutual induction** a high voltage (several thousand volts (kV)) is generated across the ends of the secondary winding.

Secondary circuit

Figure 10.5 shows the secondary circuit as well as the primary circuit of the simplified system. One end of the secondary winding (thousands of turns of fine copper wire) is connected to the HT terminal in the coil tower; the other end is connected to the primary winding at one of the low tension (LT) connections. When the primary winding is connected to the secondary winding it is known as 'auto transformer' connected. The induced primary voltage is added to the secondary voltage.

Capacitor (condenser)

The simplified ignition system described above would not work very well because the induced voltage in the primary winding would be strong enough to bridge the contact breaker gap and carry current to earth. This would reduce the secondary voltage and also lead to excessive sparking at the contact breaker points; the points would 'burn' and the efficiency of the system would be seriously impaired. This problem is overcome by fitting a suitable **capacitor** across (in parallel with) the points. Figure 10.6 shows the capacitor in circuit. One terminal of the capacitor is connected to the low-tension connection on the distributor and the other terminal is earthed.

Capacitors store electricity so that when, in the

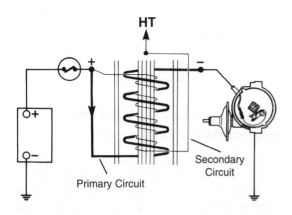

Fig. 10.5 Typical primary and secondary circuits of a coil

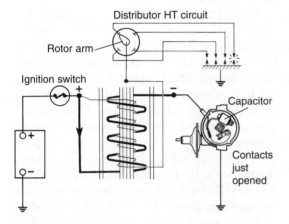

Fig. 10.6 The ignition circuit with the capacitor in place

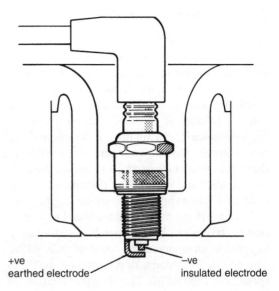

Fig. 10.7 Polarity of spark plug electrodes

case of the coil ignition system, the contact points begin to open, the self-induced current from the primary winding will flow into the capacitor instead of 'jumping' across the points gap. This flow of current will continue until the capacitor is fully charged. When the capacitor is fully charged it will automatically discharge itself back into the primary winding. This **capacitor discharge current** is in the opposite direction to the original flow and it helps to cause a rapid collapse of the magnetic field. This in turn leads to a much higher HT voltage from the secondary winding.

Coil polarity

Electrons flow from negative to positive and thermal activity (heat) also aids electron generation. For this reason the insulated (central) hotter electrode of the spark plug is made negative in relation to the HT winding (see Fig. 10.7). The result of this **polarity direction** is that a lower voltage is required to generate a spark across the plug gap. To ensure that the correct

coil polarity is maintained the LT connections on the coil are normally marked as + and −.

The coil polarity is readily checked by means of the normal garage-type **oscilloscope**. Figure 10.8 shows the inverted waveform that results from incorrect connection of the coil, or the fitting of the wrong type of coil for the vehicle under test. Figure 10.9 shows the scope pattern for a correct connection.

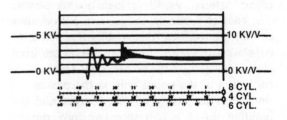

Fig. 10.8 The incorrect (inverted) waveform on the oscilloscope screen

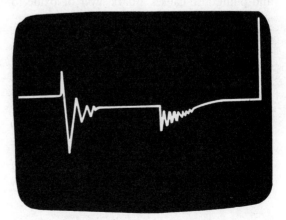

Fig. 10.9 The correct waveform on the oscilloscope screen

Contact breaker points

Each time a spark is required the contact breaker points must open and close. For a four-stroke engine this means that a spark is required once for each two revolutions of the engine crank. To achieve this the **cam** that operates the contact breaker is normally driven from the engine **camshaft**. For multi-cylinder engines the cam normally has the same number of lobes as there are cylinders. Figure 10.10 shows the contact breaker and cam in the distributor that is used on a four-cylinder, four-stroke engine.

In order to get an idea of the speed of operation of the contact breaker points, consider what happens at an engine crank speed of 3600 RPM. The cam of the distributor is rotating at half this speed, i.e. 1800 RPM. That is equivalent to 30 revolutions per second. In our four-cylinder engine the contact points will open and close four times for each revolution of the cam and this means that they will open and close $30 \times 4 = 120$ times a second. This speed obviously varies with engine speed but it is evident that the contact breaker and its operating mechanism is subject to a lot of hard work.

To give reliability and durability the cam is made from high quality **steel** with a hard wearing surface. The moving contact is operated by a heel made from hard wearing, electrically insulating material, usually a high quality **plastic**. The **contact points** are made from a **steel alloy** containing **tungsten**; this enables the points to cope with the burning action that arises from electrical action as the points open. This electrical action at the points will, in the passage of time, lead to pitting of one contact and the building up of a corresponding 'pip' on the other point; this is known as **pitting and piling**. The electrical action that leads to this pitting and piling also causes a dark layer of oxide to form on the contact point faces. These factors lead to a deterioration of ignition system performance and require the 'points' to be checked and, if they are pitted and blackened, the usual procedure is to replace them.

Sliding contact (self-cleaning) type of contact breaker

A method that is used to overcome the problem of pitting is to use **sliding contacts**. In sliding contacts the fixed contact has a larger face area than the moving one. In addition to the normal opening and closing action, the moving contact is made to slide across the face of the fixed contact.

Figure 10.11 shows a sliding contact assembly. The contact breaker heel has two ribs at its base and these ribs rest in ramps formed in the forked heel actuator. This forked heel actuator pivots on the contact breaker pivot post. This fork in the heel actuator engages with a pin which is fixed to the distributor base plate. When the vacuum advance and retard mechanism rotates the bearing plate, the heel ribs ride up the ramps in the actuator plate and cause the moving contact to slide across the fixed contact, as shown in Fig. 10.12(a). This action is controlled by a small coil spring which is secured to the end of the pivot post. The principle of operation of the sliding contact is shown in Fig. 10.12(b).

10.2 Distributor drives

Two types of **drive** are commonly used to rotate the **distributor shaft** that rotates the cam. One of these is the **skew gear** and the other is an **Oldham-type coupling**. The slot in the Oldham coupling is normally offset a little to one side of the distributor shaft centre. This aids re-timing

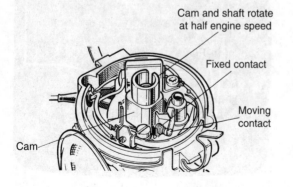

Fig. 10.10 The distributor cam and contact breaker

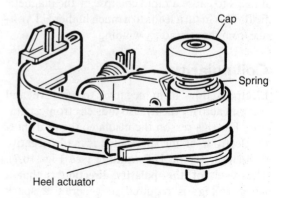

Fig. 10.11 A sliding contact assembly

(a)

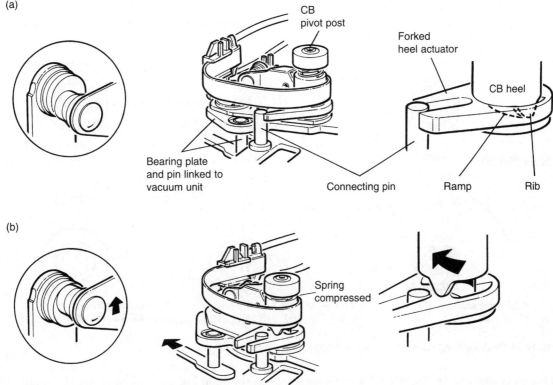

CB pivot post

Forked heel actuator

CB heel

Bearing plate and pin linked to vacuum unit

Connecting pin

Ramp

Rib

(b)

Spring compressed

Fig. 10.12 The sliding contact mechanism (a) static position, (b) advanced position

should the distributor be removed from the engine. Both types of distributor drive are shown in Fig. 10.13.

10.3 Dwell angle

The **dwell angle** is the period of time, as represented by **angular rotation** of the cam, for which the contact breaker points are closed. Figure 10.14 shows the dwell angles for the cams of four-, six-, and eight-cylinder engines.

The dwell angle is important because it controls the period of time during which the **primary current** is energizing the primary winding of the coil. In order for the magnetic field to reach its maximum strength the primary current must reach its maximum value, and this takes time.

In an inductance, which is what the primary coil is, it takes several milliseconds for the current to rise to its maximum value, as shown in Fig. 10.15. The actual time of current build up is dependent on the inductance (henrys) and the resistance (ohms) of the primary winding. For a typical ignition coil the time constant is of the order of 15 milliseconds.

The dwell angle, which determines current build-up time, is affected by the position of the heel of the moving contact in relation to the cam, as shown in Fig. 10.16. Figure 10.16 also shows how ignition timing is affected by points gap.

10.4 Distributing the high-voltage electrical energy

The timing of the spark is achieved by setting the **points opening** to the correct position in relation to **crank** and **piston position**, or the **rotor** in

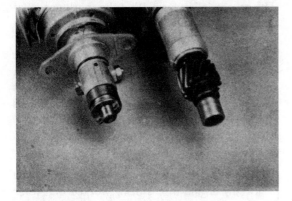

Fig. 10.13 Two types of distributor drive

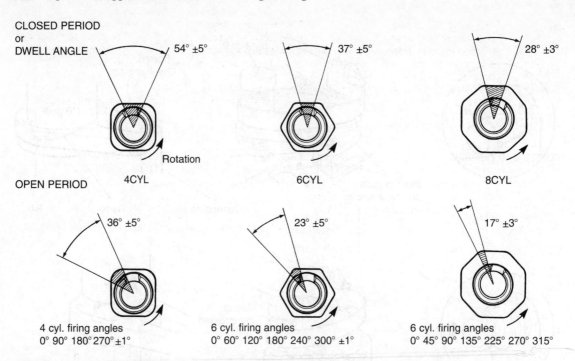

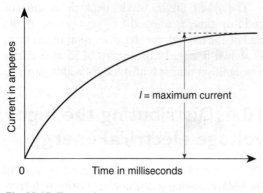

CLOSED PERIOD or DWELL ANGLE

54° ±5°   37° ±5°   28° ±3°

Rotation

OPEN PERIOD   4CYL   6CYL   8CYL

36° ±5°   23° ±5°   17° ±3°

4 cyl. firing angles
0° 90° 180° 270° ±1°

6 cyl. firing angles
0° 60° 120° 180° 240° 300° ±1°

6 cyl. firing angles
0° 45° 90° 135° 225° 270° 315°

Fig. 10.14 Dwell and firing angles for four-, six- and eight-cylinder engines

a rotary engine such as the **Wankel**. Distributing the resultant high-voltage electricity to produce the spark at the required cylinder is achieved through the medium of the **rotor arm** and the **distributor cap** as shown in Fig. 10.17.

In Fig. 10.17, a spring-loaded carbon brush is situated beneath the king lead (the one from the coil). This carbon brush makes contact with the metal part of the rotor and the high-voltage current is then passed from the rotor via an air gap to the plug lead electrode and, from there, through an HT lead to the correct sparking plug. Figures 10.18 and 10.19 show interior and exterior views of a distributor cap for a four-cylinder engine.

The rotor arm shown in Fig. 10.20. is typical of the type in common usage. It is sometimes the case that the metal nose of the rotor is extended

as shown in Fig. 10.21. This is intended as an aid to preventing the engine running backwards by making the spark occur in a cylinder where the piston is near bottom dead centre, should the engine start to rotate backwards.

Note the slot above the cam. Inside the rotor arm, in the insulating plastic, is a protrusion which locates the rotor arm in the slot on the distributor cam. The rotor is thus driven round by the distributor cam. The HT leads are arranged in the cap so that they are encountered in the correct firing sequence, e.g. 1342 for a four-cylinder and probably 153624 for a six-cylinder in-line engine.

10.5 Timing of the spark

The process of ensuring that the spark occurs at the right place and at the right time is known as **timing the ignition**. In the first place there is **static timing**. This is the operation of setting up the timing when the engine is not running. Ignition timing settings are normally expressed in **degrees of crank rotation**. The static timing varies across the range of engines in use today. A reasonable figure for static timing would be approximately 5° to 10°.

Note: This setting is critical and must be verified for any engine that is being worked on. Never guess.

Fig. 10.15 Time and current in a coil

Current in amperes

I = maximum current

0   Time in milliseconds

The points gap chosen is a compromise which must be made in order to balance out the advantages with the disadvantages at very high and at very low engine speeds.

Results in small dwell angle, good for ignition at low engine speeds; results in less arcing at contacts with less contact wear but gives poor high speed performance.

Results in large dwell angle, good for ignition performance at high engine speeds; more energy stored in the HT coil, increased arcing and contact

POINTS GAP CORRECT

POINTS GAP LARGER THAN SPECIFIED wear at low speeds.

POINTS GAP SMALLER THAN SPECIFIED

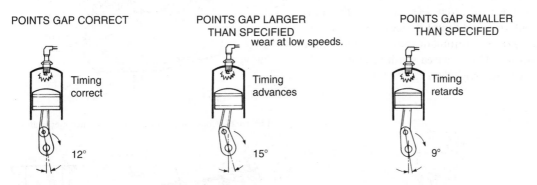

Timing correct

12°

Timing advances

15°

Timing retards

9°

Fig. 10.16 Effect of contact points gap variations on dwell angle and ignition timing or engine performance

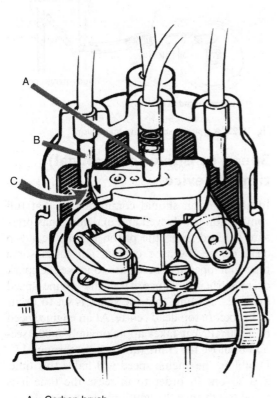

A – Carbon brush
B – Plug lead electrode
C – Rotor gap

Fig. 10.17 The HT circuit inside the distributor cap

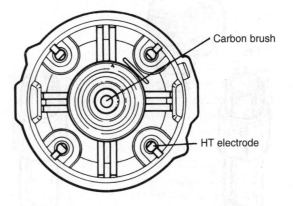

Carbon brush

HT electrode

Fig. 10.18 Interior view of a typical four-cylinder distributor cover

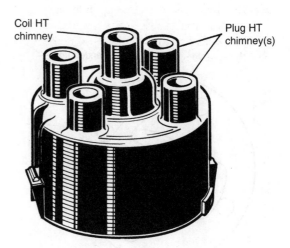

Coil HT chimney

Plug HT chimney(s)

Fig. 10.19 Exterior view of a typical four-cylinder distributor cover

When the spark is made to occur before this static setting it is said to be **advanced**, and when the spark occurs after the static setting it is said to be **retarded**.

Because vehicle engines are required to operate under a wide range of conditions it is necessary to alter the ignition timing while the vehicle and engine are in operation. The devices used for this purpose are often referred to as the **automatic advance and retard devices**. There are two basic forms of automatic advance and retard mechanisms. One is **speed sensitive** (Fig. 10.22), the other **load sensitive** (Fig. 10.23).

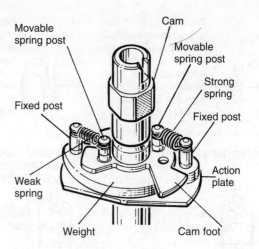

Fig. 10.22 Construction of automatic advance mechanism

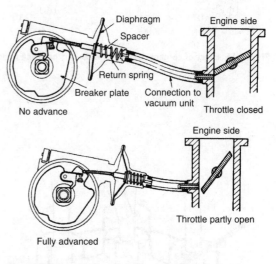

Fig. 10.23 A typical load sensitive mechanism

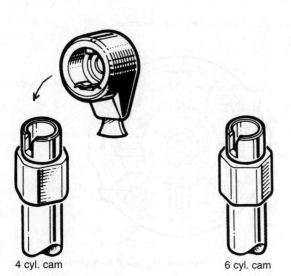

Fig. 10.20 Typical four- /six-cylinder rotor arm and cams

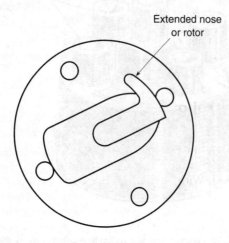

Fig. 10.21 The extended metal nose

Speed sensitive (centrifugal) timing device

Ideally ignition should commence so that full combustion is achieved and maximum gas pressure reached when the piston is very near top dead centre. Because combustion takes some time to happen it is necessary to make the spark occur earlier (advance it) as the engine speed increases. Assume that the spark is set to occur at 15° before top dead centre. At an engine speed of 1200 RPM it takes approximately 0.002 second to move the crank (and piston) through 15°. Doubling the engine speed will halve this time, and so on. In order to increase the time it is usual to advance the ignition to compensate.

Figure 10.22 shows the construction of a typical automatic advance mechanism. The whole assembly shown here is rotated at half engine speed by the distributor drive shaft. The arrangement allows the cam to rotate relative to the distributor drive shaft and it is thus possible to open the points earlier according to the position that the cam is moved to, by the action of weights.

In Fig. 10.24, the weights are pulled in by the springs and the cam is in the static timing position. As the engine speed and the distributor shaft speed increase the weights are forced outwards by centrifugal force against the tension of the springs, as shown in Fig. 10.25. Through the mechanism of the action plate, the weights and the cam foot, the cam is moved round slightly, in the direction of rotation, on the distributor shaft. This has advanced the ignition timing by 16°, in the case shown. The extension on the cam foot eventually contacts one of the fixed posts

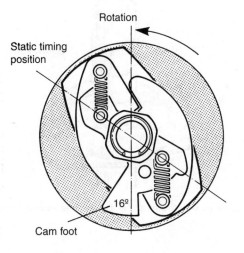

Fig. 10.24 A plan view of the automatic timing mechanism – zero centrifugal advance

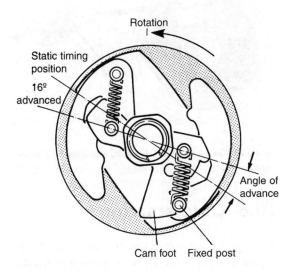

Fig. 10.25 A plan view of the automatic timing mechanism – 16° of centrifugal advance

on a weight and this prevents further advance; evidently the design of this cam foot extension will determine the maximum amount of advance for a given application.

The mass of the weights and the strength of the springs determine the way in which **automatic centrifugal advance** is related to engine speed. Figure 10.26(a) shows a graph of angle of distributor advance against distributor RPM. Remember that 1° at the distributor is 2° at the crankshaft. The two lines represent the upper and lower limits of tolerance that is acceptable. If you were to test a distributor on a test machine you should expect to get a single line that falls about midway between the two lines shown here.

Figure 10.26 (b) shows the automatic advance mechanism fitted with one weak spring and one stronger spring. This feature permits a faster rate of advance at slow engine speed and a more gradual rate above an engine speed of approximately 1000 RPM.

Load sensitive automatic timing control

Under light load, cruising conditions it is possible to improve fuel economy by weakening the mixture. Weak mixtures take longer to burn and, if economy devices are to work effectively, it is necessary to provide **extra spark advance**. In a throttle controlled engine there is a relationship between the level of vacuum (absolute pressure) in the manifold and the load on the engine.

Figures 10.27 and 10.28 show how the contact breaker plate is rotated by the action of the manifold vacuum on the diaphragm in the unit. Figure 10.29 shows how the strong vacuum at light load and small throttle opening operate to give maximum load sensitive advance. Figure 10.30 shows how low vacuum at full throttle provides no pull on the diaphragm and the spring in the diaphragm unit returns the cam to zero vacuum advance.

Control of emissions

It is known that retarding the ignition under certain conditions can help to reduce exhaust emissions. To achieve this a **vacuum retard** unit may be used. With such a device the contact breaker plate would be rotated in the same direction as the cam thus causing the points to open later, i.e. the ignition would be retarded. Such a device is usually effective during idling and over-run

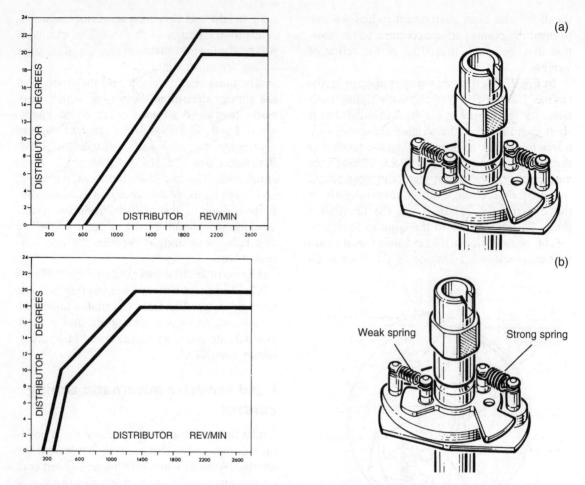

Fig. 10.26 Modern automatic advance mechanisms together with typical curves (a) with similar springs, (b) with one weak and one strong spring

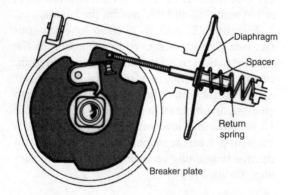

Fig. 10.27 The action of the vacuum operated timing control – no advance

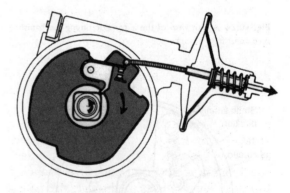

Fig. 10.28 The action of the vacuum operated timing control – fully advanced

conditions. A further development of this is a **double acting vacuum unit**. These units provide the normal load sensitive advance and an automatic retard for emission control purposes. Fig 10.31 shows such a double acting device which is distinguishable by its two vacuum pipe connections.

10.6 Cold starting

When an engine is cold the lubricating oil in the engine is more viscous than when it is hot. This requires greater torque from the starting motor and this, in turn, places a greater drain on the

Manifold pipe connection
for vacuum unit

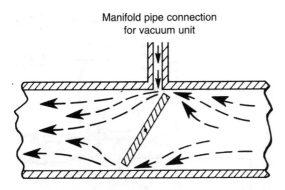

Fig. 10.29 The effect of load on the manifold vacuum – throttle partially open

Manifold pipe connection
for vacuum unit

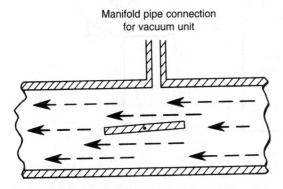

Fig. 10.30 The effect of load on the manifold vacuum – throttle fully open

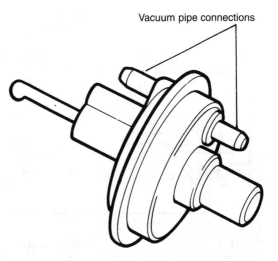

Vacuum pipe connections

Fig. 10.31 Typical double-acting vacuum unit for advance and retard operation

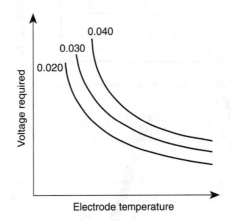

Fig. 10.32 Spark voltage and plug temperature

battery. Figure 10.32 shows how the voltage required to produce a spark at the spark plug gap varies with temperature. A much higher voltage is required for cold temperatures.

These are among the factors that sometimes make an engine more difficult to start when it is cold than when it is hot. To ease this problem, **coil ignition systems** are often designed to give a more powerful spark for starting up than is used for normal running. This process is achieved by the use of a **ballast resistor** and a coil that gives normal operating voltage at a voltage value lower than the battery voltage, e.g. an 8 V coil in a 12 V system. Under running conditions the coil operates on current supplied from the ignition switch, through the ballast resistor, to the primary winding. The size of the ballast resistor, in ohms, is that which produces the desired operating voltage for the coil. Under starting conditions the ballast resistor is bypassed and the coil is supplied with full battery voltage. This gives a higher voltage spark for starting purposes.

Figure 10.33 shows the circuit for a ballasted ignition system. In this system the ballast resistor is a separate component; but some other sys-

tems use a length of resistance cable between the ignition switch and the coil which achieves the same result. Whichever type of ballast resistor is used its function will be the same, and that is to produce a voltage drop that will give the coil its correct operating voltage. If the coil operates at 8 V and the battery voltage is 12 V, the ballast resistor will provide a voltage drop of 4 V.

Sparking plugs

The **sparking plug** is the means of introducing the spark into the combustion chamber of internal combustion engines.

Figure 10.34 shows the main details of a widely used make of sparking plug. In order to function effectively, sparking plugs must operate under a wide range of varying conditions. These conditions are considered next together with some features of sparking plug design.

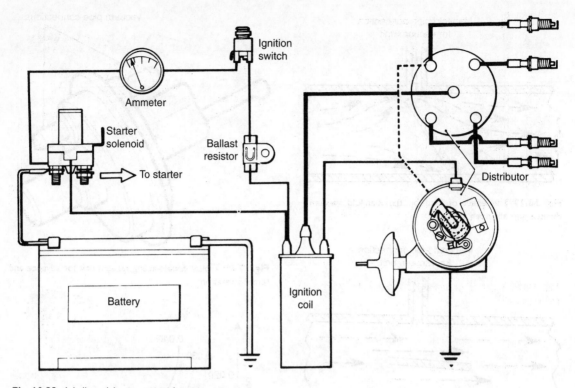

Fig. 10.33 A ballasted (series resistor) ignition circuit

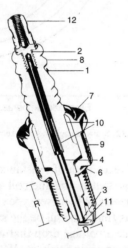

1 – Brand name and product code
2 – Cement
3 – Core nose
4 – Centre electrode
5 – Earth electrode
6 – Attached gasket
7 – Hexagon
8 – Anti-flashover 5-ribbed insulator
9 – Shell
10 – Gas-tight 'sillment seals
11 – Spark gap
12 – Terminal
D – Thread diameter
R – Thread reach

Fig. 10.34 Sparking plug construction

Temperature

In very cold weather the sparking plugs may be at sub-zero temperature whilst at operating temperatures the sparking plug temperature may be in the region of 1000 °C. The voltage required to provide the spark is affected by the temperature of the electrodes. Figure 10.32 gives an indication of the voltage required to produce a spark for various plug gaps and electrode temperatures. Note that the voltage required falls as the electrode temperature increases.

Compression pressure

The voltage required to provide a spark at the plug gap is affected by the pressure in the combustion chamber. It is approximately a linear relationship, as shown in Fig. 10.35. Note that the higher the compression pressure the higher the voltage required to produce a spark.

Within these ranges of gas pressure and temperature, the plug must continue to work and several factors contribute to the performance.

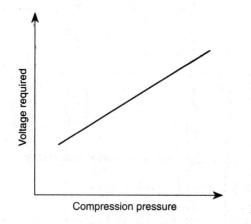

Fig. 10.35 Variation of sparking voltage with compression pressure

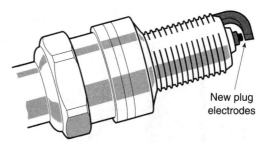

Fig. 10.36 The spark plug electrodes gap

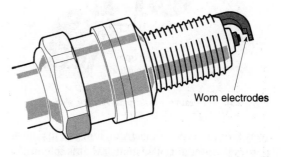

Fig. 10.37 Worn electrodes

The spark gap (electrode gap)

An **optimum gap width** must be maintained. If the gap is too small the spark energy may be inadequate for combustion. If the gap is too wide it may cause the spark to fail under pressure. Both the centre electrode and the earth electrode are made to withstand **spark erosion** and **chemical corrosion** arising from combustion. To achieve these aims the electrodes are made from a **nickel alloy** the composition of which is varied to suit particular plug types. For some special applications the alloys used for the electrodes may contain rarer metals such as silver, platinum, and palladium.

Figure 10.36 shows the spark gap on a new plug. In time the electrodes will wear and this means that spark plugs should be examined at regular intervals. The type of electrode wear that might occur in use is shown in Fig. 10.37. The shape of worn electrodes varies. Small amounts of wear can be remedied by bending the side electrode to give the required gap but, in cases of excessive wear the only remedy is to replace the plug.

For good performance the spark plug insula-tor tip must operate in the range from approximately 350 °C to 950 °C. If the insulator tip is too hot, rapid electrode wear will occur and pre-ignition may also be caused. If the insulator tip is too cool the plug will 'foul' and misfiring will occur. The heat range of the spark plug is important in this respect and we will have a look at that next.

Heat range of sparking plugs

Figure 10.38 shows the approximate amounts of heat energy that are dissipated through the various parts of the spark plug. By far the greatest amount passes through the threaded portion into the metal of the engine.

A factor that affects the dissipation of heat

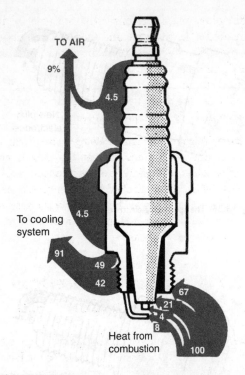

Fig. 10.38 The heat flow in a typical sparking plug

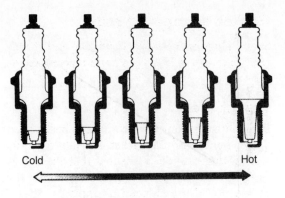

Fig. 10.40 Hot and cold running plugs

away from the centre electrode and the insulator nose is the amount of insulator that is in contact with the metallic part of the plug. This is known as the **heat path**. Spark plugs that 'run' hot have a long heat path and spark plugs that 'run' cold have a short heat path. Figure 10.39 demonstrates the principle and Fig. 10.40 shows the general form of the heat path for a range of cold to hot running plugs.

In general, hot running plugs are used in cold running engines and cold running plugs are used

in hot running engines. The type of plug to be used in a particular engine is specified by the manufacturer. This recommendation should be observed. In order not to restrict choice it is possible to obtain charts which give information about other makers' plugs that are equivalent to a particular type.

Plug reach

The length of the thread, shown as dimension R in Fig. 10.34, is a critical dimension. If the correct type of plug is fitted to a particular engine there should be no problem and the plug will seat as shown in Fig. 10.41.

However, if the reach is too long the electrodes and threaded part of the plug will protrude into the combustion chamber and will probably damage the valves and piston.

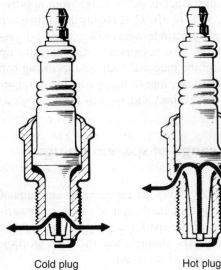

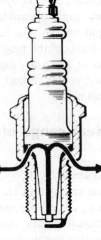

Cold plug   Hot plug

Fig. 10.39 The heat path

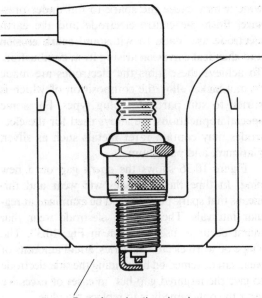

Part of combustion chamber

Fig. 10.41 The importance of plug 'reach'

Gasket or tapered seat

Spark plugs will be found with a **gasket-type seat,** as shown in Fig. 10.42, or a **tapered seat** as shown in Fig. 10.43.

Gasket seat

Plugs with a gasket-type seat need to be installed 'finger tight' until the gasket is firmly on to its seat, having previously ensured that the seat is clean. The final tightening should be to the engine maker's recommended torque.

Tapered seat

These do not require a gasket (commonly known as a plug washer). The tapered faces of both the gasket and the cylinder head need to be clean.

Fig. 10.42 A gasket-type plug seat

Fig. 10.43 A tapered-type plug seat

The plug must be correctly started in its threaded hole, by hand, and then screwed down finger tight. The final tightening must be done very carefully because the tapered seat can impose strain on the thread. As with the gasket-type seat, the final tightening must be to the engine maker's recommended torque.

> *Note:* Alignment when screwing a spark plug in is critical. Always ensure that the plug is not cross-threaded before exerting torque above that which can be applied by the fingers. In aluminium alloy cylinder heads it is very easy to 'tear' the thread out. Repairing such damage is normally very expensive.

10.7 Contact breakerless (electronic) ignition

The **contact breaker-type** of ignition systems served vehicle engineers well for many years. However, they suffered certain weaknesses such as wear at the contacts or contact breaker 'fling' where, at high engine speeds, the contact breaker return spring was not able to keep the heel of the moving contact point in contact with the rotating cam.

When **electronic switches** (transistors) became available they were quickly adopted for use in ignition systems because they offered improved switching performance without mechanical moving parts. Under electronic principles (Section 9.12) we have shown how the transistor can be used as a switch and also as an amplifier. It is these two properties of transistors that are made use of in the ignition systems that will be considered in this section.

In considering electronic ignition systems it is important to remember that their main purpose is to fulfil the requirements that we considered in the study of the contact breaker-type ignition, i.e. 'to provide a reliable spark in the right place, at the right time'. At this stage we will cover two of the earlier types of electronic ignition system because this seems to be the best way to introduce the topic. Those readers who are familiar with vehicles will know that other systems, such as distributorless or lost spark, are common, and other systems using a separate HT coil for each cylinder are not unknown. These are mentioned here but not discussed in detail because they are considered to be more suitable for study at the next stage.

10.8 The electromagnetic reluctance pulse generator type coil ignition system

At its simplest level the **electromagnetic generator** produces an electric current. This electric current provides the base current for a **bi-polar transistor**. The provision of base current to the transistor permits a larger current to flow through the **collector–emitter circuit** of the transistor. This collector–emitter current is also the primary winding current of the **ignition coil**. The electric current pulses from the **pulse generator**, thus switching the ignition coil primary current on and off; this achieves the same effect as the contact breakers in the contact breaker-type of ignition system. Figure 10.44 shows a simplified breakerless ignition system that demonstrates the respective operating principles. It should be noted that the pulse generator and transistor switch replace the contact breaker and cam.

The pulse generator produces switching pulses that turn the transistor on and off whenever a spark is required. However, it is not quite that simple and it is necessary to take into account several other factors.

An electronic ignition system

Figure 10.45 shows an electromagnetic pulse generator (variable reluctance) of the type that is used in electronic ignition systems. This pulse generator produces a **waveform** of approximately the same shape as the one shown in Fig. 10.46. This waveform has to be processed to make it suitable for operating the ignition circuit.

Electronic processing of the waveform

For precise switching 'on and off' of the current in the coil primary circuit it is necessary to convert this waveform to a more suitable **rectangular** form. The processing stages that the pulse generator voltage passes through in order to generate the high-voltage spark at the spark plug are shown in Fig. 10.47. The conversion of the curved wave from the pulse generator into the rectangular form required for accurate switching can be performed by a circuit known as a **Schmitt trigger**. In the simplified circuit shown in Fig. 10.48 the Schmitt trigger comprises two bi-polar transistors (T_1 and T_2) and five resistors.

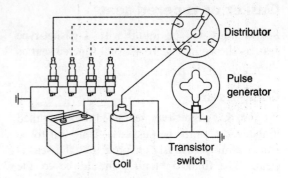

Fig. 10.44 A simplified electronic ignition system

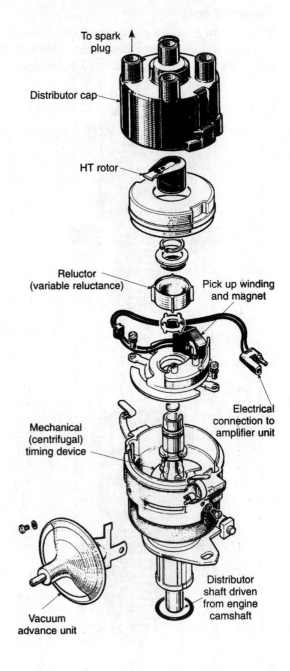

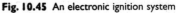

Fig. 10.45 An electronic ignition system

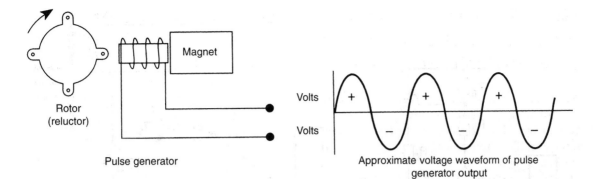

Fig. 10.46 The generator voltage waveform

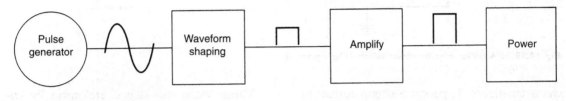

Fig. 10.47 The processing stages of the ignition circuit

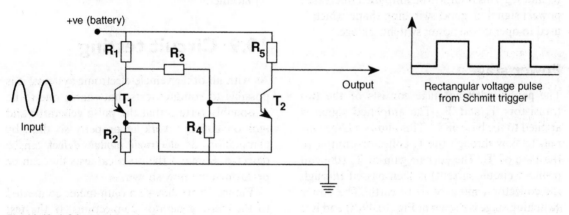

Fig. 10.48 A Schmitt trigger circuit

When the pulse generator voltage is positive (above a certain value), T_1 will conduct through R_1, the collector–emitter and R_2 to earth. This has the effect of removing current from R_3 and R_4; T_2 is not conducting current. The voltage at the bottom of R_5 is high and this gives the top part of the rectangular wave pattern.

When the pulse generator wave is negative T_1 is not conducting; this means that voltage is applied to the base of T_2. The voltage at the bottom of R_5 is now practically zero and this gives the bottom part of the rectangular wave. The vertical edges of the waveform would be seen on an oscilloscope because they represent the fall from high voltage to low voltage. They are sometimes referred to as the rising edge and the falling edge.

The rectangular wave pattern shown here is idealized. Practical waveforms, from the type of circuit shown, tend to be a little less sharply defined.

Amplification

The second stage of the electronic ignition circuit is to amplify the signal so that it is strong enough to operate the final, power switching stage. Figure 10.49(a) shows the **amplifier stage**; it comprises four resistors and two transistors (T3 and T4). It should be noted that T4 is of the p-n-p type.

When the base of T_3 receives a voltage pulse from the Schmitt trigger, current will flow through its collector–emitter circuit and R_6 and R_7. These two resistors form a voltage divider and this permits T_4 to become active. The transistor

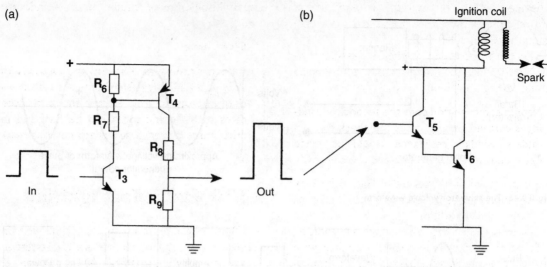

Fig. 10.49 (a) Amplifier stage, (b) power switch – Darlington pair

characteristics of T_4 permit a strong current to flow through the emitter–collector and resistors R_8 and R_9. This results in an amplified (increased power) signal of good switching shape which is used to operate the power switching stage.

Power stage

The **power switching** stage consists of the two transistors T_5 and T_6. The amplified signal is applied to the base of T_5. This allows a large current to flow through the T_5 collector–emitter to the base of T_6. The current gain of T_6 (the coil primary circuit current) is then passed through the collector–emitter of T_6 to earth. The power switching stage is shown in Fig. 10.49(b) and it is the **Darlington pair**.

These 'electronic stages' are normally encapsulated in a module which is repaired by replacement.

10.9 Circuit testing

As with all other vehicle electronic systems, it is possible to conduct tests that enable one to be reasonably certain that the pulse generator and ignition coil are working properly so that, by elimination, an **electronic module defect** can be detected. Some of the practical tests that can be performed are now shown.

Figure 10.50 shows an ohm-meter connected to the pulse generator connections. If the test shows infinity on the ohms scale, a broken coil is

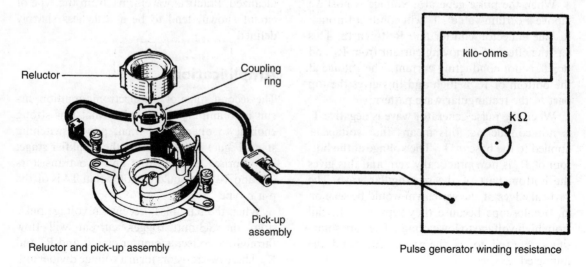

Reluctor and pick-up assembly

Pulse generator winding resistance

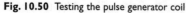

Fig. 10.50 Testing the pulse generator coil

indicated; and if the reading is very low a shorted coil is indicated. In either case the pulse generator is defective.

The ignition coil can be checked as shown in Fig. 10.51. The secondary winding resistance should be high, probably 10 kilo-ohms.

> *Note:* In some ignition coils the secondary winding is earthed. In such cases the check for secondary winding resistance would be made between the HT connection and the coil earth.

The primary winding resistance should be very low (the meter needs to be set to a very low ohms scale), 0.5 ohms to 1 ohm.

The tests shown here are of a general nature, i.e they do not apply to a specific system; as with most other work on vehicle systems, it is important to have the figures that relate to the specific system being worked on. However, they do show the practical nature of tests that can be applied with the aid of a good quality multi-meter, sound knowledge of circuits and the relevant information.

Safety note

Ignition systems generate many thousands of volts at the HT side. Great care must be exercised in order to avoid electric shock. In some cases such electric shock can be fatal and in other cases it may cause a sharp nervous reaction which, in turn, can lead to an accident.

10.10 Hall effect ignition

The **Hall effect** relies on the fact that when a small electronic device, known as a **Hall element**, is exposed to a magnetic field the output voltage of the element changes with the strength of the magnetic field.

Figures 10.52(a) and 10.52(b) show a simplified Hall-type ignition system. In the applica-

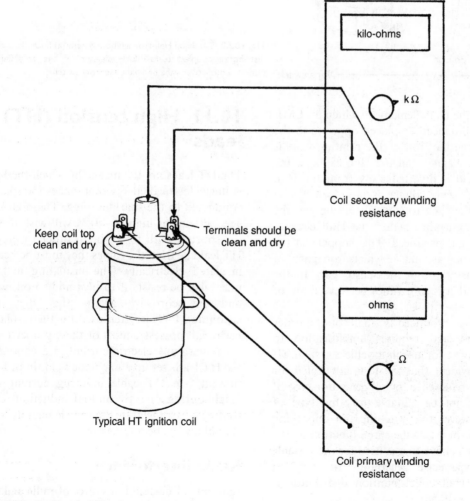

kilo-ohms

k Ω

Coil secondary winding resistance

Keep coil top clean and dry

Terminals should be clean and dry

Typical HT ignition coil

ohms

Ω

Coil primary winding resistance

Fig. 10.51 Checking the HT coil

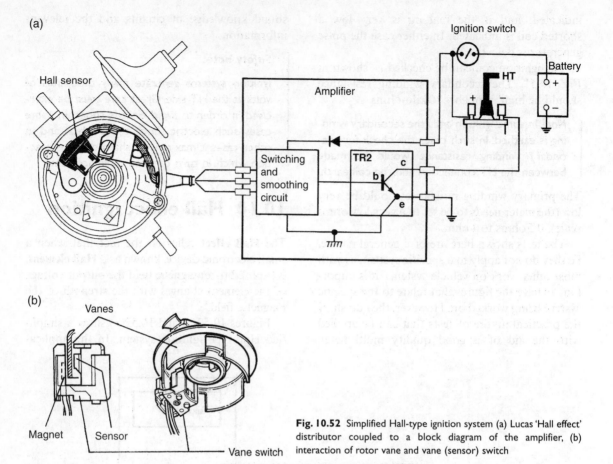

Fig. 10.52 Simplified Hall-type ignition system (a) Lucas 'Hall effect' distributor coupled to a block diagram of the amplifier, (b) interaction of rotor vane and vane (sensor) switch

tion shown the Hall element, in which an EMF (voltage) is produced, is placed opposite to the magnet. When the iron of the rotating vane is between the magnet and the Hall element, the magnetic field is diverted away from the Hall element and zero voltage is produced by the sensor. As the vane rotates out of the gap the magnetic flux again reaches the Hall element and a voltage is produced. This happens at the same frequency as that at which iron parts of the vane pass through the sensor gap. In the case shown that is four times per revolution of the shaft.

The voltage produced is small, of the order of millivolts, and requires amplification to make it suitable for use in a vehicle system. (It should be evident that the tests advocated for the variable reluctance 'pulse' generator-type of sensor will not be suitable for this type of sensor.) However, the switching and smoothing circuit perform much the same function as the one described above that is used for the **variable reluctance-type pulse generator**. An exploded view of a Hall effect ignition distributor is shown in Fig. 10.53.

10.11 High tension (HT) leads

The **HT leads** are the means by which the high-voltage electrical energy that makes the spark is conducted to the sparking plug. The high voltage, perhaps as high as 40 kV, will wish to seek the shortest path to earth. In order to prevent **HT leakage** from the cables they must be heavily insulated electrically. The insulating material must also be resistant to heat and to oil, water and any corrosive agents that they may encounter. **PVC** is often used for the insulation because it possesses most of these properties.

As with any electric current in a conductor, the HT leads set up a magnetic field. In order to prevent one HT cable inducing current in a neighbouring one, by mutual induction, cable routing as arranged by the vehicle manufacturer should always be adhered to.

Radio interference

Ignition HT current is a source of **radio and television interference** and for many years now it has been a legal requirement to adequately suppress this on the vehicle. A method that is commonly used to perform this suppression is to introduce extra electrical resistance into the HT circuit; and one means of achieving this is to make the conducting part of HT cables from a resistive material. The resistance of such cables varies considerably, a rough guide being 18 000 ohms per metre length. This means that an HT cable of 300 mm length would have a resistance of 5400 ohms. It is a value that can be checked by means of an ohm-meter and the resistance values and tolerances will be given in the workshop manual.

10.12 Some practical applications, i.e. doing the job

A substantial amount of background theory has been covered and we have shown how this theory is used to make vehicle systems work. When systems break down or cease to function correctly it is the job of the vehicle service and repair technician to find out what is wrong and to put it right and this is where practical skill, or competence, comes into play. In a book of this type it is not possible to cover every type of vehicle system and we will not attempt to do that.

As with all work, proper safe working practices must be observed. Personal safety and the safety of others nearby must be ensured and the vehicle itself must be protected against damage by following the correct procedures prescribed by the manufacturer and using wing and upholstery covers, etc.

Because of the global (international) nature of the industry vehicle technicians will encounter a range of products. It is unwise to attempt even simple work without having good knowledge of the product, or access to the information and data relating to the vehicle and system to be worked on.

The practical work described in this section generally relates to a specific product and that is made clear in the text. However, the devices chosen and the work described have been selected because they highlight types of practical procedures and tests that can be applied across a range of vehicles. It is intended that this book should be used in conjunction with courses of practical instruction and learning on the job.

The main source of information and guid-

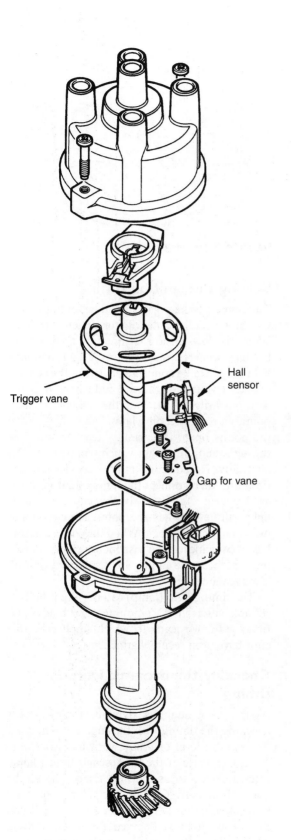

Fig. 10.53 A Hall effect distributor

Trigger vane

Hall sensor

Gap for vane

ance about repair and maintenance procedures is the manufacturer's workshop manual which is often available on CDROM.

Ignition timing

Because ignition timing varies with engine speed it is necessary to check both the static timing and the **dynamic timing**.

Static timing

The following list shows the ignition timing details for a four-cylinder in-line engine.

- firing order 1 3 4 2
- static advance 10°
- contact breaker gap 0.40 mm
- dwell angle 55°

For static advance setting the figures of interest are the static advance angle of 10°, the contact breaker gap of 0.40 mm and the firing order.

When resetting the static timing after performing work on the engine, such as removing and refitting the distributor, it is necessary to ensure that the piston in the cylinder used for timing (usually number 1) is on the **compression stroke**. The firing order helps here because in this case the valves on number 4 cylinder will be 'rocking' when number 1 piston is at top dead centre (TDC) on the compression stroke. The 10° static advance tells us that the contact breaker points must start to open at 10° before TDC. Engines normally carry **timing mark**s on the crankshaft pulley and these are made to align with a pointer on the engine block, or timing case, as shown in Fig. 10.54.

To position the piston at 10° before TDC the crank should be rotated, by a spanner on the crankshaft pulley nut, in the direction of rotation of the engine. This ensures that any 'free play' in the timing gears is taken up. To make the task more manageable it is probably wise to remove the sparking plugs. If the alignment is missed the first time round, the crank should continue to be rotated in the direction of rotation until the piston is on the correct stroke and the timing marks are correctly aligned.

When the piston position of number 1 cylinder is accurately set the distributor should be replaced with the rotor pointing towards the HT segment in the distributor cap; that is normally connected to number 1 sparking plug. This process is made easier on those distributors that have an off-set coupling as shown in Fig. 10.13.

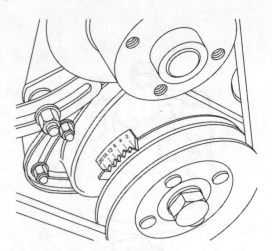

Fig. 10.54 Engine timing marks

Setting the ignition timing

The **contact breaker gap** should be set to the correct value and the **distributor clamp** loosened. When the low-tension terminal of the distributor has been reconnected to the coil, a **timing light** may then be connected between the contact breaker terminal of the coil and earth. With the ignition switched on and the contact breaker points closed the timing lamp will be out. When the points open, the primary current will flow through the timing light which will light up. An alternative is to disconnect both coil LT connections and then connect the timing light in series, as shown in Fig. 10.55. In this case the timing light will be on when the points are closed and off when they are open. When the correct setting has been achieved the distributor clamp should be tightened, the timing light removed and all leads reconnected.

The timing light (lamp) can be a light bulb of suitable voltage (12 V) mounted in a holder and fitted with two leads to which small crocodile clips have been securely attached.

Checking the dynamic ignition timing

As the name suggests, dynamic timing means checking the timing with the engine running. At this present level of study we will restrict ourselves to the use of the **stroboscopic timing lamp**, often referred to as a **strobe lamp**. The strobe lamp 'flash' is triggered by the HT pulse from a sparking plug, usually number 1 cylinder. When the strobe light is directed on to the timing marks the impression is given that the mark on the rotating pulley is stationary in relation to the fixed timing mark.

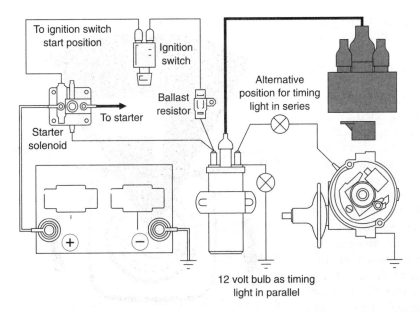

Fig. 10.55 Using a timing light

Safety note

This useful stroboscopic effect carries with it potential danger because the impression is given that other rotating parts such as fan blades, drive belts, etc. are also stationary. It is therefore important not to allow hair and clothing or any part of the body to come into contact with moving parts. It is also important to avoid electric shock. As with other work that involves running engines exhaust extraction equipment should be used.

Checking the static timing with the engine running

The **static timing setting** can be checked by means of the strobe lamp because, at idling speed, the centrifugal advance and the vacuum advance mechanisms should not be adding to the static advance angle. The static timing mark on the engine should be highlighted with white chalk, or some other suitable marking substance. This will enable you to locate the correct marks when conducting the test. Figure 10.56 shows the strobe light; this one incorporates an advance meter being used to check the static timing. For this test the engine will be run at the manufacturer's recommended speed, probably idling speed. If the marks align correctly no further action is required. However, if the marks do not align then the distributor clamp must be slackened and the distributor body rotated until the marks are aligned correctly. When the correct alignment is achieved the clamp must be retightened.

Checking the centrifugal advance mechanism

The timing details that we are using as an example gave us a static advance figure of 10° and the following for vacuum and centrifugal:

- automatic centrifugal advance 25°
- vacuum advance 12°

If the vacuum advance is disabled by disconnecting the pipe at the engine end, and blanking off the hole with a suitable device, the maximum amount of advance obtainable will be 35°, i.e.

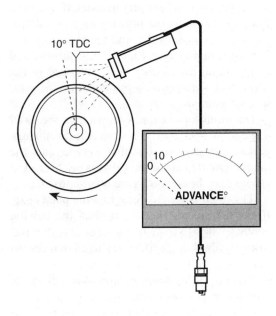

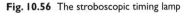

Fig. 10.56 The stroboscopic timing lamp

25° from the centrifugal device and 10° static. In this example this maximum advance occurs at 4300 RPM of the engine and a **tachometer** (rev counter) will be needed to record the engine speed.

With the vacuum pipe disconnected, the tachometer and strobe light connected and all leads checked to ensure that nothing is touching moving parts or hot exhausts the check may proceed. It will probably require another person to operate the accelerator and observe the tachometer. The strobe light should be aimed at the timing marks and when the engine is brought up to the correct speed the control on the advance meter is adjusted until the timing marks align. The number of degrees shown on the advance meter should then show the maximum advance angle. If this is correct the vacuum advance mechanism can be tested.

Checking the vacuum advance mechanism

After removing the **blanking device**, the **vacuum pipe** should be reconnected. The engine speed will increase slightly if the vacuum device is working.

Dwell angle

In contact breaker-type ignition systems the dwell angle is the period during which the contact breaker points are closed. The dwell angle is the period during which the electrical energy builds up in the **coil primary winding**. If the dwell period is too short the primary current will not reach its maximum value and the HT spark will be accordingly weaker. Figure 10.57 shows dwell angle, which has already been discussed in the context of the operating principles of the ignition system.

On a four-lobed cam as shown here the dwell angle is 54° + or − 5°. However, the dwell angle varies according to distributor type and the manufacturer's data should always be checked to ensure that the correct figure is being used.

The dwell angle is affected by the **points gap**. If the gap is too large the heel of the moving contact will be closer to the cam and this will cause the dwell angle to be smaller than it should be.

Figure 10.58 demonstrates the effect of points gap on dwell angle.

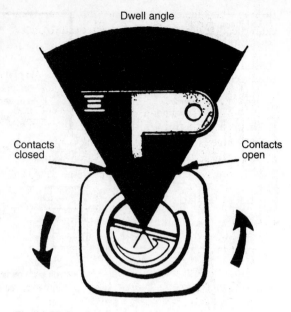

Fig. 10.57 Dwell angle

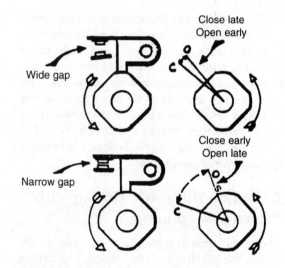

Fig. 10.58 Points gap and dwell angle

10.13 Adjusting the contact breaker points gap

Not only does the points gap affect the dwell angle but it also affects the ignition timing. A wide points gap advances the ignition and too small a gap retards the ignition. Setting the contact breaker points to the correct gap is, therefore, a critical engineering measurement in a technician's work. Figure 10.59 shows a set of **feeler gauges** being used to check the gap and the small inset shows a method of achieving the fine adjustment.

In performing this task it is essential to use clean feeler gauges and we think it worth mentioning that feeler gauges do wear out. For example, if feeler gauges have been used to check valve clearances with the engine running, it is quite possible for the blades to be 'hammered' thin. An occasional check with a micrometer will verify the accuracy of the feeler gauges.

Back to the points gap setting. The points gap is checked with the ignition switched off. The feeler gauge is inserted between the contacts, as shown in Fig. 10.59. Very light force should be used to 'feel' the setting and care must be taken to keep the feeler gauge blade in line with the contact face. If the points gap is set accurately the dwell angle should be correct. However, it is common practice to check the dwell angle by the use of a dwell meter and tachometer. These instruments are normally part of an engine analyser such as the Crypton CMT 1000 shown in Fig. 10.60. It is possible to purchase individual instruments similar in appearance to those shown in Fig. 10.61.

In this instance the dwell meter shows dwell angle of 51° at an engine speed of 1000 RPM. If the dwell angle is correct, no further action is required. However, should the dwell angle fall outside the permitted limits it is adjusted by altering the contact points gap. On some distributors this can be achieved from outside the distributor.

Dwell variation

Figure 10.63 shows the dwell angle at 2000 RPM to be 57°. If you compare this with the 51° at

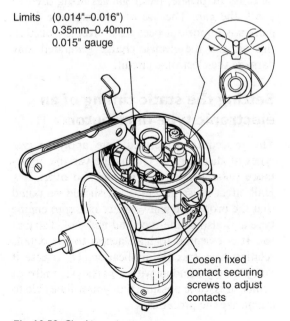

Limits   (0.014"–0.016")
0.35mm–0.40mm
0.015" gauge

Loosen fixed contact securing screws to adjust contacts

Fig. 10.59 Checking points gap

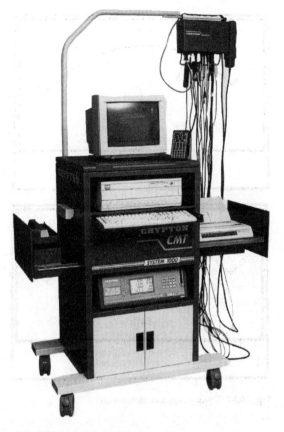

Fig. 10.60 A full size diagnostic machine

1000 RPM you will see that there is a dwell variation of 6°. In this particular case a variation of 6° is too large and it shows that the distributor is defective. The types of defect that can cause dwell variation include:

- a worn cam
- worn or bent shaft or bearings
- loose base plate

The remedial action required will depend on the severity of the problem. If it is a loose base plate the cause of the looseness should be investigated and it may be found that tightening a couple of screws will cure the problem. In the case of worn bearings (bushes) and/or shaft the time involved in making a repair will have to be taken into account and it may be advantageous to opt for a replacement unit.

Servicing a contact breaker-type distributor

Figure 10.63 shows the main points that require periodic attention. Oil should be applied sparingly and care taken to prevent contamination of the **contact points**. While the distributor cap is

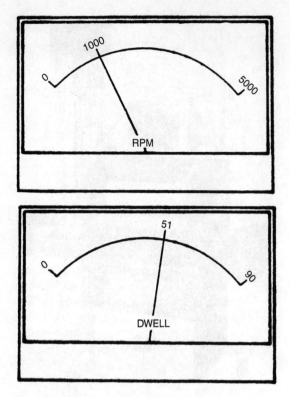

Fig. 10.61 Dwell meter and tachometer

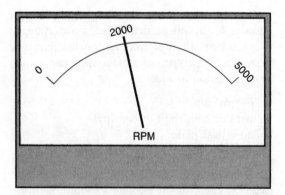

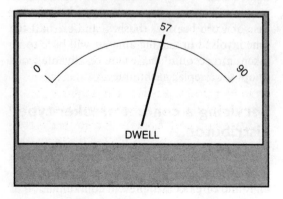

Fig. 10.62 Dwell variation

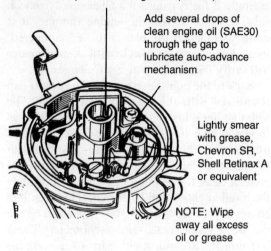

Add 2 or 3 drops of clean engine oil (SAE30)

Add several drops of clean engine oil (SAE30) through the gap to lubricate auto-advance mechanism

Lightly smear with grease, Chevron SR, Shell Retinax A or equivalent

NOTE: Wipe away all excess oil or grease

Fig. 10.63 Service details for a distributor

removed it should be wiped clean, inside and out, and checked for signs of damage and tracking (HT leakage). The rotor arm should also be inspected.

10.14 Servicing an electronic-type distributor

The **rotor** (reluctor) to **magnetic pick-up air gap** on an electronic ignition distributor is an important setting that requires occasional checking. Figure 10.64(a) shows the rotor and magnetic pick up and Fig. 10.64(b) shows non-magnetic, i.e brass or plastic, feeler gauges being used to check the gap. The use of **non-magnetic feeler gauges** is important because if steel is placed in this air gap the electric charge generated may damage the electronic circuit.

Setting the static timing of an electronic type distributor

The procedures described here apply to two types of distributors. One is the variable reluctance pulse generator type and the other is a Hall effect pulse generator. It should be noted that the procedure will vary according to engine type and also to the type and make of distributor. It is essential to have access to the details relating to a specific application. Of course if you are very familiar with a particular make of vehicle it is quite possible that you will be able to memorize the procedures.

Static timing – variable reluctance pulse generator

The cylinder to which the distributor is being timed must be on the **firing stroke** and the timing marks on the engine must be accurately aligned. The **distributor rotor** must be pointing towards the correct electrode in the distributor cap and the corresponding lobe of the **reluctor rotor** must be aligned with the pick-up, as in the case shown in Fig. 10.64(a). In Fig 10.64(b), the air gap is being checked with the aid of non-magnetic feeler gauges.

When the distributor is securely placed and the electrical connections made the final setting of the timing is achieved by checking the timing with the strobe light. Final adjustment can then be made by rotating the distributor body in the required direction prior to final tightening of the clamp.

Static timing Hall effect pulse generator

Figure 10.65 shows a Hall effect distributor for **digital electronic ignition** where the distributor itself is provided with timing marks. With the

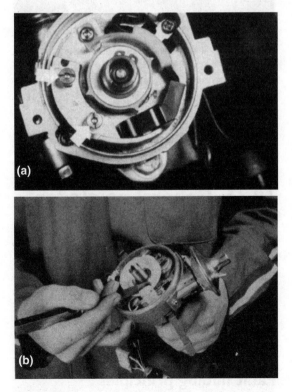

Fig. 10.64 Checking the air gap (a) alignment of reluctor lobe with magnetic pick-up, (b) using non-magnetic feeler gauges to check the gap

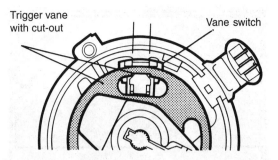

Fig. 10.65 Static timing Hall effect pulse generator

engine timing marks correctly set, the cut-out in the trigger vane must be aligned with the vane switch as shown.

Should the setting require adjustment, the distributor clamp is slackened just sufficient to permit rotation of the distributor body; the distributor is then rotated until the marks are aligned. After tightening the clamp and replacing all leads, etc. the engine may be started and the timing checked by means of the stroboscopic light.

10.15 Maintenance and servicing of sparking plugs

In common with many other features of vehicle servicing the service intervals for sparking plugs have also lengthened and it is quite common for the servicing requirement to be to keep the exterior of the **ceramic insulator** clean and to replace sparking plugs at prescribed intervals, perhaps 20 000 miles or so. However, there are still quite a few older vehicles in use and it is useful to have an insight into the methods of spark plug maintenance that may be applicable to them.

Cleaning spark plugs

Early spark plugs were made so that they could be taken apart to be cleaned. This meant that all parts could be cleaned satisfactorily by the use of a wire brush. When the non-detachable spark plug was introduced it became necessary to clean by **abrasive blasting**. This requires the use of a special machine. Figure 10.66 shows such a machine in use. It should be noted that protective eye wear must be worn for this operation because it is fairly easy to make a slip and this could lead to injury.

In addition to the abrasive (sand) blast facility, the plug cleaning machine contains an **air**

Fig. 10.66 A spark plug cleaning machine

Fig. 10.67 Filing the electrodes

blast facility that will remove unwanted abrasive from the spark plug. When the cleaning operation is completed the plug is removed from the machine. The **plug thread** can then be cleaned and the electrodes inspected. If the electrodes are **spark eroded** then the surfaces should be filed flat as shown in Fig. 10.67.

After this operation has been performed, the spark gap electrodes should be adjusted to the correct gap and this gap is checked by placing a feeler gauge of the required thickness between the electrodes. Any adjustment of the gap is carried out by bending the side contact with the aid of a small 'wringing iron' as shown in Fig. 10.68.

Testing the spark plug

The spark plug servicing machine normally includes a facility for testing the spark plug. This facility is a small **pressure chamber** into which the spark plug is screwed. A control allows the operator to admit **compressed air** to pressurize the chamber. The degree of compression is registered on a **pressure gauge**. The machine is also supplied with an **HT coil** which is connected by a suitable HT lead to the terminal of the spark plug.

When the desired test pressure is reached the 'spark' button is pressed. The pressure chamber also includes a transparent window and it is possible to examine the spark through this. A full description of the procedure will be found with the machine but this introduction must suffice in this instance.

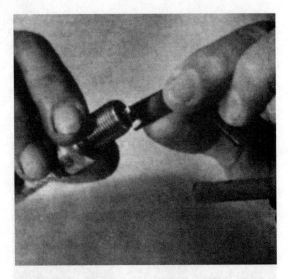

Fig. 10.68 Bending the side electrode to set the gap

10.16 General points for checking coil ignition systems

Figure 10.69 shows the main areas where visual checks of the HT parts of the coil ignition system may show up areas requiring attention. Some further checks are shown in the section on fault finding.

Fault finding principles

Before considering ignition system faults and how to deal with them it is wise to remember

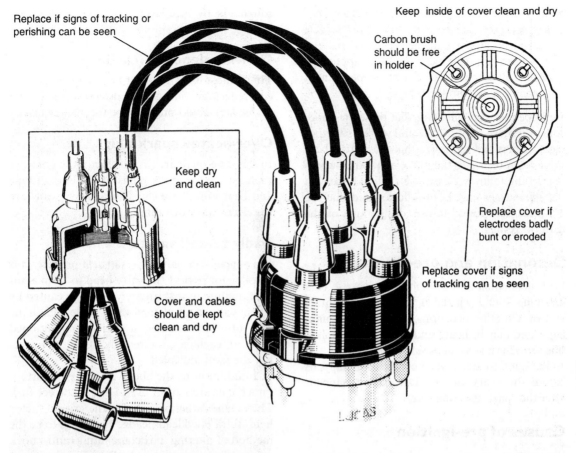

Replace if signs of tracking or perishing can be seen

Keep inside of cover clean and dry

Carbon brush should be free in holder

Keep dry and clean

Cover and cables should be kept clean and dry

Replace cover if electrodes badly bunt or eroded

Replace cover if signs of tracking can be seen

Fig. 10.69 The areas for visual checks of an ignition system

that much of the skill required to perform diagnosis and repair of electrical and electronic systems is the same as that which is required for good quality work of any type. By this we mean it is important to be methodical; it is unwise to start testing things randomly or even to try changing parts in the hope that you might hit on the right thing by chance.

Many people do work methodically and they probably employ a method similar to the six step approach, which is a good, common sense approach to problem solving in general. The six step approach provides a good starting reference, although it requires some refinement when used for diagnosis of vehicle systems.

We will briefly consider the six steps and at a later stage take into account the refinements that are considered necessary for vehicle systems.

The six step approach

This six step approach may be recognized as an organized approach to problem solving in general. As quoted here it may be seen that certain steps are recursive. That is to say that it may be

necessary to refer back to previous steps as one proceeds to a solution. Nevertheless, it does provide a proven method of ensuring that vital steps are not omitted in the fault tracing and rectification process. The six steps are:

1. collect evidence
2. analyse evidence
3. locate the fault
4. find the cause of the fault and remedy it
5. rectify the fault (if different from 4)
6. test the system to verify that repair is correct

Just to illustrate the point, take the case of a vehicle with an engine that fails to start. The six step approach could be as follows.

1. Is it a flat battery? Has it got fuel, etc?
2. If it appears to be a flat battery, what checks can be applied, e.g. switch on the headlamps.
3. Assume that it is a flat battery.
4. What caused the battery to become discharged?
5. Assume, in this case, that the side and tail lights had been left on. So, in this case, recharging the battery would probably cure the fault.

6. Testing the system would, in this case, probably amount to ensuring that the vehicle started promptly with the recharged battery. However, further checks might be applied to ensure that there was not some permanent current drain from the battery.

We hope that you will agree that these are good, common sense steps to take and we feel sure that most readers will recognize that these steps bear some resemblance to their own method of working. In the following cases we shall assume that the above steps have been followed and that the fault has been found to exist in the area of the ignition system.

Detonation and pre-ignition

Both **detonation** and pre-ignition give rise to a **knocking** sound which, at times, can be quite violent. On other occasions a high pitched **pinking** sound may be heard and as the term implies, this sound is known as pinking.

Pre-ignition arises when combustion happens before the spark occurs. Detonation happens after the spark has occurred.

Causes of pre-ignition

Pre-ignition may be caused by **'hot' spots** in the combustion space. These 'hot' spots may be caused by sharp edges and rough metallic surfaces, glowing deposits (carbon), overheated spark plugs or badly seated valves.

As a result of ignition starting before the spark occurs the pressure and temperature in the cylinder rise to high levels at the wrong time. This gives rise to poor performance, engine knock and eventual engine damage. In addition to these problems the exhaust emissions will be affected and this will add to atmospheric pollution. There are, therefore, several reasons why pre-ignition should be prevented.

When it comes to tackling the problem of pre-ignition it is necessary to consider the probable causes. If we take the factors quoted above it is possible to suggest remedial action.

Sharp edges and rough metallic surfaces

These are likely to be caused by manufacturing defects and they are normally rectified at that stage. However, if an engine has been opened up for repair work it is possible that careless use of tools may damage a surface. Should this be the case, the remedy would be to remove the roughness by means of a scraper, a file or a burr.

Glowing deposits (carbon)

This is most likely to occur in an engine that has covered a high mileage. **Decarbonizing** the engine (a decoke) would probably be the answer here.

Over-heated spark plugs

In this case there are various factors to consider such as: are the spark plugs of the correct type and heat range? are the spark plugs clean? are the electrodes worn thin?

Badly seated valves

If a **poppet-type valve** does not seat properly it is possible for part of the valve head to form a hot spot. Failure to seat squarely could be caused by a bent valve, a misaligned valve guide and, in the case of older engines, a badly reconditioned valve. In each case the remedy would be to rectify the fault indicated.

In addition to the above defects combustion knock can arise from use of the incorrect fuel. The **octane rating** of a fuel is the critical factor here. Tetra-ethyl lead (leaded fuel) used to be the method of altering the octane rating (anti-knock value) of petroleum spirit. But now that most spark ignition engines are fitted with **catalytic convertors** for emissions control leaded fuels cannot be used. There are different octane grades of unleaded fuel and many electronically controlled engines are provided with a simple means of altering settings if a driver wishes to use a different octane rating fuel from the one that she/he has been using.

10.17 Poor starting or failure to start

For current purposes we will assume that the fuel and electrical systems are in good order, in particular that the battery is fully charged and that the starter motor is capable of rotating the engine correctly. We shall also assume that the mechanical condition of the engine is good and that the fault has been identified as being in the area of the ignition system.

Poor starting

If the controls are operated correctly, the engine should start promptly. The time taken to start up may vary with air temperature. For example, when it is very cold the cranking speed of the engine will be affected by the viscosity of the lubricating oil; and the mixture entering the engine is affected by contact with cold surfaces. Generally, an engine will start more promptly when it has warmed up than it will when it is cold.

For 'poor' starting we are, therefore, looking at cases where, taking account of the above factors, the engine either takes a long time to start or is reluctant to start at all. The following ignition system faults have a bearing on the problem of poor starting.

Weak spark

This could be caused by loss of electrical energy in the ignition circuit, or failure to generate sufficient energy for a spark in the first instance. Loss of electrical energy could be due to defective connection and/or defective insulation in either the **low-tension circuit**, or the **high-tension circuit**. A range of tests and checks that can be carried out is described in the section on servicing and repair.

Spark occurring sometimes but not at others

This is known as an **intermittent fault**. Here again, the problem could lie in either or both the LT and the HT circuits.

Spark occurring at the wrong time

In most cases this means that the ignition timing is incorrectly set.

Failure to start

As it is ignition faults that we are considering the obvious place to start is the **sparking plug gap**. Failure to start is probably due to there being no spark, or a spark that is too weak to cause combustion. However, if the ignition timing is not correct, or the HT leads have been wrongly connected (not in accordance with the firing order), the engine may also fail to start.

10.18 Fault tracing in ignition systems

Safety note

The HT voltage is of the order of many thousands of volts, perhaps as high as 40 000 V. The danger of electric shock is ever present and steps must be taken to avoid it. In addition to electric shock the involuntary 'jerking' of limbs, when receiving a shock, may cause parts of the human frame to be thrown into contact with moving parts such as drive belts, pulleys and fans. Care must always be taken to avoid receiving an electric shock. It is possible to obtain special electrically insulated tongs for handling HT cables when it is necessary to handle the cables of running engines.

With this cautionary note taken care of we can now proceed to consider some practical tests.

Visual checks

Figure 10.70 shows a preliminary check of the type that is advised in most approaches to fault tracing. Here the technician is looking for any obvious external signs of problems such as loose connections or broken wires, cracked or damaged HT cables, dirty or cracked distributor cap and coil tower insulator or dirty and damaged spark plug insulators.

HT sparking

A suitable **neon test lamp** is useful for this purpose. However, Fig. 10.71 shows the **king lead** removed from the top of the distributor. Here it is held 6 mm from a suitable earth point. The engine is then switched on and the starter motor operated. There should then be a regular healthy spark each time the contact breaker (CB) points open. A regular spark in this test shows that the coil and LT circuits are working properly and that the fault lies in the HT system, i.e. the rotor arm, the distributor cap, the HT leads or the spark plugs.

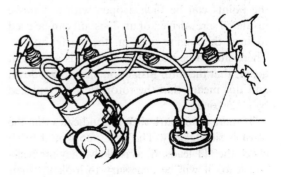

Fig. 10.70 Performing a visual check

(a)

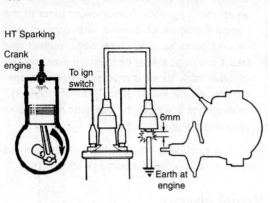

(b)

Fig. 10.71 (a) Checking coil output, (b) YDB116 high tension tester

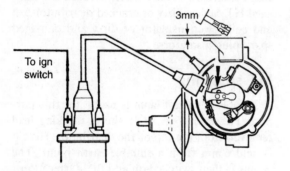

Fig. 10.72 Checking the insulation of the rotor

Checking the rotor

The rotor arm can be checked by the procedure shown in Fig. 10.72. Here the distributor cap end of the king lead is removed from the distributor cap. The end of the king lead is held about 3 mm above the metal part of the rotor. With the CB points closed and the ignition switched on the points can be flicked open with a suitable insulated screwdriver, or an assistant can be used to turn the engine over on the starter motor. There should be no spark. If there is a spark it means that the rotor insulation has broken down and this means that the rotor must be replaced by a new one.

If there is no spark then this indicates that the rotor is satisfactory. The next step would be to check the HT leads. If, as is likely, they are resistive leads it will be necessary to look up their permitted resistance before performing an ohmmeter test. The resistance value must fall within the stated limits. If they are not resistive, a straightforward continuity test will prove the conductivity of the HT leads. If these checks prove satisfactory the sparking plugs must be examined. We have already described the procedure for checking sparking plugs; if these facilities are not available the only solution may be to inspect the plugs internally and the most likely step will be to fit a new set of spark plugs. It is unusual to find that a set of spark plugs has failed completely.

Checking the condition of the contact points

Should the first test, Fig. 10.71, have failed, i.e. no spark, it is advisable to check the contact breaker condition. The contact surfaces should be clean and not badly pitted and piled and the gap should be checked to ensure that it is within the recommended limits. The securing screws should be checked for tightness and there should be no evidence of fouling of cables inside the distributor. If the points are badly worn and burnt a new set of contacts should be fitted. After this the first check for HT spark should be repeated. If this is successful then there may be no need to proceed further. However, if there is still no spark further tests will be required. These tests are now described.

Figure 10.73 shows the position of a suitable voltmeter 20 V DC. The distributor cap should be removed and the engine rotated, with the ignition off, until the CB points are closed.

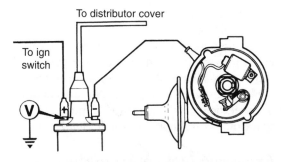

Fig. 10.73 Voltmeter check on coil supply

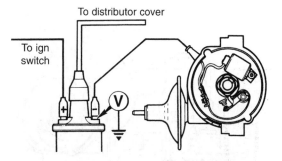

Fig. 10.74 Voltmeter check on CB side of coil

The voltmeter is then connected between the switch side of the coil and earth. The ignition should then be switched on. The voltmeter should then read battery voltage (very closely) or, if it is a ballasted coil, a lower voltage, probably 6 V.

Checking the voltage on the CB side of the coil

If these tests are satisfactory the next step is to proceed to check the voltage at the contact breaker side of the coil. The voltmeter position for this test is shown in Fig. 10.74. The CB contacts must be open. The voltmeter is then connected between the CB terminal of the coil and earth. The ignition should now be switched on and the voltmeter reading observed. If the coil primary circuit is satisfactory a reading that is very close to that obtained in the test shown in Fig. 10.73 should be seen.

If the voltage reading is zero, disconnect the LT lead to the distributor. The voltmeter should now read the same voltage as on the switch side of the coil. If it still reads zero it indicates that there is a broken circuit in the primary side of the coil and this calls for a new coil.

Voltage at the CB terminal of the coil – point closed

If the reading is correct proceed to test the voltage at the coil CB terminal with the contact points closed.

This test, shown in Fig. 10.75, checks the condition of the contact points and also checks whether there are any current leakages to earth. The voltmeter should show a zero reading if all is correct, or less than 0.2 V if it is a very sensitive meter. If the reading is more than zero volts the contacts should be checked to see if they are clean and properly closed; the insulation on the contact to condenser lead and on the LT lead

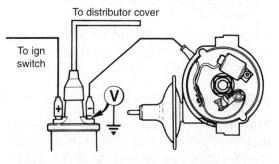

Fig. 10.75 Voltmeter test for voltage drop across the points

should also be checked. If these are in order it may be that the capacitor itself is providing a leakage path to earth.

Checking the coil for HT

If all of the above tests have been satisfactory then the **coil HT output** should be checked. A new test HT lead of known good quality is required for this test. This test HT lead is connected into the ignition coil outlet and the free end is held 6 mm from a known good earth. An assistant should then rotate the engine on the starter motor. If satisfactory sparking occurs repeat the test with the original lead and if there is no spark the HT lead should be replaced.

Testing the capacitor

Now that the HT lead has been checked, if there is still no spark from this test then the capacitor should be tested.

Figure 10.76 shows how a test capacitor can be connected, temporarily, to perform this test. The original capacitor is unscrewed and lifted away so that its casing does not make contact with earth. A test capacitor with suitable crocodile clips and leads is then connected as shown. The ignition is switched on again and the engine turned over, on the starter motor. If a spark is obtained this is fairly convincing evidence that

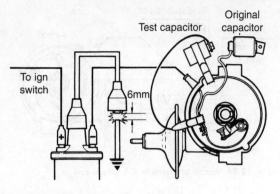

Fig. 10.76 Connecting a test capacitor

the capacitor should be renewed. If there is still no spark after checking the capacitor, the coil should be replaced.

Misfiring

Misfiring is a term that is normally applied to the type of defect that shows up as an occasional loss of spark on one or more cylinders. It can be caused by almost any part of the ignition system and the cause is often difficult to locate. Much depends on the way in which the fault occurs. If it is a regular and constant misfire one could start by checking for HT at each sparking plug. If each plug is receiving HT then the most likely cause is a spark plug. Plugs should then be removed and tested. In some cases, where the engine has not been running for very long, the insulator of a non-firing spark plug will be significantly cooler to the touch than the other plug insulators. This may be a help in locating the misfire. Here again, an electronic engine analyser is much more satisfactory because a power drop test will show which cylinder is not firing.

Cutting out

Cutting out is a term that is used to describe the type of fault where the engine stops completely, perhaps only for a split second. The most likely cause here is that there is a broken or loose connection that breaks the circuit momentarily. Careful examination of all connections and 'wiggling' of cables whilst conducting a voltage drop test across the connectors should help to locate such faults.

Hesitation

This normally happens under acceleration. The symptoms are that the engine does not respond to throttle operation and it can cause problems when overtaking.

The voltage required to produce a spark rises with the load placed on the engine. Figure 10.77 shows the relationship between compression pressure and voltage required. A probable cause of **hesitation** is, therefore, wide plug gaps or spark plugs breaking down under load.

Excessive fuel consumption

Incorrect ignition timing is usually associated with high fuel consumption.

Low power

Incorrect ignition timing, weak spark, dirty or badly adjusted plugs are defects associated with low power.

Over-heating

The ignition defect most often associated with over-heating is the ignition timing. But other defects that cause pre-ignition and detonation can also lead to over-heating of the engine.

Running on

This happens when the engine continues to run even after the ignition is switched off. An obvious cause is that parts of the engine interior remain sufficiently hot to cause combustion. This may be caused by a dirty engine with heavy carbon deposits in the combustion chamber, dirty, worn or an incorrect type of sparking plugs. It is overcome, to some extent, by fitting a

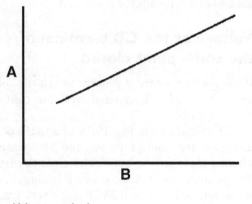

A – Voltage required
B – Compression pressure

Fig. 10.77 Spark plug voltage versus cylinder pressure

cut-off valve in the engine idling system. This prevents mixture from entering the combustion chamber through the engine idling system, this being the probable source of fuelling as the throttle is virtually closed.

10.19 Radio interference

Electromagnetic waves of a frequency that interferes with radio and TV are emitted from ignition systems. It has long been a legal requirement that vehicles are fitted with **suppression devices**. The resistive HT leads are one such device. The vehicle radio itself is subject to the same type of interference and capacitors are often used to overcome the problem (see Fig. 10.78).

10.20 Distributorless ignition systems

Electronic devices, such as the **microprocessor** and the **ECU**, allow the distributor to be dispensed with. This eliminates mechanical parts that are prone to wear and improves the reliability of the ignition system. A common approach to the design of a **distributorless system** is the **lost spark system** – so called because a spark occurs on the exhaust stroke as well as on the firing stroke. Figure 10.79 shows the basic principle of a system which utilizes two coils. Cylinders 1 and 4 are connected to one coil and cylinders 2 and 3 to the other. When cylinder number 1 is on firing stroke, cylinder number 4 is on its exhaust stroke so the spark in number 4 cylinder has no effect. Dispensing with the rotor arm reduces radio-type interference because the only sparks that occur are inside the cylinders.

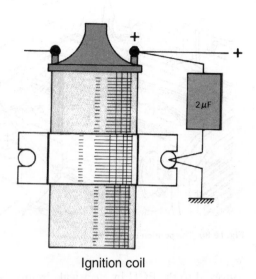

Ignition coil

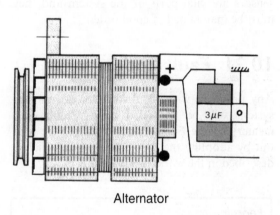

Alternator

Fig. 10.78 Some typical applications of capacitors for reducing radio interference

Figure 10.80 shows how the two ignition coils are placed on the engine of a KIA car. Figure 10.80 also shows the inputs to the ECU. These inputs are generated by sensors and are

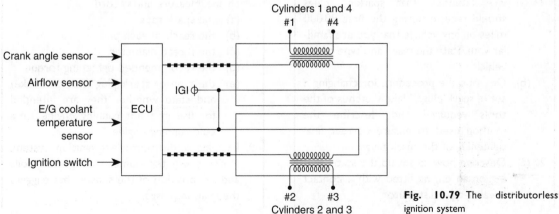

Fig. 10.79 The distributorless ignition system

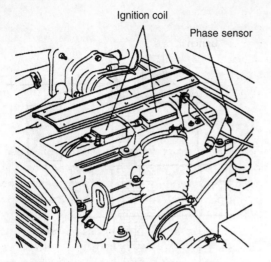

Ignition coil

Phase sensor

Fig. 10.80 The position of the ignition coils

conveyed to the ECU by electrical circuits. and sensors are vital parts of the system and they must be maintained in good order.

10.21 Fault codes

Any problems with the distributorless ignition system will be registered in the **fault code memory** of the ECU. These codes can be read out by adopting the correct procedure which is described in the workshop manual.

Learning tasks

In order to support your learning it is recommended that you keep a record of work. You are, therefore, advised to complete practical exercises of the type shown here. You should use this book to help you to complete these tasks.

1. (a) Give details of the recommended service attention that sparking plugs should receive during the first 80 000 miles on any vehicle that you are familiar with. State the make and type of the vehicle.

   (b) Describe the procedure for changing a set of spark plugs. Make sketches of the tools required and describe the method used to ensure correct final tightening of the spark plugs.

2. (a) Describe how to set up the static timing on an engine fitted with a contact breaker-type distributor.

   (b) State the dwell angle for the distributor and use sketches to show how dwell angle is affected by the size of the contact points gap.

3. Describe the type of meter that would be suitable for measuring the resistance of a length of resistive type HT ignition lead. Take such an HT lead, measure its length and, using an appropriate meter, determine the resistance of the HT lead in ohms per 10 cm of length.

4. (a) Describe how an oscilloscope can be used to check coil polarity. Explain how incorrect polarity affects the spark.

   (b) Make sketches to show the oscilloscope patterns for; (i) correct coil polarity; (ii) incorrect coil polarity.

5. Write down details of the safety precautions that must be taken when working on spark ignition systems. State the reasons why such precautions are necessary.

6. (a) State the purpose of a ballast resistor in the primary circuit of a coil ignition system.

   (b) Draw a simple circuit diagram of a ballasted ignition system to show the path of the coil primary current: (i) when the engine is running; (ii) when the starter is being operated to get the engine running.

7. (a) Describe how to set the air gap in an electronic ignition distributor. State clearly the type of feeler gauges used for this operation.

   (b) Describe how the electronic part of the distributor provides the 'shaped' pulses that allow abrupt 'make and break' of the current in the coil primary winding.

8. Examine a set of sparking plugs from an engine. Measure and record:
   (a) the spark gaps
   (b) the reach of each plug
   (c) the thread diameter
   (d) the recommended tightening torque
   (e) the type of spark plug (not the make) and state whether they are intended for use in a hot running engine, or a cold running engine.

9. Examine a distributorless ignition system. Write down the number of ignition coils and the position of the sensor that triggers the ignition pulses.

10. Describe, with the aid of diagrams, a simple practical test that can be used to check the electrical condition of a rotor arm.
11. Perform a test to check the electrical output of a magnetic pulse type generator that is used in an electronic ignition system.
12. Obtain an ignition coil and measure the resistance of the primary winding and the secondary winding. Record the figures and compare them with the figures given in this book, then write down your opinion about the condition of the coil. State whether or not the coil is for use in a ballasted ignition system.

The answers to these exercises should be kept neatly in a file so that they can be used in your assessment process.

Practical assignment – ignition systems

Objective

The purpose of this assignment is to give you practice in working on electronic ignition systems, to improve your knowledge of the subject and to help you to add to your file of evidence for the NVQ.

Tools and equipment

- a vehicle, or an engine, equipped with a variable reluctance type of ignition distributor
- wing and seat covers
- tool kit
- multi-meter
- non-magnetic feeler gauges
- clear bench space
- instruction manual
- exhaust extraction equipment
- pencil and note pad

Activity

Follow the instruction manual and/or your supervisor's advice to remove the distributor from the engine. Note carefully the need to disconnect the vehicle battery before doing any electrical work on the vehicle. High tension ignition voltage is dangerous. Take note of the precautions that you must observe. Beware of losing settings in electronic memories and note the procedures to be followed in such cases. When you have satisfied your supervisor about these matters, do the following:

(a) check the condition of the ignition pulse generator winding;
(b) check the condition of the drive gear and distributor shaft;
(c) check the air gap between the reluctor rotor lobes and the pick up;
(d) check the condition of the distributor cap, rotor and HT leads;
(e) make a note of your readings and other observations;
(f) report to your supervisor and perform any approved repairs;
(g) when the repairs are completed and the distributor is re-assembled, refit the distributor to the engine, making sure that the ignition timing is correctly set.

Glossary of NVQ terms

The meaning of terms used in the NVQ portfolio

Occupational standards

These are a collection of Units that make up the qualification you are trying to get.

Units

These describe what you are expected to do in any area of your job. It is the smallest part or section for which you can gain a credit from the City and Guilds.

Elements of competence

Units are divided into elements of competence or details which describe the abilities and knowledge you should have to pass that unit.

Performance criteria

These explain the level you must come up to (called outcomes) to be able to show that you can do the job properly, e.g. correct identification of fault and use of equipment.

Range statements

These will be found in each element and are the different circumstances in which the jobs should be performed, e.g. the vehicles on which the task is done, the methods used to perform it, the equipment used to do the task and the areas in which the task was completed.

Underpinning knowledge

This is the minimum you should know about the system on which you are working to be able to competently complete the task, e.g. how the engine basically works before taking it apart.

Performance evidence

You must provide evidence of what you are capable of doing. If the task is successfully completed you must record your work on a recognised job sheet which is signed by the person in charge of your work. This is kept as evidence or proof for the assessor or verifier.

The assessment process

When you feel that you are capable of completing one of the tasks, having practised it several times, then you can ask your assessor for a formal assessment. He will then record this on an assessment sheet.

Observation

You will be watched during the assessment (but not all the time). You may also be asked questions to enable the assessor to test your knowledge and understanding of the task.

Evidence specification

The job sheets produced by you must show that you are capable of doing a particular task repeatedly to a set standard. You also must show that you understand the range of knowledge that cannot be assessed by just doing that task; e.g. removing and replacing a cylinder head gasket, what would you do if the stud/bolt stripped the threads whilst completing the task, or if the gasket was leaking between two adjacent cylinders what other tasks would be performed to ensure that the fault would not occur again immediately afterwards?

Portfolio

This will usually take the form of an A4 ring binder in which the information from the City and Guilds and your evidence is collected. You keep this with you at all times to enable you to collect all the job sheets (both at work and off the job training) and keep the achievement record sheets up to date.

In the portfolio there are words that can be quite difficult to understand especially when used in a sentence that specifies what you have got to achieve. The following is a list of some of the more difficult ones and their meaning in relation to the motor vehicle.

Parameter

This is the limit in the specification usually laid down by the manufacturer for say a measurement of a component.

Tolerance

This is the upper and lower limits added together, e.g. the timing may be 6° +/− 2° giving a tolerance of 4°.

Deviation

This is movement away from say a line or measurement, e.g. a disc brake has a maximum deviation of 0.01 mm from revolving dead true.

Symptom

This is what the driver will notice when driving and something on the vehicle goes wrong, e.g. he/she may come into the workshop and say the engine is knocking.

Fault

This is what is actually wrong with the vehicle, e.g. the engine is knocking; therefore the fault could be the big-end bearings are worn out.

Cause

This is what has caused the fault to occur, e.g. the engine was allowed to run with too low an oil level resulting in little or no oil pressure.

Appropriate

Suitable information is noted by the mechanic from up to date data issued by the manufacturers.

Evaluate

This is to judge, assess or weigh up information gathered from different sources, e.g. getting from the customer, vehicle and manufacturer information to identify work that needs to be carried out on a vehicle.

The best way to show the use of these words and what they mean is to look at the performance criteria (PCs).

Competence

This is the skill and capability with which you do the task.

Criteria

This is the standard you must meet when completing a set task.

Assessor

This is the person responsible for evaluating whether the task is completed in the correct manner and to the correct standard

Verifier

This is the person who checks that everyone is doing the work correctly and up to the correct standard. The verifier checks the evidence and ensures that the work meets the recognized criteria for the NVQ.

Unit A8 – L2 Element A8.2 Evaluate Information and Data To Confirm Diagnosis of System Faults

Performance criteria

8.2.2 Diagnostic information on components/ systems performance is compared with known parameters to identify source of deviation

This means that the mechanic has talked to the customer, has tested the vehicle, checked the manufacturer's data and collated (put together) all the information and has identified the problem. Here is an example.

The customer complains the car has lost its pulling power. On checking the vehicle it was found that the CO was 0.05%, the ignition timing was 6° BTDC. When checking the manufacturer's data for the vehicle the CO should read 1.5% and the ignition timing should be 10° BTDC. On further investigation it was found that the spark plugs were corroding away.

In this case the mechanic now has to decide in view of all this information what should be done to put the fault right.

This process of gathering information and identifying exactly what is required applies to all the elements of the course. One of the most important requirements is the gathering of evidence and putting together the portfolio. Most students do not like the paperwork involved but once you have the system working it becomes easier and in the end worthwhile.

Examples of typical NVQ assessment sheets

NVQ repair and servicing of road vehicles assessment schedule

Example 1

This is a typical assessment report for those undertaking an NVQ assessment. A series of questions may also be asked under the underpinning knowledge section based on the engine section of this book. Evidence of the worksheet together with this assessment would give a pass in the engine dismantling module at level two.

TITLE A9.1 Dismantle A9.2 Inspect A9.3 Replace A9.4 Evaluate

TASK 3.1 Removing and refitting pistons and crankshaft

Candidate's Name

Action	Competent	Comments
Communication		
Consulted appropriate service manual before starting work.		
Maintained a log of measurements made on components.		
Completed job sheets with recommendations.		
Planning		
Personal safety hazards are identified.		
Found relevant technical data/information.		
Worked in a logical sequence within approved time scale.		
Used protective clothing.		
Specialist tools are identified.		
Components are marked before removal.		
Doing		
Pistons are removed and stored in the correct order together with bearings and caps.		
Main bearings and caps are removed and stored in order.		
Crankshaft is removed.		
All components are cleaned in the appropriate way.		
Components are measured and faults are identified.		
Crankshaft, pistons and bearings are assembled.		
Bolts/nuts are correctly tensioned with torque spanner.		

Checking
Crankshaft rotates freely.
Pistons are correctly assembled in the cylinder block.

Underpinning Knowledge

Competence Credited	Date

Assessor's Signature	Student's signature

Example 2

This is a typical assessment report sheet for those undertaking an NVQ assessment on cooling systems. A series of questions may also be asked under the underpinning knowledge section based on the cooling system section of this book. Evidence of the worksheet together with this assessment would give a pass in the cooling system module at level two.

TITLE *A9.3 Competence in Assembly and Dismantling*

TASK *3.2 Servicing a conventional cooling system*

Candidate's Name

Action	Competent	Comments

Communication
Consulted appropriate service manual *before* starting work.
Maintained a log of checks made on cooling system.
Tabulated results of tests together with data collected.
Completed report sheet together with recommendations.

Planning
Personal safety hazards identified.
Relevant technical data located.
Worked in a logical sequence within approved time scale.
Used protective clothing and vehicle coverings.

Doing
Safety precautions were followed.
Pressure test system using relevant equipment.
Remove and test operation of pressure and vacuum valve.
Remove and test operation of thermostat.
Remove/refit drive belt and adjust tension.
Test system for antifreeze content.
Top up system to correct level.

Checking
Run engine and check the following for correct operation:

- Electric fan
- Water pump
- Temperature sensor

- Interior heater including controls
- Condition/security of hoses and clips
- Coolant level

Underpinning knowledge

Competence Credited   **Date**

Assessor's Signature   **Student's Signature**

Examples of marking schedules

MARKING SCHEDULE

NAME SELECTED CRANKSHAFTS, CAMSHAFTS AND TIMING DRIVES

Mark ✓ or ✗

1. How many cylinders would example No 1 serve?
   ANSWER: _____ ☐

2. What provision is made on a crankshaft to support a gearbox primary shaft?
   ANSWER: _____ ☐

3. Why are holes drilled into the crankshaft journals?
   ANSWER: _____ ☐

4. State the number of main journals (example No 1)
   ANSWER: _____ ☐

5. State the number of big end journals (example No 2)
   ANSWER: _____ ☐

6. How many camshaft bearings are there on each camshaft?
   ANSWER: _____ ☐

7. How many engine cylinders would this camshaft serve?
   ANSWER: _____ ☐

8. Give one other component that may be driven by the camshaft
   ANSWER: _____ ☐

9. Which of the three camshaft drives require lubrication?
   ANSWER: _____ ☐

10. Where are the valve timing marks situated?
    ANSWER: _____ ☐

11. At what ratio does a camshaft revolve to a crankshaft?
    ANSWER: _____ ☐

12. Name the type of camshaft drive (example No 1)
    ANSWER: _____ ☐

13. Name the type of camshaft drive (example No 2)
    ANSWER: _____ ☐

14. Name the type of camshaft drive (example No 3)
    ANSWER: _____ ☐

CIRCLE RESULT = Pass or Referred

MARKING SCHEDULE

ADJUST ALL ENGINE VALVE CLEARANCES

Mark ✓ or ✗

1. Select the correct tools   ☐

2. Use tools correctly   ☐

3. Select the correct feeler gauges   ☐

4. Use feeler gauges correctly   ☐

5. Work systematically   ☐

6. Work with care   ☐

7. Set each valve in correct cam position for **adjustment**   ☐

8. Use the manufacturer's recommended adjustment **sequence**   ☐

9. Adjust valve clearances within manufacturer's limits   ☐

10. Recheck valve clearances   ☐

11. How is the gudgeon pin lubricated?
    ANSWER: _____   ☐
12. State one method of securing/locating the **gudgeon pin example No 1.**
    ANSWER: _____   ☐
14. State a second method of securing/locating the **gudgeon pin example No 2.**
    ANSWER: _____   ☐

CIRCLE RESULT = Pass or Referred

MARKING SCHEDULE

NAME SELECTED PISTONS, GUDGEON PINS AND PISTON RINGS

Mark ✓ or ✗

1. Where is a piston fitted?
   ANSWER: _____ ☐

2. How is a piston secured on a crankshaft?
   ANSWER: _____ ☐

3. Name skirt type on piston example No 1.
   ANSWER: _____ ☐

4. Name skirt type on piston example No 2.
   ANSWER: _____ ☐

5. What is the purpose of a top piston ring?
   ANSWER: _____ ☐

6. How is a piston ring lubricated?
   ANSWER: _____ ☐

7. Name piston ring example No 1.
   ANSWER: _____ ☐

8. Name piston ring example No 2.
   ANSWER: _____ ☐

9. Name piston ring example No 3.
   ANSWER: _____ ☐

10. What is the purpose of a gudgeon pin?
    ANSWER: _____ ☐

11. Where is the gudgeon pin fitted?
    ANSWER: _____ ☐

12. How is the gudgeon pin lubricated?
    ANSWER: _____ ☐

13. State one method of securing/locating the gudgeon pin example No 1.
    ANSWER: _____ ☐

14. State a second method of securing/locating the gudgeon pin example No 2.
    ANSWER: _____ ☐

CIRCLE RESULT   =   Pass   or   Referred

Index